SOUL HACKERS

The Wave Series by Laura Knight-Jadczyk

Riding the Wave
Soul Hackers
The Terror of History
Stripped to the Bone
Petty Tyrants
Facing the Unknown
Almost Human
Debugging the Universe

Other books by Laura Knight-Jadczyk

The Secret History of the World and How to Get Out Alive
9/11: The Ultimate Truth (with Joe Quinn)
High Strangeness: Hyperdimensions and the Process of Alien Abduction

LAURA KNIGHT-JADCZYK

SOUL HACKERS

THE HIDDEN HANDS BEHIND THE NEW AGE MOVEMENT

Red Pill Press

Copyright © 2000, 2010 Laura Knight-Jadczyk
Cassiopaean materials Copyright © 1994–2010
Arkadiusz Jadczyk and Laura Knight-Jadczyk

http://www.cassiopaea.org/

ISBN-13: 978-1-897244-54-8

All Rights Reserved. No part of this publication may be reproduced, stored in a retrieval system, or transmitted in any form or by any means, electronic, mechanical, or otherwise, other than for "fair use", without the written consent of the author.

Red Pill Press
10020-100 Ave.
Grande Prairie, AB
T8V 0V3, Canada
http://www.redpillpress.com/

TABLE OF CONTENTS

Part I: The Truth Is Out There, But... Trust No One! 14
Roses Grow Best In Manure 63

Part II: All There Is Is Lessons... 80
Some Further Remarks 102
Candy Will Ruin Your Teeth! 126
He Hideth My Soul in the Cleft of the Rock 160
Laura Finds Reiki And Ends Up In the Soup... Pea Soup, That Is 182
Wandering Around In 3rd Density Can Be Hazardous to Your Health! 223
A Trip to "Alligator Alley"! 254
Dr. Greenbaum And The Soul Hackers... 269

Afterword 308

Recommended Reading 310

INTRODUCTION

Soul Hackers is a part of The Wave Series of books. While it was originally written and published directly after the first volume, *Riding the Wave*, for the convenience of readers who have purchased this book without having read any of my other works, I will attempt to give a short summary of that work's main points. It will also serve as an introduction to my work in "superluminal communication", which forms the 10% inspiration behind the 90% perspiration of the research of our organization, Quantum Future Group, Inc. Here, I will insert some comments about the central inspiration for this book written by my husband, theoretical/mathematical physicist, Arkadiusz Jadczyk:

> The term "Cassiopaeans" appears in several places in this book and requires some explanation. After a two-year-long experiment using a spirit board, a source identifying itself as the Cassiopaeans told us, "we are you in the future." Modern physics does not provide us with practical means for this type of communication and theories on this subject are not yet well developed; they are, in fact, inconclusive and controversial. While communication into the past cannot be dismissed in current theories as impossible, it is perhaps improbable. However, the more improbably is a given phenomenon, the more information is carried by its occurrence, and for this reason we did not dismiss the possibility of the truth of the source. Instead, we decided to continue the communications as a form of a controlled experiment in "superluminal thought transfer", even if it was clear that the term should be considered as a tentative indication of only one out of several possible interpretations.[1]
>
> The information received from this experiment is presented in the context of broad ranging historical, scientific and other metaphysical material and offers the clues that have led to the worldview and inferences presented by us in our numerous publications on the Web and in print. Perhaps it is only our on subconscious mind that presents itself as a source, but even if it is so, does that tell us more? Do we really know what "unconscious" or "subconscious" mind is and of what it is capable?
>
> We sometimes ask ourselves if the C's are who they say they are, because we do not take anything as unquestionable truth. We take everything with a grain of salt, even if we consider that there is a good chance that it is truth. We are con-

---

[1] I tell the story of the beginnings of our experiment in the introductory installment of our *Knowledge and Being* video series, which can be viewed for free at www.cassiopaea.org/knowledge_and_being/ and on YouTube.

INTRODUCTION

stantly analyzing this material as well as a great quantity of other material that comes to our attention from numerous fields of science and mysticism.

We invite the reader to share in our seeking of Truth by reading with an open, but skeptical mind. We do not encourage "devotee-ism" or "true belief". We do encourage the seeking of Knowledge and Awareness in all fields of endeavor as the best way to discern lies from truth. The one thing we can tell the reader is this: we work very hard, many hours a day, and have done so for many years, to discover the "bottom line" of our existence on Earth. It is our vocation, our quest, and our job. We constantly seek to validate and/or refine what we understand to be either possible or probable or both. We do this in the sincere hope that all of mankind will benefit, if not now, then at some point in one of our probable futures.

In *Riding the Wave* we introduced The Wave, a subject of some scope and complexity! As the C's describe it, The Wave is a term used to describe a Macro-Cosmic Quantum Wave Collapse. This is presumably a naturally occurring cosmic phenomenon that produces both physical and "metaphysical" changes to the Earth's cosmic environment, theorized to be statistically probable sometime in the early 21st century. It is variously described by other sources as the planetary shift to fourth density, the "shift of the ages", "ascension", "the harvest", etc., and is most often slated to take place at the end of 2012 (as per the Mayan calendar). However, contrary to what the New Agers are saying about this event, it doesn't look like it's as simple as Earth and all its inhabitants spontaneously entering a new era of spiritual awakening and rebirth. There's no free lunch!

To sum up what we've learned so far concerning the context in which to understand The Wave, the C's tell us that *gravity* is the root and totality of all creation, "God" or Seventh Density, which holds together or *binds* all of creation. This macrocosmic gravitational *field* or *sea* acts as the medium for gravity waves, which fill up and give substance to the totality of creation by the processes of collection and dispersion. This duality of collection and dispersion is reflected at all levels – from the gravitational pull of a black hole and the expansion of a supernova, to the natures of service-to-self and service-to-others, light and darkness, being and non-being, thus forming the *Grand Cycle* of creation in both short- and long-wave cycles.

In this context, the C's relate that light and matter are energy expressions of gravity – Divine Consciousness – the root of All. Seventh-density consciousness creates matter, which is constantly recycled along with anti-matter. As the vibrational frequency of 7D "light" slows down, it "collapses" the wave, causing photons to manifest. The result, congealed light, is gravity expressed: *matter*.

The terms used, those related to mathematics and physics, should not be taken with their textbook meanings. Our scientific understanding of the Universe is evolving and, a century after the revolutions of quantum theory and relativity of the early 20th century, we may well be on the brink of a new revolution. Physicists, cosmologists, mathematicians, philosophers, as well as those multidisciplinary scientists dealing with consciousness research are searching for a new, unified framework for solving the present-day contradictions and for understanding of what we call today "anomalous phenomena". For many of the technical terms used in the C's transmissions we may find, with a proper interpretation, their counterparts in the current leading-edge physics research. Yet the "physics of the Wave" is still on the drawing board, and only when it finally gets it shape, only then it will be possible to check our present understanding, as outlined in "The Wave" against the new paradigm.

Keeping the above in our mind one can say that the utilization of gravity waves makes them unstable, and these *unstable gravity waves* bind together all that is ethereal with all that is material, the two complementary "Faces of God". It seems that the active *use* of these waves by consciousness units (beings) of creation is what holds together the ethereal realm of *ideas* and the material world of *experience*. In the long-wave cycle of evolution via Natural Selection alone, this process is less conscious, while in the short-wave cycle of self-aware beings, it is more conscious and actively directed. Without dynamic experience—the ever-changing and growing *lessons* of life—the universe would remain static and lifeless. It is through these unstable waves that *you can access other densities*—other realms of awareness—and *merge* with them. Consciousness collapses the waves' many probabilities out of a state of potential and into actuality, making new realities accessible.

The seven densities of materiality/spirituality in our cosmic system are hyperdimensional and interpenetrate one another. That is, all realities exist at the same "time", at least in potential, with lower dimensions (i.e. densities) enmeshed in higher ones just as lower spatial dimensions are enmeshed in higher spatial dimensions. For example, the Earth exists in both third and fourth densities simultaneously, although we at present only experience its third level reality, due to our restricted awareness. These realms cycle/fluctuate with the Wave, and our region of space-time cycles between realms in a period of 309,000 years (approximately 12 precessional cycles), at which point the macro-Wave "collapses", producing an all-encompassing energy reality change.

The entire cosmos exists in a constant state of balance between the opposing principles of gravity collection and dispersal. However, different sectors of the cosmos express different wave-properties at any given location in space and time. This accounts for the vast multiplicity of forms and qualities expressed throughout this grand cosmos, and the observable fact that they all exist at different points on the Grand Cycle. While at most positions on The Wave different realms inhabit their "space" in a relatively stable manner, as in rock and mineral life, at certain junctures in the cycling of this wave, the "border" or "curtain" between realms opens, making "realm border crossings" possible. These allow entire sectors of space-time, including planets and their inhabitants, to "move" between realms, either "horizontally" (i.e. between dimensions) or "vertically" (i.e. between densities). These junctures occur at critical times in the evolution of "consciousness units" or life forms in a specific region, and otherwise these "conduits" for the most part remain closed to movement. *Conduits* or *doorways* to ethereal existence are formed by an antimatter universe which exists in balance with the material universe. Utilizing antimatter by creating an *EM field*, which collapses the gravity wave, allows antimatter to unite with matter, creating a portal through which space-time can be bent, or traveled through via this "bending." In other words, producing an EM field, which results in access to antimatter, *is* the bending of space/time. However, "new worlds" can only be accessed along a conduit which has been established by groups anchoring a specific frequency.

Events happening due to the approach of the Wave are causing changes across densities and realities. In third density, these changes have third density explanations, but they are a manifestation of hyperdimensional phenomena. We see them as third density because that is our current point of reference. All reflects in and across all density levels. As such, much of the information about upcoming "changes" is symbolic, and relates to spiritual and awareness factors rather than the much publicized physical meanings.

Fourth density bleed-through produces many "3D" effects caused by electromagnetic wave changes which have their root in the approaching Wave, e.g. UFO activity, "dimensional-window fallers", extreme weather, global warming, depleting ozone, volcanoes, earthquakes, crop circles, increasing gamma ray bursts in upper atmosphere, social upheaval, personality disintegration, and various "paranormal" experiences. Specifically, climate change is caused by a gap in the "surge heliographic field". Also, temporarily overlapping densities electromagnetically charge the affected area, and are experienced by those able to perceive them as anomalous "thunder" or "skyquakes", equally dispersed over the affected area. Increased EM waves also produce anomalous "humming". These vibrational frequency changes are a function of the close arrival of The Wave. The C's recently commented on many of these issues:

January 9, 2005

Q: (L) Regarding the recent earthquake and tsunami, there is a huge buzz on the net that this was not a natural phenomenon. Some say it could have been a meteor; others say it was a US nuke; others say it was India and Israel playing around in deep sea trenches. Then there is the speculation on an EM weapon of some description. The New Agers are saying it was the start of the final "Earth Changes". So what really caused this earthquake that happened one year minus one hour after the earthquake in Iran?

A: Pressure in earth. Not any of the proferred suggestions. *But remember that the human cycle mirrors the cycle of catastrophe and human mass consciousness plays a part.*

Q: In what way does mass consciousness play a part?

A: When those with higher centers are blocked from full manifestation of creative energy, that energy must go somewhere. If you cannot create "without" you create "within".

October 20, 2005

Q: (J) I want to know about these strange formations on the radar image of Hurricane Rita.

A: 4th density "battle." Also includes some "practice."

Q: (L) They're practicing with new weapons. (J) Some people said Katrina was the product of HAARP heating up the waters in the Gulf.

A: We've already dealt with HAARP and weather. Read transcripts.

Q: (W) (Quoting transcripts) "HAARP has nothing to do with the weather or EM associated with same." (H) Which suggests that there is EM associated with the weather. There could be some EM stuff associated with the weather that isn't part of HAARP. (L) Fourth density. (J) Were any of the storms manufactured from third density or was it a natural storm?

A: Mfg in 3D? No. As we have said... 4D battles represent as weather. But the "veil" is thinning.

June 20, 2009

A: 5 more years! 2 go! 0 new year! [...]

Q: (L) Is there any particular reason you made the announcement about 5 years to go?

A: Just reminding you.

Q: (L) You normally have never been date-specific.

A: This is not "day" specific but close enough for horseshoes.

Q: (J) A lot of the New Agers are gonna be disappointed in 2012.

A: 2012 is a distraction. We have repeatedly talked about the open nature of the future. It is always open until the probabilities begin to collapse, such as now. But macro-collapses take some "time".

Q: (L) So you're saying that there is a macro-collapse that has already begun?

A: Yes. [...]

Q: (L) What is the relationship [between the apparent deterioration in the minds of two correspondents, i.e. incoherent, paranoid, threatening]?

A: It is not just "waves" beamed by such things as HAARP or microwaves, it is also a quickening of the cosmos. Those who are not integrated will disintegrate at an even faster rate than ever.

Q: (L) Are there any kinds of negative spirits or attachments involved here?

A: Not necessary when the personality is so fragmented.

Various denizens of hyperdimensional realms are also "riding" this Wave, using its energy to pass through space-time, and set to arrive after the regularly occurring cometary cluster which orbits in our solar system every 3,600 years. The precise time of this electromagnetic transfer cannot be accurately measured because of the large numbers of beings and craft, the mass of which warps space-time, making for a long time cycle. As I discuss in *High Strangeness*, many of these beings do *not* have our best interests at heart.

INTRODUCTION

As the C's describe, the predicament of humanity is as old as time itself. They describe us, the human race, as "Lucifer" who fell from the heavens into the world of matter. As they describe it, half of creation desires, and therefore "falls" into matter, losing its ethereal, STO state and entering the STS state of physicality. That is, the STS thought center (sixth density) expresses itself primarily in the material half of creation, thus identifying with the "Left" branch of the Tree of Life, (i.e., the "Lizzies"). It is the goal of STO candidates to reclaim their Divine nature by battling their own STS nature and learning the lessons of this density.

If our 3D life is drawn as a straight line, 4D exists perpendicular to that linear reality, just as 3D exists perpendicular to 2D. I think we can understand that everyone has a "connection" to The Wave, or *realm border*, via a fourth dimension-like "cut" or wormhole called a "Perpendicular Reality." Whether they can access it or not is another question. And, whether it needs more than one person to "produce" or "manifest" the "cut" is still another. If the latter idea is correct, we might conjecture that groups of seven individuals, if they are the *right* seven individuals (determined by each group dynamic) can interact in such a way as to bring exponential knowledge and awareness to each and every member of the group, thereby "opening" the cut, or wormhole.

The "catch" in the whole 2012 myth is that humanity will *not* just "ascend" to a higher state without any real effort. The Wave is not something that just *happens* to us; it is something we interact with *consciously*. The truth of the matter is that the individuals theorized above must be highly "polarized" in order to make the shift and not simply repeat third density reality in this or another sector of the universe. In order to experience The Wave in a positive way, we need to change our core assumptions about reality, breaking out of our alignment with "this world" and coming more into resonance with the STO frequency.

Part of preparing oneself to anchor the STO frequency is to transform our STS essence. This essence exists in other realms as predatory creatures, among others, which will be encountered in the process of transformation. At the time of the Wave we will "merge" with our essence parts, high and low. The C's have told us that many ride the Wave to "merge" with us (the C's themselves on the "crest" of the Wave). Our "merging" with that "hyper-spatial energy" reality, and the *nature* of that merging, depends on *us*, and the work we do here. Mass thought patterns *can* become reality, *if they are strong enough and rooted in objective reality*. The Wave is a "facilitator" for that plasticity, and different groups and belief systems will manifest certain realities at the point in time that it "hits," thereby "collapsing" the wave-form of our macrocosmic reality according to those belief systems. We must choose which reality that is!

The Cs have said that "Life is religion" and then followed that by defining what they meant: "Life experiences reflect how one interacts with God. Those who are asleep are those of little faith in terms of their interaction with the creation. Some people think that the world exists for them to overcome or ignore or shut out. For those individuals, the worlds will cease. They will become exactly what they give to life. They will become merely a dream in the "past." *People who pay strict attention to objective reality right and left, become the reality of the 'Future'."* In other words, those *bind themselves to truth*. This is the true meaning of the word "religion".

If you think about the word *ligand*, you find that it is from Latin *ligandus*, gerundive of *ligare*, 'to bind', and in chemistry, it is an ion, molecule, or functional group that binds to another chemical entity to form a larger complex. Now, if we consider that the C's (and other traditions) say that the human race is a "fragmented soul" of a higher density—that we are "soul units" or "wave-reading consciousness units"—then figuring out how to put ourselves back together as what Ra referred to as a "social memory complex" is our problem. The Cs have said that networking is a fourth density principle and that we need to "connect our chakras". Both of these ideas relate to principles of "binding."

Networking is re-establishing our social bonds to one another as a "Body of Christ" so to say. In *Secret History*, I spend some time talking about the function of ligands and our need for "binding ourselves to the truth", that believing a lie is, effectively, being bound to entropy, STS. In other words, The Wave is a study of True Religion, which means to "re-connect" and that's what we most desperately need to do, individually and collectively.

This volume, *Soul Hackers*, deals with the issues of Religion, of binding the lower self with the Truly Spiritual. We can only "reconnect" by learning the lessons of life in third density, and this means coming to some understanding of the true nature of simple karmic understandings. Though these understandings *are* simple, it's amazing how often we misread reality, giving it an interpretation that is wholly opposite to its true nature. *Soul Hackers* begins the process of breaking down those false interpretations, and I hope it will help to open your eyes to the wonderful possibilities that lie behind the terrible realities of life in the cosmos!

PART I:
THE TRUTH IS OUT THERE, BUT…
TRUST NO ONE!

1999: As I write these pages, the e-mails come fast and furious with questions. I recently received a communication from a correspondent that said, in part:

> After all your efforts and all the information [the Cassiopaeans have given you], have you yourself come up with a synopsis of what we can expect more or less? Here's mine:
>
> Aliens will invade in some form or other between now and 2018 [the actual date given by the Cassiopaeans was 18 years from 1994, or 2012] or something, causing even more fear and confusion than there is already, then try to take us over or annihilate us or let the earth changes do that and then seed earth with their own race. About the same time this is all happening The Wave will strike and half of the world or more (people and landmass) is wobbling in and out of 4th density and then transitions completely. Those of us who have not been wiped out by earth changes or the busy Lizzies and gone to 5th density dead zone (there to decide what to do next) will find ourselves in 4th density earth which will look very weird to us and will take some getting used to, only to find ourselves in the same situation environmentally, [with] 4th density Orions or Lizzies trying to manipulate and control us there as they have been doing here for millennia.
>
> In short, as you said to the Cassies, the picture looks ugly. They said that you seem to think that only good experience is useful, well no, but at least there is usually a mix of good and bad but in their scenario we are all for the high jump with no mat on the other side though. (Splat)
>
> They are asking us to accept the fact that we are the spirit and that our bodies should not matter and we shouldn't be worried about dying horribly en masse. OK, to come to this realization about ourselves is possible I believe, but for the whole world to try to do it by 2018!! [2012] This is asking a bit much! I mean we haven't as a race really made any inroads into this way of thinking at all!!
>
> The biggest deal for me is to conceptualize all this. Say for a second that I decide that all this makes sense to me and I'm buying it, it is gonna happen. I then look up from my computer bleary eyed and look at my fellow earthlings (!) and look at the world outside and say...no way!! I mean, there is nothing in what I see around me that is even hinting that any of this could be happening!
>
> This smacks to me yet again of the type of blind faith needed for the Christian church! Blind faith is a con. If [something] exists, then we should be able to experience it. For me that is a much better way to get people to act: give them something to act on, not a story that requires belief without any proof.
>
> An example is that Sahaja Yoga is gathering more and more people because it is an actually experienceable phenomenon, people can feel their own spirit and are prompted to pursue further. Why can't we have some proof?

For the most part, the questions I receive are questions we have already asked the Cassiopaeans, only I have not yet managed to transcribe, edit, and otherwise clean up and publish all the material. Personal names and other details need to be removed, typing errors corrected, and so on.[2]

---

[2] In fact, after a series of events described in *Petty Tyrants* and *Facing the Unknown*, these unedited transcripts were stolen and published illegally on the Internet, violating the privacy of many individuals. I am currently in the process of putting the complete transcripts – minus any personal information about guests to our sessions – on my forum: http://www.cassiopaea.org/forum/index.php?board=51.0

Other questions are of the kind that really can be answered by us, with *no* intervention, if we will just take the time to study the matter and think. I will never forget the occasion when the Cassiopaeans responded to a general melee of rapid-fire group questions with the following:

> January 14, 1995
> We are trying to tell you something important, and you keep asking questions. Now, please, silence for a moment!!!!
> We have told you many times to *communicate with each other and network and share ideas, because that is how you LEARN and PROGRESS!* But, you are beginning to rely on us for all your answers, and you do not LEARN that way!!!!!!!
> Now, try this, you will be thunderstruck with the results: Each of you has stored within you unlimited amounts of factual and "Earthshaking" information. This information was put into your consciousness in order for you to retrieve it in order for you to learn. Now just start by holding a discussion about the last series of questions you were trying to ask us, and "let it flow".

In and amongst our group, we have learned gradually to implement this type of activity. Yes, it means that we have to put forth effort, and much material must be researched and compared, but it has strengthened our confidence in our abilities to evaluate and make choices based on hidden variables.

Many of the questions I have received have been about other sources of information whose scenarios or interpretations of our reality vary somewhat from the Cassiopaean presentation. I have avoided talking about these things for a variety of reasons, the main one being that each individual learns something from every interaction and we all seem to learn best when we directly experience something for ourselves. In fact, in terms of our reality, each and every source of information has its place and purpose. Everyone who is seeking is at some point on the learning cycle. The old saying, "When the student is ready, the teacher will appear," is appropriate in this respect. It would do no good for a child in second grade to work with a teacher who specializes in sixth grade material – he or she simply would gain nothing from the interaction but confusion. The Cassiopaeans have commented on this factor:

> January 10, 1995
> Q: (L) Now, I have some articles in this magazine here: This is Lyssa Royal and she has "channeled for thousands around the globe since 1985." Her books and magazine articles are published in six languages worldwide, etc. She writes here: "The human consciousness is roughly divided into three different areas for the sake of this illustration: the conscious mind, the subconscious mind and the unconscious mind." Now, are these labels generally correct?
> A: Roughly.
> Q: (L) She says: "The unconscious mind is a link to your greater self, it is also used as a wasteland where scary, dark things are stored that you really don't want to bring up." Is this a fairly accurate statement?
> A: Semi-accurate.

Q: (L) Is there anything you can say to make the statement more accurate?

A: The unconscious mind is also a conduit for connecting with the higher self, other selves, and the universal mind.

Q: (L) Lyssa also says: "When you are a child and have a traumatic event, the subconscious not only finds a way to immediately process the information and store it, but also to protect you from further fragmentation. It must seek to create a balance." So, she says, the "very intense raw energy that is generated from trauma gets stuffed into the unconscious mind." Is this true?

A: Close enough.

Q: (L) She then goes on to say: "When an extraterrestrial looks at us, we seem like multiple personality cases to them because of our mind divisions." Is this true?

A: Irrelevant.

Q: (L) Why is that irrelevant? Is it because when a higher density being looks at us they know what they are looking at?

A: Yes. They know and understand the separations of your minds quite precisely. That would be like saying "when a human looks at a rodent, they notice that they are excessively furry."

Q: (L) She goes on to say: "The ET often does not know how to communicate with a fragmented human. Sometimes they fly their ships by and few people may see them, but the greater percentage do not see them as that data gets sucked into the subconscious and the triage occurs." She means triage in the sense of the mind being so flabbergasted that it immediately shunts information into the unconscious. Is this true, that ETs are having problems communicating with us because we are the ones blocking contact?

A: No.

Q: (L) Is it true that some people may not see ETs or UFOs because they block it from their own minds?

A: This can happen or the blockage may be inspired by the alien.

Q: (L) Now, she says: "For the most part, the average person in society does not know how to interpret telepathic contact... (Lyssa's alien talking) in the moment you start perceiving us reality starts shifting because, remember, you are one frequency and we are another." Is this true?

A: It is irrelevant.

Q: (L) Why is that irrelevant?

A: This is not an obstacle, as suggested by this statement.

Q: (L) Anyway, the article goes on: "So an ET walks up to you in your backyard and for a fragment of a moment you may perceive us. But what commonly happens is that the human will suddenly shut down usually by becoming very sleepy and falling into a sleep or type of trance state such as one that is produced by alpha or theta brain waves." Is this true? When a person sees an ET do they just turn off from the shock? Is this why most ET contact is not remembered?

A: It can happen but does not usually.

Q: (L) It says that when you start clearing out the stuff in your subconscious mind that the first layer that comes out of the subconscious is simply the top layer of priorities that were given to your subconscious mind to store and process. For the most part the first layer is not scary. It represents procrastinated perceptions that are waiting for processing by the conscious mind... then you start peeling off more layers through hypnosis or meditation and then...

A: We do not wish to further critique this as we can give all relevant and related information when needed. You are "comparing notes" which is fine if in moderation, but remember, separated sources are subject to variable corruption.

Q: (L) What is a separated source?

A: That which is separated from yours.

Q: (L) Somebody different from us? Okay, let me work on this. Our source is you, correct?

A: Yes.

Q: (L) So, the source this person is getting her information from is separated from you?

A: From you, thus unverifiable.

Q: (L) Well, I don't exactly get what you mean. The whole point of this article is to say that ETs who abduct people are here to help us evolve and that it is only us, if we have dark and dirty unconscious minds, who perceive them as negative.

A: Wrong, you do not need "help" evolving, nor does anything else.

Q: (L) Well, the thing that concerns me about this particular point of view is that a lot of people are using this to rationalize seeing the ETs and the abductions... Can I read you just a little more?

A: Overall gist is enough for us.

Q: (L) This other woman here, Dorothy Ann, claims she channels dolphins and whales. Dolphins and whales are telling her that they are here to keep frequencies and to awaken energy centers on the earth, and that they are very high level beings, for eons they have kept the electromagnetic grids in the oceans, they follow the old paths, etc. The grids are now in the process of being reset and the whales will be instrumental in this change of the vibrational patterns on the planet.

A: No.

Q: (L) The dolphin kingdom has been empowered to communicate more easily with humans; the whales are awakening to their mission of greater contact and communication with other beings...

A: Nonsense.

Q: (L) So, I don't really need to go on because all of this is nonsense. Now, this guy here who channels this being called Kryon writes an article about the metaphysical Christ. I read this article and really liked it. It made me feel nice and good and pleasant. Well, I'm not even going to ask you because I like him. It says here on another page that the Milky Way galaxy is part of a system of loosely twenty other galaxies. Is this true?

A: Too vague, all systems can be measured thusly if desired.

Q: (L) So that is too arbitrary.

A: Also a system of every conceivable combination.

Q: (L) In any event, it says that all of these universes expand at the rate of 90% of the speed of light. The ultimate central sun of it all is what we vaguely call God.

A: We have already covered these areas and "God" is "Everything", not a central sun.

Q: (L) Well, he is talking about this 25,000-year cycle where the earth passes into a photon belt that circles the Pleiadean system, and, when this photon belt hits us it is going to make all kinds of changes and it one of the small cycles, and the harmonic convergence is...

A: Fragmented channel.

Q: (L) This guy is a fragmented channel? Is there such a thing as the harmonic convergence?

A: If you wish to converge harmonically, you may.

Q: (L) So there is no photon belt circling around the Pleiades that hits us every 25,000 years?

A: If this was true, don't you think we would have informed you by now?

September 2, 1995

Q: (L) Now, could you talk to us a little bit about the purported "Photon Belt"?

A: The key issue remains one of interpretation. The messages are genuine; interpretations are variable in their accuracy. So, when one speaks of the "Photon Belt", one may really be thinking of a concept and giving it a name.

Q: (L) So, you mean that various persons are seeing something and only describing it within the limits of their knowledge?

A: At one level, yes.

In other cases, the comments have indicated that the channel is not clear, as it were, saying that this or that individual is working with a fragmented transmission. I would think that this means that the channel *is* getting valid information mixed with noise or even deliberate disinformation. On other occasions, comments have been made that this or that channel is simply making it up at some level in their subconscious minds, even if they are sincere in their conscious thinking. In a couple of instances, the individuals in question were described as agents of disinformation and agents provocateur. Rarely have we found the answer to be that the individual was just simply acting fraudulently for purposes of monetary gain, though that *has* come up a time or two.

July 11, 1998

Q: (L) I want to ask about the Dan Winter web site. He uses a lot of keywords that are very familiar to us. His whole site is devoted to pyramids, golden ratio, geomagnetic grid, geometry, bees, bloodlines, etc. The question is: everything that happens, I consider that it happens for a purpose. What is the purpose of being directed to this site? Is this all his own nonsense, or is he channeling this?

A: Extract.

Q: (L) He extracts his stuff?
A: Yes.
Q: (L) And we should extract from there the pertinent information?
A: Yes.
Q: (L) Well, he seems to be real hung up with this Drunvalo Melchizedek guy...
A: No. No good.
Q: (L) Drunvalo is no good?
A: Yes.

July 4, 1998

Q: (L) Now, we want to ask about this "Zeta Talk" web material [by Nancy Leider].
A: Specifics.
Q: (L) Okay, we wanted to know if it was a legitimate source but corrupted by a lot of noise, or if it is a major disinformation campaign?
A: Not legitimate.
Q: (L) What is the energy behind this woman who claims to channel these Zetas?
A: Ego.
Q: (L) Well, from what I read, it is pretty much an amalgamation of stuff from other sources... I mean, there was nothing that would validate it as higher density material... There was stuff from Sitchin, Velikovsky, Cayce... There is nothing there she couldn't have gotten from other sites. Ra, our stuff...
A: Yes.
Q: (L) And it is just a mishmash of all this stuff along with erroneous stuff that must have come right out of her own head.
A: Yes.
Q: (L) And, there is a huge amount of garbage coming out of her own head...
A: Yes.
Q: (L) But, as Ark pointed out, it is a very well organized site, mirror sites, she obviously has supporters and fans and all of that.
A: Any one seeking this can accomplish it. Do you really believe the "Zetas" would expend energy warning humans about impending earth changes?
Q: (L) Well, if they wanted humans to perceive the gray aliens as the good guys they would! That's what occurs to me when I think about it.
A: How much energy do you expend warning squirrels about fires?
Q: (L) Okay, point taken. None.

August 5, 2000

Q: (L) I do have a question. It says here in this Top Secret document penned by the so-called Nexus Seven:
"The bottom line is, ARC has discovered that it is very possible that confirmation, validation and consensus scientific acceptance equals an open invitation to invasion. Think about it. Denial may be one of the most powerful measures

we have at our disposal to prevent the overt acceptance of the reality of advanced alien presence into the consensus consciousness. Denial is a munition."

They are saying that as long as the whole idea of alien presence remains "in the realm of the fantastic and kooky, the implausible and mentally ill" that it is a line of defense against aliens. They see this as just a little "guided free will" to protect consensus belief using "popular deployable psychological munitions of belief."

They are saying that denial is a psychological weapon, a "deterrent of aliens into mainstream reality since the aliens seem to respect the stance of individual and group consciousness and acculturation free-will more than military might and power. Therefore, we can, by accepting alien presence and existence above board in enough mainstream public, unwittingly turn off the restrictions against overt contact the aliens are following. The overt invasion trigger is our general human acceptance."

Could you comment on the idea that denial of the reality is protection? Is that, in fact, so?

A: No. Protection comes from awareness, not the other way around.

Q: (L) That was an interesting idea to me, so I did want to pose it. Another idea in this document was that the patriarchal, monotheistic religion brought some measure of blanket protection. From this assessment, as soon as the patriarchal monotheism was installed on the planet, the alien presence withdrew. Is this a valid concept? Does the patriarchal monotheism act as a deterrent of alien intrusion into our reality?

A: This is a confused concept. Why would aliens install monotheistic principles if the result is to close off the contact opportunity?

Q: (L) That's what I thought myself. I mean, what better contact opportunity than under the guise of God, Jesus, angels, or the Holy Ghost. Alien intrusion into our reality was, in my opinion, facilitated via the monotheistic religions. But, they did note that after the institution of monotheism, the *apparent* alien contact became much less, thus the conclusion they drew.

A: The two events are either coincidental or inaccurately measured.

Q: (L) Well, it is clear that the whole monotheistic religion was a perfect front for the alien contact to continue to feed on humanity within the holy of holies of the temples. It did *not* stop, as this document suggests. The whole animal sacrifice thing, the offerings to the gods, the chanting and praying and all that; it just gives a whole new meaning to cattle mutilations! Sheesh!

Okay, there *is* something very interesting in this document.

"What is the final ontological matrix of hidden truth? What elucidates all the aspects of the true-to-life UFO phantasm in our past, present and future? What are the critical goals of Echelon beyond information suppression and technological catch-up? What are the hyper-intelligence focal points for the future?

"The sun, our sun, is dying, and too soon.

"This was caused by regional dimensional vortex shutdown some 90,000 years ago. Solar instability can cause much life on Earth to be unsustainable in 40 years. Ancient astro-theology calendars all end around now. There are also dangerous interplanetary bodies, with civilization threatening capability due to cause more serious damage to Earth in another 150 years.

"One way or the other we are slated to leave Earth, sooner or later, or else. This is a prevailing secret truth. Those in control would rather save themselves and a few elite than worry about the whole of mankind, despite the presence of a few well meaning but deluded true human patriots amongst the bunch."

Is, in fact, our sun dying?

A: Yes, and so is everything else.

Q: (L) Is it going to do it in 40 years?

A: You do not understand our attempted allusion. What is not dying?

Q: (L) Well, I *know* that, but they are saying that our sun is dying too soon.

A: No. What is "too soon"?

Q: (L) Well... (A) Forty years is certainly too soon!

A: Why?

Q: (A) Because scientists would normally give the sun much longer...

A: But do "scientists" really know?!?

Q: (L) You are *not* helping here! Are you saying this guy is right?! I don't want to talk about it anymore!

A: Be patient, Laura, this is a lesson.

Q: (L) Is our sun slated to burp and blink out in 2012 with the Mayan calendar?

A: We asked YOU a question. It is impolite to not answer!

Q: (A) Well, no, scientists don't really know; but they conjecture.

A: Ah hah! Conjecture!

Q: (L) So, what's your point?

A: Our point is: what is too soon and why?

Q: (L) Too soon would be... well, I guess that in completely objective terms, there is no such thing as "too soon". When things happen, it is exactly the right time for it to happen. When something happens, everything is perfect.

A: Okay.

Q: (L) So, in the deepest sense, nothing is ever too soon... However... (C) What situations would have to be in place for this to happen within forty years?

A: There are unlimited numbers of situations...

Q: (L) Are any of the situations that would have to be in place for the sun to burp and go out in forty years actually present and activated in our present time-line?

A: Burp?

Q: (L) Well, you know what I mean! Expand, become a red giant, burn out, run out of gas, go supernova...

A: Some of those possibilities are always present, especially when combined with multitudinal external factors.

Q: (L) What would the external factors be?

A: Energies, or cosmic forces present in space at various locators which the sun would pass through in its journey through space, for one example.

Q: (L) Are we slated to pass through any of those energies or forces?

A: Wait and see.

Q: (L) You guys can't do that to me!
A: Yes we can!
Q: (L) Well, let me ask the next question on that subject. Does any of this have to do with dimensional vortexes that were shut down 90 thousand years ago in the area of Sirius?
A: We are interested in knowing the "dimensional shutdown of vortex process". Could you explain, please?
Q: (L) Is there such a thing as a dimensional vortex?
A: Semantics.
Q: (L) What would you call a dimensional vortex?
A: Once again, this is not flowing because you are navigating haphazardly through subjective proclamations.
Q: (L) So, you are saying that all of this analysis of what the deep ontological truths are, is just subjective proclamations. Was there ever something that happened that might have been perceived by the person who wrote this material, as a dimensional vortex shutdown 90 thousand years ago?
A: What is that?!?
Q: (L) So, basically, you are trying to point out that there is no such thing as a dimensional vortex shutdown. But, you have said that the planet Kantek exploded between 70 and 80 thousand years ago, right?
A: If so, that is not what the writer is attempting to portray.
Q: (L) Could it have been a supernova?
A: Look here! This is pointless.
Q: (L) So, all of this stuff is nonsense?
A: No.
Q: (L) Are you telling me that I am too dense to get what you are trying to say here?
A: We would normally not suggest something as harsh as that.
Q: (L) Well, the only thing you didn't say was "but".
A: Okay; "but".
Q: (L) So, I am really missing the point here. Okay. What I am getting from what you are and are not saying, is that this person is clearly trying to portray something, and that there *is* something behind what he is saying, but I am just too dense to figure out the right question so you can download the answer.
A: Dense? No my dear! You are just learning, as are we all.
Q: (L) 90 thousand years ago. Is the 90,000 a parameter for something? Can I start there?
A: We doubt it!
Q: (L) Now, I did have a thought that this 90,000-year cycle could be the period of the companion brown star you have said is on it's way into the solar system. Is that what they might be talking about?
A: Closer.

Q: (L) So, what they are really talking about, or may have seen in some way, is the companion star, rather than the death of our own sun. (A) Let me just ask a simple question. Can you estimate the likelihood that the sun will die in 40 years?

A: That is unlikely.

Q: (L) Well, what a relief! (A) We are done! How unlikely?

A: There is one chance in 189 million.

Q: (L) Well, when I read this Top Secret document and they said this business about the sun, I just really wondered where they were getting all this! I mean, does the secret government really believe this crap? And if they do, and all their actions are geared around that, then that would explain a lot. But, if they don't believe it, then they might even be responsible for putting out this kind of disinformation just to make people panic and get even more anti-government so they can have more excuses to clamp down on the masses and take away more freedoms! This Nexus Seven says right up front: "This document is a clear and present danger to the mental health of unstable persons!" Well, they *did* warn us! (Laughter.)

(A) Well, it's a Val Valerian source! The fact that one or more things are wrong does not mean that everything is wrong!

A: Arkadiusz is right on the money!! There is much accurate information there and some disinformation mixed in!

Q: (L) Yes. I figured out that as long as the Nexus Seven guys were talking about the secret government echelons, the ideas of the compartmentalization, the views of the different factions about how to manage the alien threat, and so on, he was on pretty safe ground.

But, when he launched off onto the many things that were clearly borrowed from a number of channeled sources, including Billy Meier, he really missed the boat.

But, it made me aware that there are people in the government who really are following channeled material, who are using it to make their assessments, because they really don't have much choice. They are as much against a brick wall as most everyone else in figuring out the whole scenario! I guess that Billy Meier and now this Anna Hayes, are their favorite guys because it appeals to their STS hierarchical mindsets.

But, when they start to rely on channeled sources for their explanations, they run off the road because most of that sort of information is put out by the very beings they are trying to second guess, who clearly, from all their behaviors, have a serious vested interest in remaining behind the curtain, so to speak. It's hardly likely that they are going to go to all the trouble doing wicked things in secret, and then blab all their secrets to every Gray-hugger on the planet who sits down with a pyramid on their head!

And, when the abductors come and "take you to their leader" to "explain the facts of life" to you, because you have been "demanding answers" all your life, don't expect them to tell the truth. It's like the Wizard of Oz when he finally was unmasked: he was still a humbug and gave out fake hearts, fake diplomas and worthless testimonials. There is a deep lesson in that scene!

If the aliens are maintaining a covert operation, but then *do* contact people, do they expect them to tell the truth? Sheesh! You'd think these big shots in the military would figure *that* one out! It's pretty standard intelligence maneuvers!

I think that Nexus Seven runs afoul of his objective, unless his objective *is* disinformation. I would like to know: what is the possibility for Sirius to go supernova?

A: Sirius is indeed a supernova candidate.

Q: (L) Well, it's about 8 light years away. I don't think the human race would survive that one!

A: In the words of a wise philosopher: you would fry!

Q: (A) That's a wise philosopher. (L) What is the likelihood of Sirius doing the supernova number in the next hundred years or so?

A: Not good.

Q: (L) So, we can forget that one for now.

Now, it's all fine and good for the Cassiopaeans to say this or that in regard to other sources, but the question then becomes: how reliable are the Cassiopaeans *themselves*? If a person were to write to me and ask about their weekly "channel o'choice", and I were to inform them that the Cassiopaeans had said that the individual was just patching together their own theories about things from their reading and presenting it as channeled information (which was the explanation in the Zeta Talk case), what would be the point? If the reader *likes* that source and *likes* their material, and further, based on their knowledge at the time (which may be greater or lesser, depending on the amount of research they have done into the subjects being talked about by their chosen source), believes it to be an accurate representation of reality, even if what is being talked about is a hidden reality, then they are perfectly right to adhere to their choice of belief systems.

If, however, after a certain period of time of studying any such material, doing corollary research and comparisons to what can be observed and known through other disciplines, they discover that the presentation by the given source no longer holds up to scrutiny, then they are perfectly right to discard that belief system and expand their scope of understanding.

This is why I say repeatedly that it is our responsibility to do the work, examine the material, observe, research in the fields being discussed, compare, and most of all, *think*. When you strip away all the lies, what is left is Truth. And, in some teachings, you find that when you peel the onion, there is nothing in the middle!

The question then arises: can and do benevolent sources at other levels of reality *lie*?

Yes.

I can hear the sharp gasps of horror and negation at this statement. I realize that many people have had channeling experiences with beings of "love and light" who infuse every word, every contact, every interaction with insuperable sensations of "love and well-being", which amounts to "proof" that their source is a truly higher being. And then, how often have I heard the story from hypnosis subjects who have come to me for help, telling me that when they began their channeling experiments, performing the prescribed exercises of "surrounding the self with love and light" and "calling on my guides and higher self for protection," the resulting contacts and information were "transcendent" and truly "love oriented;" and then something "went wrong"? Something turned around and there were energy drains, the messages that initially were so positive and beautiful soon became oddly different or off key. In some cases, it turns ugly and intervention is necessary. In others, the percipient is convinced that they must suffer the side effects for the sake of the work, and no intervention is desired. But at the same time they wanted me to fix their stress problems or help them work on their energy levels, or find out if the real problem was in *them*, their past lives, or anything other than the fact that they were hooked up with vampiric "guides".

Sometimes the percipient doesn't have such problems as this. The problem becomes apparent in other ways. Their source tells them that they are special or chosen in some way – that they are really a great teacher who is a "walk-in" or an "incarnation" who was stimulated to awaken on the day they serendipitously decided to "channel my higher self". They are given titles, such as "Lord Ramananda" or "Lady Krishnagupa" or whatever. They are given to know that they are to be the new purveyors of the long hidden science of "Keyturn" or whatever, and the dance begins. The words pour forth in awesome syntactical matrices of great profundity and beneficence. And all the listeners agree that they are somehow changed or "uplifted and inspired" by the presence of so great a master in their midst. They follow the teachings, invest their time and money in predicted events of "mass landings" or "photon belts" or cometary companions who are going to airlift them to glory, and then – what? The predicted rapture goes kaflooey, and the excuses begin in an effort to find someone or something to blame for the disappointment.

Somewhere along the way I received the following e-mail reproduced here exactly as I received it except that I have left out the name of the correspondent:

> Under the Law of Synchronicity I have been put in contact with Sheldan Nidle. For very deep personal reasons I stayed with him before and after the "photon belt affair".
>
> Recently a friend of mine send me the address of your site. I read Earth Changes. Very interesting indeed. To be honest though, I did not appreciate the fact that your Contact made a singular comparison between Nidle and Bo and Peep [the leaders of the Heaven's Gate cult].
>
> Now let me ask you a direct question. Your Contact is from the 6th density. Nowhere in your transcript have I seen any mention of Love. Cycles, numbers, dates, no dates, time, no time, jokes sometimes, funny by the way, mention about bases, a very and extremely complicated series of scenarios of what is coming: a cold and cruel pessimism involving giants and monsters, sort of Clyde Barker Movie or

> even worst, the infamous War between Good and Evil, sort of cosmic western that reminded Star Wars, Dune, or Lovecraft for instance. The Lizards, awful creatures that ruin our hope to transcend because they are just waiting for us to eat our ass alive. Wow! No love, no hope, a peculiar definition of what STO is all about with a total disrespect for the Spirits we are under our skin. Where is God (us) doing in that kind of business?
>
> Something is wrong somewhere cause I know hope and love are making the world and all the Universes what they are and there is no love coming out from those Cassiopaeans. Who is conducting disinformations here? You or Nidle. My mind is set on that. All you need is love is the answer. As far as I am concern, Love can get anyone out of commission and we will proceed as planned, for us, for Us, and for All.

I wrote back and simply asked where was the love in promoting mass landing rumors and photon belt rumors that resulted in the suicides of 39 people? Further, where was the love in presenting aliens as saviors of mankind, when clearly, that was not the case? I received no reply.

In the book of Joel, the prophet talks about the End Times in the following way:

> I will pour out My Spirit upon all flesh, and your sons and your daughters shall prophesy, your old men shall dream dreams, your young men shall see visions. And I will show signs and wonders in the heavens and on the earth, blood and fire and columns of smoke. The sun shall be turned to darkness, and the moon to blood, before the great and terrible day of the Lord comes. (Joel 2:28, 30, 31; Amplified, Zondervan)

In the book of Acts, this prophecy is declared to be activated in the Christian context (about which I have my doubts!) with some slight amplification:

> And it shall come to pass in the last days, God declares, that I will pour out of My Spirit upon all mankind, and your sons and your daughters shall prophesy – telling forth the divine counsels – and your young men shall see visions, and your old men shall dream dreams... and they shall prophesy – telling forth the divine counsels and predicting future events pertaining especially to God's kingdom. And I will show wonders in the sky above and signs on the earth beneath, blood and fire and smoking vapor; the sun shall be turned into darkness and the moon into blood, before the obvious day of the Lord comes, that great and notable and conspicuous day. (Acts 2:17-20; excerpts; Amplified, Zondervan)

At the same time, 2nd Thessalonians says:

> The coming of the Antichrist is through the activity and working of Satan, and will be attended by great power and with all sorts of miracles and signs and delusive marvels – lying wonders – and by unlimited seduction to evil and with all wicked deception for those who are going to perish because they did not welcome the Truth but refused to love it that they might be saved. Therefore, God sends upon them a misleading influence, a working of error and a strong delusion to make them believe what is false... (2 Thessalonians, 2:9-11; Amplified, Zondervan)

In Matthew 24, when Jesus was asked, what will be the sign of the end – the completion, the consummation – of the age? He answered:

> Be careful that no one misleads you – deceiving you and leading you into error... And many false prophets will rise up and deceive and lead many into error... for false Christs and false prophets will arise, and they will show great signs and wonders, so as to deceive and lead astray, if possible, even the elect... (Matthew 24:4,11,24; Amplified, Zondervan)

So, we have some ancient traditions about this time of the "End", (or so we suppose it to be due to our many current observations about the state of the world), that support the idea of many, many channeled teachings and messages being "poured out" on the Earth in that given time. We note, in the first place, that it is described as a "pouring out of God's Spirit on all flesh" so that many are inspired to prophesy or have dreams and visions.

Okay, that's all fine and good. But then we are told that a *lot* of this will be *"unlimited seduction to evil and with all wicked deception"* brought through by false prophets and wonder workers. Further, it is clearly stated that this influence is as a result of that very same Spirit of God when it is stated: "God sends upon them a misleading influence, a working of error and a strong delusion to make them believe what is false..." The final piece of the puzzle is "false prophets will arise, and they will show great signs and wonders, so as to deceive and lead astray, if possible, even the elect..."

It's pretty clear, I think, that the Elect, whoever and whatever they are, must be considered to be the prime targets of this activity, so we have to consider that it is *not* going to be an easy task to sort the wheat from the chaff! We can expect the deceptions and delusions to be *very* subtle and clever.

Again, I would like to call your attention to the remark: "*God sends* upon them a misleading influence, a working of error and a strong delusion..."

Don't you think that this is an *astounding* statement? I do. It certainly makes it understandable why so many sources can come across as teachers of "love and light" when, in fact, they are purveyors of error and "strong delusion". In effect, we are being told that these are *tests*!

And how do you pass a test? A really difficult one? At the very least, you have to have some knowledge of the subject. In most cases, it requires a great deal of study and effort.

The point is: *there is an ancient tradition that tells us that deception is going to be the keynote of the times.* Those who have not done their homework, and who are not *aware* of this, look upon the expanding spiritual concerns of the New Age movement as a sign that the world is going to be transformed by love and light and the aliens are here to help us, and we should all embrace every new avatar that comes down the pike showing us signs and wonders or telling us that we are special and chosen, as our savior and way-shower to the Elysian Fields of sanctity and bliss.

According to the Koran, God is the "Best of deceivers". In Chapter 231 of Ibn al-'Arabi's *Futuhat*, ("Unveiling"), which is entitled "On Deception", there is a long description of the various forms that God's deception may take. It is said that God's deceptions appear as the wiles of Satan and the lower soul which often consist of:

> The continuation of favors in spite [of the servant's] opposition [to God's command]. [God allows the "state" to continue] in spite of the servant's discourtesy in the manifestation of miraculous signs without divine command and without being punished.
>
> In our own view, God's deceiving "the servant" is that He should provide him knowledge which demands practice, and then deprive him of the practice; or that God should provide him with practice, and then deprive him of sincerity in the practice. When you see this in yourself or recognize it in someone else, know that he who has such an attribute is the object of deception.[3]

In this chapter, Ibn al-'Arabi discusses various manifestations of deception, especially as it affects the general spiritual seeker, the "elect" and the "elect of the elect". These last can be the ones who are tempted by the desire to convince others by manifesting "signs".

To attempt to sidestep the natural laws of the world in which we have our being is considered to be a very great discourtesy toward God because it suggests a judgment on the creation or a breaking of the natural laws without a direct command from God. It seems that, as a test, God bestows upon some people the "power to break the laws of nature," and then places within such a person an urge to manifest these signs in such a way that he is unaware that this is a deception. Hence, he is inspired in his soul to manifest the signs as a kindness to "attract the creatures to God." Such a person does not understand that, by so doing, he is depriving the witnesses of "acting upon insight".

In other words, such a person has deprived his devotees of Free Will.

The dangers come, of course, when a person deliberately seeks to channel higher beings or the higher self before being well educated in the history and forms and results of such activities. Such practices become, in effect, a "piercing of the veil", or as Ibn al-'Arabi calls it, "unveiling".

The experience of unveiling opens up an infinite expanse of previously unseen realities to the heart of the spiritual seeker. The realm into which the adept first enters is, after all, the World of Imagination, whose byways never end. *It is the domain of the Satans and other deceiving forces.* The traveler needs to keep a clear head during his journeys and not be misled by the swirling forces, which lie just beyond the horizons of stability and balance.

> Nowadays most people interested in the spirituality of the East desire the "experience," though they may call what they are after "intimate communion with

---

[3] William C. Chittick, *The Sufi Path of Knowledge* (Albany: State University of New York Press, 1989).

God." Those familiar with the standards and norms of spiritual experience set down by disciplined paths are usually appalled at the way *Westerners seize upon any apparition from the domain outside of normal consciousness as a manifestation of the "spiritual"*. In fact there are innumerable realms in the unseen world, some of them far more dangerous than the worst jungles of the visible world. No person familiar with the teachings of Sufism would dare lay himself open to such forces...[4]

On a number of occasions, the Cassiopaeans have referred to other sources of information and have suggested that we read them so as to save time in dealing with specific concepts. The two sources are Elkins, Rueckert and McCarty's *The Ra Material* and Barbara Marciniak's *Bringers of the Dawn*.
Yes, they have mentioned that other material is connected to The Wave, but with varying degrees of corruption and distortion imposed by the recipients' wishful thinking and assumptions. Apparently, these two, mentioned here, have suffered the least from distortion – but it doesn't take long for the negative forces to act upon those who are in tune. As the Cassiopaeans have said: "Remember all channels and those of similar make-up are identified, tracked, and 'dealt with'."

In this respect, I think it is the long period of training I underwent in the areas of spirit release, depossession, exorcism, and identifying and dealing with STS/negative/demonic energies that may, initially present themselves as STO sources that has helped to prevent this very same corrupting element that worms its way in and gives that slight twist that derails the most positive of channels.

I studied for over 30 years before I began to "practice" anything. In the beginning, my practice consisted of prayer and meditation, the object being to achieve Divine Insight rather than to experience anything of a material manifestation. In 1985, when I was 33 years old, I began to meditate as an adjunct to my studies. Those who have read *Amazing Grace* are aware of some of the results of this period.

During this same time, there was a great deal of what could only be called psychokinetic activity. Many people saw this as a sign of spiritual achievement.

I didn't.

To me, it was useless and distracting. My studies had shown me that most, if not all, such events were a result of "short circuited" kundalini type forces; energies of the soul, entering via the basal chakra, diverted by the brainstem into the environment. I was distressed that they were being diverted at this juncture, rather than flowing, as was proper, in the Shepherd's Crook configuration to the third eye.

It was then, only by following the path as it developed, that the channeling experiment commenced (bringing to an end the PK activity, I should add). Even at this point, the experiment was more an attempt to bring up to conscious

---

[4] Ibid.

awareness, and then merge, the conceptualizations and possible insights of the subconscious mind. We *did* have the idea that our experiment might be a path to contact with truly higher beings, but we felt that this could only be accomplished via this "merge of conscious with subconscious" and clearing away the detritus of contradiction between the two.

I guess it would be safe to say that, until I had studied for 40 years, I did not feel competent to attempt channeling. Many people, apparently, *do* feel competent to do it with very little study – perhaps a weekend workshop or seminar at the local New Age Emporium – or because they have been contacted and told that it is their destiny. I am afraid that if I had been thusly informed that I was going to be doing such a thing, it would *never* have happened! (I guess I am a rebel at heart!)

At the same time, I don't for a minute delude myself by thinking that we are immune to corruption. On the contrary, I am *always* on the watch for information that is "off". I expect it, watch for it, and take all measures possible to prevent it on a continual basis. I am convinced that the instant this kind of vigilance is relaxed, you can pretty much say "goodbye" to objective channeling.

Nevertheless, Barbara Marciniak apparently tuned in and her first book, *Bringers of the Dawn,* contained a good percentage of useful material.

In the case of the *Ra Material*, this was also a group effort as is ours, which also began with a somewhat scientific perspective. When analyzing their material, it seems that Don Elkins was the contact with Ra, and Carla, the channel, was merely a sort of conduit. Another way to describe it would be that Don was the tuner/receiver and Carla was the speaker.

When Don died, Ra came no more.

This brings up the question that many people have written to ask me: if the *Ra Material* was such a good source, as the Cassiopaeans state, why did Don Elkins commit suicide? If Ra was supposed to be Serving Others, why didn't he[5] help Don?

Good question.

The problem, as I see it, was the distortion of judgment placed on the receiving of the material. In many ways, it was a very useful thing that this group was so aware of possible corruption, and took so many precautions. But, it may have been, in fact, these very limitations that they deliberately placed on *what* could be communicated rather than *how* it could be communicated that was responsible for Don's deteriorating mental state and, ultimately, his decision to end it all.

There was the circle ritual that was instituted for Carla's comfort. She did not feel safe otherwise. This ritual and feeling of safety may have been related to the group's idea of *what* was and was not acceptable in terms of subject matter. Or, it may simply have been Carla's own bias.

---

[5] While the being(s) known as Ra present themselves as a "social memory complex", much as the C's present themselves, I have referred to them as "he" for the ease of the reader.

Carla wrote honestly about this:

> That Ra worked with these deeply ingrained biases within me is, to me, a signal characteristic of this unique source. I felt loved, accepted and cherished by having these items placed near me, and that they thought this out was a constant blessing during this contact.

From all the reading I have done in these side remarks of the group, a great deal of activity revolved around Carla's biases. It was a major operation just to get anything through at all! But then, there was the bias as to *what* was acceptable in the way of questions and answers:

> Early in the Ra contact we received answers to our questions which fell into a controversial portion of our third density illusion.
>
> The following information falls into this category and resulted from a follow-up question Don asked about UFOs and their sources. You will note Don's incredulous attitude throughout this portion of his questioning.
>
> It was our decision to remove this information from Book One of *The Law of One* because we felt it to be entirely unimportant and of a transient nature since knowing it adds nothing to one's ability or desire to seek the truth and the nature of the evolutionary process, whether the information is true or not.

I have to say that the above remark astonished me to no end. Here they are talking about seeking the truth about the evolutionary process, and information pertaining to same has been deemed "entirely unimportant… whether it is true or not." We notice in the next paragraph how easy it is to begin to classify truths according to human criteria.

> In fact, knowing and continuing to seek this kind of information can become a major stumbling block to one's spiritual journey because it removes one's attention from the eternal truths which may serve anyone's journey—at any time—and places it upon that which is only of fleeting interest and of little use spiritually.
>
> Concentrating on conspiracy theories and their participants tends to reinforce the illusion of separation and ignores the love that binds all things as One Being. If we had continued to pursue this particular line of questioning, or any other line of questioning of a transient nature, we would soon have lost the contact with those of Ra because, as Ra mentioned in the very first session, Ra communicated with us through a "narrow band of vibration or wave length."

The fact seems to be that the contact with Ra was, indeed, lost because sufficient questions were *not* asked about those very things that might have served to protect Don.

Let's go back to the remark I already noted:

> It was our decision to remove this information from Book One of *The Law of One* because we felt it to be entirely unimportant and of a transient nature since

knowing it adds nothing to one's ability or desire to seek the truth and the nature of the evolutionary process, whether the information is true or not.

As much as I admire the material and the group and their efforts, I have to say that the above remark was clearly a judgment. When you start judging, you begin constriction and limitation of what may or may not come through according to your idea of truth. Yes, indeed, one must evaluate the intent and nature of the entities transmitting, but one must *not* judge as unseemly any material, which is, in fact, a *fact*! If there is corroboration from other directions, even scientific or historical, yet you judge it to be not worthy of discussion, you have effectively closed down a receptivity to truth.

As we have discussed in *Riding the Wave*, *all* knowledge is knowledge of God. At whatever level it exists, it is a manifestation of the Faces of God. Carla writes that they made a decision to remove this information because they felt it to be "entirely unimportant... whether true or not."

This is one of the cleverest deceptions going in the modern New Age teachings. In effect, it *promotes* the subjective and wishful thinking version of reality, suggesting at the same time that learning about the world as it is, is somehow dangerous.

This is similar to the Christian Fundamentalist teaching that you never need to read any book but the Bible – everything you need to know is there. They contend that knowing anything outside of that, as Carla wrote about knowledge of anything outside of "love and light" questions, "adds nothing to one's ability or desire to seek the truth and nature of the evolutionary process."

Yet, it is abundantly clear that knowing such things is *crucial* to understanding the truth of the evolutionary process! It may not add anything to the "desire", but it adds *everything* to one's *ability* to seek the truth. And that truth might have saved Don's life.

Carla wrote:

> In fact, knowing and continuing to seek this kind of information can become a major stumbling block to one's spiritual journey because it removes one's attention from the eternal truths which may serve anyone's journey—at any time—and places it upon that which is only of fleeting interest and of little use spiritually.

I certainly agree that "continuing to seek" this kind of information can become a stumbling block. But knowing it in the first place is essential to navigate one's way on the spiritual journey. And, in point of fact, the negative existence, the STS hierarchy *is* part of the "eternal truths", and is therefore, of considerable interest, spiritually speaking.

The next remark:

> If we had continued to pursue this particular line of questioning, or any other line of questioning of a transient nature, we would soon have lost the contact with those of Ra.

At this point in time, it is clear that the restricted line of questioning this group *did* follow ultimately led to the loss of the contact with Ra through Don Elkin's suicide even though they thought that their precautions would produce the opposite result.

Our own experience has shown us that pursuing the very lines of questions that the Ra group eschewed has been our only source of defense against the forces that have sought to destroy us. Had the Ra group also pursued this line of information, Don might have had the means of evaluating what was happening to him in the crushing psychic attack he underwent, and would thereby, very likely, have been able to resist the assault.

I can tell you that the psychic attack, the mental pressure, the emotional manipulation, that one undergoes in this kind of work can be utterly brutal. There are no words to describe it. But it seems that doing it and surviving it are essential to broadening and deepening the communication band.

Carla wrote: "as Ra mentioned in the very first session, Ra communicated with us through a "narrow band" of vibration or wave length."

This remark of Ra's undoubtedly referred to the restrictions placed on the conduit as a result of Carla's fears and biases, and the very judgments expressed in the above comments. I hardly think that such an entity as Ra claimed to be would be confined to, or experience reality as a "narrow vibration or wave length." It would, therefore, stand to reason that the "narrow band" was at the receiving end. The band of communication might very well have been broadened at the receiving end if such judgments and choices had not been made as those we have examined.

The Cassiopaeans commented on this broadening of the channel on one occasion. In one of the earliest sessions, we were told about the experiments being performed on children by "aliens", and this was truly a horrible thing to be discussing. I later asked *why* such a thing was being told to us. Like Carla, I was of the opinion that a good source would only say nice things. I was horrified and my first reaction was to terminate the contact immediately. But I didn't, and later I came back to ask about this initial shocking material.

October 20, 1994
Q: (L) We got some information from an early session which said some awful things about bits of children's organs being removed, etc. What was the source of that information? Did that come from you guys?
A: Yes. Sorry for shock but necessary for broadening channel.

On the subject of rituals, the Cassiopaeans are very clear that, for the most part, they, too, are restrictive.

July 16, 1994
Q: (L) Do any of the rituals we perform provide protection against further abduction?

A: Maybe. Some crystals with energy fields. Don't need protection if you have knowledge.
Q: (L) How do we get this knowledge?
A: It is deep in the subconscious
Q: (L) When did we get it?
A: Before birth.
Q: (L) Is there anything else we can do for protection?
A: Learn, meditate, read. Need to awaken.

The following was one of their earliest explications of "Knowledge Protects".

October 22, 1994
Q: (L) Are there any rituals that can be performed to provide protection for one against intrusion by the Lizzies.
A: Rituals are self-defeating.
Q: (L) Are there any technological means we can use?
A: The only defense needed is knowledge. Knowledge defends you against every possible form of harm in existence. The more knowledge you have, the less fear you have, the less pain you have, the less stress you feel, the less anguish you feel, and the less danger you experience of any form or sort.

Think of this very carefully now for this is very important: Where is there any limitation in the concept behind the word "knowledge"? Being that there is no limitation, what is the value of that word? Infinite.

Can you conceive of how that one concept, that one meaning frees you from all limitation? Use your sixth sense to conceive of how the word, the term, the meaning of knowledge can provide with all that you could possibly ever need. If you think carefully you will begin to see glimpses of how this is true in its greatest possible form.
Q: (L) Does this include knowledge learned from books?
A: This includes all possible meanings of the concept of the word.

Can you think of how it would be that simply with one term, this one word could carry so much meaning?

We sense that you are not completely aware. You can have glimpses of illumination and illumination comes from knowledge

If you strive perpetually to gain and gather knowledge, you provide yourself with protection from every possible negative occurrence that could ever happen.

Do you know why this is?

The more knowledge you have, the more awareness you have as to how to protect yourself. Eventually this awareness becomes so powerful and so all encompassing that you do not even have to perform tasks, or rituals if you prefer, to protect yourself. The protection simply comes naturally with the awareness.
Q: (L) Does knowledge have a substance or an existence apart from its possession or its acceptance?
A: Knowledge has all substance. It goes to the core of all existence.
Q: (L) So acquiring knowledge includes adding substance to one's being?

A: Indeed. It includes adding everything to one's being that is desirable. And also, when you keep invoking the light, as you do, truly understand that the light is knowledge. That is the knowledge, which is at the core of all existence. And being at the core of all existence it provides protection from every form of negativity in existence. Light is everything and everything is knowledge and knowledge is everything. You are doing extremely well in acquiring of knowledge. Now all you need is the faith and realization that acquiring of knowledge is all you need.

Q: (L) I just want to be sure that the source that I am acquiring the knowledge from is not a deceptive source.

A: If you simply have faith, no knowledge that you could possibly acquire could possibly be false because there is no such thing. Anyone or anything that tries to give you false knowledge, false information, will fail. The very material substance that the knowledge takes on, since it is at the root of all existence, will protect you from absorption of false information that is not knowledge.

There is no need to fear the absorption of false information when you are simply openly seeking to acquire knowledge. And knowledge forms the protection – all the protection you could ever need.

Q: (L) There are an awful lot of people who are being open and trusting and having faith that are getting zapped and knocked on their rears.

A: No. That is simply your perception. What you are failing to perceive is that these people are not really gathering knowledge. These people are stuck at some point in their pathway to progress and they are undergoing a hidden manifestation of what is referred to in your terms as obsession. Obsession is not knowledge; obsession is stagnation. So, when one becomes obsessed, one actually closes off the absorption and the growth and the progress of soul development, which comes with the gaining of true knowledge. For when one becomes obsessed one deteriorates the protection therefore one is open to problems, to tragedies, to all sorts of difficulties. Therefore one experiences same.

October 28, 1994

Q: (L) The ideas of candle burning, salt, sage, shamanistic rituals and so forth? Is all this useless?

A: Maybe. You are learning; remember when we say "good: no ritual"?

Q: (L) In other words, your knowledge and your strength, which comes from your knowledge and knowing, are the point and the protection?

A: Precisely. This is extremely important. Ritual drains directly to Lizard beings.

Q: (L) Even our saying of the Lord's Prayer?

A: It is okay to pray. Why do you think organized religion is obsessed with rituals?

Q: (L) Is the same thing true of shamanistic practices and so forth?

A: Exactly.

The following excerpt shows us how focusing on the positive aspects can be as limiting as focusing on the negative. Once you know what the situation is, how it developed and came into being, you can then more easily control your own reaction to it. This excerpt also deals with the issue of sharing information.

You might even say that, at this point, I was experiencing much of the type of attack that Don Elkins undoubtedly experienced, though my way of dealing with it was to ask more questions and get to the bottom of the problem.

July 23, 1995

Q: (L) Why have I been under such severe physical, material, and emotional attack in the past six months? Frank thinks that I am under such attack because I work and move too fast in the gathering of information and attempts at sharing it; that I charge ahead and do things, thereby exposing myself to retaliatory attacks.

A: That has the potential for being partially correct in the sense that you disseminate information, perhaps less carefully than you should. The gathering of information holds no potential for attack from any particular realm. However, dissemination DOES, because those whom become aware, become empowered. And, in any struggle between opposing forces, there is always danger in allowing anyone to become empowered without realization of the ramifications.

Q: (L) So, I can continue to seek information, as long as I keep it to myself?

A: You have free will to do that which you please. But, when you are framing it in terms of the question: where is the danger, this presupposes that you are concerned about dangers to yourself. And, if this be the case, we will be happy to give advice where and when needed.

Q: (L) Well, right now it is needed. I am almost completely debilitated physically and materially, which creates a severe barrier to focus and concentration, and also my ability to assist other people.

A: Well then, perhaps it is true that you should be careful as to how you disseminate the information and how you disseminate knowledge gained, and where, and when. This is not to say that you must stop, but rather to think carefully before you do it, as to what the ramifications will be. And then your instincts will lead you in the proper direction. The dangers are always that when one proceeds too quickly, the instincts may be overrun and become confused with other thought pattern energies, and thereby opening one up to attack and other unpleasant possibilities.

Q: (L) Well, if I promise not to tell, make a vow, can't we just stop all this other?

A: It is not necessary to stop, it is just to be careful as to how one does it. The flow of information is never a harmful thing. As we have previously described, the Service to Self involves the constriction and restriction of energies, and the focusing within. The Service to Others orientation involves an outward flow of energies, the focus being from within to without. Therefore, the passage of information, or dissemination is very helpful and is of Service to Others orientation. But, one must also be aware of the dangers involved. One must not lose control of the flow and the possibilities that can result. This is where you need to be more careful. You need to regulate.

And, attack can come from any number of sources for any number of reasons. It is not always for the same reason. And, of course, there is the short wave and long wave cycle. The short wave cycle is one which closes rather quickly. The long wave cycle is one that closes more slowly, therefore take a longer amount of time, as you perceive it, to close. Therefore it also involves a more complicated issue. This is just one example as to how attack can be the result of what we were just describing.

Q: (L) Can attack be a left over from another cycle?

A: That is one possibility, certainly.

Q: (L) Can you give us any advice as to how to navigate our way out of such situations?

A: That is a VERY vague thought concept.

Q: (L) Well, I seem to repeatedly face the financial flow issue, and it seems to be one of the primary modes of attack against me at this point. How can I overcome this?

A: Are you asking us how to make more money?

Q: (L) Yeah!

A: My dear Laura! You are already in possession of literally thousands of possibilities to accomplish that end, are you not?

Q: (L) Everything takes money!

A: There goes that prejudice again. We have given much food for thought in that area to help you to learn, to contemplate, to meditate.

Q: (L) It is rather difficult to do that when one is worried about how to keep the lights on and feed the children.

A: That is interesting. You can't meditate or contemplate when you are worried about your next meal. I guess then that this means that no one on third density has ever been able to contemplate or meditate while worrying what was going to be eaten at the next meal. Hmmmmmm.

Q: (L) The point is that a constant state of worry, another crisis every day, the perpetual worry, eventually wears a person down to the point where one can no longer focus on any other issues.

A: Perhaps one can solve the crises by focusing on other issues? You see, when you constrict the flow, you constrict the channel. And when you constrict the channel, you close down possibilities. And, you make it difficult, if not impossible for you to see that which is there. In other words, the obvious becomes oblivious because of constriction of the flow.

This is why we have recommended against all rituals, because ritual restricts the flow, thereby restricting the possibilities. And, what you are describing is a situation of "dire straits," as you call it – and pressures of great magnitude – which is restricting you.

But actually, it is your concentration on same that is restricting, not the situation itself. And we realize that it is difficult for you to focus your attentions, or, more importantly to open up the flow of the channel. But, it is certainly not impossible. Especially for an individual as strong as yourself. It is what you choose to do, not what you MUST do. It is what you CHOOSE to do.

Indeed, I spent so much time worrying that I could hardly think about anything but how dreadful things had gotten in my life since the Cassiopaean communications had begun and I had been sharing the material. And so it was that I could not see any solution at all.

A practical example of this is the well-known PMS syndrome. I had a friend who used to joke that "For years I suffered from PMS. Then I went through menopause. Now I realize I never had PMS. I'm just a natural bitch."

Well, that's pretty funny, but it emphasizes something important. Many women have remarked how much easier it is to control their PMS reactions *knowing* what is going on. Before the defining of this syndrome, many women suffered horribly at the hands of friends and family who thought they were crazy or just simply bad tempered. When you know it is the hormone mixture in your body affecting the permeability of cell membranes, which affects the electrical balance or synaptic response, it is a *lot* easier to say to yourself, "This will pass. I am only seeing things through the distortion of hormonal influences." It is also a lot easier to concentrate on normalizing your actions and reactions when you *know* you have to compensate for a physiological condition.

The same is true in terms of psychic attack – whether it comes from third, fourth or fifth density sources. Once you know how these things work, when it happens to you, you are *aware*, and thus able to withstand the assault and put your attention where it belongs – on continuing to operate in a stable and clear-headed way – which you *now know* is going to require extra exertion on your part for a period of time – so that the attack passes much more quickly and with less damage.

For example, consider an individual who is under attack from a purely third density source – say, an ELF (Extremely Low Frequency) transmitter is nearby causing severe fluctuations in their physiological system which then leads to internal sensations and perceptions that are distorted. So, the person goes to church to pray or gets out the sage and lights it up and waves it around. This may or *may not* have an effect.

If, on the other hand, they become aware of the ELF transmitter, or the *possibility* that it could be of such a nature, then their knowledge, combined with application – such as putting up some kind of shielding device or moving away from the transmitter – might have better results.

August 12, 1995

Q: (L) We would like to know a bit more on the subject of rituals, which you have warned us are restricting on many levels. Why is this?

A: If one believes in one's activities sincerely, to the greatest extent, they certainly will produce SOME benefit, at SOME level. But, merely following patterns for the sake of following patterns does not produce sincerity and faith necessary for ultimate benefits to result.

So, therefore, as always, one must search from within, rather than from without, to answer that question. Do you understand?

> To give you an example, to be certain, you meet this all the time. If you read material in the pages of a book that advises one form of ritual or another, and you follow that form of ritual because you have read words printed on the pages, does that really give you the true sense of satisfaction and accomplishment within yourself to the greatest extent possible?
>
> Whereas, if you, yourself, were to develop an activity, which one or another could interpret or define as a ritual, but it comes from within you, it feels RIGHT to you, and you have a sincere and complete faith in it, whatever it may be, does that feel right to you?
>
> Q: (L) Yes.
> A: Have we answered the question, then?
> Q: (L) Yes, thank you.

Note, however, the caveat in the above comments: "SOME benefit, at SOME level." In the end, knowledge of the true nature of the attack, and specific actions formulated in response to that knowledge, will be the most effective "ritual".

Now, in the case of the Ra channeling experiment, it seems that the rituals put in place to make Carla comfortable certainly were of benefit to her. But, the question that must be asked is: did Don believe in them? If he had, then perhaps the protection would have extended to him as well. But, either he didn't believe in them, *or they were objectively ineffectual.*

Knowledge of the methods of psychic attack, knowledge of negative experience in *this* density, and how to deal with it by being *aware*, would probably have saved Don's life. We asked the Cassiopaeans about it, specifically, at one point:

> July 24, 1999
>
> Q: (L) I have been having a dialogue with a fellow on the net in the last week or so who is very well versed in the *Ra Material*. He sent me a large chunk of Volume 5 of the Ra books, which was material that had not been released earlier.
>
> It seems that during the times that Don Elkins was asking some questions about different conspiracies and the nature of the fourth density STS manipulations and some other rather grim subjects, there was some sort of judgment made by this group, or members of this group, that such subjects were not appropriate lines of questioning for an STO channel. They were, apparently, considered to be a "focusing on negative aspects", therefore they were not of "love and light". Such questions and directions of questions were, therefore, discouraged or agreed by this group to be not desirable to pursue. Don Elkins *did*, however, commit suicide. Can you tell us why?
>
> A: Suicide is a chosen pathway for the purpose of close realization of shutting off the noise.
>
> Q: (L) I would like to understand. Here, these folks had this marvelous contact with Ra.
>
> A: Contact with Ra does not preclude the possibility of attack.

Q: (L) Why did Ra not convey to him the information necessary to understand that he was under attack, and what kind of attack it was, and how to deal with it?

A: The questions were not asked.

Q: (L) Why were the questions not asked that would have protected him?

A: "Love and Light" focus.

Q: (L) So, because they were so focused on the love and light aspects...

A: There is no positivity without negativity. There is always negativity present, whether acknowledged or not.

Q: (L) So, you are saying that if it is not acknowledged, placed on the table, so to speak, that it sort of "bites you" no matter what? That, in some way it will manifest, and if a person goes to an extreme in terms of love and light, the negativity will come in the back door?

A: Close.

It is such a tragedy that this happened to this groundbreaking, trail-blazing group. But, it is a lesson for all of us to realize that when you begin to deal with the realms of knowledge of the cosmos, and you start to limit or place your subjective assumptions in the way so that the information is constricted or limited, that energy/information that you filter out *still* exists, objectively, and is still a part of *you*.

It is *not* true that evil is created by the mind of man except insofar as the mind of man is the mind of God and all else.

A simple way to understand this is: when you have a current of energy, it normally is a wave with crests and troughs – up and down, positive and negative. Those sources that focus on any one aspect of the energy become like a diode, which converts alternating current to direct current. The current can flow through the diode only one way, and part of the current is blocked and is converted to heat. This is, essentially, the process of a DC converter and it is also why DC converters have to be frequently replaced: they burn out.

The "heat" produced in Don as a result of the diode function of Carla was that which "burned out his circuits" because the information being transduced in Don was so much greater than that which could be received and channeled by Carla.

I understood this instinctively when I was studying the *Ra Material*. Yes, I had many of the same biases as Carla in the beginning, but I was also aware of something else – something that was crucial to my understanding and which had resulted from my work in spirit release and exorcism – and that was a simple principle which amounts to this: putting attention on negative forces does *not* make them stronger *if the intent is to diminish them*. And one can only learn to diminish darkness by learning exactly what *is* of darkness. And that amounts to, as we have already discussed, learning to identify our reality through its symbols, and learning to give each thing its due.

In another respect, a focus on love and light can, in some cases, reflect an inner fear of the darkness. And that fear will attract unpleasant experiences and events into one's life. *Only knowledge can dispel that fear.*

In our own channeling, do we have a diode functioning? Do we filter the information?

It is clear that, in the early days, Frank played the role of the ground wire, the actual conduit of the material into this realm, and that the connection to the Cassiopaean nexus is something that takes place through my physiology. I never hear anything in my mind, I am always as interested in having the comments read back to me as everyone else; I am constantly conscious and active, while Frank is generally in a sort of semi-conscious state.

For a long time, we thought that this meant Frank was the source. But then, gradually, through experimentation, we discovered that, yes, Frank can channel just about all the time by virtue of his uniquely neutral nature and physiology. He was the clearest and cleanest open channel I have ever encountered or heard of.

But this condition presents unique problems. Being an open channel means exactly that: an open channel – empty – and it is the question of what person he is channeling with that determines what is channeled through him. When he channels alone, he is subject to the whims and forces of everything and anything in the psychic atmosphere. He seems to have *no diode function*. He merely connects and amplifies like a radio tuner and set of speakers. This was, of course, very fortunate for me.

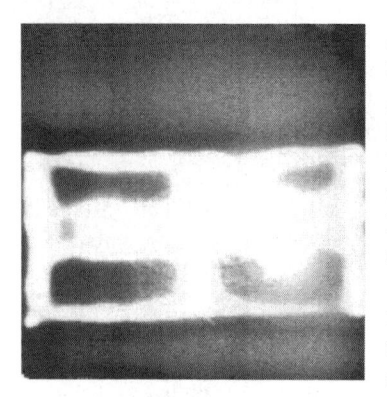

In the image left, that I have already discussed in *Riding the Wave*, notice that the bright glow on the right is my left hand. The glowing image on the left is Frank's right hand. Note the gap in the flow in the area of Frank's wrist where some of the flesh shows through. This photo seems to indicate some level of blockage on Frank's side, but it was minimal.

What does this mean? Well, it is interesting the ways in which we have come to these conclusions. In the early days of the experiment, we noticed a curious phenomenon: if there were persons present who had strong emotional agendas or assumptions, these things would color the transmission. It was as though Frank were picking up on bleed through from the particular individual sort of like cross talk on a radio or telephone when another conversation is being heard in the background. When he channels alone, having no orientation of his own, Frank is as subject to pure STS information as STO. His function as a tuner and speaker means that he can be connected to any transmission source. It also makes him uniquely able to do individual psychic readings by simply tuning into the individual with a clarity unsurpassed by any other psychic I've ever known.

For many years, prior to our association, Frank was channeling. He began doing it as a young child when he discovered that using a stick to beat out a rhythm could entrance him, and then his mind would receive endless streams of information. We experimented with him doing this alone, and examined the material produced thereby, and it was exactly the type of mindless psychobabble that comes through so many other sources.

It was clear that Frank was definitely a conduit, but he was not connected to any particular source. One way of describing it would be like a radio tuner constantly running the scan function. This *can* produce problems when people are present at the sessions who have strong biases or emotional agendas. Doing the channeling under such conditions is rather like trying to watch television with the vacuum cleaner running. The static manifests as certain turns of phrase or grammatical constructions that are not usual, and even certain slants on the material. In some cases, it has resulted in the Cassiopaeans declining to answer some questions at all because the guest was only asking for confirmation of a subjective opinion.

On a couple of occasions it was pretty obvious to me that they were declining to answer because the individual was an STS "mole". These answers usually come as "open", "up to you", or other non-answers; but not always.

At one point, I started counting the number of non-answers and relating it to the people present, and I began to realize that we had a real problem with this. I then began to try to screen guests before they were invited to attend a session. But, even with screening, you don't really know until you do it. There are many people who say all the right things to get invited to a session, but once there, the energy sort of forces them out in the open and their biases become quite evident. I had to laugh on one occasion when the participant was blocked over and over again by the Cassiopaeans who were hinting that he had some strange affiliations. The man became more and more uncomfortable and actually turned quite rude and aggressive thinking that to attack would divert the attention.

The man in question was a director of a MUFON group with the initials G.B. and the following is the excerpt of the strange responses in question:

February 25, 1995

Q: (GB) I had a very strange experience when I meditated a while back. Was that positive or negative?

A: You have had many "strange" experiences. Would you like to share any with those present, GB?

Q: (TM) I think I know which one you are talking about. (L) What was the nature of that experience?

A: Entity reflection through curtain.

Q: (GB) Was the entity reptilian that I manifested behind me? Or was this a positive or negative energy?

A: Both and neither. Reflection. Projection.

Q: (L) What was it a projection of?

A: Complicated.

Q: (L) What was the source of this projection?

A: STS.

Q: (GB) What were the loud whacks behind my chair? What did they try to tell me?

A: It was not a message, it was a "curtain breach".

Q: (J) Kind of like a dimensional sonic boom. (GB) Well, I heard a tremendous crack behind my chair when I asked for a sign. About seven large whacks on the floor. (J) Was there an entity standing behind his chair?

A: Yes, but again, GB has had a most interesting life, apparently he does not want to divulge this.

Q: (L) Well, three times they have hinted about this! (Laughter.) (BP) And I thought I knew you! (TM) Yeah, he doesn't even know about it! (BP) Is GB a so-called "abductee"?

A: In more ways than one.

Q: (BP) Please clarify.

A: That is up to GB.

Q: (L) There are about six different kinds of abductions ranging from physical to telepathic contact and triggering.

A: And there are human abductions too.

Q: (L) You mean humans abduct people too? (J) Have humans abducted GB?

A: Up to GB.

Although Terry and Jan were the first to notice and bring up the subject that Frank's function was other than being the source contact, I wasn't too sure. (I tell the whole story in *Petty Tyrants* and *Facing the Unknown*.) However, a curious exchange occurred at one point that began to give me a better perspective on what was going on.

It was shortly after my husband, Ark, found me through the Cassiopaean material, and, at that point, we were really pressing the C's for answers as to exactly *what* was going on; what was our purpose, and so forth. The obviously "maneuvered" connection with Ark – a physicist – certainly made it clear that this was not your ordinary, garden-variety channeling. It was becoming more and more evident that there was a purpose even though the Cassiopaeans declined to suggest as much, preferring to leave such realizations to our own pathway of discovery.

So, there we were, asking questions about the plans of the fourth density STS forces with the objective of trying to get a handle on our proper response. The questions were focused on activities in alleged underground bases:

August 31, 1996

Q: (L) What do these guys plan on doing?

A: This is where "The Master Race" is being developed.

Q: (L) And what is the time frame they have planned for this activity?

A: Never mind.

Q: (L) Is Ark going to be able to help us with technology, to help other people, or to protect ourselves in some way? In this really bizarre stuff going on on our planet?

A: Too much, too soon, my dear. Curiosity killed the cat.

Q: (L) Well, satisfaction brought him back!

A: Not in this case!!!

Q: (T) He's coming to protect you. That's what he said.

A: Maybe, but there is so, so, so much more in store than that!!!!!!

Q: (L) Is that an ominous, "maybe, but there's so, so, so much more in store?" Or is that a positive, there is so, so, so much more in store?

A: Why would you think it ominous?

Q: (L) Well I don't know… Because I'm scared of what I don't know!

A: What have we helped you to discover so far? Would you rather discontinue this operation?

Q: (L) Oh, hell no! (T) After two years, you know she's always going to ask those kinds of questions!

A: Not two years, eternity. We have helped you build your staircase one step at a time. Because you asked for it. And you asked for it because it was your destiny. We have put you in contact with those of rare ability in order for you to be able to communicate with us. […]

Q: (T) It is destiny for you to find out what your path was, and you had to make this contact, because it was what you were supposed to do. (L) Are we talking about Frank in terms of being put in contact with someone who enables me to communicate with you, so you can put me on my path, which is building the staircase, etc.? Is that what we've got going here?

A: He is one, but not the only one, just the one who awakened your sense of recognition.

So, we studied that passage and came to the realization that Frank does, indeed, have a rare ability to act as a "broad-band frequency transducer". But his tuning is entirely dependent upon the strength of the vector, which, respecting the Cassiopaeans, seems to be me.

But, getting back to the *Ra Material*, Carla made the remark, "Concentrating on conspiracy theories and their participants tends to reinforce the illusion of separation and ignores the love that binds all things as One Being."

I agree that one should not concentrate on "conspiracy theories". The Cassiopaeans have said as much. But the fact is, they are a very real part of our world, and conspiracy is part and parcel of the STS pathway, and the reality in which we live. It is also apparent that we are here to learn the lessons of this reality as completely as possible in order to graduate. To consider this aspect of our world as being "outside" or "not a part" of God, is doing the very thing

Carla was trying to avoid: in effect, by *not* learning about such things, she was *reinforcing the illusion of separation* and ignoring the love that binds all things as One Being – including conspiracies and their participants.

To this day, Carla focuses in that direction, and suffers incredibly from many physical ailments and, seemingly, other mental/emotional torments. She has stated in her writings that these sufferings are the price she must pay in her efforts to hold her focus on love and light. This is very commendable, but misses the point, I think. As we have talked about already, it is not that a person is supposed to *manifest* negativity in their lives in a deliberate way. There is always choice. That is the key. But it is in judging the negativity to be an error or a mistake or something to be "fixed" in others or the self that one goes astray. And when you exert effort to "create love and light via focus on same," it becomes a tacit admission that there is some lack of it in your reality.

Folks have a lot of problems in distinguishing between "judgment" and "assessment and personal choice". I can look at and assess any number of things as negative and choose to act otherwise, or, in other words, learn to give negativity its due by *non-participation*. But, I don't have to think that I must impose my choice on anyone else, nor do I have to think that the negativity needs to be fixed or done away with. It is the choice of some beings to follow that path. They have the right to choose it just as I have the right to choose what I choose. And, the only way I *can* choose *is to know the difference*! And I cannot know the difference if I do not have the deepest knowledge possible about every aspect of the reality in which I live.

And that is not to say that we can ever fully know the *truth*. But it is our job to Love the Creator, and we cannot love the Creator/Self without *knowing* Creator/Self. When we deny fully half of Creation, we are choosing to love only *our image* of what the Creator *should* be, according to *our* judgment. And by blocking, or ignoring information that would instruct us about the many Faces of God, we are actually *taking action against God*. We are judging and *carrying out a sentence of exclusion*. And that which we exclude from acknowledgement comes back to us over and over again in our lessons in life.

Now, having talked about the *Ra Material* source in some detail, I want to suggest that those who have not read it try to get a copy because it is a rare and amazing thing what this group did, in spite of the pit they fell into and the tragedy that resulted. Don paid a very high price for the purity of the material and it deserves first place in the higher-level transmissions.

Here are some of the comments of the Cassiopaeans about the Ra channeling:

October 23, 1994

Q: (L) We want to know about the *Ra Material* by Elkins, Rueckert and McCarty. Where is the *Ra Material* coming from?
A: Sixth Density.
Q: (L) Would you say that the *Ra Material* comes through a clear channel?
A: Yes.

August 11, 1996

Q: (L) Okay, since the *Ra Material* is considered to be a kind of primer to the Cassiopaean material, could you give us a percentage on the accuracy of this material?

A: 63.

Q: (L) 63%, well, that's pretty good, considering... (T) A lot of it is very good stuff... (L) Can you talk to us a little bit about the concept of Wanderers? In the Ra teaching about Wanderers, it is said that Wanderers are individuals who feel alienated in the world system...

A: Yes but they can partially adapt.

Q: (L) Okay, do they also sometimes have physical...?

A: Revulsion to physicality.

Q: (L) Okay, is that always a clue?

A: Yes.

Q: (J) Revulsion to physicality, does that refer to a dislike of the fact that in third density all is physical, and it's fixed, as opposed to upper densities, where there are variables?

A: 3rd density is not "all" physical.

Q: (L) I think that what they're getting at is like a fine division between somebody who focuses on physical sensation as opposed to spiritual or mental or emotional sensation as being the point of reference.

A: Yes. 3rd density natives tend to concentrate and, to an extent, revel, in the physical.

Q: (J) I think the point that I was trying to make was, having to stay in third density, would they miss the variability of physicality? (L) Well, Wanderers, remember, are sixth density beings.

A: The lack.

Q: (T) The lack of physicality?

A: Yes. Is missed. Not so much "miss," as much as difficulty of adjustment.

Q: (T) If you were used to the freedom of non-physicality, and then became limited by being physical, you'd miss the non-physical state.

This is another area where there are some misunderstandings in the spiritual life. Many seekers believe that their inability to function in the real world is like a badge of merit – a proof of their great spirituality. Physical ailments, loss of function, inability to manage ordinary daily affairs, and so on and on are all excused because the person is so "spiritual" that they cannot be expected to be bothered with such things.

Well, that's all fine and good but wouldn't you think that a person who is supposed to have graduated to higher spiritual realms did so because they mastered the lower ones? And, if that is the case, what is so hard about remembering those lessons and activating them at a higher level of competence this time around? If you have graduated to sixth grade, surely you can ace all the tests of third grade?

In *Amazing Grace*, which chronicles my path toward the C's, I have written about my specific work as a hypnotherapist and the things I learned as an exorcist that gave me insight into the ins and outs of the spiritual realms. I'm not going to go into that here except to say that I knew what I was dealing with when we began the channeling experiment.

For those who have asked the questions about my spiritual hygiene, I can assure you that I used some pretty sophisticated techniques to maintain a state of psychic cleanliness at the inception of the project, throughout the past 15 years or so, and at present. I constantly monitor the flavor, feel and "fruits" of the contact – making adjustments or shifts to accommodate. And, most of all, we look on it as "play". We don't now, nor did we ever, take it as true believer material. It sure is interesting because of the many areas that have independent corroboration, but some of it is, by its very nature, unverifiable.

There are many things we have learned, and not just from being informed via hard work, but also by having a suggestion given to us, which we then observed, experimented with, and developed more fully on our own. This is one of the keys to the uniqueness of the Cassiopaeans; they don't just hand it out. As I have noted again and again, they give clues, but not roadmaps. Their position is that if we don't do the work to gather the detailed knowledge, it is useless; like candy: empty calories. Clearly, this approach is designed to make the practice of channeling ultimately unnecessary and obsolete. We will, eventually, "become" them. Repeatedly they tell us that leading us by the hand is detrimental; they have laid the groundwork, given us the boost because we *asked* (and did so repeatedly, consistently, and with dedication for over two years before the contact initiated), but that the real purpose is to get us to learn to walk on our own.

Most channeled sources want folks to channel just so they can channel more and more and on and on. The Cassiopaeans have actually been becoming less and less communicative, preferring to tell us "you have the tools, we have taught you, now figure it out yourself!"

A lot of people don't like that. They want to have everything handed to them. They don't want to think or work or do anything except just lie down and have everything poured into their heads. Then, they just "believe" and get eaten alive (which generally manifests as all sorts of physical, emotional, mental and relationship type problems).

There is another curious thing about channeling and current day channeled material, and that is the excessive, archaic, or convoluted syntactical verbiage! As Michael Topper described it:

> Consider, for example, the most common means of establishing the "inner plane" or channel connection: meditation.
> This is the method most recommended both by channelers *and* the given channeled source.

Meditation is of course, as we should all know by now, a means of stilling the mind so that our ordinary thinking faculties are temporarily vetoed. This provisional silence of the otherwise constant "interior monologue" is the means whereby the one meditating is supposed to bypass the conditioning screen of (culturally programmed) concepts. In so doing he becomes ideally receptive to holistic dimensions otherwise recessed into the unconscious beyond the focus of ordinary "notice".

However, as the very object of channeling, out of those ostensibly more holistic zones of being comes charging: more verbiage!

Out of the meditator's mouth issues another voice.

In fact, the phenomenon is so prevalent that it seems every other face has "someone else's" voice coming out of it (although this is apparently such a commonplace of Filmland that "channeling" seems more a logical extension than an abrupt break).

And a great deal of the content of such channeled information from coveted "higher sources," is composed of odd syntactical constructions, inflected in the upper registers of nasality, extolling the virtues of meditation!

This of course can only mean *one* thing, ultimately, (amounting to a largely unnoticed metaphysical tautology), and that is: you're being encouraged to meditate in order to still the noise of the verbal mind, thus putting you in the properly receptive condition to pass a sonorously rolling Voice, (*not* your own) around the glottis, in elicitation of a Speech which invariably extols the virtue *of meditation*, as means of extracting a verbal instruction that tells you...

As Topper notes, that is really SPOOKY!

Many people who read the *Ra Material* complain that they are irritated by the strange syntactical constructions and unusual word use. There seem to be extra and redundant words; there are confusing definitions, and so forth.

This is *not* the same thing as occurs in other channeled material where there are endless ramblings that go on and on and on consisting of nice, pleasant sounding words that say, in effect, nothing of significant value.

People send me *reams* of this stuff. They will find a new web site that posts such "wonderful channeled messages" from Swami Beyonda or Coot Whosits or whomever, and they will download entire files and then send them to me to discover if I am aware of this great information and will I please read it and offer up an opinion; or surely I should join forces with these people because, clearly, we are all saying the same thing!

So, I open the files and begin to read what different people send me.

Now let me say up front here that I am *not* perfect in terms of grammar, word selection, punctuation, or even spelling. I'm pretty good, but there are many people who are *excruciatingly* correct! I'm not one of them. But, I *do* have a great love and respect for language and its ability to communicate marvelous ideas so that people can be more intimately connected in *this* density which is, I think, one of the lessons before us and a major *point* of being in this density. I also really detest misuse of the language that results from carelessness and lack of concern for the spirit of communication. Furthermore, I can say that one thing I *do* know is the difference between subject and verb and how to diagram a sentence. (Thank *you* Miss Thompson and Mrs. McCurdy for *making* me do it in 9th and 10th grades!)

So, one of the first things I do when I start reading these "great" channeled exposés, is to take some sentences at random and diagram them to determine what they are *really* saying. I was amazed to discover, over and over again, such great contradictions and misuse of terms that, in effect, most of these passages consist of what is politely termed "word salad". We jokingly refer to it as "salad shooter channeling".

In a recent example, the material contained the following remark: "Our karmic purification is speeding up as the positrons that we hold in our bodies release and collide with their corresponding electron twins."

Having a husband who is a physicist is very helpful in sorting out a lot of this mishmash. Ark replied to the individual who wrote to us inquiring about the above channeled message, as follows:

> Dear _____,
>
> I was reading this Nibiru stuff with some amusement.
>
> I am open towards unconventional thinking but sometimes it is just funny. Positrons are antiparticles and they annihilate rather soon. So there is no way there can be any positrons in human bodies, unless they are constantly created by highly energetic processes!
>
> For instance: several positrons have certainly been created in me today because I was in the lab and pretty close to a high-energy neutron source. Some of these neutrons went into my body and have been captured by Carbon, Hydrogen, Oxygen and whatever. Then my atoms created energetic photons; then these photons created pairs: positron-electron, and then these positrons annihilated again. But once I was out of the lab, there were no more positrons in me.
>
> Making a universal Galactic story out of the positrons is just disinformation. It misinforms all who are not physicists. And it is a typical disinformation pattern: truth between lies, and lies between truths.
>
> It is true that that electron-positron pairs annihilate, emitting photons (sometimes two, sometimes three). It is a lie that positrons (in any significant number) are in our bodies (except temporarily for those people who are exposed to energetic radiation as I was in the lab today). Thus all the justifications of the "photon belt" are disinformation and traps.

Which brings us back to the problem of assessing different material. At one point we really wanted to nail this problem down. Ark decided to "interrogate" the Cassiopaeans about it.

> December 31, 1997
>
> Q: (A) Now, at some point you said when we asked about the *Ra Material*, you gave the number that it was 63 per cent accurate. Do you confirm this now?
>
> A: Yes.

Q: (A) Now, I want to know exactly how you got this number 63, how you computed it, why is it 63 and not 62 or 64?
A: The divination process always breaks down to mathematical processes, as this is the only true universal language.
Q: (A) But, I want to know what mathematical process you were using to get this number 63?!
A: Add the total number of words published; divide the sum by the number reflecting accurate conceptualizations.
[Note: the original transcript reads "divide by" rather than "divide into", which serves pretty well as an example of possible distortion due to non-universality of meanings.]
Q: (A) Okay, if we have 100 words, and 25 are used in the description of a concept that is accurate, is that what you mean?
A: Close.
Q: (A) How do you determine if a given word is accurate?
A: By the verity of the issuer.
Q: (A) So, words, even though words can mean different things, the verity of the speaker can give...
A: Yes, because if monitored in a state of pure non-prejudice, the accuracy level will be perceived correctly.
Q: (A) Okay, I want to read a sentence: "the first, the Great Pyramid was formed approximately 6,000 of your years ago." I want to go through this word-by-word. The word "the", accurate or inaccurate?
A: Accurate.
Q: (A) "First".
A: Inaccurate.
Q: (A) "The".
A: Neuter.
Q: (A) "Great".
A: Accurate, in this case because of conventional agreement.
Q: (A) Now, you describe a word as neutral, but in the mathematical algorithm you gave for computing the numbers, you didn't mention neutral words, so, what do you do with neutral words?
A: They belong to the 37 percent, as they cannot be counted subjectively as accurate.
Q: (A) "was".
A: Accurate.
Q: (A) "formed".
A: Accurate.
Q: (A) "approximately".
A: Accurate.
Q: (A) 6,000.
A: Accurate.

Q: (A) "of".
A: Neuter.
Q: (A) "your".
A: Accurate.
Q: (A) "years".
A: Accurate.
Q: (A) Okay, if we apply the same formula to the C's, your material, what percentage would you give?
A: Not up to us to measure.
Q: (A) Okay, you gave, concerning the pyramid the following sentence: "The Great Pyramid was built 10,643 years ago." Is it accurate? (L) Yes, I think there is a problem. You confirmed the *Ra Material* on a point that contradicts what you gave yourselves!
A: Problem is not with "us," problem is trying to compare to different frames of reference. Look for clues in terms of definition.
Q: (A) I don't understand what you are saying. Either it was built 10,643 years ago or it was built 6,000 years ago.
A: Formed/built… you think it means the same thing, eh???
Q: (L) It was built before it was formed? (A) According to this *Ra Material*, was never built at all, it was formed by thoughts…
A: If your house is remodeled, then it takes a new form. Now, reread sentences in question carefully.
Q: (L) "The first, the Great Pyramid, was formed approximately 6,000 of your years ago. Then, in sequence, after this performing by thought of the building or architecture of the Great Pyramid, using the more local or earthly material rather than thought form material to build other pyramidal structures." Now, C's say: "The Great Pyramid was built by Atlantean descendants 10,643 years ago."
A: No, Laura, no, no, no, no!!!!! If your house is remodeled in 1998, is that when it was built?
Q: (L) No, that is not when it was built. Okay, I get your point. Subtle clues have to be discerned. Can we use this process to analyze all the material?
A: You can, but senior citizenhood awaits its completion.
Q: (L) Is there some issue about asking this question of accuracy that needs to be addressed? One main thing we note is: Some sessions were more accurate than others depending upon who was present…
A: You got it!!!
Q: (L) Therefore, it would be difficult to assess an accuracy rating for the C's themselves…
A: Bingo!
Q: (L) But, we *can* assess the material itself up to the present, keeping in mind that some parts can be more accurate than others…
A: 71.7.
Q: (L) Okay, that takes into account corruption from different people, long passages of comment from the participants, typos, reconstruction, and so forth.

And, the same applies to the *Ra Material*... (A) Okay, suppose I have a sentence that "the Great Pyramid was built 10,000 years ago," but really it was built yesterday, and you would give 70 per cent accuracy to this statement?
A: No.

Q: (A) But only one word is inaccurate... (L) No, only four words are accurate. If you have "The Great Pyramid was built 10,000 years ago," you have eight words. Of those eight words, the only ones you can consider to be accurate are "Great Pyramid was built." The word "the" is neuter, and "10,000" is inaccurate, so you divide the six words into the total and you have an accuracy rating of 75 percent. I think that, in the case of the problem you propose, it says it pretty well!

A: You are searching for a concrete formula within a vacuum of abstraction. The only way to get an accurate measurement is to wait until you can include the sum total of all the words, and then determine accuracy as a percentage of the total. With the total of all words, and each individual word as the unit of measurement.

Another way to consider this problem that the C's are trying to convey to us in the above is to look at two nearly identical sentences.

1) There was rain over my house today.
2) There was no rain over my house today.

In different contexts, each statement can be true. But on a given day when it rained, to say that there was no rain would be a false statement. And yet, except for the single word, every other word in the sentence is "accurate". You could say that it is 87 percent accurate, but it is still completely false in its context!

The bottom line seems to be: use your brain to figure it out!

Getting back to the *Ra Material*, we have discussed the filtering and the judgments of that group, and we have discussed a process by which percentages of accuracy can be divined, with the result that *The Law of One* still holds a very high place as one of the first, if not *the* first, Sixth Density Communication into our realm that was maintained over a consistent period of time in our modern era. So, don't sell it short because of the unusual verbiage; apparently there was a reason for it.

It is my opinion that Ra spoke as he did because it was necessary in order to get the information through the various constrictions and biases of the channel. Otherwise, I cannot justify why a Sixth Density being would not be able, considering their "lofty attainments", to communicate in terms that are more generally comfortable to the Third Density mind. As I said before, if you are in 6th grade, it shouldn't be too hard to go back and do 3rd grade stuff. It may take a little adjustment period, but it can be done.

Yes, in the beginning of the Cassiopaean contact, there were some rather archaic and stiff sentences – but as time passed and the channel grooved, the communication became more natural, and even gently humorous. I asked the Cassiopaeans about this:

November 11, 1995

Q: (L) I noticed that in the beginning of these transmissions that the language was very formalized, and that as time has gone by, the language used has become more colloquial. Why is this?

A: Formalized? Colloquial? Define your judgment, please!

Q: (L) Well, what I meant was, that in the beginning it seemed that certain colloquial expressions that we are accustomed to were unclear to you. And now, not only is there great familiarity with our expressions, but you seemed to often come up with rather clever and original witty sayings.

A: Familiarity breeds contentment!

Q: (L) Okay. I want to get on with the questions for tonight...

A: Do you not wish to reflect upon our witticism?

Q: (L) (Laughter.) Yes! I thought that was a very clever witticism!

A: It seemed as if you were not impressed?!? Give us a break, Laura?!? We're only sixth density!

We have also discussed our own material and its flaws and shortcomings, and even with awareness and constant monitoring, we are only making a little over 71 percent – at least that was the figure at the time. I am certainly working on ways of improving and purifying the material all the time. In regard to this, the Cassiopaeans have many times commented on the need to actively learn and acquire knowledge. The effort put forth in this respect is sort of equivalent to exercising your soul/mind muscle. The more you exercise it, the stronger it gets:

> Subtle answers that require effort to dissect promote intensified learning. Learning is an exploration followed by the affirmation of knowing through discovery. Learning is necessary for progress of soul... this is how you are building your power center... Patience serves the questor of hidden knowledge... Search your "files"... Learning is sometimes best accomplished by study and exploration... There are other clues that you can discover by your own study... (Cassiopaeans)

This is why the many sources that drone on and on in such extraordinary detail, even if *some* of what they are saying is truth, can be doing a great disservice to their devotees due to the fact that they are not encouraging them to think for themselves.

So, what's the difference, other than the obvious? Some people would say that they "learn differently" – that it is "right" for them to learn by simply "receiving the inflow of information", and because they receive it in this way, that makes it right.

Well, I am not going to say that this is not possible, for sure! My experience has been that there *are* people who have "done the work" in many lifetimes prior to this one, and at some magical moment, they hear something or see something, or something happens and the key gets turned and it all opens up! This is why the Sufi masters talk about some seekers who can begin the process and rapidly achieve enlightenment, and others can "stand at the door and knock" their entire lives and it is never opened to them. On the surface it seems unfair, but behind it is a reality of long and diligent labor on the part of the soul who "achieves" so quickly.

I guess you could apply the same principle to persons who demonstrate great artistic talent – they didn't just get it without a reason; it was the result of possibly many lifetimes of work as an artist before the present one. So, it *can* and *does* happen!

We still have to be concerned about this because, in some cases it can be true, and in others it may not be true! My experience has been that this can be used as a stumbling block, and very often the concept is utilized to assure the recipient that the channeled information is true or STO, simply by virtue of the fact that it is channeled, when, in fact, it is not true. In the end, the only way to validate any information is by *work* – reading, studying, research – exercising the gray matter!

As I write this, I have received another e-mail from a reader asking about still another source of channeled teachings. He writes that this information "can be difficult to understand because it is written in such a way as to be accessed through the emotional body and if you aren't in touch with that you won't get it."

That, right there, sets off warning bells in my head. Information that requires emotion to understand is, by definition, distorted. As I have already mentioned, any woman of childbearing age will tell you that emotions are chemical and very definitely color how you think. A very neutral personality trait that could be described as "slowness to act", can be seen as either commendable caution or cowardice depending on which hormone is in the upper ranges of distribution in the female body at the moment. A mild joke can be funny or tragic depending on what day of the month it is!

So, if emotion is what is necessary to understand the referenced work, I don't think it has much objective validity. The Cassiopaeans have made many comments about emotion, but the following one is, I believe, most appropriate in regard to the idea that emotion is necessary to learn truth:

> November 21, 1998
>
> Q: (L) The question is: in reality, what is it that really exists? What are things that really exist?
>
> A: Gravity is the key. Now, plug in your wave functions.
>
> Q: (L) How can you describe gravity mathematically?
>
> A: Must be possible! Review texts re: gravity.
>
> Q: (L) We did... and either we are so dense, or we can't get it...
>
> A: Not dense, emotionally clouded. When one is in a defensive mode, all is "skewed," including this conduit. Review texts and meditate to clear consciousness of emotional poison!

The correspondent further writes, "Apparently one of the agenda's the ET's have is to recover and reintegrate [themselves] with their wills that they denied and separated from long, long ago."

So, we begin to understand the motivation... it is an *apologia* for the nasty critters invading our world and an attempt to garner sympathy for them. This is further amplified with:

> One of the books in the series is about original cause that was the trauma experienced when God split into male and female and that the trauma from then is still affecting us now. A point made is that we can not get to that trauma with our minds alone because Mind did not exist then and as far as our minds are concerned this trauma never happened and doesn't exist!

Well, that was a curious statement and I decided to go to the web site in question and see if I couldn't get a bit of clarification on that idea. I won't describe the gory details of the story of creation presented there, I will only say that the upshot is that, once again, our reality is being described as the result of an error or mistake; something that has to be "fixed", and, again, it is basically attributed to the female. Of course, this source is going to teach everybody to channel so they can "fix things"! This is really just a variation on what David Icke writes:

> November 21, 1998
>
> Q: (L) David Icke says: "The imbalanced consciousness that I will call Lucifer is not an essential part of the positive/negative balance. He is a disrupting, disharmonious aspect of consciousness, which is not necessary for human evolution. More than that, Lucifer's efforts to close off the channels that link humanity to its higher understanding have blocked, not advanced, our evolution." Is this a correct assessment of this Luciferian Consciousness, that it is not part of the positive/ negative balance of the universe, and that it has blocked our evolution?
>
> A: No. It is part of the lesson plan.
>
> Q: (L) That was my thought as well, but he says that because of this problem with the Luciferian consciousness, the "higher levels of creation began to intervene because Lucifer was imposing its misunderstandings on others and breaking the universal law of free will. Is this true?
>
> A: No.
>
> Q: (L) I have read about this "decision to intercede" by higher levels of consciousness who look down upon mankind and feel sorry for our terrible suffering, and that somehow, if something isn't done, the whole universe will be overcome by this evil... so it has got to be "stopped". A number of sources promote this idea, which then leads, generally, to claims that this or another alien group is part of the "good guys" or "bad guys", or whatever. Is any of this idea accurate?
>
> A: No.
>
> Q: (L) So, what is *is*, and we only suffer exactly as much as we need to learn? Is that it?
>
> A: There is more to it than that, but at this point, you would be unable to comprehend.

Q: (L) Icke says, "This Luciferian consciousness is a large aspect of Divine Consciousness which chose to work against the Source." Is this true?

A: Not really. It is balancing where needed.

Q: (L) He says: "Other volunteers, aspects of very highly evolved consciousness, came into the universe and this galaxy in an effort to restore harmony. They did not incarnate in physical bodies on the earth, they arrived in spacecraft, some of them miles in length, while others simply manifested themselves here. These were extraterrestrials who came to bring knowledge to this planet hundreds of thousands of years ago." Is this true? Yes or no?

A: Neither.

The point is: it is all about balance, and cycles and timelessness. To believe in error or something that needs to be fixed, even if that fixing is to be managed by ignoring, is to further add to the creation of that reality. Remember what the Cassiopaeans have said about belief:

> Most all power necessary for altering reality and physicality is contained within the belief center of the mind. This is something you will understand more closely when you reach 4th density reality where physicality is no longer a prison, but is instead, your home, for you to alter as you please. In your current state, you have the misinterpretation of believing that reality is finite and therein lies your difficulty with finite physical existence. We are surprised that you are still not able to completely grasp this concept.

The crucial point to understand here is this: if you *believe* that something is broken, that something needs to be fixed out there, that is exactly the reality you will experience.

If you spend your days and nights saying prayers and mantras, sending love and light here and there, or visualizing change or something different than what *is* at the given moment, if you assign a day to "pray for peace" or "heal the Earth", or "converge harmonically", you are, effectively, acting from the belief that there is something wrong, broken, needing change, needing peace, needing healing, or needing harmony. You are proclaiming, in a clear and present way, what *is* is not acceptable, God screwed up.

Now, let's deal with that. Obviously, there is a *lot* of stuff that goes on here on the Big Blue Marble that we don't *like*! There is death and decay and darkness. There is poverty and want and suffering. There is war and pestilence and disaster after disaster. What kind of a crazy person would want things to continue that way?

Not me.

But I know something from experience that gives me a different perspective. I know that the Universe is a self-regulating mechanism of which I, as a third density human being, am only a tiny, insignificant part. I also know that when I keep my judgments *out* of it, (remembering that judgment conveys the idea of taking some action), the Universe knows better what is needed at any given point in space-time than my limited, feeble human brain could ever conceive.

Further, I know that when I get myself out of the way, when I sit back and observe what *is* with appreciation, with awe and wonder; with curiosity as to what clever and wonderful thing "God" is going to do next in this marvelous, endlessly changing reality in which we have our existence, I am n*ever* disappointed.

Nevertheless, at this point, I would like to comment on the idea that "in the beginning," *mind* did not exist. This is quite contrary to what the Cassiopaeans say, which is, in fact, that the *only* thing that is real is *mind*.

February 25, 1995
Q: (GB) Could you explain the process of the soul?
A: Soul is consciousness, period.

October 18, 1994
Q: (L) Are you part of the collective subconscious, unconscious, or consciousness? Are you part of our higher consciousness?
A: So is everything else.

November 16, 1994
A: There is no time, as you know it; it's all just lessons for the collective consciousness.
Q: (L) So at the closing of this grand cycle everything will just start all over again?
A: Not exactly. You see; there is no start.

November 13, 1999
Q: (L) Next question; a reader writes: "In [certain teachings], man is viewed as a composite entity comprised of one being, supposed hopefully to be 'in charge', and an enormous number of separate entities in various states of consciousness/unconsciousness, not completely dissimilar to the description given in Ouspensky's *In Search of the Miraculous*. One of the critical differences between what the Cassiopaeans are saying and what is given as fact in [those teachings] is that, in [the referenced teachings], one is taught that one is not ultimately One, that an individual remains an individual to the upper reaches of evolution, and evolves as a "god". [I cannot vouch for this being the actual teachings of the mentioned source; I am only reading the question as the reader wrote it.]
A: The Grand Pulsation makes individuality a temporary state of being.
Q: (L) By saying that the Grand Pulsation is only a temporary state of individuation, this means that all are One and return to the state of Oneness.
A: Yes. If so, it is always true. All are ultimately "god".
Q: (L) But they don't evolve as a god by remaining *individual* in the upper reaches of evolution?
A: What would be the purpose?
Q: (L) I guess they are hung up on remaining individuals and becoming as "gods" for purposes of power and control issues… sort of ultimate STS.

A: Maybe that would work if time and linear reality were correct, but...

May 27, 1995

Q: (L) What is the link between consciousness and matter?

A: Illusion.

Q: (L) What is the nature of the illusion? (T) That there isn't any connection between consciousness and matter. It is only an illusion that there is. It is part of the third density...

A: No. Illusion is that there is no link between consciousness and matter.

Q: (L) I got it! The relationship is that consciousness *is* matter.

A: Close. What about vice versa?

June 7, 1997

Q: (L) All right There are a lot of people teaching that there are divisions of ethereal being such as spirit, soul, consciousness, etc. What is the difference between the spirit and the soul?

A: Semantics.

But, curiously, going back to the former statement that consciousness is matter and matter is consciousness, the Cassiopaeans *have* defined four "bodies", so to speak:

October 10, 1998

A: And remember, your consciousness operates on four levels, not just one!

Q: (L) And what are these four levels?

A: Physical body, consciousness, genetic body and spirit-etheric body.

Q: (L) Are those the four composites of the human manifestation in third density?

A: 3rd *and* 4th. One leads oneself, through physical actions, as well as psychic ones, to develop these "problems" when one is preparing to "bump it up" a notch.

October 23, 1999

Q: (A) The question is: is this theory that I have been developing with Blanchard for the past ten years or even more, is it a step forward; can it be made a step forward by completing it?

A: Yes.

Q: (L) Okay, if it can be a step forward, the main question that we don't know the answer to is: what is classical? Gravity or consciousness or something else? What? Or, perhaps everything is classical...

A: Classical [physics] negates consciousness, regarding the mind as merely a function of chemical functions and electrical impulses occurring within a vacuum, rather than being interfaced with the rest of creation at all levels of density and all dimensions, which is of course, the case.

Wheeler writes:

"The universe viewed as a self-excited circuit. Starting small (thin U at upper right), it grows (loop of U) to observer participancy – which in turn imparts 'tangible reality' to even the earliest days of the universe"

"If the views that we are exploring here are correct, one principle, observer-participancy, suffices to build everything. The picture of the participatory universe will flounder, and have to be rejected, if it cannot account for the building of the law; and space-time as part of the law; and out of law substance. It has no other than a higgledy-piggledy way to build law: out of statistics of billions upon billions of observer participancy each of which by itself partakes of utter randomness."[6]

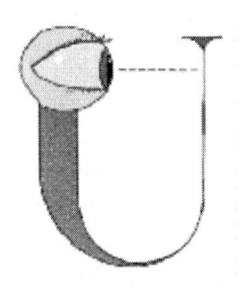

Gravity is the "glue, which binds all aspects of reality, physical and ethereal. Nothing would exist without consciousness to perceive it. Classical physics assumes, among other things, that consciousness and the brain are one and the same, or that one exclusively facilitates the other. In actuality, the brain is merely that conduit which facilitates conscious expression in the physical state of human third density states and similar manifestations.

December 9, 1995

Q: (L) Carlos Castaneda talks about the "Eagle's emanations", the Eagle being, I suppose, Prime Creator that emanates down through all the densities, and that the Nagual who can "see", sees the Eagle as a large black and white object. Are they seeing the source, or are they seeing something on just another density?

A: Source? There is no such thing. You are Prime Creator.

Q: (L) But that is so esoteric... I am talking about...

A: The point is: stop filling your consciousness with monotheistic philosophies planted long ago to imprison your being. Can't you see it by now, after all you have learned, that there is no source, there is no leader, there is no basis, there is no overseer, etc. You literally possess, within your consciousness profile, all the power that exists within all of Creation!?! You absolutely have all that exists, ever has, or ever will, contained within your mind. All you have to do is learn how to use it, and at that moment, you will literally, literally, be all that is, was, and ever will be!!!!!!!!

Q: (L) That is all fine and dandy and sounds wonderful, except for one little item. You also say that the monotheistic concepts were *imposed* on us to prevent us from knowing this. So, if we are all that *is*, how can something exist that can impose something so unpleasant on us?

A: Choices follow desire-based imbalances.

---

[6] J.A. Wheeler, "Beyond the Black Hole", in *Some Strangeness in the Proportion*, Ed. Harry Woolf (London: Addison-Wesley, 1980).

Q: (L) If that is the case, why can't any one just turn off the lights, end the illusion, and everything becomes nothing?

A: Well, first of all, everything does not become anything. Secondly, some have already become everything.

December 19, 1998

Q: (L) If, at fourth density, there is variability of physicality, and the Lizzies, as you have previously said, are engineering new bodies for themselves to occupy in some sort of mass transition at the time of this realm border crossing; in this state of variability of physicality, why do they need to engineer new bodies for themselves? Why, in point of fact, are Lizzies, Lizzies? Why do they look like Lizards?

A: They do not.

Q: (L) Well, why do we call them Lizard Beings? I mean, *you* named them that!

A: We label in accordance with your familiarity. If we had called them "Drachomonoids," what would be your point of reference??

Q: (L) What do they *really* look like? You said they resemble upright alligators with humanoid features, six to eight feet tall...

A: Yes.

Q: (L) So, why do they look like that?

A: Biology.

Q: (L) Does biology exist at fourth density?

A: Yes.

Q: (L) Yet, it is a variable physical density, right?

A: Yes, but what is your assumption here?

Q: (L) I don't know what my assumption is. I guess that I am assuming that if it is a variable state, they could have a different biology very easily. Isn't that the case?

A: No.

Q: (L) Can they appear as something else? Change their physicality?

A: Temporarily.

Q: (L) When you say "temporary", what exactly do you mean? Temporal relates to time.

A: We have explained before that the biggest single factor regarding densities is the awareness level.

Q: (L) Okay, how does that relate to them only being able to temporarily change their appearance. Is this because they can control *our* awareness?

A: Closer. Are you not yet aware that absolutely everything, we repeat: everything is an illusion?!?

Q: (A) They say here that everything is an illusion, and on the other hand they say there is consciousness and matter. Everything is an illusion? Even this?

A: Yes.

Q: (A) God is also an illusion?

A: Yes.

Q: (A) Illusion to whom?

A: *To those not on Level Seven.* Your learning naturally dictates your experiences. Once you no longer require something, you naturally move beyond it. However, you retain it as a function of understanding.

Q: (A) And I am also an illusion! And understanding is also an illusion! (L) Back to my question: who created Lizzies *as Lizzies*? (A) Our illusion...

A: Everything is real; therefore, illusion is reality.

Q: (L) If everything is an illusion, from what does this illusion spring, and into what space does it spring?

A: Your consciousness.

Q: (L) Where did this consciousness originate?

A: Consciousness is the absolute, the center point.

Q: (L) Where is it centered?

A: Within the Access. The prompt that begets energy.

Q: (L) Of what is this energy made?

A: The consciousness.

Q: (L) Was there ever a time when this consciousness did not exist?

A: No, but there never was a time.

Q: (L) What prompted this consciousness to dream up all these illusions?

A: Need for balance. Energy cannot exist within a vacuum, therefore it must pulse. Hence you have waves.

Q: (L) What was the impetus for the need for balance?

A: Not a need, per se, just a natural function.

Q: (L) Well, when you have a pulse, you have a wave, and if you have a wave, that implies time.

A: Therein lies the crux of your 3rd density illusion. Why assume that any given aspect of the pulse is not occurring simultaneously with any other. And if any are, all are. Until you once and for all break free from the illusion of time, you will not advance.

Q: (L) Well, back to my question...

A: No, your question cannot be answered unless you stop assuming the range of acceptable answers.

See how easy it is to get off the track and switch from the subject of "accuracy" to "consciousness"? But, I think that I will just go with the flow here, and make some final remarks. It is good to read and study many things. As a member of our discussion group has said:

> So read the Bible. Read the Koran. Read the Three Little Pigs. Read EVERYTHING! You'll be certain to read a lot of silly things, but you'll also stand a chance of seeing bits and pieces of TRUTH.

ROSES GROW BEST IN MANURE

THE ROSE
(Amanda McBroom, sung by Bette Midler)

Some say love, it is a river
That drowns the tender reed

Some say love, it is a razor
That leaves your soul to bleed

Some say love, it is a hunger
An endless aching need

I say love, it is a flower
And you its only seed

It's the heart, afraid of breaking
That never learns to dance

It's the dream, afraid of waking
That never takes a chance

It's the one who won't be taken
Who cannot seem to give

And the soul, afraid of dying
That never learns to live

When the night has been too lonely
And the road has been too long
And you think that love is only
For the lucky and the strong

Just remember in the winter
Far beneath the bitter snows
Lies the seed, that with the sun's love
In the spring becomes The Rose

There are other issues involved with the subject of accuracy and deception during the present period of human history that I would like to examine. Let's look at the excerpt we presented at the beginning of this chapter:

> September 2, 1995
>
> Q: (L) Now, could you tell us a little bit about the purported "Photon Belt"?
>
> A: The key issue remains one of interpretation. The messages are genuine; interpretations are variable in their accuracy. So, when one speaks of the "Photon Belt," one may really be thinking of a concept and giving it a name.
>
> Q: (L) So, you mean that various persons are seeing something and only describing it within the limits of their knowledge?
>
> A: At one level, yes.
>
> Q: (L) Was there a harmonic convergence as was advertised within the metaphysical community?

A: For those who believed there was a harmonic convergence, indeed there was a harmonic convergence.

Q: (L) Did anything of an objective, material nature happen on or to the planet to enhance or change the energy?

A: Did you notice any changes?

Q: (L) No. Except that it seems that things have gotten objectively worse, if anything.

A: Did you notice any clear, obvious, material changes?

Q: (L) No. But that could just be me. I could just be a stubborn and skeptical person.

A: Did anyone else in the room notice any clear or obvious changes?

Q: (S) What date was it? (L) 8/8/88, I believe. (S) I thought it had something to do with 11/11 ninety-something...

A: Well, obviously if the recollection of the calendar date was difficult, one would suppose that material changes on the planet did not take place. For, if they had, would you not remember the calendar date ascribed to them?

Q: (L) Yes. The claim has further been made that, for a month, following the harmonic convergence that no abductions were taking place. Is this true?

A: No. There has been no cessation in what you term to be abduction in quite some time as you measure it.

In our efforts to maintain accuracy and purity of the source, we have consistently resisted the standard channeling techniques of trance or telepathy, etc. It is far too easy to substitute subjective, emotional thinking for objective reality, particularly when the objective reality is, from the human perspective, unpleasant. As you will have noted in the previous discussions, there is greater potential for corruption when there is also a great deal of verbiage. In other words, it seems that the wordier the source, the more easily corruption can enter it.

Now, let's go back again to the concerns of the correspondent who wrote:

> Aliens will invade in some form or other between now and 2018 [2012] or something, causing even more fear and confusion than there is already, then try to take us over or annihilate us or let the earth changes do that and then seed earth with their own race.
>
> About the same time this is all happening the wave will strike and half of the world or more (people and land mass) is wobbling in and out of 4th density and then transitions completely. Those of us who have not been wiped out by earth changes or the busy Lizzies and gone to 5th density dead zone (there to decide what to do next) will find ourselves in 4th density earth which will look very weird to us and will take some getting used to, only to find ourselves in the same situation environmentally, [with] 4th density Orions or Lizzies trying to manipulate and control us there as they have been doing here for millennia.
>
> In short as you said to the Cassies the picture looks ugly. They said that you seem to think that only good experience is useful, well no, but at least there is usually a mix of good and bad but in their scenario we are all for the high jump with no mat on the other side though. (Splat)

As a way of dealing with this issue, I want to present here sections of a particular session in which an experience of my own was being discussed (the same incident described in *High Strangeness*). To give you a little background, as I have said before, I do not ever remember seeing or experiencing an alien being or an abduction that could be clearly stated to be such – although at one point, I did have an experience in an altered state of consciousness that I have never been able to decide whether it was physical or imagined. I also *have* made disconcerting discoveries about my state when awakening, or have dreamlike memories of very strange things, which then corresponded to some sort of physical or material anomaly that I would immediately sweep under the rug. But, in the case I want to talk about here, I *did* wake up in the night – in an extraordinary state – to very strange activity.

The background of the event is that I had been in an auto accident on Christmas Eve 1994. The accident itself was strange because I was hit from behind by a car that *was not there*. I was stopped, waiting to make a left turn, looking in my side view mirror, which gave me a broad view of what was behind me, and I am certain that no car was approaching. What is more, the driver of the car that hit me driving at full speed, claimed with great puzzlement that he did not see me at all. For him, I was not there! His car was completely destroyed, but he had an airbag and was not hurt. I, on the other hand, suffered several severe injuries when my body "whiplashed" and my head hit the back window of the pick-up truck I was driving.

During the course of the following year, I was in therapy every other day and had numerous medical exams to determine the nature of the injury and possible progress of the therapy.

The first unusual thing that showed up was a set of X-rays taken by a chiropractor. It showed a strange object that looked like a small straight piece of something that was situated at the front side of two of my cervical vertebrae. The chiropractor was a bit puzzled, but suggested that it was a calcium spur and I needed to have more tests done. He referred me to a neurologist. The neurologist did a thorough series of tests over a period of about three hours, and then ordered a set of MRIs (Magnetic Resonance Imaging).

On the night before I was supposed to go in for the MRIs, I woke up in a startled state, feeling like I had been thrown off a cliff. I thought I had bitten my tongue because the only thing I was aware of was a terrible sensation of something crunching in the back of my mouth, accompanied by terrible pain. This pain was so intense that the only thing I could think about in this altogether unusual state of waking up in that condition was to stop the pain. Also, my mouth seemed to be full of fluid, and I assumed I had bitten my tongue so severely that it was bleeding.

Now, certainly, this explanation I gave to myself in those first moments of waking up blinded by pain was reasonable. I had certainly bitten my tongue in my sleep a time or two during my life – especially when I was a child. But nothing quite like this had ever happened.

Since I was choking on the fluid in my mouth, I struggled to get up and get to the bathroom as quickly as possible. I leaned over the sink and spit out large quantities of blood. Quickly mixing up some warm salt water, I gargled and rinsed my mouth thoroughly until it seemed that the bleeding had stopped. Then, getting a flashlight so that I could see better, I began to examine my mouth to see exactly how much damage was done. What I found was that there was, indeed, an injury in my mouth, but it was at the back of my throat in a place that it was impossible for my teeth to have produced it! The pain was coming from this area, and was so severe that I had initially been unable to distinguish it from my tongue. But, now that things had calmed down a bit, now that the pain was receding, it was clear that it was localized at the very back of my throat.

Even though, at this point in time, I was fully aware of the many strange things that were reported by so-called abductees, I didn't even want to consider such a thing. I kept trying to think of ways I could have injured my throat so severely during my sleep. Nothing seemed to make any sense, and I was left with a mystery.

The next morning, the MRIs were duly made. The only unusual thing that showed up on the films was the bulging of several discs that was a result of the injuries sustained in the accident. There was no sign of any strange object at the front of my cervical vertebrae.

Several months went by and the case was being passed back and forth between doctors and attorneys and a request came from the insurance company for the films to be sent to another doctor. The only problem was, they seemed to be missing.

Now, I never, at any time, had possession of these films. They were being sent around via standard methods of transferring files between medical offices. They had been sent directly to the neurologist who had ordered them, which is where I saw them. He then referred me to a neurosurgeon who wanted to operate on me, but I refused surgery. They were then, supposedly, sent back to the testing institution which was where they were supposed to be filed and kept. This is where they turned up missing.

Over a period of two weeks, I was contacted by the three separate medical offices where the films had passed through, each of them asking me for details about where I thought they might be. I was assured that each of them were employing their full staff to search for this expensive set of films. But still, they were nowhere to be found.

Finally, since the insurance company was exerting pressure to have them, and since no one could come up with an explanation for what happened to them, it was decided that the hospital where the films were taken – and where they had finally been lost – was obligated to replace them at their own expense. The young lady in charge of this department called me with many apologies to ask me if I would please come in to have a second set made. She explained all the things they had done to try to locate the films, and I could tell that there had been a lot of pressure on her about this because it was a lot of money.

I agreed to come in the following morning, and she would fit me in early. She apologized over and over again for the inconvenience.

In any event, as I went to bed, I was slightly worried about being able to go to sleep due to the strange events surrounding this loss of the films. After lying down, as I was thinking about the MRIs, there was a sudden sort of blank-out, and then I came to myself suddenly – again coming to awareness like I had been thrown off a cliff – and I realized that there were three spidery type creatures pulling and tugging on me, and it seemed that they were trying to float me out of the bed. What was even stranger was that I was fighting them like crazy. I had a death grip on the brass headboard, and it was like my body was being subjected to a tug of war! One of the creepy creatures was pulling on me by my ankle and I could distinctly feel a sort of cold fuzziness in the grip. The other two seemed to be trying to exert some kind of mind control on me, like trying to use their mental powers to make me submit. All of my body, except for my shoulders and head which were anchored by my grip on the bed, was suspended in air and seemed to be being sucked toward a small window (which I could not possibly have fit through!) and there seemed to be a sort of beam of light coming through this from the outside of the house! The bed was shaking and bouncing with the struggle taking place.

I was certainly a bit groggy and disoriented at first, as anyone would be to discover themselves in the middle of a violent fight in which their body is participating, only they haven't been at all aware of it. It felt like the effects of a sleeping drug was wearing off. As it did, I became more alert and thought to myself, "Oh ho! So abductions *do* really happen! And here I am, being abducted! Well, guess what? I don't like this, I don't want this, and I am *not* going to cooperate. If those creepy jerks abduct me, it won't be with my assistance!" In short, I was mad as heck!

The creatures seemed to be aware that I was awake and things were rapidly going south. At this point, one of them placed his hand on my head and a powerful paralysis began to spread over me from the head down. This seemed to be causing my eyes to close forcibly, as though the powerful sleeping drug was being re-administered.

I realized fully that I was somewhat helpless against this kind of technology but I still wasn't going to give up. I was going to fight this sleep right to the last. I became even angrier and I threw down the mental gauntlet, so to say. I decided to "speak" to these creatures with my mind. I said, "You may be able to paralyze me and overcome my physical body, but I'll fight you with everything I have, every chance I get, so don't turn your backs on me or you'll regret it!"

And then, with every bit of will I could muster, I struggled to curse them out loud. The only thing I actually managed to do was emit a strangled groan. But as I did this, as I achieved even this small bit of mastery over a small part of my physical body, a strange thing happened. With the uttering of this sound, the creatures seemed to become confused and disoriented and began to chatter in strange clicking sounds to each other and they dropped me as though I had become a hot potato! Then, they clustered together like frightened, twittering insects and just melted into a shimmery curtain beside the bed. This shimmering thing was very much like the heat waves you see on the highway far ahead when driving on a hot day.

Now, there are several strange things about this event that, I admit, could have just as well have been a sort of dream. One of these things is the fact that I was gripping the headboard with my left hand raised up above my head. What is so strange about that? Well, fact is, my left arm had been severely injured in the accident and was partially paralyzed. I hadn't been able to lift it much above my waist for over a year much less use it to grip anything at all. I actually had to reach up with my right hand, uncurl my fingers from around the curling tubes of the headboard, and remove my hand and place my arm back at my side because I was unable to perform these small motions with that arm itself! Needless to say, I spent most of the night sitting up in a chair.

The next morning, the phone rang at about 7:30 as I was getting ready to go out the door. It was the hospital testing facility, the same young woman I had been talking to the previous day. She told me I didn't have to come in, that the films had been found. The only thing she could not explain was how, and by whom, they had been found.

I was so curious about this strange turnaround of events that I asked questions. It turned out that the films were right there on her desk when she arrived that morning to open up the place. When I asked, "Who could have put them there?" her voice was a bit shaky as she explained that it was really impossible to figure out since she had locked up the night before, no one else could have been there except the janitor, and she was sure he hadn't put the films on her desk because she asked him.

The whole thing is still a mystery.

Naturally, I asked the C's about the event, though I didn't want to be too specific in my questions because I didn't want anyone else in the room, or at the board, to have any data that might skew the answers:

July 23, 1995

Q: (L) The first thing on my mind is an experience I had several nights ago. It seemed as though there was some sort of interaction between myself and something "other". Could you tell me what this experience was?

A: Was eclipsing of the realities.

Q: (L) What is an eclipsing of the realities?

A: It is when energy centers conflict.

Q: (L) What energy centers are conflicting?

A: Thought energy centers.

Q: (L) Whose thoughts?

A: Thoughts are the basis of all creation. After all, without thought nothing would exist. Now would it?

Q: (L) True.

A: Therefore, energy centers conflicting involve thought patterns. You could refer to it as an intersecting of thought pattern energies. [...]

Q: (L) I also seemed to be aware of several dark, spider-like figures lined up by the side of the bed. Was this an accurate impression.

A: Those could be described as specific thought center projections.

Q: (L) I seemed to be fighting and resisting this activity.

A: That was your choice. [...]

Q: (L) At what level of density do these thought centers have their primary focus?

A: Thought centers do not have primary focus in any level of density. This is precisely the point. You are not completely familiar with the reality of what thoughts are. We have spoken to you on many levels and have detailed many areas involving density level, but thoughts are quite a different thing because they pass through all density levels at once. Now, let us ask you this. Do you not now see how that would be possible?

Q: (L) Yes. But what I am trying to do is identify these conflicting thought centers. If two thought centers, or more, conflict, then my idea would be that they are in opposition.

A: Correct. [...]

Q: (L) Okay, in the experience I felt a paralysis of my body. What caused this paralysis?

A: Yes. Separation of awareness, which is defined as any point along the pathway where one's awareness becomes so totally focused on one thought sector that all other levels of awareness are temporarily receded, thereby making it impossible to become aware of one's physical reality along with one's mental reality. This gives the impression of what is referred to as paralysis. Do you understand?

Q: (L) Yes. And what stimulates this total focus of awareness?

A: An event that sidetracks, temporarily, the mental processes.

Q: (L) And what event can sidetrack the mental processes to this extent?

A: Any number.

Q: (L) In this particular case, what was it?

A: It was an eclipsing of energies caused by conflicting thought centers. Whenever two opposing units of reality intersect, this causes what can be referred to as friction, which, for an immeasurable amount of what you would refer to as time, which is, of course, non-existent, creates a non-existence, or a stopping of the movements of all functions. This is what we would know as conflict. In between, or through any intersecting, opposite entities, we always find zero time, zero movement, zero transference, and zero exchange. Now think about this. Think about this carefully.

Q: (L) Does this mean that I was, essentially, in a condition of non-existence?

A: Well, non-existence is not really the proper term, but non-fluid existence would be more to the point. Do you understand?

Q: (L) Yes. Frozen, as it were?

A: Frozen, as it were.

Q: (L) Was there any benefit to me from this experience?

A: All experiences have potential for benefit.

Q: (L) Was there any detriment from this experience?

A: All experiences have potential for detriment. Now, do you see the parallels? We are talking about any opposing forces in nature, when they come together, the result can go all the way to the extreme of one side or all the way to the extreme of the other. Or, it can remain perfectly, symmetrically in balance in the middle, or partially in balance on one side or another. Therefore all potentials are realized at intersecting points in reality. [...]

Q: (L) Was one of these conflicting thought centers or energies some part of me?

A: Yes.

Q: (L) And was it eclipsed by interacting with a thought center energy that was part of or all of something or someone else?

A: Or, was what happened a conflicting of one energy thought center that was a part of your thought process and another energy thought center that was another part of your thought process? We will ask you that question and allow you to contemplate.

Q: (L) Does it ever happen that individuals who perceive or think they perceive themselves to have experienced an "abduction", to actually be interacting with some part of themselves?

A: That would be a very good possibility. Now, before you ask another question, stop and contemplate for a moment: what possibilities does this open up? Is there any limit? And if there is, what is that? Is it not an area worth exploring? For example – just one example for you to digest – what if the abduction scenario could take place where your soul projection, in what you perceive as the future, can come back and abduct your soul projection in what you perceive as the present?

Q: (L) Oh, dear! Does this happen?

A: This is a question for you to ask yourself and contemplate.

Q: (L) Why would I do that to myself? (J) To gain knowledge of the future.

A: Are there not a great many possible answers?

Q: (L) Well, this seemed to be a very frightening and negative experience. If that is the case: a) maybe that is just my perception, or b) then, in the future I am not a very nice person! (J) Or maybe the future isn't very pleasant. And the knowledge that you gained of it is unpleasant.

A: Or is it one possible future, but not all possible futures? And is the pathway of free will not connected to all of this?

Q: (L) God! I hope so.

A: Now do you see the benefit in slowing down and not having prejudices when asking questions of great import? You see when you speed too quickly in the process of learning and gathering knowledge; it is like skipping down the road without pausing to reflect on the ground beneath you. One misses the gold coins and the gemstones contained within the cracks in the road. [...]

Q: (L) Okay, when this experience occurred, am I to assume that some part of myself, a future self perhaps, of course they are all simultaneous but just for the sake of reference, came back and interacted with my present self for some purpose of exchange?

A: Well this is a question best left for your own exploration, as you will gain more knowledge by contemplating it by yourself rather than seeking the answers here. But a suggestion is to be made that you do that as you will gain much, very much knowledge by contemplating these very questions on your own and networking with others as you do so. Be not frustrated for *the answers to be gained through your own contemplation will be truly illuminating to you and the experience to follow will be worth a thousand lifetimes of pleasure and joy.*

What can we deduce about the Eclipsing of Realities discussion?

The first thing that occurs to me is a result of a conversation I had with an individual who visited me a few days ago. There are a number of events in my life that I am not yet ready to talk about publicly, but which I shared with this lady in the course of our discussion.[7] At one point, she made the remark that, in her opinion, my life experiences had been a sort of microcosmic example of the battle between the forces of good and evil – that my very physical body, soul and mind had been the battleground. It was her opinion that the "good guys" had won because, in the end, all the physical, mental and spiritual destruction that had been effected against me had been healed, reversed, and/or restored to proper function and balance.

This is, in some sense, true. But, what does it mean if we wish to apply it globally? Or even just for some others?

The Cassiopaeans said I experienced a conflict of thought centers. This was further elaborated:

> We are talking about any *opposing forces in nature*, when they come together, the result can go all the way to the extreme of one side or all the way to the extreme of the other. Or, it can remain perfectly, symmetrically in balance in the middle, or partially in balance on one side or another. Therefore all potentials are realized at intersecting points in reality...

I was told to contemplate the issues involved and that "answers to be gained through your own contemplation will be truly illuminating to you and the experience to follow will be worth a thousand lifetimes of pleasure and joy".

In the simplest of terms, the experience of "Eclipsing Realities" led to my full perception of reality in the so-called objective view that we have already discussed. More than that, it also led to my making choices – life changing choices – that effectively *changed my reality.* Perhaps in a very literal sense. Within eight months of the Eclipsing of Realities event, I had asked for a divorce from my husband, and within four months of that event, I had met Ark. Two years later, we were married. There was a remark made at one of the sessions that emphasized this point:

---

[7] I have since written about many of these things in my autobiography, *Amazing Grace*.

January 4, 1997
A: Because of already given data that is elementary my dear, Martin, elementary!
Q: (L) I am *not* Martin anymore! So there!
A: You are in an alternate reality.

Martin was my former married name.

So, when the realities eclipsed, some sort of choice was made at a deep level as to whether I was going to continue to live in STS-oriented wishful thinking that all would become "love and light", if I just kept trying to "fix it", which constitutes the ongoing condition of being food for higher density beings; or if I was going to open my eyes and *see*. It seems that my choice to resist the activity taking place was the symbol of the shift that then began to manifest in my ordinary life as life-changing choices.

> What if the abduction scenario could take place where your soul projection, in what you perceive as the future, can come back and abduct your soul projection in what you perceive as the present?

It seems that, if I had continued in the old life, the wishful thinking subjective version of reality, where I was still Martin, I would have progressed to a point in space-time when I *became* those horrible creatures that were trying to abduct me (through the incarnational processes, of course)!

Now, I did *not* change my reality by visualization, or affirmations or any of the standard teachings about creating your own reality. In fact, if anything, I did exactly the opposite. What actually happened was, I opened my eyes and I completely lost hope in the world as it is ever being anything other than full of darkness and deception and horror and pain, and I chose to continue to live in this world, to do what I could, but not be "of the world".

I wonder if this was what Don Elkins saw? If so, it is indeed sad that he did not have the information about how this state is essential, how this state can be used by dark forces to derail the spiritual seeker who *must* go through it in order to be "born again".

How does one become born again"? It is just as traumatic as being born the first time, if not more so!

Taking my first breath in the new reality, I made a conscious choice to *limit my participation* in this deception foisted on mankind. I consciously decided that I was no longer going to lie – to myself or to anyone else – about how I felt or what I wanted. I was no longer going to lie about what I liked or didn't like or what I did or did not want to do. I was no longer going to lie to myself that my suffering and sacrifices had any benefit for anyone whatsoever; because it was clear to me that this was *not* true. It was all an illusion or delusion. In short, I was no longer going to lie to myself about reality at all.

When I looked at a flower I was going to remember the decay and death in the soil from which the flower drew its nourishment. When I looked at a cat or a dog, I was going to remember the fleas and parasites and killing and eating of other creatures that goes on all the time in the animal world. When I looked at a beautiful and peaceful lake, I was going to remember the loads of disease causing organisms multiplying prolifically beneath the shining, mirrored surface.

Sounds pretty bizarre, yes? But it had a strange effect.

Because I was no longer lying to myself about anything that existed, least of all myself, my nature, my being, I was free to choose *what* to manifest in every instant. Knowing that all of these shadows existed within me, in my very DNA, my flesh, my evolved self; knowing that I had experienced many lifetimes dealing death and destruction on my own, or suffering the same at the hands of others, I was free to *choose*. And further, I knew that the choice *was* free! If I had chosen to follow the path of STS, to dive back into the illusion, there would be no blame. As Ra said: The ALL blinks neither at the darkness nor at the light.

There was no longer any blame for anything. It was just *what is*. This is *nature*. This is *God*. And God has two faces: Good and Evil. We can love them both, but we can choose which face we manifest, while always loving unconditionally both faces.

This state of the world is masterfully depicted in Tennessee Williams' play *Suddenly Last Summer* where Mrs. Venable says:

> We saw the Encantadas, but on the Encantadas we saw something Melville hadn't written about. We saw the great sea turtles crawl up out of the sea for their annual egg-laying... Once a year the female of the sea turtle crawls up out of the equatorial sea onto the blazing sand-beach of a volcanic island to dig a pit in the sand and deposit her eggs there. It's a long and dreadful thing, the depositing of the eggs in the sandpits, and when it's finished the exhausted female turtle crawls back to the sea half-dead. She never sees her offspring, but we did. Sebastian knew exactly when the sea-turtle eggs would be hatched out and we returned in time for it...
>
> Terrible. Encantadas, those heaps of extinct volcanoes, in time to witness the hatching of the sea turtles and their desperate flight to the sea! The narrow beach, the color of caviar, was all in motion! But the sky was in motion too... Full of flesh-eating birds and the noise of the birds, the horrible savage cries of the – carnivorous birds... Over the narrow black beach of the Encantadas as the just hatched sea-turtles scrambled out of the sandpits and started their race to the sea... to escape the flesh-eating birds that made the sky almost as black as the beach!
>
> And the sand all alive, all alive, as the hatched sea turtles made their dash for the sea, while the birds hovered and swooped to attack and hovered and swooped to attack! They were diving down on the hatched sea-turtles, turning them over to expose their soft undersides, tearing the undersides open and rending and eating their flesh. Sebastian guessed that possibly only a hundredth of one per cent of their number would escape to the sea...
>
> My son was looking for God, I mean for a clear image of him. He spent that whole blazing equatorial day in the crow's nest of the schooner watching this thing on the beach till it was too dark to see it, and when he came down the rig-

ging he said "Well, now I've seen Him!" and he meant God. And for several weeks after that he had a fever, he was delirious with it.[8]

There I was, having my own "sea-turtle" experience and yes, I was sick for a long time after. What happened was, my entire system nearly shut down completely. It is curious to me that, faced with the destruction of every fairy tale I ever believed in about the world, I couldn't cry. At least not in the regular way. The pain was far too deep for ordinary tears. I literally cried blood. My eyes swelled up with inflammation that did not respond to medical treatment of various sorts that were tried. (I even went to a specialist, and nothing helped.) My eyes constantly poured what is called sero-sanguinous fluid – blood and serum – in such quantities that it ran down my cheeks continuously for weeks. I really understood what it meant to say, "Let this cup pass from me!" I was looking at reality, and it nearly killed me.

The life changing difference was what I eventually chose to do with this vision. The key is in the above extract from the Cassiopaean material where it says:

> ...Is it one possible future, but not all possible futures? And is the pathway of free will not connected to all of this?
>
> Q: (L) I seemed to be fighting and resisting this activity.
>
> A: That was your choice... Be not frustrated; for the answers to be gained through your own contemplation will be truly illuminating to you, and *the experience to follow will be worth a thousand lifetimes of pleasure and joy.*

Now, we are brought back face to face with our objective view of reality and our *free will*.

I *knew* I was "*Seeing* God". But, in the end, my *choice* was to *love* Him anyway. More than that, my choice was to *make manifest* those aspects of God *in myself*, that were of Love and Beauty and Truth as a *free will choice*. I was not choosing out of *fear*, even a hidden fear, such as is present in most people who adhere to the love and light routine and eschew any knowledge of the darkness.

If one were present at such an event as the hatching of the turtles, would it be right to rescue the turtles, to kill or scare away the birds? Both represent aspects, or Faces, of God, and both have a right to exist in their own context and to survive in their own way, so it would be wrong to interfere. But I would be hoping that some of the baby turtles would have the sense to wait until dark to make their dash to the sea! Perhaps I might walk back and forth along the beach to act as a "scarecrow" against the devouring birds. Perhaps that is how knowledge can work in our lives? Perhaps that is how the Cassiopaeans relate to us – only with somewhat more complexity.

---

[8] Tennessee Williams. *Suddenly Last Summer* (Huffer, 1958).

When you love your cat or dog, do you love them less for eating or killing other creatures? So what that he doesn't need to do it in his nice, warm, human home where dinner comes in a can. Leave him outdoors and on his own for a bit and he will soon enough eat whatever is there. Will you then reject him, love him less, or pretend that he – and dogs in general – do not exist?

Is this consuming aspect of our reality less acceptable when it reaches a conscious level, such as that of human beings? Are we not still to love all that exists as part of Nature, as part of God, and to accept it and allow it to *be* as it *is* – even while managing the delicate aspect of ensuring our own continuing right to exist and be?

And, if we do this, and further, if we *choose* to limit our participation in the consuming aspect to as great a degree as possible, can we think that we have learned one of the most valuable lessons of our reality? The lesson of what Love truly is? That Love is to love ALL, unconditionally, with no need or desire to change anything? That only in this state of Love – *objective* Love – can we truly have Free Will?

In point of fact, that is the true meaning of the much-touted "unconditional love". If you are going to love anything or anybody in spite of what it is or what they do, thinking that your love *changes something*, then you do *not* love unconditionally. You are loving your illusion of what might be, not what *is*.

Further, loving unconditionally means to love the self in the same way. If your "unconditional love" of another means that you must act in any way other than what is authentic to you, then you haven't gotten it. Further, if this other person does not love you in the same way, allowing you to be fully accepted *as you are*, and you think that by continuing to hold them close and love *them* unconditionally, that they will finally figure it out and change, then you have already violated the law of unconditional love. In terms of daily living, *you can only live in unconditional love with another who understands it in exactly the same way you do.*

I realized this. And I made my choice, as I said, to limit my participation in the lies and delusions to as great an extent as possible. This meant that I could no longer remain in close relationships that were less than fully reciprocal in terms of this kind of love. I understood clearly that this probably meant living entirely alone and loving the world and others unconditionally from a distance which was the only way I could see that it would be possible in practical terms. I could see that allowing myself to be used for energy food in a personal relationship of compromises was *not* in the best interests of anyone I loved, nor was it in my best interests. (And the same applies in practical considerations of law and order as well.)

Thus, I made the decisions I made, acted on them, and the result was nothing short of amazing.

Now, how does this apply globally to our question?

It means that in the upcoming times, we may be very much like the newly hatched turtles on the Encantadas. There are beings all around us who are like the ravenous, carnivorous birds. We *do* have a chance to get to the sea. What's more, with awareness, we can do a lot more than that! We may, in fact, with growing awareness, be able to change one probable future to another.

Why would there be so much deception in our world if it were not for the fact that there is some quality, some aspect of ourselves that the ones who seek to keep us blind and unaware wish to keep hidden? Why else would there be such a plethora of teachings in the present day that tend to soften and weaken our resistance by appealing to our love of ease and comfort and status quo? Further, why is the teaching about Love, itself, so horribly distorted?

February 24, 1996

Q: (L) Mike Lindemann[9] has proposed that we submit the channeling to "rigorous testing".

A: Mike Lindemann does not channel, now does he? What sort of rigorous testing does he propose?

Q: (L) He didn't say. I guess they want short-term predictions and all sorts of little tests...

A: Precisely, now what does this tell you?

Q: (L) It tells us that he wants proof.

A: Third density "proof" does not apply, as we have explained again and again. Now, listen very carefully: if proof of that type were possible, what do you suppose would happen to free will, and thusly to learning, Karmic Directive Level One?

Q: (L) Well, I guess that if there is proof, you are believing in the proof and not the spirit of the thing. You are placing your reliance upon a material thing. You have lost your free will. Someone has violated your free will by the act of *proving* something to you.

A: If anyone CHOOSES to believe, that is their prerogative! And what would constitute proof?

Q: (L) Predictions that came true, answers that were verifiable about a number of things. Physical phenomena.

---

[9] The most recent "bio" on Mike tells us: "From Dec 1994 to June 2000 he was editor and publisher of the online journal CNI News (www.cninews.com), reporting the latest in UFO research and the scientific quest for life in the universe; and from Jan 1999 to May 2000 he was editor and publisher of Global Situation Report (www.gsreport.com), covering events and trends shaping the new millennium. He discontinued those publications in June 2000 in order to join a new media company called Project Voyager (www.projectvoyager.com) that will focus on global trends and the human future. Michael is also author of the book *UFOs and the Alien Presence: Six Viewpoints* (1991; revised edition 1997) and has been a featured speaker at scores of UFO conferences across the U.S. and abroad. In October 1998 and again in July 1999, Michael co-organized and participated in a private think-tank project called the Contact Planning Sessions, in which business executives, NASA scientists, military officers, academicians, media professionals and futurists came together under confidential conditions to discuss the real social and political outcomes of contact with extraterrestrial intelligence. Michael has a passionate side interest in the planet Mars and plans to visit the moon as a tourist by the year 2020, preferably with his wife Deborah Lindemann, a professional hypnotherapist." (projectvoyager.com) My own opinion is that he may very well be part of the COINTELPRO of the New Age Movement.

A: Those would still be dismissed by a great many as mere coincidences. We have already given predictions, will continue to do so, but remember, "time" does not exist. This is a 3rd density illusion. We do not play in that sandbox and cannot and never will. The primary reason for our communication is to help you to learn by teaching yourselves to learn, thereby strengthening your soul energy, and assisting your advancement.

Q: (L) Are you saying that your primary reason is just to teach us? This small group?

A: Because you asked for help.

Q: (L) So, you came through because we asked. Is this material being given to others, or is it designed to or intended to be shared with others?

A: If they ask in the necessary way. Otherwise, the sharing of the messages we give to you will teach millions of others.

Q: (L) What is the "necessary way"?

A: How "long did it take you?"

Q: (L) Well, it took all our lives and a *lot* of hard work.

A: Okay, now what did we mean when we referred to "millions of others"?

Q: (L) Are you saying that this information will be transmitted in some way to millions of others?

A: In what way?

Q: (L) Well, the only thing I can think of is through writing.

A: Bingo!!

Q: (W) That's a lot of work.

A: The work has been ongoing, W!

Q: (W) Well, it all has to be typed, and edited, and correlated and put in a cohesive form, and it will be a couple of years. [...]

A: All will be taken care of, and no, W!

Q: (W) Well, I was thinking of the time frame and so many things are getting ready to happen any time now. It seems like the information needs to get out there soon, or it will be obsolete.

A: Prejudice serves no purpose! Also, who says that the information is going to be obsolete? Wait and see.

And more on the subject of proof versus strength:

April 18, 1998

A: We wish to reiterate something further on this subject A***, and for anyone else in need of the following message: we are not communicating with you in order to "prove" our existence. If one has faith and is willing to learn, to explore new realms and to discover what will one "day" be commonplace awareness profile, then no "proof" is necessary. If, on the other hand, one is of the opposite psychic orientation, then no amount of proof is adequate.

Q: (A) Yes, I think it is like the story of the magic crocodile skin where you can make wishes on it, and with every wish it becomes smaller. And, you are told that when it becomes too small, then you die. And, of course, you try, and say "let me do one more wish..." and that is it. Once you make the choice to ask and not do the work, then it becomes easier and easier and you want more and more... and your own will and force becomes smaller and smaller...

Q: (L) I think that the most important thing that has come out of this channeling is that sometimes the C's sort of trick me into trying something and they pique my curiosity and I go out and *do* something that results in a learning experience that is truly awesome. And the important thing is, getting out and doing the work actually makes you stronger. And, like you just said, each time you make the choice to *not* go after the answer yourself, to try and get it the easy way, it makes you weaker and lessens who you are. It is sort of a nonlinear principle that can lead to all kinds of things. If they gave us all the conceptual truths, we would have lost something *huge* in the way of strength and free will. Like those sources that supposedly gave the secrets of the bomb... and other sources that just give and give all sorts of things and you can clearly see the deterioration of those involved... (F) Yes, and the crucial point is the robbing of free will *initiative*. (L) So, it is a *very subtle* thing.

June 19, 1999
A: Have we not already indicated? Knowledge is power. If we give it to you like Halloween candy, it is diffused.

Again, I want to repeat what the Cassiopaeans have said about studying and learning by work and effort:

Subtle answers that require effort to dissect promote intensified learning. Learning is an exploration followed by the affirmation of knowing through discovery. Learning is necessary for progress of soul... this is how you are building your power center... Patience serves the questor of hidden knowledge... Search your "files"... Learning is sometimes best accomplished by study and exploration... There are other clues that you can discover by your own study...

In more recent times, they have specifically addressed Ark and yours truly with the following:

Combine energies in pursuit of answers, and the rest falls into place. You and Arkadiusz are complementary souls. Karmic Destiny Level One Mission.

Thus, we work, we pursue answers, and we experiment in many ways to discover the secrets that can be shared with others on the same path. And it is in this process that many interesting ideas have come forth. Remember the scenario of my correspondent:

In short as you said to the Cassies the picture looks ugly. They said that you seem to think that only good experience is useful, well no, but at least there is usually a mix of good and bad but in their scenario we are all for the high jump with no mat on the other side though. (Splat)

Relating this to the Eclipsing of Realities, it seems that from the descriptions of The Wave, it must be a macro-scale Eclipsing of the Realities. It has been described in many of the same terms as my own experience that resulted in changing my reality. If that is the case, and resistance was my choice, and that resistance resulted in the seeding of a new state of existence, would it then follow that similar actions in regard to the future of the human race could have the same effect?

To put it another way, as a member of our discussion group pointed out:

> The [spider-like beings] aspect might have been there to provide you with the experience to "nudge" you in the direction you are upon to provide yet again, balance; and this may have been actually a necessary contribution to obtain it.

Thus, by being presented with the objective truth of our reality, are we not being nudged to make a choice? And if, in fact, we do actually get invaded by aliens, will that not also be an experience that stimulates choice?

The question becomes: why are we supposed to be building strength of soul and will and awareness if we are not supposed to *do something with it*? I leave you with that question.

PART II:
ALL THERE IS IS LESSONS…

November 24, 1994

All there is is lessons. This is one infinite school. There is no other reason for anything to exist. Even inanimate matter learns it is all an "Illusion". Each individual possesses all of creation within their minds. Now, contemplate for a moment. Each soul is all-powerful and can create or destroy all existence if [they] know how. You and us and all others are interconnected by our mutual possession of all there is. You may create alternative universes if you wish and dwell within. You are all a duplicate of the universe within which you dwell. Your mind represents all that exists. It is "fun" to see how much you can access.

Q: (L) It's fun for *whom* to see how much we can access?

A: All. Challenges are fun. Where do you think the limit of your mind is?

Q: (L) Where?

A: We asked you.

Q: (L) Well, I guess there is no limit.

A: If there is no limit, then what is the difference between your own mind and everything else?

Q: (L) Well, I guess there is no difference if all is ultimately One.

A: Right. And when two things each have absolutely no limits, they are precisely the same thing

The above remarks by the Cassiopaeans reflect the general core of many teachings down through the ages. So what's the difference between what the Cassiopaeans are saying and what has already been said?

Perhaps we can answer that question with another one: what good is it to know all the other things that the Cassiopaeans have told us? What practical purpose does it serve?

I am a *very* practical person. For me, and for my husband, Ark, it is the *results* that count. I guess you could call it the "Fruits agenda" derived from the saying: "By their fruits you shall know them." It's all fine and good to have a philosophical view of the world that admits to an underlying unity of everything, but for all practical purposes, despite the claims of numerous teachers and gurus down through history, including a plethora of New Age promoters of the "You create your own reality" ilk, we can see that this is somehow not precisely applicable in our world.

Yet, the Cassiopaeans have just said it. But, they said something else: "IF YOU KNOW HOW."

Clearly that is the problem. We don't know how. And it is in the knowing how, the developing of the tools of the mind and psyche that there seems to be a difference. In plain words: what the Cassiopaeans are saying about our reality, when applied in the ways that become obvious when one is aware, *works*.

We have been dealing with this issue from a couple of different perspectives already, and now I want to go in a different direction to see if we can't get a better handle on all of this.

In addition to my idea of the Fruits agenda, there is also what I call the "Mumbo Jumbo factor". I have two six foot tall, three foot wide, bookcases here in the house filled with what I jokingly refer to as the Mumbo Jumbo category. I am not sure what the Dewey decimal system would make of this, but after I read a book, I can generally tell if it goes in that particular section.

I really don't like ambiguity. And it seems that much, if not most, information that comes down to us from so-called higher sources is *very* ambiguous. Terry once asked a question that opened a door to helping me understand this:

November 26, 1994

Q: (T) One last question. How do I know you are telling me the truth?

A: Open. *For you to decide*. Listen: Now would be a good "time" for you folks to begin to reexamine some of the extremely popular "Earth Changes" prophecies. Why, you ask. Because, remember, you are third density beings, so real prophecies are being presented to you in terms you will understand, i.e., physical realm, i.e., Earth Changes. *This "may" be symbolism*. Would most students of the subject understand *if prophecies were told directly in fourth density terms?*

Q: (L) Is this comparable to my idea about dream symbolism? For example, the dream I had about the curling cloud, which I saw in a distance and knew it was death dealing and I interpreted it to be a tornado, but it was, in fact, a dream of the Challenger disaster. I understood it to be a tornado, but in fact, what I saw was what I got: a death dealing force in the sky, a vortex, in the distance. I guess my dream was a fourth density representation but I tried to interpret it in terms I was familiar with. Is this what you mean?

A: Close. But it is easy for most to get bogged down by interpreting prophecies in literal terms.

Q: (L) In terms of these Earth Changes, Edgar Cayce is one of the most famous prognosticators of recent note. A large number of the prophecies he made seemingly were erroneous in terms of their fulfillment. For example, he prophesied that Atlantis would rise in 1969, but it did not, though certain structures were discovered off the coast of Bimini, which are thought by many to be remnants of Atlantis. These did, apparently, emerge from the sand at that time.

A: Example of one form of symbolism.

Q: (L) Well, in terms of this symbolism, could it be that [when you tell us things about our reality], you read events from third density into sixth density terms and then transmit them back into third; and while the ideation can be correct, the exact specifics, in third density terms, can be slightly askew due to our perceptions. Is that what we are dealing with here?

A: 99.9 per cent would not understand that concept. Most are always looking for literal translations of data. Analogy is: novice, who attends art gallery, looks at abstract painting and says, "I don't get it."

Q: (L) Well, let's not denigrate literal translations or at least attempts to get things into literal terms. I like realistic artwork. I am a realist in my art preferences. I want trees to look like trees and people to have only two arms and legs. Therefore, I also like some literalness in my prognostications.

A: Some is okay, but, beware or else "California falls into the ocean" will always be interpreted as California falling into the ocean.

Q: [General uproar.] (F) Wait a minute, what was the question? (L) I just said I liked literalness in my prophecies. (F) Oh, I know what they are saying. People believe that California is just going to go splat! And that Phoenix is going to be on the seacoast; never mind that it's at 1800 feet elevation, it's just going to drop down to sea level; or the sea level is going to rise; but it's not going to affect Virginia Beach even though that's at sea level! I mean... somehow Phoenix is just going to drop down and none of the buildings are going to be damaged, even though its going to fall 1,800 feet... (T) Slowly. It's going to settle! (F) Slowly? It would have to be so slowly it's unbelievable how slowly it would have to be! (T) It's been settling for the last five million years, we've got a ways to go in the next year and a half! (F) Right! That's my point! (T) In other words, when people like Scallion and Sun Bear and others who say California is going to fall into the ocean, they are not saying that the whole state, right along the border is going to fall into the ocean, they are using the term "California" to indicate that the ocean ledge along the fault line has a *probability* of breaking off and sinking on the water side, because it is a major fracture. We understand that that is not literal. *Are you telling us that there is more involved here as far as the way we are hearing what these predictions say?*

A: Yes.

Q: (T) So, when we talk about California falling into the ocean, we are not talking about the whole state literally falling into the ocean?

A: In any case, even if it does, how long will it take to do this?

Q: (LM) It could take three minutes or three hundred years. (T) Yes. That is "open" as you would say.

A: Yes. But most of your prophets think it is not open.

Q: (T) Okay. So they are thinking in the terms that one minute California will be there and a minute and a half later it will be all gone. Is this what you are saying?

A: Or similar.

Q: (T) So, when we are talking: "California will fall into the ocean," which is just the analogy we are using, we are talking about the possibility that several seismic events along the fault line, which no one really knows the extent of...

A: *Or it all may be symbolic of something else.*

Q: (L) Such as? Symbolic of what?

A: *Up to you to examine and learn.*

Q: (L) Now, wait a minute here! That's like sending us out to translate a book in Latin without even giving us a Latin dictionary.

A: No it is not. We asked you to consider a reexamination.

Q: (L) You have told us that there is a cluster of comets connected in some interactive way with our solar system, and that this cluster of comets comes into the plane of the ecliptic every 3,600 years. Is this correct?

A: *Yes. But, this time it is riding realm border wave to 4th level, where all realities are different.*

Q: (L) Okay, so the cluster of comets is riding the realm border wave. Does this mean that when it comes into the solar system, that its effect on the solar system, or the planets within the solar system, (J) or us... (L) ...may or may not be mitigated by the fact of this transition? Is this a mitigating factor?

A: *Will be mitigated* [made less severe].

Q: (L) Does this mean that all of this running around and hopping and jumping to go here and go there and do this and do that is...

A: That is strictly 3rd level thinking.

Q: (L) Now, if that is third level thinking, and if a lot of these things are symbolic, I am assuming they are *symbolic of movement or changes in energy.*

A: Yes.

Q: (L) And, if these changes in energy occur does this mean that the population of the planet are, perhaps, in groups or special masses of groups, are they defined as the energies that are changing in these descriptions of events and happenings of great cataclysm? Is it like a cataclysm of the soul on an individual and or collective basis?

A: Close.

Q: (L) When the energy changes to fourth density, and you have already told us that people who are moving to fourth density when the transition occurs, that they will move into fourth density, go through some kind of rejuvenation process, grow new teeth, or whatever; what happens to those people who are *not* moving to fourth density, and who are totally unaware of it? Are they taken along on the wave by, in other words, piggybacked by, the ones who are aware and already changing in frequency, or are they going to be somewhere else doing something else?

A: Step by step.

Q: (T) In other words, we are looking at the fact that what's coming this time is a *wave that's going to allow the human race to move to fourth density?*

A: *And the planet and your entire sector of space-time.*

Q: (T) Is that what this whole plan is about, then, if I may be so bold as to include all of us here in this. We could be beings who have come here into human form, to anchor the frequency. Is this what we are anchoring it for, for this Wave; so that when it comes enough of us will be ready, the frequency will be set, so that the change in the planet can take place as it has been planned?

A: Yes.

Q: (T) Okay, when the people are talking about the earth changes, when they talk in literal terms about the survivors, and those who are not going to survive, and the destruction and so forth and so on, in fourth, fourth, and fifth level reality, we are not talking about the destruction of the planet on fourth level physical terms, or the loss of 90 per cent of the population on the fourth level because they died, but because they are going to move to fourth level?

A: Whoa! You are getting "warm".

Q: (T) Okay. So, we are anchoring this. So, when they talk about 90 per cent of the population not surviving, it is not that they are going to die, but that they are going to transform. We are going to go up a level. This is what the whole light thing is all about?

A: Or another possibility is that *the physical cataclysms will occur only for those "left behind" on the remaining 3rd level density earth.*

Q: (T) Okay, what you are saying, then, is that we are anchoring the frequency, so that when the Wave comes, we move to fourth level density as many people as possible, in order to break the hold the "Dark T-shirts" (as Barbara Marciniak calls them) have got on this planet. Those who remain behind will not have enough energy left for the "Dark T-shirts" to bother with the planet any longer. There will be less of them so the planet will be able to refresh and they will be able to move on in their lessons without interference?

A: Close.

Q: (L) Let me get this straight. At this point of dimensional transition, is what we are doing, anchoring a frequency, are we creating a sort of network that will literally create another earth in fourth density, which will then exist in fourth density, and the old fourth density earth – almost like the splitting of a one celled organism, only in this splitting one half of it moves into another dimension and is energized and quite literally created by the anchoring frequency, while the old one remains and experiences fourth density reality?

A: Step by step.

Q: (L) Are we anchoring frequency to create a split?

A: One developing conduit.

Q: (L) We are developing a conduit?

A: Yes. One.

Q: (J) How many conduits do we need?

A: Open.

Q: (T) Is this conduit going to allow those who remain behind to be able to move to fourth density easier when they are ready?

A: No.

Q: (T) What is the conduit for?

A: You and those who will follow you.

Q: (L) This conduit. Is this a conduit through which an entire planet will transition?

A: You are one. There are others.

Q: (J) So, at this point we are developing a conduit?

A: Yes.

Q: (T) There are other groups on this planet developing their own conduits?

A: Yes. *Knowledge is the key to developing a conduit.*

Q: (T) I am working on the assumption that all of us here are part of the family of light, is this true?

A: Yes.

Q: (T) And we have been drawn together in order to develop this conduit from where we are?

A: Yes.

Q: (T) Are there others in this area?
A: Yes.
Q: (T) Are they supposed to join with us or are they working on their own?
A: Open.
Q: (T) Okay, so it is up in the air as to whether we join with them, they join with us, or we all work independently. We're developing a conduit to move us from fourth density to fourth density. Once we have moved through the conduit does that mean we have completed what we came here to do, and that is anchor the frequency?
A: Partly.
Q: (T) Is the conduit kind of like an escape hatch for us?
A: Close.
Q: (L) Let me get this straight. When we move through this conduit, are the other...
A: You will be on the 4th level earth as opposed to 3rd level earth.
Q: (L) What I am trying to get here, once again, old practical Laura is trying to get a handle on practical terms here. Does this mean that *a fourth density earth and a third density earth will coexist* side by side...
A: *Not side-by-side, totally different realms.*
Q: (L) Do these realms interpenetrate one another but in different dimensions...
A: Close.
Q: (L) So, in other words, a being from say, sixth density, could look at this planet we call the earth and see it spinning through space and see several dimensions of earth, and yet the point of space-time occupation is the same, in other words, simultaneous. (J) They can look down but we can't look up.
A: Yes.
Q: (L) So, in other words, while all of this cataclysmic activity is happening on the third density earth, we will be just on our fourth density earth and this sort of thing won't be there, and we won't see the third density people and they won't see us because we will be in different densities which are not "en rapport", so to speak?
A: You understand concept, now you must decide if it is factual.

Well, I tried! I was really getting close and then they went ambiguous on me! But the important thing is the fact that the Cassiopaeans were trying to get a point across about *Symbols of Reality*. They are proposing to us the idea that our reality is a *symbolic* one. But, remember the first quote:

> Each soul is all-powerful and can *create or destroy all existence if [they] know how*. You and us and all others are interconnected by our mutual possession of all there is. *You may create alternative universes if you wish and dwell within.* You are all a duplicate of the universe within which you dwell. Your mind represents all that exists. *It is "fun" to see how much you can access.*

We have already talked about reality being pseudo-symbolic; that is, our world is most likely a limited version of a greater reality like Plato's shadows on the wall of the cave were symbols of a greater reality; but even when talking about hyper-dimensional space and fourth density, we are still speaking in a *material* sense. Remember the tesseract?[10] Well, now we are going to talk about *all* of it being symbolic in another sense: *symbols of ideas and energies* in a strictly non-material sense.

Further, as we go along (in this book and others in the Wave series), we are going to talk about the possible realities behind these symbols of third and fourth density – and most importantly, the *reason* it is the way it is. And this, we will find, relates directly to the ambiguity of information from higher realms. Michael Topper writes about this ambiguity, or Mumbo Jumbo factor in the following:

> We consult the channeler because, basically, we are concerned, in a very ordinary conceptual way, like every personality anxiously poised on the psychological tight wire spanning the temporalized chasm of existence. [...]
>
> It would always be oh so helpful if we could see the future in advance, be informed of the respective consequences in the alternatives confronting the present perplexing moment of decision.
>
> We would like if possible, to be underwritten not only for our monetary but also for our psychic commitments; insured in advance against the usual contingencies. And the channeler proffers the prospect of just this excelsior potential. [...]
>
> The myriad channeled voices to which we have been opened in recent years do indeed present an avalanche of prediction, of advice on principle and in particular, and a massive characterization of planes, states, levels and dimensions of reality which introduce whole other magnitudes to the ultimate questions of purpose and consequence.
>
> Through the innumerable contributions of channeled sources we have been, in a certain sense, asked to reappraise the whole matter of success in terms beyond the conventional, so that the horizon upon which the grail of accomplishment rests has been, as it were, elevated; the sights raised to the prospect of a more comprehensive and crucial, indeed sacred, focus.
>
> On the "plus" side then, the phenomenon of channeling has supplied a verbal chorus of confirmation tending collectively to install our usual questions and concerns in a setting offset by distinct considerations of Soul.
>
> The "answers" to our most mundane queries as to future, choice and result have been furnished a whole additional dimension of meaning.
>
> The most casual skimmer of "channeled" material can't help but perceive, at least implicitly, the bearing, which every conventional ego-choice has upon the larger destiny of soul-growth. Never mind for the time being that such emphatic intimations result from a cutting in, an abrupt verbal tunneling of the basic meditative stream that was ostensibly moving toward the unique value of personal (unmediated) cognition and direct perception of those very, spiritual and high-psychic modes now presented by descriptive approximation.

---

[10] A tesseract is a four-dimensinoal cube or hypercube. Just as a three-dimensional cube is made of 6 two-dimensional faces, a hypercube is made up of 8 cubes. Four-dimensional space is hard to comprehend at first, so I refer the reader to discussions in *Riding the Wave* and the recommended reading listed there.

Never mind that the whole phenomenon seems, in a certain light, to express the impatience of higher-dimensional intelligence long waiting for the sluggish personal development characteristic of this "material plane".

And so, they simply intrude with the necessary packets of information at the minimal achievement of some meditative quietude.

To be fair, some "channeling" circumstances seem to promote the actual personal progress of the channeler in gaining direct access to the planes, states, phenomena and degrees of mind-body integration otherwise only described or verbally characterized by ventriloquist voice-transmission (cf. the Seth material, and the late Jane Roberts' occasional description of her personal development in "inner plane" understanding).

But for the most part, the expressed Ryerson[11] attitude prevails. This amounts to a curious dissociation between the person of the channeler and the content of the communication resulting practically in an overall substitution of the description for the thing described.

More immediately, on the minus side of the phenomenon we end up (in this avalanche of description from various sources) with *a collision rather than a smooth confluence of materials.* At the "higher" levels of consciousness (not limited to the space-time framework of the blindered channeler) there still seems to be *contention or discrepancy in the respective characterizations of Reality*; there still seems to be division regarding that which is perceived or known even in these greater and more allegedly comprehensive Domains of Knowing.

Any who've scanned more than one of these sources in print, or compared notes with "live" sessions attended, are bound to notice (if minimally conscious) that, beneath the general agreement as to the existence of higher states and planes, of different orders of knowledge and action from those assumed in the context of strictly physical expression there is *a welter of large and small divergences ranging from minor variations to an embarrassment of glaring contradictions.*

This is explained in one such source. *Cosmic Revelation* "channeled" by Virginia Essene and Ann Valentin, as the inevitable condition of confusion resulting from the urgent/unprecedented need of the higher dimensions to disseminate changing patterns of information belonging to "revamped educational programs," brought about by this *critical epoch of transition* through which we're hesitantly passing.

Such confusion, according to this source results from the requirement of transmission along the spiritual hierarchy of inner plane beings through which such "information", formulated at the highest levels, must pass.

---

[11] The reference that Topper is making here is to the fact that Ryerson's personal life and behavior is not in keeping with that of a spiritual seeker, that his normal speech is full of prurient and scatological remarks. From Patrick O'Reilly's "Channeling: A Skeptical View" (http://www.michaelteachings.com/ skepticism _channeling.htm): "Kevin Ryerson is a "trance channel" who has achieved fame and riches. He was brought to the public's attention through the books of Shirley McLaine. Ryerson's message is that we are all divine and he has created a strange cosmology that includes, among many other aspects, chakras, intuition and ecology. Ryerson has frequently been on television talk shows, has written popular books about his channeled messages, and holds workshops at which he channels his particular entities. According to him, our society is devoid of healing psychic imagery, so we allow ourselves to be overwhelmed by technology. We must step out of our world into a sacred mandala. Kevin Ryerson – at one time – charged '$250 per session, has had so many inquiries at his San Francisco office that he is referring business to other channelers.'"

Consistent with what may be gathered from other source-channels, the various levels along which the orders of intelligence transmit the flow of data "downward" formulate the patterns of information *according to the understanding of their particular plane.* Tinctured already by that qualification, *the information may receive its most noticeable distortion at the level of the channeler* where, according to the variable of the given "linkage" there may be greater or lesser reliance on the personal memory-record, conceptual matrix or vocabulary of the channeling agent.

The resultant verbal product is, in any case, several dimensional steps removed from the originating Intention.

Add to this the recognition that all such knowledge emanates in its highest form from levels of creative intelligence that are basically nonverbal and that conduct all processes of knowing in abstract spiritual terms not directly translatable into concepts congenial to a physically-focused framework, and we seem to have on the surface a convenient explanation as to why Seth and Hilarion don't agree, why Ramtha and the "Christ" material of The New Teachings apparently quarrel on the shelves. (Emphases added.)

Well, that certainly seems to explain the problem: different sources say different things because of the filtering down process from the higher realms. And, of course, when it reaches the channel, it gets its greatest twist from the knowledge, vocabulary and assumptions of the specific channel. So, the obvious solution is to seek the information from the highest source possible with the least noise.

This was, in fact, the problem that prompted me to approach my channeling experiment in the way I did. I was not going to be satisfied with "dead dudes", who generally have very little more information or insights than we do ourselves in our state of third density illusion. In fact, as I learned from many hypnosis subjects and many conversations with dead dudes, the level of ignorance at that stage of existence is often abysmal! I very definitely did *not* want to waste my time with dead dudes, because it was a sure path to deliberate obfuscation, innocent disinformation, or useless speculation. As Cayce said: "A dead Presbyterian is just that: A dead Presbyterian." And, the fact of the matter is: as dead dudes, most of them are *still in the prison*!

But getting back to the Symbols of Reality as mentioned by the Cassiopaeans above:

November 26, 1994

Q: (T) So, when we are talking: "California will fall into the ocean, which is just the analogy we are using, we are talking about, as far as earth changes, is the possibility that several seismic events along the fault line, which no one really knows the extent of...

A: Or it all may be symbolic of something else.

Q: (L) Such as? Symbolic of what?

A: Up to you to examine and learn.

This places the responsibility squarely in our laps.

But, at the time, because I was still influenced by the teaching that the higher truths ought to be free and easily acquired, this question drove me crazy. Why couldn't I get a straight answer about *anything*? Well, that is not entirely fair. The Cassiopaeans gave us many straight answers about many things, both of the verifiable and *un*verifiable sort. But on certain subjects, the ambiguity was left hanging there like the proverbial Sword of Damocles. It seems that it was something I had to figure out on my own.

As I have written before, I had read Ouspensky's *In Search of the Miraculous* back in the mid-eighties and many of the things said in that book outraged me so completely that I would literally throw the book away from me.

At the time, I was bedridden and had little else to do but think. So, I would slam the book against the wall across the room, and fume indignantly at what Gurdjieff had said – very much in the way Carlos Castaneda reacted to many things said by don Juan Matus – until, gradually, I would cool down and a very small voice inside would suggest that I think about the matter without the heat of my emotions. I would ponder a bit longer, examining many experiences of my life in my mind, and soon would come to the realization that what Gurdjieff was saying, if not the whole picture, was certainly going in the right direction.

So, I would call someone to come and retrieve the book for me and settle down to read another few pages until – yes, over and over again – I felt outraged and blasphemed, and then the book went flying! That very book is sitting in front of me at this moment, held together with duct tape.

What was it Gurdjieff said that was so outrageous to me?

> You do not realize your own situation. You are in prison. All you can wish for, if you are a sensible man, is to escape. But how to escape? It is necessary to tunnel under a wall. One man can do nothing. But let us suppose there are ten or twenty men – if they work in turn and if one covers another they can complete the tunnel and escape.
>
> Furthermore, no one can escape from prison without the help of those who have escaped before. Only they can say in what way escape is possible or can send tools, files, or whatever may be necessary. *But one prisoner alone cannot find these people or get into touch with them.*
>
> ...It is necessary to understand that man's being, both in life and after death, if it does exist after death, may be very different in quality. The "man-machine" with whom everything depends upon external influences, with whom everything happens, who is now one, then next moment another, and the next moment a third, has no future of any kind; he is buried and that is all. Dust returns to dust. This applies to him. In order to be able to speak of any kind of future life there must be a certain crystallization, a certain fusion of man's inner qualities, and a certain independence of external influences. If there is anything in a man able to resist external influences, then this very thing itself may also be able to resist the death of the physical body...
>
> Fusion, inner unity, is obtained by means of "friction", by the struggle between "yes" and "no" in man. If a man lives without inner struggle, if

everything happens in him without opposition, if he goes wherever he is drawn or wherever the wind blows, he will remain such as he is.

But if a struggle begins in him, and particularly if there is a definite line in this struggle, then, gradually, permanent traits begin to form themselves, he begins to "crystallize".

But crystallization is possible on a right foundation and it is possible on a wrong foundation. "Friction", the struggle between "yes" and "no", can easily take place on a wrong foundation.

For instance, a fanatical belief in some or other idea, or the "fear of sin", can evoke a terribly intense struggle between "yes" and "no", and a man may crystallize on these foundations. But this would be a wrong, incomplete crystallization. Such a man will not possess the possibility of further development. In order to make further development possible he must be melted down again, and this can be accomplished only through terrible suffering.

Crystallization is possible on any foundation. Take for example a brigand, a really good, genuine brigand. I knew such brigands in the Caucasus. He will stand with a rifle behind a stone by the roadside for eight hours without stirring. Could you do this? All the time, mind you, a struggle is going on in him. He is thirsty and hot, and the flies are biting him; but he stands still.

Another is a monk; he is afraid of the devil; all night long he beats his head on the floor and prays. Thus crystallization is achieved.

In such ways people can generate in themselves an enormous inner strength; they can endure torture; they can get what they want. This means that there is now in them something solid, something permanent.

Such people can become immortal. But what is the good of it? A man of this kind becomes an "immortal *thing*", although a certain amount of consciousness is sometimes preserved in him. But even this, it must be remembered, occurs very rarely.

In what way can one evoke the struggle between "yes" and "no" in oneself?

Sacrifice is necessary. If nothing is sacrificed nothing is obtained. And it is necessary to sacrifice something precious at the moment, to sacrifice for a long time and to sacrifice a great deal. But still, not forever. This must be understood because often it is not understood. *Sacrifice is necessary only while the process of crystallization is going on.* When crystallization is achieved, renunciation, privations, and sacrifices are no longer necessary.[12] (Emphasis added.)

When I began to think about the *why* of the symbols of reality, I remembered this passage. Somehow, I felt, there was a connection. This passage seems to be saying, in opposition to many current teachings, that, as third density human beings, we may not be as special and chosen and wonderful as we have been taught to believe by most of the world's religions and their offshoots. Gurdjieff's comments just *fly* in the face of the standard New Age dogma, which, for the most part, says we are "special beings" even if we may have made a few nasty mistakes; it's okay. A few lifetimes will straighten it all out and we will

---

[12] P.D. Ouspensky, *In Search of the Miraculous: Fragments of an Unknown Teaching* (San Diego: Harvest/HBJ, 1977).

be right as rain. If we just think about good things, we can create a good reality because what we focus on is what we "create", so we must forget altogether about bad or negative things, and "love is all you need". La la la la la!

But Gurdjieff is saying that we are in *prison* and we have *no hope* of escaping without certain knowledge, *the primary realization being that we ARE in prison.* Further, that we cannot escape without help and group effort, and that *this help cannot even be obtained or accessed without a certain "crystallization"* or effort. He also seems to be saying that our concepts about our souls being integrated and consistent may be a bit egotistical, and possibly not a fact at all!

That's pretty scary stuff!

At one point, Carlos Castaneda's Don Juan told him:

> We have a predator that came from the depths of the cosmos and took over the rule of our lives. Human beings are its prisoners. The predator is our lord and master. It has rendered us docile, helpless. If we want to protest, it suppresses our protest. If we want to act independently, it demands that we don't do so… You have arrived, by your effort alone, to what the shamans of ancient Mexico called the *topic of topics*. I have been beating around the bush all this time, insinuating to you that *something is holding us prisoner*. Indeed we are held prisoner! This was an energetic fact for the sorcerers of ancient Mexico.
>
> "Why has this predator taken over in the fashion that you're describing, don Juan?" I asked. "There must be a logical explanation."
>
> "There is an explanation," don Juan replied, "which is the simplest explanation in the world. They took over because we are food for them, and they squeeze us mercilessly because we are their sustenance. Just as we rear chickens in chicken coops, the predators rear us in human coops. Therefore, their food is always available to them."
>
> I felt that my head was shaking violently from side to side. I could not express my profound sense of unease and discontentment, but my body moved to bring it to the surface. I shook from head to toe without any volition on my part.
>
> "No, no, no, no," I heard myself saying. "This is absurd, don Juan. What you're saying is something monstrous. It simply can't be true, for sorcerers or for average men, or for anyone."
>
> "Why not?" don Juan asked calmly. "Why not? Because it infuriates you?"
>
> "Yes, it infuriates me," I retorted. "Those claims are monstrous!" […]
>
> "I want to appeal to your analytical mind," don Juan said. "Think for a moment, and tell me how you would explain the contradiction between the intelligence of man the engineer and the stupidity of his systems of beliefs, or the stupidity of his contradictory behavior. *Sorcerers believe that the predators have given us our systems of beliefs, our ideas of good and evil, our social mores. They are the ones who set up our hopes and expectations and dreams of success or failure. They have given us covetousness, greed and cowardice. It is the predators who make us complacent, routinary, and egomaniacal.*"
>
> 'But how can they do this, don Juan?' I asked, somehow angered further by what he was saying. 'Do they whisper all that in our ears while we are asleep?'
>
> 'No, they don't do it that way. That's idiotic!' don Juan said, smiling. 'They are infinitely more efficient and organized than that. In order to keep us obedi-

ent and meek and weak, the predators engaged themselves in a stupendous maneuver – stupendous, of course, from the point of view of a fighting strategist. A horrendous maneuver from the point of view of those who suffer it. *They gave us their mind!* Do you hear me? The predators give us their mind, which becomes our mind. *The predators' mind is baroque, contradictory, morose, filled with the fear of being discovered any minute now.*[13]

Don Juan continues:

"I know that even though you have never suffered hunger... you have food anxiety, which is none other than the anxiety of the predator who fears that any moment now its maneuver is going to be uncovered and food is going to be denied. Through the mind, which, after all, is their mind, the predators inject into the lives of human beings whatever is convenient for them. And they ensure, in this manner, a degree of security to act as a buffer against their fear."[14]

Note, most particularly, don Juan's remark:

The predators have given us our systems of beliefs, our ideas of good and evil, our social mores. They are the ones who set up our hopes and expectations and dreams of success or failure. They have given us covetousness, greed and cowardice. It is the predators who make us complacent, routinary, and egomaniacal.

Essentially, what is being said here is that "nothing is as it seems and *never* has been!" We can trust almost nothing, if anything at all, about our reality, if we try to read it through the lenses of our "systems of beliefs, our ideas of good and evil, our social mores."

We are being informed by Gurdjieff, don Juan, and the Cassiopaeans, that our jailers are the ones who set up our beliefs, our hopes and expectations and dreams of success or failure – and we note that these things – our beliefs, hopes, dreams and ideas of good and evil – are all ideas that have been derived, over millennia, from essentially channeled sources. We consult priests, priestesses, pastors, the Bible, the Koran, the Vedas, and nowadays endless channeled books because we are, as Mr. Topper noted, "*concerned*, in a very ordinary conceptual way... It would always be oh so helpful if we could see the future in advance, be informed of the respective consequences [of our choices]..."

And the many sources that we consult do, indeed, offer us the "answers". Michael continues:

The myriad channeled voices to which we have been opened in recent years do indeed present an avalanche of prediction, of advice on principle and in particular, and a massive characterization of planes, states, levels and dimensions of reality which introduce whole other magnitudes to the ultimate questions of purpose and consequence.

---

[13] Carlos Castaneda, *The Active Side of Infinity* (HarperCollins, 1998), pp. 213-20.
[14] Ibid.

So, what's wrong with that? Isn't it a good thing that we are being guided to think of our reality in something other than material terms? Isn't it a generally good thing to be made aware that our lives have meaning in a larger, cosmic context? Isn't it a good thing to have some hints and descriptions of higher levels of reality to which we may ascend if we adhere to the spiritual principles being presented to us? Don't they pretty much agree, in principle, and does it matter one way or another whether one subscribes to this or that system? Don't most of them say that there are "many paths to the mountain top?" Don't they encourage us to "create your own reality", to "get saved", or whatever version is being offered?

Yet Gurdjieff, don Juan, and the Cassiopaeans are saying that we are prisoners, in opposition to the vast majority of other teachings.

The Cassiopaeans have said:

January 21, 1995

Q: (L) [Has the government been engaged in faking UFOs, abductions, and cattle mutilations] to protect themselves from the public knowing that they were engaged in alien interactions?

A: They do it to protect the public from knowing that which would explode society if discovered.

Q: (L) What is this item that they were protecting so that society or the public wouldn't know about it. What activity is this?

A: *Humans eat cattle; aliens eat you.* […]

Q: (T) [You say] the government, our government, the U.S. government, is holding 36 alien craft of one kind or another that they have gotten in one way or another. How many other governments have craft?

A: All is one.

Q: (L) We already have a one-world government is what they're saying. (T) Yes, they're just waiting to make it official somehow.

A: Has been so for long time, as you measure time.

Q: (L) What is the "ultimate secret" being protected by the Consortium?

A: *You are not in control of yourselves; you are an experiment.*

December 26, 1998

Q: (L) Is the "buried treasure" of the Templars or Cathars, or whoever, manuscripts from the Alexandrian library telling about the true origin and nature of man?

A: Well if so, maybe that would explain the structure you live under.

Q: (L) What structure do we live under?

A: *Forced choices.*

This is *not* sounding very friendly, for sure! And there is something else to consider. The coming of Ra was, as far as I know, the first exposition of densities via a *channeled source*. But the idea of the "octaves of reality" as *seven* levels of experience was already being taught by Gurdjieff and in later offshoots of his work, and was certainly present in the ancient Sufi teachings. As far as anyone knows, Gurdjieff was taught in some of the secret Sufi centers of Asia Minor. He often alluded to man being "food for the Moon", and what he was saying is pretty much equivalent to saying that third density is the prison and the only way to get out is to graduate to fourth density.

He made another curious remark that really grabbed me at one point.[15] For the sake of comprehension, Gurdjieff described these different worlds, obviously meant to suggest densities, as:

1) Absolute
2) All Worlds
3) All Suns (Stars)
4) Sun
5) All Planets
6) Earth
7) Moon.

How these relate to densities can be understood by reading *In Search of the Miraculous*, however the point that gave me the shock came during the following exchange between Ouspensky and Gurdjieff. Ouspensky writes:

> G. drew a small diagram and tried to explain what he called the "correlation of forces in different worlds". This was in connection with the previous talk, that is, in connection with the influences acting on humanity.
>
> The idea was roughly this: humanity, or more correctly, organic life on earth, is acted upon simultaneously by influences proceeding from various sources and different worlds... All these influences act simultaneously; one influence predominates at one moment and another influence at another moment. And for man there is a certain possibility of making a choice of influences; in other words, of passing from one influence to another... It is impossible to become free from one influence without becoming subject to another. *The whole thing, all work on oneself, consists in choosing the influence to which you wish to subject yourself, and actually falling under this influence. And for this it is necessary to know beforehand which influence is the more profitable.*
>
> "In what relation does the intelligence of the earth stand to the intelligence of the sun?" I asked.
>
> "The intelligence of the sun is divine," said G. "But the earth can become the same; only, of course, it is not guaranteed and the earth may die having attained nothing."
>
> "Upon what does this depend?" I asked.
>
> G's answer was very vague.
>
> *"There is a definite period,"* he said, *"for a certain thing to be done. If, by a certain time, what ought to be done has not been done, the earth may perish without having attained what it could have attained."*

---

[15] I recommend the reader obtain a copy of Ouspensky's *In Search of the Miraculous* to get a good background in these matters. I have condensed his thoughts in the following.

"Is this period known?" I asked.

"*It is known*," said G. "But it would be no advantage whatever for people to know it. It would even be worse. Some would believe it; others would not believe it, yet others would demand proofs. Afterwards they would begin to break one another's heads. Everything ends this way with people."[16] (Emphasis added.)

Gurdjieff is obviously, in my opinion, alluding to The Wave and the possibility of the Earth moving into fourth density and the graduation or "harvest" of some individuals to the fourth density state.

As we have noted, there are any number of probable futures at any given point of universe branching. It seems that these options may narrow as one approaches the moment of singularity – or branching. And it also seems that *the direction the earth is heading, judging by the signs we observe in our environment, is NOT the future we want to manifest.* The fact may be that it is the very work of our religions and beliefs and many of the current day channeled messages that have brought us to this perilous point, and that continue to propel us in this direction, so to say.

So, what I want to say is this: just as the teachings of the Cassiopaeans have produced a *real* change in my personal reality of so dramatic a nature, as well as having had similar effects in the lives of others who have begun to use this "Blueprint of Reality", *it may be that we have an opportunity to select a different future by becoming aware,* and that this is also represented in Gurdjieff's talk about being in prison.

First, one must become aware that one is in prison in order to even begin to think about how to get out. At some level, yes, it is a prison we have chosen when we entered third density. But, by entering, we have agreed to forget our true nature and to operate in the reality we are given for the purpose of learning. It does no real good to speak in terms of "cosmic oneness" and "we are, in our true natures, all-powerful beings," because *we don't have access to those realities BY CHOICE.* The chain of circumstance, the chain of choices, it seems, must be followed in logical steps of access. We may be able to accelerate our progress, but apparently, it is frowned on to try to "skip" over the lessons.

Very few there are who can meditate on Cosmic Oneness and – POOF! – just hop back to seventh density and be done with the whole mess. And, in real terms, it may be that this is not what is wanted at a deep level. I once asked the Cassiopaeans:

December 28, 1996

Q: (L) Well... is there any activity a person could do to stimulate their DNA to become superconductive?

A: No need. You would like to find an activity to stimulate [your youngest child] to grow up faster?

Q: (L) Of course not! She's just a *baby*! She needs to have fun! Oh, I get it.

---

[16] Ibid.

Remember what the Cassiopaeans said at the beginning of this section: "It is 'fun' to see how much you can access." So, I don't think the point is to just look for a short-cut to seventh density. The point is to "follow the Yellow Brick Road," to engage in the adventure, and the task, at this moment, seems to consist in the fact that we are in prison and it is up to us to figure out how to get out.

But, it is impractical, for the sake of the lesson, to think of the prison as being non-existent unless we have created it. It has obviously been constructed from a level of reality that we are not yet capable of accessing, (again, because at a much higher level, we have chosen this drama); so it is useless to say, "If you don't think about or focus on it, the prison won't exist." That becomes nonsensical when we consider the larger scope of the problem. We are *in the prison*. But, we are *not* in it because we think about it or focus on it at *this* level. In fact, if we *don't* think about it or focus on it, learn all we can about it and the ways and means of escape, we will be choosing, by default, to continue to live within its walls!

If we are seeing our present state of limitation as a prison, and making efforts to escape, we have a hope of doing so – of learning the present lesson. If we decide to sit in our prison, in our present state of limitation – which is self evident – and "think it away" by *not* seeing it as a prison, we have done nothing but change the color of the walls or something similar. We have changed the appearance of the prison to that of a park or a luxury hotel. But, we have done *nothing* to emerge into the larger universe.

And it seems that we are misinformed by those sources that teach us that we can do this – just focus on or think about nice things – that you have access to all, that you are all "one" or whatever. To do so is to simply "take the blue pill" of *The Matrix,* to refuse to wake up, to remain available to feed more and more energy to the system that operates to keep us blind and captive. Yes, if you just think nice thoughts and "surround yourself with love and light," you may certainly manifest an illusion of a paradise. But such illusions have a nasty way of collapsing. That is not to say that the makers of such illusions don't have seemingly endless desire to patch such illusions and reconstruct them after each calamity; and, perhaps, after many lifetimes of such experiences, they reach the point of ultimate disillusionment that causes them to seek the *true* nature of reality as it *is*, and not as they would *wish* it to be, and then they begin to realize that they are in prison.

Most teachings and systems of belief are designed to perpetuate just such illusions. These systems are built almost exclusively on "faith". And there is the rub, the *real* reason for the teaching that "you create your reality by what you think and focus on." It is a *defensive maneuver* to conceal the true nature of the Cosmos!

In such teachings, nothing is allowed to challenge the system. The reason is: it is a fragile world that has to be protected at any cost. It is a theological domino that, if it is allowed to fall, all the rest of the lies and illusions begin to fall soon after. In such a system, all of life has to fit into place. That is, there really is no evil, and if there is apparent evil, it is only because you have allowed it to be apparent by thinking about it. No ambiguity on this point can be tolerated. Mystery is outlawed and doubt is exiled. All who believe differently are a threat and such persons must keep up their guard to protect themselves from such contamination. Of course, the best idea is to convert them by bombing them with love and light.

Faith, as it is generally understood, always seeks order in the midst of disorder; it builds habitable worlds in the midst of chaos and absurdity. Better to live in Awe of the *mystery*, to *choose* in the face of doubt, than to have faith in an illusion. Doubt is not the rival of faith. It is its sister. The opposite of faith is self-righteousness.

When we observe such systems built on faith, what do we see?

We see that such systems do a very funny thing: they end up producing acute guilt in those who don't manage to manifest all they need and desire – which is generally everybody some of the time, and most people most of the time. And then, they proceed to sell the remedy for the guilt in the form of more teachings, more workshops, more seminars, more books, and more verbiage that is supposed to solve the problem. In effect, they are producing a syndrome, which they then "cure". Only nobody seems to be noticing this little fact. In the beginning, for the drowning soul, such teachings seem to be a lifejacket – but they end up being a straitjacket.

Think about this: many people who are advocates of the "faith trip", whether in the garb of standard religious teachings, or New Age versions of "you create your own reality", (which amounts to the same thing), encounter the usual spate of life's disappointments and heartbreak. The response is generally a pious assumption that God/the Self sent the experience for a purpose. When something positive happens/manifests, it is assumed that God/the Self has answered the prayer/affirmation.

The only problem with this is: when you begin to count the number of disappointment and successes, you find that the number is evenly distributed *regardless of belief.* You begin to understand that there is something else going on behind the scenes and those disappointments and successes are *symbols* of something else.

Yes, human failures and immaturity are an adequate explanation for about any of it, and that is the point: to learn about human failure and immaturity, to learn about the origins and causes of same, that it is a prison described by don Juan:

> "Think for a moment, and tell me how you would explain the contradiction between the intelligence of man the engineer and the stupidity of his systems of beliefs, or the stupidity of his contradictory behavior.
>
> "Sorcerers believe that the predators have given us our systems of beliefs, our ideas of good and evil, and our social mores. They are the ones who set up our hopes and expectations and dreams of success or failure. They have given us covetousness, greed and cowardice. It is the predators who make us complacent, routinary, and egomaniacal."

When you begin to think about it this way, when you begin to think about third density and the domination of beings who represent "forces", then you begin to realize that it *is* a prison – a maze – that has been chosen in order to learn.

One correspondent wrote:

> I'm beginning to see what I can most simply call a "cult of the Lizzies", i.e., an overwhelming concentration and fascination with same, to the point where endless rumination, endless "what if's", endless speculation on the causes of this and results of that begin to take over one's daily thoughts.
>
> *We are here as sentient, aware beings, born into a physical world which is sometimes frustrating to some of us – but of which we are a part, and we cannot divide ourselves from the laws of our nature or the world's nature, for it is not the right time.*
>
> This is very simple and should be obvious to all.
>
> So as far as I am concerned, the Lizzies be damned, nor am I setting up the C's as another substitute for a guru or godhead or all-wise source of wisdom. I personally find much of great interest in what they have to say, and I have learned to look around me with more open eyes than before, but keeping in mind what they have taught me, I shall continue to make my own decisions and follow my own conscience and personal intuition on life, love and the pursuit of happiness until I am wafted – wherever. Or left behind.

The point the writer is making, and which is valid, is this: it is as dangerous to use the Lizzies as a crutch or explanation for lack of success, as it is to say that we didn't have enough faith in this or that exposition of reality.

But, it is also dangerous to say "the Lizzies be damned," because that is not taking the full import of the imprisonment into account. Until we know the full nature of the prison and the habits and powers of the jailers, we have no hope of escaping. And, for some – it is true – it is not the right time. They have no desire to see or to examine the situation in the depth and detail required to become free.

But the examination of the situation must *lead to something,* or again, there is no point. And this is the crux of the matter: the Fruits agenda.

There is an interesting discussion of these matters in Ouspensky's *The Fourth Way*. It is clear from obvious implications that we can infer that Gurdjieff knew about Lizzies, to one extent or another, though that may not have been the symbol system he was working with. Gurdjieff was Ouspensky's teacher, and it is clear from research and hints given by Gurdjieff himself, that he was more or less putting his own spin on far more ancient teachings. In the following dialogue, it is Ouspensky answering the questions put to him by the audience at one of his meetings in the decade before his death in 1947:

> Q: Do the many laws under whose influence we are produce the different "I's" in us?
>
> A: Yes, very many. Forces pass through man and he takes this as his own desires, sympathies, and attractions. But it is only forces passing through him from all directions.

Q: You said we are under the law of accident. From what source of influence does this law come? Can we be free from it?

A: Accident has many different manifestations. *The simplest forms begin to disappear very quickly if we are more awake.* But you cannot take this literally: this law is very big and many sided. It is a question of degree. Only in the Absolute are things absolute. For us it is a long stairway and on each step one is freer. If you are below, you cannot speak about what will happen when you are at the top. You can only say: "If I begin to work so as to be free from the law of accident, would my life be less chaotic?" Certainly if you have a permanent aim, you will be free from accidental aims.

Q: How can one extricate oneself from bad influences?

A: Before we can even think about "doing" we must try to understand what these influences are. This is a constant mistake that everybody makes always to think they can "do". We cannot "do", but *if we know, we may change something.* [And we can begin to know when we open ourselves to higher forces]... Higher forces or higher influences are normal, cosmic; but we can open ourselves to receive them, or shut ourselves off from them. If we are asleep, we are more closed to them, and the more we are asleep the more we are closed. If we awake, we open ourselves to higher influences.

Q: As we have not developed our higher centers, how do we receive the influences coming from higher worlds?

A: Our ordinary state is relative; in our best moments we are receptive to higher influences. They reach us through centres. Though we are not permanently connected with higher centres; they influence us if they are not too deeply buried, and something manages to reach us through them.

Q: What is the purpose of man's existence?

A: Man and even mankind does not exist separately, but as a part of the whole of organic life. The earth needs organic life as a whole – men, animals, and plants. The Ray of Creation is a growing branch, and this communication is necessary in order that the branch may grow further. Everything is connected, nothing is separate, and smaller things, if they exist, serve something bigger... Organic life is a particular cosmic unit and man is a unit in this big mass of organic life. He has the possibility of further development, but this development depends on man's own effort and understanding. It enters into the cosmic purpose that a certain number of men should develop, but not all, for that would contradict another cosmic purpose. Evidently mankind must be on earth and must lead this life and suffer. But a certain number of men can escape; this also enters into the cosmic purpose...

Q: Did you say it was intended that some of us should develop?

A: As far as we can see it is under the same law as, for instance, street accidents. It is well known that in every big town a certain number of people will be killed by traffic. Who will be killed is not determined, it need not necessarily be one or another person, but a certain number. In the same way, *a certain number of people MAY have a chance of escape – but there is no must about it in this case.* This is the difference.

Q: Are we given the possibility or must we create it in the teeth of circumstances?

A: The possibility is given. Every normal person has this possibility. The rest depends on us.

Q: How many laws does a man live under?

A: We do not know... It is not a question of catalogue but of understanding what the idea means. Man is not under one type of law but under many different types. First of all man, life, every creature on earth, lives under physical laws, which means that he can live only within certain limits of temperature. Then, there must be a particular amount of humidity in the air, and the air must be of a special chemical consistency for man to breathe. Man is also limited to a certain kind of food, which he can digest. These things are all laws for man. Then, coming to quite simple laws, there is, for instance, our ignorance. We do not know ourselves – this is a law. *If we begin to know ourselves, we get rid of a law.* We know that all men live under the law of identification... Those who begin to remember themselves begin to get rid of the law of identification. *So in order to free oneself from laws it is first necessary to find one law from which one can liberate oneself, and get free from it. Then, when one has freed oneself from this law, one can find another. Again one liberates oneself, and so on. This is the practical way to study laws...* There are laws, which hinder us on all sides or keep us in subjection...

Q: Can we get free?

A: We can – on conditions. The Ways enter here. The four Ways are ways of liberation from unnecessary laws. You can be shown the Way... but you must work yourself. Most of the laws we have to obey are the result of our sleep and our unconsciousness. Every step we make in becoming more conscious sets us more free. Suppose a man is satisfied with mechanical life; then he cuts himself off from higher influences [that could teach him how to awaken] and receives only influences [from lower levels, including his own inclinations]. Certainly he is then in a worse position than a man who receives influences from higher worlds. Many influences can be received mechanically, but many others need effort...[17] (Emphasis added.)

Note particularly the following remarks extracted from the above excerpt:

> The simplest forms [of accident or attack] begin to disappear very quickly if we are more awake. ... If we know, we may change something. Every step we make in becoming more conscious sets us more free.
>
> So in order to free oneself from laws it is first necessary to find one law from which one can liberate oneself, and get free from it. Then, when one has freed oneself from this law, one can find another. Again one liberates oneself, and so on. This is the practical way to study laws.

Thus, to know about the forces/laws, i.e., Lizzies, acting against us in the great Cosmic Drama of Creation is a *crucial* step in becoming Free. And we are going to begin to get into some of these examples in a very practical way. You remember that I said I was a practical person. I don't like mumbo jumbo and

---

[17] P.D. Ouspensky, *The Fourth Way* (New York: Vintage Books, 1971).

nebulous, ambiguous statements that lead to no useful result, so I am going to share with you some of the things that we have learned along the way of becoming aware.

SOME FURTHER REMARKS

The idea that the material world in which we live, move, and have our being is really a symbol system for a deeper reality is, for some people, pretty obvious. The interpretations, however, are many and varied.

Some people believe that the symbol system is a self-created reality that manifests in order for the higher self to communicate with the conscious mind. When you consider that All is, ultimately, God/One, that is the simplest and truest explanation. And there are certainly manifest capabilities of human beings that show us that this can be directly the case, e.g., psychokinesis.

But I want to talk about it from a different perspective and level. The only way I can talk about it in practical terms is to recount some strange experiences of my own. I hesitate to do this because I don't want to bore the reader, yet there is really no better way to be practical than to set forth more or less concrete examples which may find resonance in the experiences of others. I will try to make it as short as possible, while still including enough detail to convey the truly weird complexity of some of these cosmic dramatizations. Before I get to the practical application of all of this information, there are a few more important things that need to be covered.

So far, we have discussed the fact that Gurdjieff, Castaneda, and the Cassiopaeans have all talked about the prison of third density reality. Gurdjieff opines that it is because of forces that act on man to control him, and these forces are somewhat nebulous and belong to different levels or worlds of creation. According to don Juan, we are in prison because the Predator has "given us his mind" in order to feed on us. He talks about the higher worlds in terms of the unknown and the unknowable. The Cassiopaeans say we are in prison essentially because we chose it in order to learn and acquire experience – that God/the Universe more or less has "fun" in the great Cosmic Drama planned at Level Seven and executed down through the levels of density like a play with writers, producers, directors, actors, and so forth. And, all of these parts are "played" by One Being.

At the same time, Ouspensky suggests that we can also choose which of the forces or laws (or parts in the play) we live under. He notes that "Forces pass through man and he takes this, as his own desires, sympathies, and attractions. But it is only forces passing through him from all directions."

In such a case, a person lives under the "law of accident", as he puts it. The Cassiopaeans say that this condition of randomness means that man is living under a control system that is designed to keep him confused and unaware so that he can continue as food for higher density beings. Don Juan says, in effect, a similar thing. I would call it the Law of Chaos.

Then, Gurdjieff suggests that this state of confusion and accidentalness begin to disappear when we begin to wake up. He points out that "this law is very big and many sided. It is a question of degree. Only in the Absolute are things absolute. For us, it is a long stairway and on each step, one is more free." He suggests that we cannot really *do* anything – that is, have any control over our choices and direction at all, until we reach the higher levels, and that the only way to do this is to begin to try to understand these influences because, as he says: "If we know, we may change something."

What he seems to be saying is that this "knowing" is part of the process of opening ourselves to higher forces. He notes that: "Higher forces or higher influences are normal, cosmic; but we can open ourselves to receive them, or shut ourselves off from them. If we are asleep, we are more closed to them, and the more we are asleep, the more we are closed. If we awake, we open ourselves to higher influences."

This "opening ourselves to higher forces" seems to be a key element because it is then that we can begin to differentiate between what influence comes from what higher source and make some sort of consciousness shift so as to select which influence one wishes to be "under".

This goes back to the Eclipsing of Realities example, where these realities are described as Thought Centers that traverse all densities. Ouspensky remarks that:

> "Man and even mankind does not exist separately, but as a part of the whole of organic life. The earth needs organic life as a whole – men, animals and plants. The Ray of Creation is a growing branch, and this communication is necessary in order that the branch may grow further. Everything is connected, nothing is separate, and smaller things, if they exist, serve something bigger... Organic life is a particular cosmic unit and man is a unit in this big mass of organic life. He has the possibility of further development, but *this development depends on man's own effort and understanding.* It enters into the cosmic purpose that a certain number of men should develop, but not all, for that would contradict another cosmic purpose. Evidently mankind must be on earth and must lead this life and suffer. But a certain number of men can escape, this also enters into the cosmic purpose..."[18]

How this is done, the Cassiopaeans suggest, is through becoming aware of the meaning of the Symbols of Reality. We first become aware of these symbols as manifested in ourselves – physically, psychically, emotionally and mentally – and then expand this outward to understand our environment. It seems that our environment and experiences, individually and collectively, reflects our Selection of Influences. Thus, we must first begin to examine ourselves, our thoughts and actions and from whence they actually originate,

---

[18] Ibid.

that is to say, which influence is dominant, and then we can begin to make choices about whether or not we will continue to interact with – or enact – this influence. Our environment and experiences then will begin to demonstrate the results of these choices, thereby giving us a feedback system that confirms or denies the rightness of our choice. And our choices, made in relation to our reality, can be either dependent upon outward perception, or inward perception. Ouspensky says:

> "If we begin to know ourselves, we get rid of a law... So in order to free oneself from laws it is first necessary to find one law from which one can liberate oneself, and get free from it. Then, when one has freed oneself from this law, one can find another. Again one liberates oneself, and so on. This is the practical way to study laws... There are laws which hinder us on all sides or keep us in subjection..."[19]

Becoming Free of these laws of confusion and accidentalness is possible in a number of ways. This is observationally established if one studies the extensive literature that has emerged from the many religions and philosophies. But, when one studies this body of material, there are certain things that become apparent only upon comparison, and Gurdjieff enunciates these problems pretty clearly. He describes them as the "Four Ways".

We have talked about mind and illusion, and all being "One". Yes, all is mind/consciousness, but my point has been, throughout all this labor, that we need to be practical here and deal with things that are more accessible at our particular level of development.

We are at living at third density. That's a fact. Our present consciousness fragments are focused here. So, trying to jump from third density to "becoming One" in Cosmic terms is like trying to put the cart before the horse and jumping directly into seventh density concepts. Yes, we can know about them to a limited extent – we can entertain ourselves with them – but for all practical purposes, we have to learn what it is we have to learn to go the next step – here and now. This seems to be a sort of law, and this is where we fall into obfuscation. But, again, there is a reason for that, as we will see.

Many channeled sources talk about this idea of "being One" and the creation of the Illusion by the Mind, and all of that is *true*! The deception enters in when they suggest that all we have to do is sit under a Bo Tree, contemplate our navel, and become Buddha like. Yes, in some very rare instances it *is* possible, and in some other instances, acquiring of powers is also possible, but it is when you begin to examine the literature, the Fruits agenda, that you find some funny little glitches in such a teaching.

Carla Rueckert McCarty (*The Ra Material*) was recently quoted in an e-mail forwarded to our e-groups discussion list saying:

---

[19] Ibid.

> To me, there are basically two ways of working spiritually in this density, the way of love and the way of wisdom.
>
> In general, I would say that Buddhism follows the way of wisdom, and Christianity, the way of the heart.
>
> In a wisdom structure, you are going for knowledge, peace, detachment, aiming towards a feeling of emptiness and nothing. It is very peaceful and calm, but I find it the slow track compared to the way of love.
>
> In the way of love, one is going for compassion and purity of passion and the will that is behind that, aiming towards a feeling of fullness and unification of all.
>
> For myself, I find that this density's work seems to be the following of the love in the present moment, of opening the heart to that present moment and the love in it. This is usually not peaceful or calm, but it feels right. I think it's a matter of preference. Both ways of learning are useful.

This is a pretty standard New Age interpretation. It is somewhat broader and more accepting than the Fundamentalist Christian perspective, but not much. It is, in effect, the Way of the Monk or Saint.

As noted, there are actually *more* than two ways; there are, as mentioned above, four.[20] There is the Way of the Monk, the Way of the Yogi, the Way of the Fakir, and, the Fourth Way, which Gurdjieff taught and which is, apparently, derived from his long contact with Sufi teachings. The Fourth Way is, more or less, the way that is open to humanity that takes advantage of all the conditions that exist in normal life, and is certainly quite similar to what don Juan was advocating, (up to a point), as well as what the Cassiopaeans have explicated.

The Way of the Monk is much like what is described by Carla as her chosen mode. This is the way of faith, the way of religious feeling, the way of religious sacrifice. This is the way for people with very strong religious *emotions* and *imagination*. It is a long, hard way, as the writer herself notes when saying, "This is usually not peaceful or calm, but it feels right."

Such a way consists of years and years of struggling with the self, on struggling with the emotions – on feelings. The individual subjects all of his/her emotions to one emotion, and thereby develops unity in self. This person is working on developing emotional *will*. Carla states this quite clearly by saying, "In the way of love, one is going for compassion and purity of passion and *will that is behind that*, aiming towards a feeling of fullness and unification of all."

But Gurdjieff suggests that, in such a person, the physical body and the mental body may remain undeveloped and then, in order to make *use* of what the Monk/Saint has attained, attention must be focused on developing the body and the capacity to think. But, this can only be done by another series of sacrifices. The monk has to become a yogi and a fakir. Very few do this because they die before they overcome the difficulties. There is another problem with this way,

---

[20] There is actually a Fifth Way, but we are not going to discuss this just now. Suffice it to say that Fifth Way work is rare, and reserved for rare individuals who emerge at nodal points in human history. Indeed, we are at such a point, but there is little point in describing the Fifth Way for general readers.

dealing with wrong crystallizations as Gurdjieff called them in the excerpt quoted in the previous section.

The way of "wisdom", as Carla refers to it, or otherwise known as the Way of the Yogi, is the way of knowledge, the way of the mind. This way consists in developing the mind, but may result, as Carla also notes quite accurately, in leaving the body and the emotions undeveloped. She says: "In a wisdom structure, you are going for knowledge, peace, detachment, aiming towards a feeling of emptiness and nothing. It is very peaceful and calm." But, without development of the physical and emotional bodies, the individual may be unable to make use of his attainments without going back to work on the body and the emotions. Such a person "knows everything", but can *do* nothing. He/she then has to go back and work on obtaining results by means of another series of prolonged efforts of application of what he knows.

The main difference between the path of knowledge and the ways of the Fakir and Monk is that the yogi eventually has the advantage of *understanding his position*, of knowing what he lacks, what he must do, and in what direction he must go. This is more than the Way of the Monk can achieve, since the Monk dies in his belief that he has achieved something, but it is an empty victory of knowledge since, again, very few are able to take the next step because they die before achieving it.

The Way of the Fakir is the way of struggle with the physical body. It is long and difficult. The object is to attain transcendence by developing physical will and power over the body. This is attained by means of terrible sufferings, by torturing the body. The whole thing consists of various incredibly difficult physical sacrifices such as standing motionless in the same position for hours, days, months, or years. If he doesn't get sick and die before he reaches his goal, he may achieve something. What does he achieve? He has acquired *physical will*; but has nothing to which he can apply it. He can't make use of it for gaining knowledge or self-perfection because, usually by this time, he is too old and he dies.

In the Way of the Fakir, there is usually no teacher. The practitioner may have witnessed some incredible feat of will that so impresses and obsesses him that he longs to emulate it – to have such an accomplishment for his own.

In the Way of the Monk, the main thing *is* the teacher. Part of the work of the Way of the Monk consists in having absolute faith in the teacher and in submitting to him, or his teachings, absolutely in faith and obedience. Generally this way seeks faith in God, the love of God, in constant efforts to obey and serve God by only expressing love no matter what. Of course, as the history of religion shows us, such a person's understanding of the idea of God and of serving God may be very subjective and contradictory.

Fortunately, nowadays, it is becoming more and more accepted that this Way of the Monk can operate in different contexts so that people are less inclined to kill those who don't follow their particular concept of God.[21]

But still, those who follow this path generally cling to the idea that it is the "best" or a "better" path than others. Carla is essentially saying this. She says that she considers the way of the heart to be the "fast track", and for her and many others, it is – the fast track to become an "immortal thing".

In the Way of the Yogi, one starts with a teacher, or many teachers, but ends up being one's own teacher. One learns methods by study, and then begins to apply them independently.

The main thing about these three ways is that they all require a significant *retirement from ordinary life*. Much of the struggle must, of necessity, take place in "retirement" or private meditation. Each of these methods is opposed to everyday life in some significant way, so the practitioners generally have some difficulty adjusting in the "real world".

The Fourth Way, according to Gurdjieff, and that which the Cassiopaeans and Sufis seem to be advocating, is one that requires *no* retirement from the real world. It also has no definite form, as do the ways of the fakir, the monk and the yogi.

"Work" in the Fourth Way consists of utilizing life as a person finds it in their own milieu to work on all of their aspects simultaneously. They work on the physical mastery, mental development, and emotional integration and control. And this is done through *awareness* combined with *knowledge* and *will* and *love*, correctly understood. One must become master of his body, his mind, and his emotions.

The chief demand of the Fourth Way, according to both Sufi teachings and the Cassiopaeans, *is understanding*. We are to become aware of as much as possible about our reality and *do nothing* that we do not understand except as experiment to discover and understand more. The more we understand *what* we are doing and *why* and *how*, the greater our consciousness. Purification of emotions can be accelerated by understanding.

Faith – as it is commonly understood – is not required in this way. In fact, faith in the Christian sense – is opposed. In this Fourth Way, a person must "satisfy himself of the truth of what he is told" by research and investigation and experiment. Until he is satisfied, he should not act "in faith". However, faith is built in this way, faith of an altogether different kind.

Of the four ways, the way of the fakir is the crudest, as Gurdjieff remarked. The fakir knows very little and understands very little, but he has *incredible* mastery over his physical body.

The "monk" knows little better. He is driven by his religious feeling and by his chosen religious tradition, and by a desire for achievement – that is, he

---

[21] Note that this was written before 9-11 and the takeover of the U.S. by a "fundamentalist ideology" that promotes the ideals of the Inquisition: Kill them all, God will know his own.

wants salvation. He trusts his belief system, which incorporates his chosen teacher (Jesus, Buddha, whomever), and he believes that all his efforts and sacrifices are pleasing to God.

How this works is revealed in several clues in the above correspondence. Carla states that the "way of wisdom aims for ... emptiness" and the "way of the heart aims toward ... a feeling of fullness." This brings us back to don Juan's remark about the Predator:

> In order to keep us obedient, meek, and weak, the predators ... "gave us their mind! ... The predators' mind is baroque, contradictory, morose, filled with the fear of being discovered any minute now".
>
> "I know that even though you have never suffered hunger ... you have food anxiety, which is none other than the anxiety of the predator who fears that any moment now its maneuver is going to be uncovered and food is going to be denied. Through the mind, which, after all, is their mind, the predators inject into the lives of human beings whatever is convenient for them. And they ensure, in this manner, a degree of security to act as a buffer against their fear."

People who choose the way of the heart are very much aware of feeling these very sensations within: contradiction, guilt (fear of being discovered any minute now) and *hunger*. They constantly seek to manifest love in the face of these negative emotions in order to fill the void within. Carla tells us about her struggles when she says: "This is usually not peaceful or calm, but it feels right."

The usual condition of such a path can be stated as follows: "I find myself in all kinds of painful and miserable situations. I find myself feeling things about people and situations that are negative or the situations themselves that manifest in my life are negative and painful. But I am choosing to overcome this by the manifestation – via will – of *love* of everything and everybody in all of these miserable situations. By doing this, I am 'going for compassion and purity of passion and will that is behind that, aiming towards a feeling of fullness and unification of all.'"

In other words, I can be tortured inside and outside and all around, but I am going to *give love* and *feel love* so that God will love *me* and then I can concentrate on amassing this *full* feeling of *love* inside no matter what!

Thus, she is overcoming the predator's mind by refusing to accept the contradictions, the moroseness, the guilt, and the hunger. And, indeed, this is a way to overcome the laws, a way to generate the struggle between yes and no. And it certainly will have results as the literature shows. Paraphrasing Gurdjieff:

> Speaking in relative terms, the monk can attain in a week of fasting and prayer and concentration on manifesting of love, what the fakir accomplishes in a month of torture. He thus becomes free of the Predator's mind.
>
> The yogi knows considerably more. He gains knowledge of the existence of the Predator's mind, and he knows that he wants to be free of it. He knows why he wants it, so he studies to gain knowledge of how it can be done. What he

learns, eventually, if he is doing his "homework", is that to be free of the "laws" he must produce a certain "substance" in himself.

He learns that a certain kind of mental exercise or concentration of consciousness – in concert with a certain emotional state – can produce this substance in one day. Of course, it may have taken him a lifetime to learn this – the very same lifetime that the Monk has been spending on producing the necessary emotion that lacks the state of consciousness.

But generally, the progress of the Monk is much less because the yogi begins with a teacher who has already achieved a certain level and much of this knowledge can be communicated in practical ways that save time.

Thus, the result is that the relative relationships show us that a yogi can produce in one day what the monk produces in a week and the fakir in a month.

But, that is taking all things as equal. We can't leave out of the equation that any given person may have already "done the work" along one line in a given former life, and be ready to do the work in another line in this lifetime. Perhaps, for Carla, this is the case. Her attachment to rituals doesn't suggest that, but then, no one is in a position to judge what is between another individual and their "God". We might conjecture that such persons who find it to be the way that "feels right" and moves them along more rapidly, have already done the way of the yogi and the way of the fakir in a previous/simultaneous lifetime. For some, the way of the heart may be the final piece of the puzzle of self-integration. And for such, it may indeed be precisely right.

For others, the way of the heart has already been done, and they then focus on the way of the fakir or the yogi. And in still others, all three ways have been done, and they cycle very rapidly through the various ways in a single life, consolidating their various crystallizations. It is really impossible for any one person to judge one way as "right" and another as "wrong". Every individual and every situation is different.

The reader who finds the material on these pages to be resonant or in sync with what is felt and/or known deep inside, may have already proceeded along the ways of the fakir, monk and yogi, and is now looking for synthesis and practical application in order to merge this awareness.

In the Fourth Way, according to Gurdjieff, and with related Sufi texts supporting (though they are obscure and deliberately so), the seeker knows about the other ways, knows that there are definite substances that must be produced in the body – knows that they can be produced by a month of torture, a week of prayer and fasting, or a day of mental exercises. He also knows that these substances can be produced in another way: The Fourth Way, though I do not necessarily mean the Fourth Way *exactly* as explicated by Gurdjieff and Ouspensky.

What are we speaking about here?

In studying the literature of religious, paranormal and psi phenomena, one begins to note some odd connections.

There are fakirs and yogis who can control their bodily functions to a degree that passes ordinary understanding. They can slow their metabolism, control their heartbeat, produce extreme heat or cold, levitate, run for days on end without stopping, bi-locate, and apparently manifest material objects with their minds. I have even heard that there have been some who have gone into meditation and then, in the view of their students or brothers, have just gone – POOF! – disappeared instantly in a blinding flash of light, never to be seen again! Obviously, they have removed themselves from some of the laws of third density to a greater or lesser extent. At the same time, one can read about Christian saints who have done the same things. There are shamans who give evidence of the same accomplishments, and practitioners of various paths of magic or rituals. So, we can see by these road signs that there *is* a certain correlation as described by Gurdjieff.

Then, there are the anomalous miracles that just seem to occur spontaneously. In such cases, a certain reference seems to recur over and over again, and that is the relationship between psi, genetics, and DNA. Time and time again a person who had strange powers would remark that "Oh, I inherited the sight from my aunt, or grandmother, or mother, or uncle or whatever." And, it is not always "the sight". There are many powers that manifest with this comment.

Then, there is the peculiar connection of the endocrine system to psi phenomena. Many serious studies of poltergeist type phenomena note that it is most often, if not always, manifested in the presence of either a pubescent child or a sexually fluctuating woman, including those who are in one or another stage of menopause. Hormones produced by the endocrine system play a part in turning DNA on and off.

One thing is clear to me after all of these years of study: psi phenomena, whether it is healing or manifestation of matter or bi-location or whatever has *almost* no *relation whatsoever to one's state of spirituality*. In my work, I encountered a family line that could stop the flow of blood with the touch of a hand, yet nearly every member was alcoholic, promiscuous, abusive to partners and children, and generally what one would consider to be ethically deficient. Yet, certain members of this line had this interesting power and were often called upon by neighbors and friends to save lives – even if they had to be hauled out of a bar dead drunk to do it!

Another curious thing is that the many notations of psi phenomena onset after a severe trauma to the head, or a strong electrical shock. Electrical current can alter DNA by affecting the permeability of the neural membranes or by altering the balance or composition of neurotransmitters, thus turning on or off DNA. (In later volumes of this series I will get into this in more technical detail so that the reader can really apply it to their lives in individual situations.)

It seems that the thing that stands between the physical and ethereal worlds, or between third and fourth densities, and which is reflected in our awareness, is our DNA. It seems to be the interface or operating system that determines how much, how well, how completely our souls can manifest via the instrument of our bodies, in third density reality. Certain, shall we call them *ecstatic*, practices, which include the three ways discussed above, have been shown to have effects on both the electric current in the body as well as the chemicals, including hormones and neurotransmitters.

It has often been noted that only 2% of our DNA is involved in coding the proteins that make up our bodies. The rest is referred to as "junk". There are theories about why this is so, including the "Selfish Gene" theory where it is postulated that human beings are merely constructs created by DNA for the purpose of propagating DNA!

Another thing noted is that we seem to utilize only 5 to 10% of our brains – and there are many theories about why this is so as well. I would like to suggest that *there is a connection*.

So, we have a curious series of factors to contend with that all seem to point in the direction of DNA being far more interesting and mysterious than we might have supposed.

On the one hand we have such naturally transmitted powers, and on the other hand we have folks who can engage in some activity that either temporarily or permanently changes something in their physiology – and the apparent result is becoming free of the laws of third density. The only problem is, as noted above, if the change is not across the board, so to speak, it merely becomes a blip on the screen – an aberration – a signpost that something is happening, but is of no practical value without knowledge of application in the four bodies, as it were. The following excerpt from the Cassiopaean transcripts will become important as we go on with the story here. The discussion was about the Symbols of Reality as they manifest in the body as physical pain related to some pathological disorder.

October 10, 1998

A: When one receives message of pain… could it be symbolic of potential advancement of neo-physicality?

Q: (L) I have known a lot of people who had pain who are just unhappy people.

A: But why unhappy? Think, my dear… and remember, your consciousness operates on four levels, not just one! Physical body, consciousness, genetic body and spirit-etheric body.

Q: (L) Are those the four composites of the human manifestation in third density?

A: 3rd and 4th. One leads oneself, through physical actions, as well as psychic ones, to develop these "problems" when one is preparing to "bump it up" a notch.

Remember what Ouspensky said:

The four Ways are ways of liberation from unnecessary laws. You can be shown the Way… but you must work yourself. Most of the laws we have to obey are the result of our sleep and our unconsciousness. Every step we make in becoming more conscious sets us more free.

> Suppose a man is satisfied with mechanical life; then he cuts himself off from higher influences [that could teach him how to awaken] and receives only influences [from lower levels, including his own inclinations].
> Certainly he is then in a worse position than a man who receives influences from higher worlds. *Many influences can be received mechanically, but many others need effort...*[22] (Emphasis added.)

So, the whole thing seems to center around being in contact with higher influences. We have already talked about the prolific amount of channeling that is going on all over the planet, increasing in volume and variety daily. And we have been talking about the fact that some, if not most, of this is effectively influences from lower levels. What I mean by that is what I would colloquially call the difference between dead dude communications and truly higher *density* sources.

Why do I make such a distinction? Isn't a "dead dude" a "fifth density" soul? Aren't communications from "dead dudes" effectively communications from fifth density? Doesn't that make them "higher"? What about communications from fourth density beings? Clearly, they are "higher". Well, this is part of the problem of becoming aware and "choosing" which influence you wish to be under, and it is *not* as easy as one might think!

As already noted, as far as I know, until the coming of Ra via Elkins, Rueckert and McCarty, the concept of fourth density was poorly defined. Yes, Gurdjieff was obviously talking about it, and it is thought that his knowledge was derived from ancient secret mystery schools in Central Asia; but it also seems that his extrapolations about it may have given it a certain twist.

My own thoughts about it, after discussing with my husband Ark the various differences in what Gurdjieff was saying and doing, examining his writings and talks about his experiences, are that it is very likely that Gurdjieff was actually experimenting with ways to open ordinary people of Western culture to higher understanding in ways they could accommodate to their lifestyles. It may even have been that he had a mandate to do this, or it may simply have been his own idea.

Nevertheless, prior to the ideas about densities, there really wasn't much of an option about existence: it was physical or astral; dead or alive; in the body or out of the body; earth or heaven/hell. Those were the choices. When you died here on earth, you only had the option of being ethereal or astral, or something similar. You were "in the spirit" or "in the body".

Of course, it wasn't exactly that simple. Just as there are economic and class distinctions here on earth, a whole plethora of sources devised intricate and elaborate systems of levels and stages of advancement through the astral realms. Helena Blavatsky, Rudolf Steiner, Alice Bailey, and others down to the present-day weekly "channel o'choice" have added endless permutations to these planes, sub-planes and hierarchical systems.

---

[22] Ouspensky, *The Fourth Way*.

These explanations seem to have been created in response to the growing awareness that something was fishy in the other world! While everyone liked to think that, when you die, you are suddenly either taken up into heaven to sit with God or Buddha or whomever; or you descend to hell with no possibility of cooling your heels, it was increasingly apparent that this might *not* be the case. The many voices being heard from the "spirit world" made it abundantly clear that there was *very* complicated activity going on out of the range of human perception and understanding. And, some of it was distinctly unpleasant.

So planes and sub-planes, and causal planes and mid-causal planes were delivered to humanity as the solution to this problem. The key now became to determine what *level* of entity one was in communication with in order to determine the validity or usefulness of the information. Naturally, once such a hierarchy has been defined, the knowing spirit inevitably claims membership in the highest levels!

At a certain point in the confusion, there was a big step in the history of channeling: "Seth". Michael Topper writes about Seth:

> What made the Seth material so noticeable, and what allows it to stand up well today, has much to do with the channeler Jane Roberts herself who—along with the channeled text—narrated a continuous chronicle of her own internal struggle with the whole phenomenon of channeling, as well as the content of the material.
>
> The uniform quality, consistency and integrity of the Seth teachings, which spanned many years (compared to various one-shot sources today) was largely due to the strangeness and unfamiliarity of such a mode visited upon any consciousness at that "early" time, meeting head on a rational and intelligent—if critical and initially quite skeptical—personality.
>
> As Roberts herself states from the perspective of experience, it was indeed the initial deep reservations accompanying her reluctant participation in so extreme a phenomenon that kept the keel even, and helped therefore to keep the communication steadily aligned between the potential shoals of egoism on the one hand, and reductive rationalization on the other.
>
> There is, as anyone should be able to tell, a universe of difference between these carefully monitored, combed and curried sessions and the modern immoderate opus cavalierly compiled in the interval of time since the Summons of Seth, wherein the chief feature of the recent books seems to be the channeler Herself, lavishly displayed on the pages of the photo insert, coyly captioned "from childhood to the mature adult present" (in which, having donned a pyramidal dunce cap in a moment of pure caprice the subject became so suddenly Serendipitous Host to some materializing entity, quite helpfully clarifying things at the outset by announcing Its Enlightenment!)[23]
>
> In considering the Seth material as a whole, we can recommend it on the great virtue alone (taken for granted by now, but quite unique for its time), that it introduced the important key of probability to the field of psychological reality. Prior to this, the idea was exclusively an abstruse phenomenon of physics

---

[23] I really laughed at Michael Topper's veiled allusion to *Ramtha*.

occurring only at the Heisenberg-indeterminacy level, describing "position and velocity of electrons".

This concept, introduced by Seth, enabled humanity to strip the material mind from its fixation upon rigid causal conditioning and deterministic hypotheses of action. The Seth discussion of multidimensionality and the branching probable paths of conscious navigation through the wake-and-dream-state, served to shift the fulcrum of power to the psychic present, thereby helping at once to loosen the mental clamps of a dominant behaviorist psychology and to perform a long-overdue correction to the religio-spiritual emphasis on karma or the irresistible pressure of past actions, mnemonic conditioning, etc.

In this respect then the Seth material served its purpose admirably; and that purpose was to help consciousness take the next great step, the necessary step into a whole new Stage of spiritual progress and development. (Topper, "Channeling, UFOs And The Positive/Negative Realms Beyond This World", http://www.signs-of-the-times.org/signs/forum/viewtopic.php?id=1256)

That said, having spent a lot of time dealing with spirit attachment, spirit possession, obsession, and related maladies, I can assure you that entities on the other side can and *do* lie. William Baldwin, Ph.D., writes:

> Spirit attachment does not require the permission of the host. This seems to be a violation of free will. It also appears to refute the popular notion that each person is totally responsible for creating his or her reality and that there are no victims. The apparent conflict here stems from the definitions of permission and free will choice. Ignorance and denial of the possibility of spirit interference is no defense against spirit attachment. Belief or lack of belief regarding the existence of intrusive entities has no bearing on the reality of these beings and their behavior.
>
> In denial and ignorance, most people do not refuse permission to these nonphysical intruders. Individual sovereign beings have the right to deny any violation or intrusion by another being. With limited, if any, knowledge and distorted perceptions of the nature of the spirit world, the nonphysical reality, many people leave themselves open and create their own vulnerability as part of creating their own reality. It is fashionable today among many "new Age" enthusiasts to attempt to channel some higher power, a spirit teacher or master who will use the voice mechanism of any willing person to speak "words of wisdom". Some use the terminology "for my highest good" when calling for a spirit to channel through. This activity constitutes permission and welcome for a discarnate spirit. *The identifiers such as "master" and "teacher" and qualifiers such as "for my highest good" will be claimed by the entities as personally valid identifications, qualities or attributes.*
>
> ...The host is usually unaware of the presence of attached spirits. The thoughts, desires and behaviors of an attached entity are experienced as the person's own thoughts, desires and behaviors. The thoughts, feelings, habits and desires do not seem foreign if they have been present for a long time, even from childhood. This is a major factor in the widespread denial of the concept and lack of acceptance of the phenomena of discarnate interference and spirit attachment, obsession or possession.

In most cases, a person can only experience and acknowledge the reality of the condition after an attached entity has been released. The realization may come some months after a releasement session as the person suddenly notices the absence of a familiar attitude, desire, addiction or behavior.

The symptoms of spirit attachment can be very subtle. An attached spirit may be present without producing any noticeable symptoms.

...A living person can have dozens, even hundreds of attached spirits, as they occupy no physical space. They can attach to the aura or float within the aura outside the body. If any part of the body of the host has a physical weakness the earthbound can attach to that area because of a corresponding weakness or injury to the physical body of the spirit prior to death. A spirit can lodge in any of the chakras of the host, drawn by the particular energy of the chakra or by the physical structures of that level of the body.

...The mental, emotional and physical influence of an attached entity can alter the original path of karmic options and opportunities of the host. It can disrupt the planned lifeline by hastening death or prolonging life, thus interfering with any specific checkout point. An entity of the opposite gender can influence the sexual preference and gender orientation. An attached entity can influence the choice of marriage partners and the choice of a partner for an extra-marital affair.[24] (Emphasis added.)

There sure seems to be a lot of this sort of thing going on out there. Baldwin suggests that the number of people suffering one or more attachments at any given time is about 100%! I was pretty shocked when I read that figure. In fact, when I began experimenting with the techniques of the therapeutic modality, I had a *lot* of misgivings about it. It just seemed too far-fetched and wild even for my open-minded approach to reality.

So, as a sort of experiment, I began to use the differential diagnosis technique with subjects who had agreed to participate in an experimental therapy, but were not told any details whatsoever as to what this would entail. I think they were more or less expecting something dramatic rather than a small series of questions artfully designed to reveal the presence of attached entities. And, at the point I shifted into the questions designed to identify spirit attachment, I made sure to do it in a subtle way, burying the questions in a series of other innocuous questions. I certainly didn't want to contaminate my experiment, so I was being *very* careful! If this idea was a hokey theory, I was determined to expose it!

Well, the results were nothing short of astounding. In case after case, there *were* attachments – usually more than one. The most startling thing about it was that the release therapy *worked* in amazing ways! Problems that had persisted with standard hypnotic therapies utilizing repeated suggestions and/or post-hypnotic suggestions, (which sometimes worked and sometimes didn't) would virtually disappear almost instantly with the release of the attaching entity.

---

[24] William J. Baldwin, D.D.S., Ph.D., *Spirit Releasement Therapy: A Technique Manual* (Falls Church, VA: Human Potential Foundation, 1993).

In a couple of cases, individuals who were in marriages that were highly unsatisfactory and even miserable, but had been unable to extricate themselves because they would "weaken at the thought", or would "argue with themselves" over the rightness of leaving, were suddenly freed of these fears, co-dependencies, and so forth. It was established in a couple of these sessions that the subject had been invaded at an opportune moment by an entity that wanted to be with the marriage partner and that the attaching entity had influenced the subject to marry that person in the first place! Whenever the "core" person, or host, would try to leave the relationship, a full-bore inner struggle would take place, preventing the wishes of the host from prevailing. This was always perceived as the subject's *own* doubts and misgivings about leaving.

Physical ailments, fears and phobias, addictions, and personality irregularities of many kinds were dissolved almost by magic! I was completely stunned! Not only that, but all of my ideas about children being protected in their innocence from such infestation had to be tossed aside as it became more and more evident that many attachments took place during very ordinary childhood traumas!

But the point is – this may be part of the true condition of mankind's prison! As Dr. Baldwin notes above: "In *denial and ignorance*, most people do not refuse permission to these nonphysical intruders... Many people leave themselves open and *create their own vulnerability as part of creating their own reality.*" What a concept!

I hate to have to admit it, but this sentence applied to me for a very long time. In fact, it applies to all of us, to one extent or another and that is why I am going to tell you some stories about my becoming aware. These were complex interactions with many people, and at many points, the various players involved all had the same opportunities to become aware and make choices as a result of this awareness. We will see how those choices were presented and how they operated in the Symbols of Reality, and we will see what the Fruits of the various choices were. When we are done with these stories, it is hoped that there will be a very clear understanding of how to read the signs and, possibly, what the results can be, though each person will have their own idea of how to respond to the lessons and what a desirable outcome is.

As I have recounted to some extent in *Amazing Grace*, discovering the Truth and Meaning of our existence – or even just *my* existence since, for all I know, everything else is an illusion – has been the driving force behind my whole lifetime of internal and external process.

At any given time when I participated in any activity whatsoever, it was always with the idea that I might learn something about God from it. Even when I was at the stage of complete atheism, it was an experiment. In my early years I studied Wicca and various forms of shamanism, ritual magic and so forth. I was cautious about material experimentation with such things, preferring to study further and compare, so I think I saved myself a lot of grief that I have since observed in other people who did not have the same reservations about "practice".

Weaving in and out of all this study was, of course, my family's religious background (which had been inculcated at a very early age) coming from a long line of preachers and religious scholars. This influence was very strong, so my programmed inclination whenever I reached the end of a particular study that had shown itself to be, in effect, only a fragment of the answer, was to revert to this familiar religious path until some other study beckoned. What this means is that my many years of study and dedication to knowledge were punctuated by periods of The Way of the Monk. As a teenager, I even dreamed of being a nun when I grew up. I seemed to experience a cyclical fluctuation between cold cerebral analysis and passionate pursuit of an intimate emotional relationship with God. The curious thing was that I could enter into either state with equal ardor and dedication.

I know well the agonizing struggle of "going for compassion and purity of passion and will... aiming towards a feeling of fullness and unification of all." I viscerally understand "following of the love in the present moment, of opening the heart to that present moment and the love in it." And I also experienced the fact that "This is usually not peaceful or calm." I also know what it is like to achieve it to greater or lesser extent and what it costs the mind and body. I have great fondness for this way.

But I am a practical person, and finding a balanced combination of cerebration and emotion has been my particular struggle. I have to really control my urge to "give my body up to be burned," to "give all I own to the poor," and to sacrifice myself in any number of ways as a martyr. For me, that is far more difficult than subjecting all of my emotions to one emotion to develop emotional will.

As I have written in *Amazing Grace*, at a certain point in my life I decided that this way of the heart was, indeed, the path for me and I embraced it wholeheartedly. I was 30 years old and pretty worn out from seeking God in knowledge; or at least I wasn't getting anywhere with it that felt satisfying, so the urgings of my ex-husband to get back with God in the old-fashioned, fundamental way were like an anchor beckoning me to come and rest. So, to put it bluntly, I plunged headfirst into the faith trip.

Not being one to do anything halfway, I put all thinking aside, all knowledge aside, and essentially submitted myself willingly and by choice to believe that faith would take me home. To make the point of how effectively this was accomplished, I will share a funny event.

In the early days of this plunge, I was sitting in church with my ex-husband and children. I was observing the order of the service, the standing up, sitting down, turning to page so-and-so to sing a hymn, the kneeling and praying and so forth. I realized suddenly, from my training as a hypnotherapist, that this whole process was a form of hypnosis. In studying mass or group hypnosis, we had been taught about what is called the "Yes set". The yes set is designed to put people into a mild trance state, to entrain their brain function, and to make them receptive to the deepening of the trance and any suggestions that follow.

It is accomplished by getting a group of people to either respond "yes" to a series of questions, or to get them to comply with a series of innocuous requests. In so doing, they give their will to the person making the request.

One way this works for charismatic public speakers is for them to deliberately pose several questions in a row (at least three) that they are certain everyone, or most everyone, will agree with. For example: a politician might begin his campaign speech with these three questions:

> "Are you tired of high taxes?"
> "Have you had enough of crime and violence in this country?"
> "Is everyone tired of spending their hard earned dollars for less and less every week?"

Hardly anyone would disagree with any of these questions. But, by agreeing with them, by saying "yes" three times in a row – even if only mentally – the first stage of induction has just been accomplished!

So, there I was, realizing that what was being done in this church – and churches around the world and down through the centuries – was that people were being hypnotized. So, what did I think about this? Well, since I had decided to take the plunge, I decided that it was okay because it was hypnosis for the *right* reasons! Yup! That's me talking there! When I do something, I go *all* the way!

Immediately, my life began to fall apart.

Of course, being committed to this path meant that the only interpretation for this phenomenon of my life going to Hell when I was trying to get to Heaven was to think of it as a test of my faith. Not being a quitter by any stretch of the imagination, I wasn't going to let things like deteriorating physical health, long drawn out suffering and death of a loved one, or financial disaster after financial disaster stop me! No sir! I fasted, prayed, and assiduously schooled my thoughts and emotions to one thing and one thing only: "going for compassion and purity of passion and will… aiming towards a feeling of fullness and unification of all… following of the love in the present moment, of opening the heart to that present moment and the love in it."

The more things came against me, the more I suffered, the more I was attacked from within and without, the more my resolve strengthened. I refused to even ask "why?" I read the book of Job again and again to comfort myself that at least I was not alone in my suffering. I regularly sought to experience vicariously the sufferings of Christ on the cross so that, by comparison, nothing I experienced could possibly be considered suffering! I took no offense at offense, whether intended or not; I forgave and loved and comforted my hurts by transforming them in the crucible of my suffering to pure and passionate love for God, for Jesus, and for all mankind.

It's easy to talk about suffering in an abstract way, but what do I really mean by it? Suffering is relative. The old saying, "I cried because I had no shoes until

I met a man with no feet," applies here. I don't want to go through the whole scene so I will make it short:

I had been ill in 1980 with a fever that left me with damaged heart valves. In 1984, the physical labor I had been doing just to manage a home and three children, caring for my aged grandmother, and a now failing business put so much strain on my heart that I was near collapse when I found myself pregnant with my fourth child. Just to cover the bases of those who will say, "Don't you know what causes it?" let me add that I became pregnant while on contraceptives.

Being in the faith trip, of course meant that my choice was to sacrifice any health considerations for the sake of the child.[25] My kidneys began to fail, and the residual damage from two back injuries, which occurred when I was a teenager, began to manifest. (I had seriously injured the lumbar vertebrae in a fall while skating and the second was a pelvic/sacral injury that occurred in a toss from the back of a horse.) In my previous three pregnancies, I had received competent care because I had been in a position to obtain it. But now, only the minimal care was available due to the deteriorating financial state.

Also, during this time we were being plagued by some sort of haunting that my young daughter was perceiving as an alligator outside her window, and that we could sense in "cold spots" in the house as well as "see" out of the corner of our eyes. In retrospect, there were a lot of clues of abduction type activity going on, though this was not something I had in my knowledge base at the time.

In the midst of this situation, my grandmother's cancer, which had been in remission for 11 years, went metastatic. I was physically incapable of doing all that was on my shoulders, but somehow I did it anyway. (Looking back, I have no idea *how* I did it!) I was exhausted *all* the time, dealing with pre-eclampsia, gestational diabetes, a heart that wanted to back flush several times a day, three small children, a depressed husband who wandered about wondering what to do about the financial situation, and a dying grandmother who was more than a mother to me.

Meanwhile, our former business partner, *my own mother*, in whom we had placed utmost confidence, and who had maneuvered all our financial assets into her control, had emptied our bank accounts, maxed out our credit cards, and was now suing us to foreclose on our house! And did it! For all the details on that situation, I can only suggest that you read *Amazing Grace*.

Somewhere along the way during this time – much of which blurs in my memory due to the horror of it all – I had what I call my "Boat ride to Damascus."

We were bringing our commercial fishing boat down from its docking 40 miles or so north of where we lived, to put it in at the marina where it was to be sold. Because of our schedule, we made the trip at night. Forty miles is not far in a car, but a big commercial fishing boat doesn't do 60 mph, so it was several

---

[25] I probably would not make the same choice now, but I don't regret that choice at all. My third daughter and fourth child is a remarkable human being. The reader has her to thank for copyediting this manuscript.

hours of travel time. I was doing the steering while my ex-husband was on deck keeping an eye out for bird racks or other obstructions.

I was alone in the steering cabin with nothing but the red glow of the instrument panel and the low rumble of the diesel engine under the floor. This trip was sort of an admission that all was going down the tubes. I was struggling with my hurt and anger and bewilderment, praying fervently for understanding and compassion and love to fill my heart in spite of the apparent hopelessness of the situation.

I wanted to be filled with the Love of God. I wanted to subsume all of the experience into that single pointed devotion the brings the "peace that passes understanding." Over and over again I was repeating, "Help me oh Lord! Help me!" The agony of the struggle was deeper than the mind can fathom or words can express. The Apostle Paul describes it in Romans 8:26: "[F]or we do not know what prayer to offer nor how to offer it worthily as we ought, but the Spirit Himself goes to meet our supplication and pleads in our behalf with unspeakable yearnings and groanings too deep for utterance."

Well, the beginning of that verse says: "So too the Spirit comes to our aid and bears us up in our weakness..."

What happened next was a sensation of growing heat in the solar plexus, accompanied by a buzzing sound in my ears that soon became a sort of "inaudible BOOM"! The only way I can describe this is that it could be reproduced by being stone deaf and standing between two huge Chinese gongs while they are being struck simultaneously. It was a soul-deep resonating to some sort of long, slow and rhythmic internal sound that descended around me like a warm, comforting cloud.

And there was a voice; not audible, and not really in my head, so to speak, but a voice nevertheless that was supernally rich and rapturously tender.

"You KNOW that I LOVE you, my child," the voice said. "But until you remove the darkness from between us, I can do nothing."

The words vibrated every cell in my body from a depth of being that is impossible to describe.

"WHAT?!?" I cried back. My mind raced through all the aspects of my life. Like the proverbial moment before death when all of a person's deeds pass before their eyes, I reviewed every facet of my existence, enumerating all the ways in which I was endeavoring to seek only to do the will of God. I couldn't find a single breach in this "contract" where one could think that evil would enter the picture. In a sense, I was laying all this out as a sort of legal pleading in my mind.

At this point, a response came, though not in words. It was a movie being run in my mind/soul/awareness. I was shown my children in a series of vignettes that brought up the deep love and devotion I had for them, and the purpose was made clear that I was to understand that my love for my children, as great as it was, was merely a "human" love and could, in no way, equal the love of the Creator for his creation. I was being infused with this love. It was consoling and warmly caressing to a level that is impossible to express with words.

Then the scene changed and I was shown my children being warned about an ant bed; that they should leave the ants alone and not "play in the dirt" of the anthill. But, as children will, their curiosity about the anthill led them to it, and their lack of knowledge of ants coupled with their foolhardy, naive bravery caused them to begin to jump into the anthill just to see what would happen. The result was that they suddenly were covered with ants, biting and stinging them and they were running to me, screaming for relief.

Then, there I was, soothing them and brushing away the ants, and explaining that I could get rid of the ants, and I could put salve on the bites to soothe the pain, but it would do no good if they hadn't learned something from the experience about ants, and certainly, they would never forget what it felt like to be bitten by them. There might be scars on the skin, and certainly there would be scars in the mind.

Well, I certainly didn't see how my life related to children playing in an ant bed! "What are the ants?" I asked. "What is the evil in my life?"

And the voice came again, this time with overtones of sternness combined with sorrow: *"Learn!"*

And it reverberated away into silence as the sound of the engines began to return to my awareness. I was still feeling the sensation of the great infusion of love that had come with the first part of the interaction. I call it that, because it was hardly a vision in strict terms, though something happened of a visionary nature.

For weeks I was sustained by this love, and I certainly needed it.

My grandmother died two weeks after the sheriff delivered the eviction notice saying that we had been foreclosed and must vacate the house that had belonged to her for over 40 years, which she had transferred ownership to me, and which I had then trusted to my mother for tax purposes, in her name. (The taxes were lower because she could claim more exemptions).

My grandmother died as much from a broken heart at the betrayal by her daughter (my mother) as from the cancer.

We were effectively homeless and broke. We still had property of our own, but it was undeveloped and located out in the boondocks away from everything. We could have sold it and used the money to rent a house, but I knew that would be only a temporary solution. We certainly couldn't buy a house because my ex-husband was too depressed to work and our credit had been destroyed in the collapse of the business.

So we sold our equipment and used the money to buy building materials, and went to the woods to live on the land. We built a small house and moved in with the necessities, putting most of my furniture and books and other possessions in storage. The only luxury we kept at hand was my piano. There we were, in a cabin in the woods with no electricity or running water, but we had a baby grand in the corner!

At this point there was the daily struggle to see to it that there was enough food for my small children so that they would not have to go to bed hungry at night. Most of the time they didn't even have shoes to wear, and it was only by charity that they had clothes. We went from owning several homes, investment property and a business, to literally nothing.

And then, there was the work.

I don't know how many of you have tried the living on the land philosophy/lifestyle, but it's a *lot* of work. When you have a hand pump in the yard about 40 feet from the house, it is a lot of work to keep water available for all the normal uses of five people – especially when three of those people are small children.

My already compromised physical condition was really not up to that level of work. But, I was determined to maintain as normal a standard of living as possible, so it was a question of determination and will to continue to do what had to be done against the deterioration of my body.

But enough of that! The point was to establish the objectivity of suffering. Suffice it to say, that through all of this, I was sure that my faith was being tested and tried by fire. I never wavered. I will admit that I often woke up at night in so much psychological and emotional pain at the loss of my grandmother (actual) and my mother (virtual), as well as the worries for the future of my children (realistic), that I would get up and pace in the darkness, wringing my hands and crying. I would find a quiet, private place, and sit and rock and weep in the struggle to continue to find the love in the moment, so that I could go on another day.

I continued to ponder the command to "learn" that had been given so many months before on the boat. I needed that contact again. It was at this point that I decided that the only way I was going to accomplish this objective was to be able to truly open my heart to God so that he could infuse me on a permanent basis with this thing I so much lacked. Thus, the idea grew in me that I must still my own voice, both internal and external, so that I could hear daily the voice that betokens God's presence within.

I searched the Bible for clues as to how to go about this within the parameters of the religion. I knew about meditation and that this was one way to achieve a contact, but since I was in the faith trip, whatever I did had to be within the guidelines. I found a reference in Psalms where the psalmist says: "Let the words of my mouth and the meditations of my heart be acceptable unto thee, Oh Lord."

Well, that's good enough for me! There it was, right in the Bible!

I began to meditate on the love of God. That seemed to be the acceptable way to do it by the rules. And it was at this point that things began to really happen.

As I wrote in *Amazing Grace*, one Sunday during this time, I was sitting in church during the Pastoral prayer. I was praying hard along with the Minister that God would send the Holy Ghost to me to help me understand all that I needed to understand. The pastor's wife, a gifted musician, was evoking celestial harmonies in counterpoint to the mellifluous voice of the shepherd of our flock, lost in the drama of the prayer. It was my favorite part of the service because he was so erudite and articulate and she was so talented a partner in service to God.

Suddenly, I heard a buzzing noise, or a crackling sound; similar to the sound of bacon sizzling in the pan; and the voice of the pastor and the resonant "Amens" from the congregation became very far away and metallic sounding exactly as if I were hearing them broadcast from a loudspeaker under water.

This shocked me and my eyes snapped open to see if my vision was impaired because I thought I might be having a stroke or something. I was completely dismayed to see that the Minister, standing at the podium, gripping the stand with both hands, his eyes closed and his head thrown back in the profound drama of his praying, was overlaid with a shimmering, living, image of a *wolf*!

It was exactly as if a film was being projected onto him where the image of the wolf, in full color, was a sort of alter ego and all the expressions of the pastor were corrupted and twisted by the matching expressions of the wolf. When the Minister would move his hands or shake his head – so did the wolf. The gaping jaws of this toothsome figure from Hell exactly matched every move of the Minister's mouth! It was not a solid figure; it was a projection of light, so to speak.

I quickly looked around the sanctuary to see if this was a complete delusion, and was shocked to see similar overlays on all the people there. Many of them were sheep, but there were also pigs and cows and other creatures represented.

I was *horrified!* I was sure that the Devil had me now for sure! Here I was, in the middle of church, seeing our beloved Minister in the guise of a *wolf!* It was damnation for certain!

I closed my eyes and prayed harder. The sound anomaly continued and I opened my eyes to peek again. The wolf was still there dramatizing the euphoniously intoned pastoral prayer.

I squeezed my eyes tightly shut and prayed and prayed and rebuked Satan and finally began to just repeat the Lord's prayer over and over again to drive this image from my reality. Soon, it began to taper off and die away and when I opened my eyes again, the wolf was gone and I was *very* relieved to have won this battle with Satan.

A couple of Sundays later, we arrived a little late, expecting the services to be already started. We were surprised to see the congregation all gathered outside the church door, milling about like lost sheep.

We discovered that the Minister had done a midnight flit, so to speak, leaving the church in a bad way, having embezzled a huge amount of money from the funds that were supposed to pay the bills for the building and supply the various organizations. There was even a bill for dock rent for a rather large yacht that the church was also paying for, unbeknownst to all the members.

All the expensive furnishings of the luxurious parsonage were gone, the mortgages on both buildings were on the verge of foreclosure, the electricity was about to be shut off – and the Minister and his family were gone to parts unknown. A real wolf in sheep's clothing, so to speak.

I was stunned. I realized that my vision was exactly what I had been praying for: The Holy Spirit revealing the truth to me; and I had rebuked it and cast it away!

This resulted in a shift in my faith in my own ability to be "in touch" with God, or whoever was in charge of this Universe. Clearly, I had been shown the truth under the surface, and my self-doubts and belief in the authority of others had interfered with my "communion with Holy Spirit".

I understood an essential thing: if you truly pray for guidance, deeply and sincerely, it *will* come, but it may not be what you want to hear or believe and it may go against what others are saying or teaching.

But this, of course, raised other questions. The most dominant was how was one to tell when it was a misleading influence and how to tell if it was truly a Divine Revelation? If a number of people are claiming that the "Holy Spirit" is giving them revelations and these revelations are contradictory, then somebody is right excluding the others, or all of them are wrong. We have only our knowledge and reason with which to analyze and compare.

So it was back to the books.

One point that should be made here is: I had faith, I prayed diligently and fervently, I struggled and strove for that love, that subsuming of all other emotions into an all pervasive, comprehensive Love of God – and it surely did *something*!

There were actually, during that time, other events that could be termed visionary and ecstatic, but they aren't relevant, so I won't go into them now. Suffice it to say, they were supportive in every way of the idea that I had to *learn* what was under the surface in order to know what to accept as truth, or even partial truth. The only way to discern a "lying spirit" was to have some yardstick by which to determine as much of the objective truth as possible. That meant knowledge, "testing the spirits" by checking up on their accuracy.

Not long after, my fourth child was born and I was basically *forced* to spend more time studying and meditating and, as some of you know, the result of this period was my still unpublished book: *The Noah Syndrome*.

At this point, I was 33 years old and had spent three years in this experiment which did not really start as an experiment, but that is how it turned out.

What emerged in my mind was the fact that when you ask a question – if the question is a burning one – your life becomes the answer. All of your experiences and interactions and so forth shape themselves around the core of the answer that you are seeking in your soul. In this case, the question was: How to be One with God, and the answer was, Love is the answer, but you have to have knowledge to know what Love really is. As the writer of the book of James says:

> Consider it wholly joyful, my brethren, whenever you are enveloped in or encounter trials of any sort, or fall into various temptations. Be assured and understand that the trial and proving of your faith bring out endurance and steadfastness and patience. But let endurance and steadfastness and patience have full play and *do a thorough work, so that you may be perfectly and fully developed, lacking in nothing.* If any of you is deficient in wisdom, let him ask of the giving God who gives to everyone liberally and ungrudgingly, without reproaching or faultfinding, and it will be given him. Only it must be in faith that he asks, with no wavering – no hesitating, no doubting... *What is the use for anyone to profess to have faith if he has no works?* Can faith save? ... *Faith if it does not have works, by itself is destitute of power – inoperative, dead...* You see that a man is justified through what he does and not alone through faith – *through works of obedience* as well as by what he believes. (Amplified, Zondervan)

I understood that the poverty of my life, the torment and the suffering, the loss of things I loved, and the many related and complex events were *an expression of my actual state of being* the poverty of my knowledge relative to what I was capable of knowing. When I plunged headfirst into "Faith without knowledge/works" I was choosing death, for "faith without works is... dead."

But what were these works? What was it that God gives liberally and ungrudgingly? Knowledge.

> For that which is known about God, is evident to them [man] and made plain in their inner consciousness; because God has shown it to them. For, ever since the creation of the world, His invisible nature and attributes have been made intelligible and clearly discernible in and through the things that have been made – His handiwork. (Amplified, Zondervan)

According to the Sufi perspective, There is no God but God and knowledge concerns itself with knowing God. But in order to gain knowledge of God, it is necessary to utilize the intermediary of creation, which is, in fact, the purpose of all that exists. It not only *is* God, it is the path to God. It is incumbent upon the seeker to learn all he can with a view toward God. All things must be gathered into the knowledge base of the Seeker to be taken back to God exactly as described in the Parable of the Talents.

To *not* work as diligently as possible to know God through the creation – and that includes all branches of knowledge and art and craft – is defined by the apostle as passing judgment on God.

> And so, since they did not see fit to acknowledge God or approve of Him or *consider Him worth the knowing...* [His invisible nature and attributes have been made intelligible and clearly discernible in and through the things that have been made – His handiwork.] O man, whoever you are who judges and condemns another... for in posing as judge and passing sentence on another you condemn yourself, because you who judge are habitually practicing the very same things that you censure and denounce... (Amplified, Zondervan)

This seems to be precisely what I experienced. I dove into the faith/love and light trip and all Hell broke loose!

In looking back over the experiences recounted above, we can see that I was thinking about and focusing on "love and light and faith". But that is *not* what I experienced in my creation! Though, in a funny sort of way, my faith was answered! But, what an answer! Not at *all* what I was expecting!

Now, it has been recently suggested by a correspondent that I have some sort of inherent ability to manifest that is so powerful that my environment and experiences shift suddenly and dramatically in response to my inner state. This may be so, *but I don't think I am alone in this*. I think that it is true to one extent or another with everyone. It *is* true that you create your own reality and in some twisted sense, it is true that you do it by what you think and focus on... but there is a real Catch 22 involved in there and it is that factor that we are going to be investigating next!

CANDY WILL RUIN YOUR TEETH!

The writing of this book series pretty much took on a life of its own. It started out with a "plan" of only nine segments,[26] and I intended to get from a designated "point A" to a conclusion, "point B", with a minimum of words. I never dreamed that there would be so much resonance with so many people who would write to me and propose questions and subjects that pretty much fit into sub-categories of *The Wave*.

The present discussion of what it is we may be here to learn in order to graduate, was not part of the original plan. In the original plan, it was going to be mostly technical information about The Wave itself. But, clearly this concept is far more than that and I am flowing with it in response to everyone who wrote to encourage and assure me that my efforts are truly worthwhile. To all of you, I say thank you!

While, on the one hand, in response to what I am writing, there are those who are saying, "Finally, the fog is lifting," and such things, on the other hand there are those who are manifesting in a very real ways the very things I am talking about, i.e., being in prison and under the influence of the Predator's Mind.

To give an example of what I am talking about, since we are in the mode of giving concrete examples and have given Mumbo Jumbo the boot, one correspondent wrote to me:

> People have e-mailed [Carla, the Ra channel, and Jim] about your comments about them/Ra in *The Wave*... The e-mailers seem to have taken offense and thought that Carla and Jim should also. My opinion... is... that you were simply expressing your opinion as you see the situation from your own perspective, that no ill intention was involved...

---

[26] These were originally published online, and have now been published as *Riding the Wave*.

Having had a fine relation with Carla for some time, our main differences being semantical rather than actual, I naturally was stricken to think that anyone took offense at any of my remarks, since it was clear (I thought) that objective validation of their work with Ra was uppermost in my mind. But, that is how the forces of entropy work through people and it is the main subject of this essay that is shaping up here. I wrote back to this correspondent as follows:

> I would have to say that anyone who took offense – or felt motivated to urge offense – simply isn't getting it. Those are personal issues and we are not dealing with personal issues here. What we are dealing with is, in effect, a defense of the significance of the *Ra Material* as a great breakthrough in the history of channeling. I think that is clear from all my comments.
>
> But, the issue still remains in the minds of many folks who have written to me when I suggest (as I have been doing for a long time) that they read the Ra work... that if it was so good, why did Don kill himself? And why does it seem that Ra, being a "higher being who supposedly had access to realms of greater awareness" couldn't grasp the idea of conventional colloquialism and standard definitions? Added to this was the question: if Ra is trying to teach such concepts, why is it "obfuscated" to most people?
>
> The answers people form in their lack of knowledge generally consist of the idea that Ra was a "Trojan Horse" demonic who drove Don to his death, and therefore the validity of the material is compromised in the worst possible way. The next conclusion they draw is that Ra was not who and what he claimed to be and the evidence is the obscuration of language.
>
> Perhaps those who insulate themselves in cocoons of wishful thinking or "true believership" aren't aware of these concerns, or do not wish to address them – thinking that if you ignore it, it will go away.
>
> Our position is that every legitimate question and concern deserves an answer – even if the answer can only be reached by the individual asking himself or herself. But, in this case, these concerns are serious, not only for the Ra group, but for the whole field of work – channeling; the idea of not only the existence of, but the possibility of communication with, "higher beings". (For lack of a better term).
>
> Thus, I began my examination and questions from the "theoretical position" (even if it was influenced by the C's assurance that it was so), that Ra and the Ra work was exactly what Ra stated – a contact with 6th density unified thought form beings (social memory complexes), and went from there. If that hypothesis is to be validated, then there must be accommodation within it that explains what actually occurred... otherwise, it is nonsense.
>
> Those who wish to live in the land of "true believers" will, of course, find this approach to be offensive. But the history of "true believership", when analyzed and laid bare, leads to the obvious conclusion that such a position is precarious at best, disastrous at worst.
>
> A hypothesis HAS to explain the events, or it has to be thrown out! What is YOUR hypothesis for the nature of the contact and the results??????
>
> Nothing is black and white – simple observational conclusion – but there are many who prefer to see it that way. They see that the "fruits" of the Ra contact was the death of Don Elkins by his own hand, and a body of material that is tortuous and often difficult to read.

Those are facts.

How does one deal with those facts other than retreating into wishful thinking or by feats of cerebral gymnastics? We are using Ockham's Razor here...

As to whether it is just "my opinion", that may be so, but it is an opinion born of a lot of research and study and experience. But, as noted, it is more than an opinion... it is the result of much discussion and creating of a number of hypotheses that have been "tried and discarded", leaving only one that sufficiently explains the FACTS. (Assuming, of course, that Ra is who and what he says he is.)

I wrote to Carla. Even if there is a "divergence" in our approaches to how to deal with things at THIS level of reality, we are certainly in agreement as to what RESULTS are useful. I would not for the WORLD hurt Carla and Jim. My intent was exactly the opposite... to provide an adequate explanation for things that are very troubling... to validate the material itself (hopefully it will increase the numbers of people who actually will read the *Ra Material* – and that DOES seem to be a result as people are now writing to me saying "oh! I see! Okay, that makes sense... I can read it now!") And, if that happens, if it stops the rumors and whispers that have been floating around and growing – well, it has served its purpose.

In this field, you just can't have "sensitivities and personal agendas". Carla knows that and I know that. That is why, after very protracted and painful deliberation, I agreed to allow a journalist inside my life – knowing full well that the result would be to some extent "distortion and bias". The end result was, of course, that even though he could find no deception, no manipulation, no "dirt" in my work, he still had to put a "personal spin" on the story that ended up being a rather shallow and "cheesy" take on very serious work. The good thing is that it let people "inside" in a very public way and thereby attracted them to the work because they feel like they "know me".

So, enduring the "spin" was just the price that had to be paid. If you have read the article in the Times, you will note that Tom French remarked that he was always "bored" at the sessions. That says more about him than me. The same can be said for those who have taken offense at what is written in the referenced pages... it says more about them than me.

The following day, I received a response from Carla saying:

Hey there Laura –

several readers wrote me about your material, and i did look it over. i think people were upset because they felt perhaps don and i were being judged this or that way.

as far as i am concerned, and i told each person this, your opinions are rightfully your opinions, and i am totally accepting of them, not necessarily that they are right as far as i am concerned, but that they are your thoughts from the heart.

i KNOW you did not mean to offer disrespect. you and i have a good relationship, a friendship that goes beyond our being channels or in the same weird field of inquiry. i think we are both really honest people, and when we offer our thoughts, people might take them as unflattering. hey, i can take it! it's totally ok between you and me. we are both doing our sincere best to give the best that is in us in service to others. what can we ask of each other more than that?

i feel as though i just want to be a force for harmonization of all positive material. and i cannot do that by taking offense and being picky and petty with you or with anyone. let's both just redouble our efforts to serve, and let the chips fall where they may.

So, I hope the reader can see how people can be agents of Entropy and division when they are not aware of how the Predator's mind operates as *their* mind:

> The predators give us their mind, which becomes our mind… Through the mind, which, after all, is their mind, the predators inject into the lives of human beings whatever is convenient for them. And they ensure, in this manner, a degree of security to act as a buffer against their fear.[27]

And this is precisely what we are trying to talk about here. How the Predator (i.e., Lizzies, Entropic forces, et al.) influences our lives when, on the surface, and even at many deeper levels, there is *no seeming evidence.*

How do we *tell*?

I have said before and I will say it again: I have *never* seen a Lizzie! Some people claim to have seen them and I can't judge whether or not they are delusional or simply more in tune than I am and what they are reporting is a fact. But I *have* seen them through the descriptions of many people under hypnosis who have claimed to be abducted by aliens. I also see them constantly in my research – in myth and legend down through the millennia. Others have seen them in hallucinogen-induced visions, ecstatic states, dreams, and so forth. In nearly all cases, the descriptions are so similar, the dynamics of the interaction so consistent, that I cannot help but think that we are dealing with a large part of the Control System as elucidated by Jacques Vallee:

> I believe that when we speak of UFO sightings as instances of space visitations we are looking at the phenomenon on the wrong level. *We are not dealing with successive waves of visitations from space. We are dealing with a control system.*
>
> The thermostats that regulate your house temperature summer and winter are an example of a control system. In summer, a thermostat allows the air to get warmer until a certain limit is reached, and then the cooling system is triggered. But in winter, when the outside atmosphere turns cold and the temperature drops below another limit, a different mechanism, the heater, comes into play and warms the house. A naive observer might try to explain all this by assuming that warm is "good" and cold is "bad". He or she would be right half the time. Another naive observer of the opposite school might take a reversed view and decide that warm is "evil". He or she would also be right half the time. To understand the whole phenomenon one needs a grasp of the control concept, and one must be ready to understand that it needs two opposite principles for its function.
>
> I propose that there is a spiritual control system for human consciousness and those paranormal phenomena like UFOs are one of its manifestations. I cannot tell whether this control is natural and spontaneous; whether it is explainable in terms of genetics, or social psychology, or of ordinary phenomena – or if it is artificial in nature, under the power of some superhuman will. It may be entirely determined by laws that we have not yet discovered.
>
> I am led to this idea by the fact that, in every instance of the UFO phenomenon I have been able to study in depth, I have found as many rational elements

---

[27] Castaneda, *op. cit.*

as absurd ones, as many that I could call friendly as I could call hostile. This is what tells me that we are working on the wrong level. And so are all the believers, and this definitely includes the skeptics, because they believe they can explain the facts as strongly as the most enthusiastic convert to Ms. Dixon's vision of Jupiterian Amazons!

There are ways to gain access to the reference level of every control system. Even a child, if smart or daring enough, can climb on a chair, change the dial of a thermostat, and elicit a response. (The response in question might be a sound spanking from his father, of course. The road to higher knowledge has such accidents.) It must be possible to gain access to the control of the UFO phenomenon, to forget the spirits and the pranks and the claims of extraterrestrial contact, and do some real science. But it will take a very smart approach – and a very daring one.

...A newspaper column commented upon the apparent lack of reality of the whole UFO phenomenon: "It does not attack us. It does not affect our daily lives. It does not help us with our many problems. It has brought us nothing of value. It may have scared a few folks here and there, but then so do thunder storms and tornadoes. The whole thing, as a social issue, is of no consequence whatsoever." The journalist who wrote this column was superficially right, of course. But he forgot another fact:

...If UFOs are acting at the mythic and spiritual level it will be almost impossible to detect it by conventional methods. ... UFOs cannot be analyzed through the standard research techniques, if they are the means through which man's concepts are being rearranged. *All we can do is trace their effects on humans and hope that we eventually stumble on some principle that explains their behavior.*

What is the variable being controlled in this control system? Thermostats control temperature; gyroscopes control the direction in which a rocket flies. What could a paranormal phenomenon control? *I suggest that it is human belief that is being controlled and conditioned.*

My speculation is that a level of control of society exists which is a regulator of human development, and that the UFO phenomenon should be seen at this level.[28]

Did you catch that? "If UFOs are acting at the mythic and spiritual level it will be almost impossible to detect it by conventional methods."

This is my point. If "Lizzies" or "The Predator" or "Entropic Forces" act on us as is described by not only many ancient sources through myths and legends, but by Gurdjieff, don Juan, Ra and the Cassiopaeans, it will be almost impossible to detect by ordinary means.

And it is in this respect that the Cassiopaeans have been an invaluable guide in our passage beyond Scylla and Charybdis. Which is not to say that once one danger has been avoided that another does not appear. They do. And, in general, they seem to get more and more subtle.

---

[28] Jacques Vallee, Dimensions: A Casebook of Alien Contact (Ballantine, 1988).

Since we have already noted the response to my little "tweak" of the control system above, in the emails of the offended Ra fans, there is a more serious level that I would like to tell you about.

Since the day the last couple of chapters were uploaded to our website,[29] the energy has been very strange around here. And this is where I am going to tell you some of the things we look for when trying to determine the "temperature" of the Control System.

Not only did we post the "Truth Is Out There" sections, but also we have been setting up the Russian version of the site. A member of our group lives in Russia and has been working diligently on getting some basic material translated. There have been a number of glitches involved with that, and the most interesting was, of course, that as soon as he finished the first section and it was formatted by Ark and loaded onto the site, Alex's computer began to act up and we were afraid that the project would have to be brought to a halt.

The problem turned out to be overheating, which was pretty symbolic, to say the least. If you begin to see your reality as a symbol system, how are you to interpret such a thing? Did Alex's computer "heat up" because his "higher self" was communicating to him that something was "too hot", or was it a signal that his efforts were adding heat to the system; or even that his efforts were unwelcome in certain realms and denizens of same were showing him that they could "cook his goose"? And those are just the most obvious possible interpretations!

But then, things turned in a funny direction. The material that I intended to present in this chapter you are now reading was actually finished on the 30th of June. When I began the actual writing some days earlier, I hesitated over what and how much I ought to reveal about such matters. Finally, I decided to tell pretty much the whole story that was on my mind, changing only the names of those involved for protection of their privacy.

One problem remained: three of the names of the people involved were part and parcel of the Symbol system under discussion. So much a part, in fact, that one of my children contracted an illness with the name of one of these people. I was thinking how I was going to convey this dynamic and still use a pseudonym for this person. I finally resolved it by finding another name that was both a disease and a woman's first name.

As I was writing about the situation, I was asking myself some questions about this particular person's role, (and we are going to call her Candida, or Candy for short) in the soon to be revealed bizarre drama. But, let me get on with the story.

At the very period of my life when I was approaching the breakthrough to the Cassiopaean contact (though I didn't know it at the time), a great deal of opposing energy came against me, to the extent that my life was literally in danger on more than one occasion. The source of the danger seemed to be centered in two different groups, and the only thing that these two groups had in

---

[29] When they were originally written, in 2000.

common with each other was this woman, Candy. Further, the only way there was any connection at all between me and these groups, was by virtue of my friendship with Candy. (It's a truly strange story, as you will soon see.)

At the same time that I was writing this story – which started off with my experiences with Reiki – curiously, the discussion on the Cassiopaean e-groups mail list turned to the subject of Reiki! Well, that's not so unusual. I've gotten used to such "ordinary" synchronicities.

After a couple of days of intense work, (the whole thing was a struggle to get into words because of the very strangeness of it and multiple levels of interaction and complexity), I felt that it was finished and I was getting ready to switch to another program. I went to click the minimize icon at the top of the window but inadvertently clicked the close icon. Well, I realized that I had done it, so when the prompt box came up that I *assumed* said, "Do you really want to quit?" I quickly clicked no. But, what the prompt *really* said was, "Do you want to save the changes to file..."

So, the entire day's work was gone. (Yeah, I forgot to save every ten minutes or so. *Awareness* and *vigilance* were *not* being practiced!)

What is worse, this was a subject that I had never before written about; so it was all first hand work. A lot of these pages consist of excerpts from transcripts, quotes from books that are scanned and converted to text, and a few pages of connecting dialogue that I write here and there to help it all to make sense. This was the first time that I had to write everything from scratch – and it was gone.

I was *sick*. It was about 20 pages of script that I had sweated blood working through.

Well, I went outside to water the flowers and think about it a bit while Ark went through the system to see if there wasn't some way he could retrieve it. No luck. It was gonezerooni. Sayonara. Hasta la vista! And all that.

I thought about the level of exposure of the control system that I might be activating in this story, and the fact that it (the control system) certainly might not wish to be exposed in that way. I thought about the groups I was writing about and their possible connections to some really dark doings here on the Big Blue Marble.

I had stumbled upon these groups inadvertently then, had been able to read the clues and extricate myself in the nick of time, so to speak, but I had certainly seen a level of the "man behind the curtain" that most people don't see and survive. They had tried to kill me, and if it was desirable to do so then, they surely would have some sense that their maneuvers and manipulations might be being exposed now and they could sort of reach a "mind tentacle" in my direction to generate impatience and mental confusion in my state of extreme tiredness so that I was not paying close enough attention when closing my file.

I came back inside, and Ark told me that now *his* computers were acting up. Very strange behavior, loss of a file similar to my own incident; freeze ups; the server went down; e-groups were suddenly inaccessible; his halogen lamp suddenly stopped working, and so forth. And all of this on top of a flat tire on the car and an expensive brake job on the van in the days following the launching of the Russian site. I was beginning to think that maybe I was stepping over the line with my revelations.

I went into the study where we do the sessions and took out my handy dandy Russian Gypsy cards and shuffled them around for a minute while thinking what I ought to do. I began to lay out the cards.

Now, anybody who is familiar with this deck knows that each card has four segments, and each segment is a half picture. There are 25 cards and 50 pictures. The only pictures that are "read" are those that are "completed" by virtue of falling next to a card that has the other half of the picture. In such a case, even if the cards are not aligned so that the halves fall together, you are supposed to rotate the two adjacent cards so that the two halves match. Because the adjacent half of any picture can be above, below or on either side, this means that the picture can fall in one of four positions or "directions". This direction is part of the "reading" of the picture.

On any number of occasions when I have used these cards, I have always had 3 or more matches. That is pretty standard. But, as I laid the cards down this time, card after card was put in position with no matches – until I got to the very last row when picture number 26 fell... without need to rotate either card to bring the halves together. (That doesn't happen very often at all!)

And what did number 26 indicate? It is a picture of a book.

The question was whether I should just skip telling the story – certainly related to a "book" in theme. And the interpretation is:

> The secret you have been told is going to be disclosed. Either you or someone else will make it public. Knowledge and information are ever changing and what is secret one minute can be public the next. This should be of no concern to you if you have been aboveboard and honest in your dealings.

There were further permutations that didn't apply to this case, but this one certainly did. So, I resolved to rewrite the piece, and bump my awareness up a few notches.

But then, another very strange thing happened.

Ark receives all the email from the site and forwards to my computer anything that is addressed specifically to me. He had received an email at almost exactly the time that I had made the fatal error of closing the file without saving, and he had forwarded. But I had been so upset that I did not come back to the computer until the next day when I opened and read the e-mail. It said:

> Hi Laura,
>
> ...I am a friend of [Candy]. She had told me about the Cassiopaeans and that you and she started these transmissions a while back. If that is you, she wanted to get in contact with you again.

The history of the coming of the Cassiopaeans is pretty well known and witnessed by a number of people. I have written to some extent about the many people who came and went from the early experimental sessions, but who did not have the patience or inclination to stay with it. Candy was one of several dozen *occasional* participants. I find it curious that she is telling her current associates that she and I started these transmissions! As the record will show, Candy was present for only *two* of the actual early Cassiopaean sessions, though she was present at approximately four other sessions prior to the Cassiopaean contact.

Nevertheless, there is the tweaking of my reality by the Control System in that Candy is apparently telling her friends that she was more or less instrumental.

But, what is even more disturbing is the fact that Candy (through a third party – an agent – mind you) attempts contact after almost six years, at the exact time that the file *about her* is lost. Not only that, but I was exactly in the process of mulling over the question of whether or not she was an innocent dupe of the very dark groups that I encountered through her, or if she was, in fact, knowledgeable and willingly a participant.

The problem here is that I *like* her! I liked her from the first instant I met her. She is charming and friendly and vivacious and funny beyond anything. Seeing the things I saw in the series of events I was writing about was very hard.

But, further and deeper: what kind of serpentine Control System can be aware of a person's thoughts, intent and actions in the way that would be required to arrange such a series of bizarre events and synchronicities?

At this point I was thinking that it would be nice if she wanted to get in touch because she had given up her associations with those folks who are, as it appears to me, part and parcel of the manifestation of the Predator's mind, the Lizzie faction, if you want to call it that. It would be nice...

So I called Terry and Jan to share with them this bizarre little series of events. They are both as familiar as I am with the ways the energies in the environment become chaotic and even destructive when a significant change is in the air. Terry advised me to be very careful and have nothing at all to do with Candy; didn't I learn my lesson before? Weren't there enough signs detected in the former interactions, which saved my buns from the fire so that I wouldn't get burned again?

I agreed that he was right. But again, I really *like* Candy! It hurt me a lot to realize that she was just being friendly and trying to get close so that she could be a conduit of attack, so to speak. Maybe it would be different now?

Nope, Terry said. Not a chance!

But, I wondered. So, we did I Ching on this one. What is the deal with Candy?

Hexagram 39: OBSTRUCTION
Above: the abysmal water
Below: Keeping still, Mountain

The hexagram pictures a dangerous abyss lying before us, and a steep, inaccessible mountain rising behind us. We are surrounded by obstacles. But the mountain, whose attribute is keeping still, provides a hint as to how we can extricate ourselves. In the face of danger without, we must keep still within. It is by turning inward that our attention is directed to overcoming obstacles. Obstruction is not a lasting condition.

Six in the fourth place: going leads to obstruction. Coming brings about unity. Be wary of becoming entangled in conflicts and lawsuits, for they could create much trouble. If you continue to be diligent at work, you are likely to be promoted. If you are in school, you can expect to receive recognition and then a good job.

Well, a mountain "keeping still" in this case, means that I should not be moved from my "position" which is to continue to work to expose this Control System. But, obviously, I am going to have to write it very carefully so as to avoid being entangled in conflicts and, perhaps, even lawsuits, though I think the latter very unlikely.

In the case of my comments on the *Ra Material* and now, in my work on exposing one facet of the Control System, we find exactly what Dr. Vallee suggested might happen:

There are ways to gain access to the reference level of every control system. Even a child, if smart or daring enough, can climb on a chair, change the dial of a thermostat, and elicit a response.

It seems apparent to me that something *is* going on here. In learning about these things, I suffered much on my own. In *telling* about them, there seems to be an attempt to strengthen the feedback control mechanism. But, I am familiar with that response, and hopefully, I will be able to proceed with awareness.

At this point, the reader needs to be familiar with some rather disturbing material that will play a rather interesting part in the story I am going to tell. The passage is a bit longer than usual, but you will need to read it carefully . Someday, it might save your life too.

THE GREENBAUM SPEECH

Herein is the lecture by D.C. Hammond, originally entitled *Hypnosis in MPD: Ritual Abuse*, but now usually known as the "Greenbaum Speech," delivered at the Fourth Annual Eastern Regional Conference on Abuse and Multiple Personality, Thursday June 25, 1992, at the Radisson Plaza Hotel, Mark Center, Alexandria, Virginia.

Sponsored by the Center for Abuse Recovery & Empowerment, The Psychiatric Institute of Washington, D.C.

Both a tape and a transcript were at one time available from Audio Transcripts of Alexandria, Virginia. Tapes and transcripts of other sessions from the conference are still being sold but – understandably – not this one. The transcript below was made from a privately made tape of the original lecture.

The single most remarkable thing about this speech is how little one has heard of it in the two years since its original delivery. It is recommended that one reads far enough at least until one finds why it's called "The Greenbaum Speech".

In the introduction the following background information is given for D. Corydon Hammond: B.S. M.S. Ph.D (Counseling Psychology) from the University of Utah.

- Diplomate in Clinical Hypnosis, the American Board of Psychological Hypnosis
- Diplomate in Sex Therapy, the American Board of Sexology Clinical Supervisor and Board Examiner, American Board of Sexology
- Diplomate in Marital and Sex Therapy, American Board of Family Psychology
- Licensed Psychologist, Licensed Marital Therapist, Licensed Family Therapist, State of Utah
- Research Associate Professor of Physical Medicine an Rehabilitation, Utah School of Medicine
- Director and Founder of the Sex and Marital Therapy Clinic, University of Utah.
- Adjunct Associate Professor of Educational Psychology, University of Utah Abstract
- Editor, *The American Journal of Clinical Hypnosis*
- Advising Editor and Founding Member, Editorial Board, *The Ericsonian Monograph*
- Referee, *The Journal of Abnormal Psychology*
- 1989 Presidential Award of Merit, American Society of Clinical Hypnosis
- 1990 Urban Sector Award, American Society of Clinical Hypnosis
- Current President, American Society of Clinical Hypnosis

THE SPEECH

We've got a lot to cover today and let me give you a rough approximate outline of the things that I'd like us to get into.

First, let me ask how many of you have had at least one course or workshop on hypnosis? Can I see the hands? Wonderful. That makes our job easier.

Okay. I want to start off by talking a little about trance-training and the use of hypnotic phenomena with an MPD (Multiple Personality Disorder) dissociative-disorder population, to talk some about unconscious exploration, methods of doing that, the use of imagery and symbolic imagery techniques for managing physical symptoms, input overload, things like that.

Before the day's out, I want to spend some time talking about something I think has been completely neglected in the field of dissociative disorder, and that's talking about methods of profound calming for *automatic hyper-arousal* that's been conditioned in these patients.

We're going to spend a considerable length of time talking about age-regression and abreaction in working through a trauma. I'll show you with a non-MPD patient – some of that kind of work – and then extrapolate from what I find so similar and different with MPD cases.

Part of that, I would add, by the way, is that I've been very sensitive through the years about taping MPD cases or ritual-abuse cases, part of it being that some of that feels a little like using patients and I think that this population has been used enough. That's part of the reason, by choice, that I don't generally videotape my work.

I also want to talk a bunch about hypnotic relapse-prevention strategies and post-integration therapy today.

Finally, I hope to find somewhere in our time-frame to spend on hour or so talking specifically about ritual abuse and about mind-control programming and brainwashing – how it's done, how to get on the inside with that – which is a topic that in the past I haven't been willing to speak about publicly, have done that in small groups and in consultations, but recently decided that it was high time that somebody started doing it. So we're going to talk about specifics today.

[Applause]

In Chicago at the first international congress where ritual abuse was talked about I can remember thinking, "How strange and interesting." I can recall many people listening to an example given that somebody thought was so idiosyncratic and rare, and all the people coming up after saying, "Gee, you're treating one, too? You're in Seattle"...Well, I'm in Toronto...Well, I'm in Florida...Well, I'm in Cincinnati." I didn't know what to think at that point.

It wasn't too long after that I found my first ritual-abuse patient in somebody I was already treating and we hadn't gotten that deep yet. Things in that case made me very curious about the use of mind-control techniques and hypnosis and other brainwashing techniques.

So I started studying brainwashing and some of the literature in that area and became acquainted with, in fact, one of the people who'd written one of the better books in that area.

Then I decided to do a survey, and from the ISSMP&D [International Society for the Study of Multiple Personality and Dissociation] folks I picked out about a dozen and a half therapists that I thought were seeing more of that than probably anyone else around and I started surveying them.

The interview protocol, that I had got the same reaction almost without exception. Those therapists said, "You're asking questions I don't know the answers to. You're asking more specific questions than I've ever asked my patients." Many of those same therapists said, "Let me ask those questions and I'll get back to you with the answer." Many of them not only got back with answers, but said, "You've got to talk to this patient or these two patients." I ended up doing hundreds of dollars worth of telephone interviewing.

What came out of that was a grasp of a variety of brainwashing methods being used *all over the country*. I started to hear some similarities. Whereas I hadn't known, to begin with, how widespread things were, I was now getting a feeling that there were a lot of people reporting some similar things and that there must be some degree of communication here.

Then approximately two and a half years ago I had some material drop in my lap. My source was saying a lot of things that I knew were accurate about some of the brainwashing, but the individual was telling me new material I had no idea about.

At this point I decided to check it out in three ritual-abuse patients I was seeing at the time. Two of the three had what they were describing, in careful inquiry without leading or contaminating.

The fascinating thing was that as I did a telephone-consult with a therapist that I'd been consulting for quite a number of months on an MPD case in another state, I told her to inquire about certain things. She said, "Well, what are those things?" I said, "I'm not going to tell you, because I don't want there to be any possibility of contamination. Just come back to me and tell me what the patient says."

She called me back two hours later, said, "I just had a double session with this patient and there was a part of him that said, 'Oh, we're so excited. If you know about this stuff, you know how the Cult Programmers get on the inside and our therapy is going to go so much faster.'"

Many other patients since have had a reaction of wanting to pee their pants out of anxiety and fear rather than thinking it was wonderful thing. But the interesting thing was that she then asked, "What are these things?" They were word perfect – [the] same answers my source had given me.

I've since repeated that in many parts of the country. I've consulted in eleven states and one foreign country, in some cases over the telephone, in some cases in person, in some cases giving the therapist information ahead of time and saying, "Be very careful how you phrase this. Phrase it in these ways so you don't contaminate." In other cases not even giving the therapist information ahead of time so they couldn't.

When you start to find the same highly esoteric information in different states and different countries, from Florida to California, you start to get an idea that there's something going on that is very large, very well coordinated, with a great deal of communication and systematic-ness to what's happening.

So I have gone from someone kind of neutral and not knowing what to think about it all to someone who clearly believes ritual abuse is real and that the people who say it isn't are either naïve – like people who didn't want to believe the Holocaust or – they're dirty.

[Applause]

Now for a long time I would tell a select group of therapists that I knew and trusted, information and say, "Spread it out. Don't spread my name. Don't say where it came from. But here's some information. Share it with other therapists if you find it's on target, and I'd appreciate your feedback." People would question – in talks – and say they were hungry for information. Myself, as well as a few others that I've shared it with, were hedging out of concern and out of personal threats and out of death threats.

I finally decided to hell with them. If they're going to kill me, they're going to kill me. It's time to share more information with therapists. Part of that comes because we proceeded so cautiously and slowly, checking things in many different locations and find the same thing.

So I'm going to give you the way in with ritual-abuse programming. I certainly can't tell you everything that you want to know in forty-five or fifty minutes, but I'm going to give you the essentials to get inside and start working at a new level.

I don't know what proportion, honestly, of patients have this. I would guess that maybe somewhere around at least fifty percent, maybe as high as three-quarters – I would guess maybe two-thirds of your ritual-abuse patients may have this.

What do I think the distinguishing characteristic is?

If they were raised from birth in a mainstream cult or if they were a non-bloodline person, meaning neither parent was in the Cult, but Cult people had a lot of access to them in early childhood, they may also have it. I have seen more than one ritual-abuse patient who clearly had all the kinds of ritual things you hear about. They seemed very genuine. They talked about all the typical things that you hear in this population, but had none of this programming with prolonged extensive checking. So I believe in one case I was personally treating that she was a kind of schizmatic break-off that had kind of gone off and done their own thing and were no longer hooked into a mainstream group.

[Pause]

Here's where it appears to have come from. At the end of World War II, before it even ended, Allen Dulles and people from our Intelligence Community were already in Switzerland making contact to get out Nazi scientists. As World War II ends, they not only get out rocket scientists, but they also get out some Nazi doctors who have been doing mind-control research in the camps.[30]

They brought them to the United States. Along with them was a young boy, a teenager, who had been raised in a Hasidic Jewish tradition and a background of Cabalistic mysticism that probably appealed to people in the Cult because at least by the turn of the century Aleister Crowley had been introducing Cabalism into Satanic stuff, if not earlier. I suspect it may have formed some bond between them. But he saved his skin by collaborating and being an assistant to them in the death-camp experiments. They brought him with them.

---

[30] Convinced that German scientists could help America's postwar efforts, President Harry Truman agreed in September 1946 to authorize "Project Paperclip," a program to bring selected German scientists to work on America's behalf during the "Cold War".

However, Truman expressly excluded anyone found "to have been a member of the Nazi party and more than a nominal participant in its activities, or an active supporter of Nazism or militarism." The War Department's Joint Intelligence Objectives Agency (JIOA) conducted background investigations of the scientists. In February 1947, JIOA Director Bosquet Wev submitted the first set of scientists' dossiers to the State and Justice Departments for review. The Dossiers were damning. Samuel Klaus, the State Departments representative on the JIOA board, claimed that all the scientists in this first batch were "ardent Nazis." Their visa requests were denied. Wev wrote a memo warning that "the best interests of the United States have been subjugated to the efforts expended in 'beating a dead Nazi horse'." He also declared that the return of these scientists to Germany, where they could be exploited by America's enemies, presented a "far greater security threat to this country than any former Nazi affiliations which they may have had or even any Nazi sympathies that they may still have."

When the JIOA formed to investigate the backgrounds and form dossiers on the Nazis, the Nazi Intelligence leader Reinhard Gehlen met with the CIA director Allen Dulles. Dulles and Gehlen hit it off immediately, Gehlen was a master spy for the Nazis and had infiltrated Russia with his vast Nazi Intelligence network. Dulles promised Gehlen that his Intelligence unit was safe in the CIA. Dulles had the scientists dossier's re-written to eliminate incriminating evidence. As promised, Allen Dulles delivered the Nazi Intelligence unit to the CIA, which later opened many umbrella projects stemming from Nazi mad research. (MK-ULTRA / ARTICHOKE, OPERATION MIDNIGHT CLIMAX) By 1955, more than 760 German scientists had been granted citizenship in the U.S. and given prominent positions in the American scientific community. Many had been longtime members of the Nazi party and the Gestapo, had conducted experiments on humans at concentration camps, had used slave labor, and had committed other war crimes. In a 1985 expose in the Bulletin of the Atomic Scientists Linda Hunt wrote that she had examined more than 130 reports on Project Paperclip subjects--and every one "had been changed to eliminate the security threat classification." President Truman, who had explicitly ordered no committed Nazis to be admitted under Project Paperclip, was evidently never aware that his directive had been violated.

(http://www.thirdworldtraveler.com/Fascism/Operation_Paperclip_file.html)

They started doing mind-control research for Military Intelligence in military hospitals in the United States. The people that came, the Nazi doctors, were Satanists. Subsequently, the boy changed his name, Americanized it some, obtained an M.D. degree, became a physician and continued this work that appears to be at the center of Cult Programming today. His name is known to patients throughout the country.

[Pause]

What they basically do is they will get a child and they will start this, in basic forms, it appears, by about two and a half after the child's already been made dissociative. They'll make him dissociative not only through abuse, like sexual abuse, but also things like putting a mousetrap on their fingers and teaching the parents, "You do not go in until the child stops crying. Only then do you go in and remove it." [31]

They start in rudimentary forms at about two and a half and kick into high gear, it appears, around six or six and a half, continue through adolescence with periodic reinforcements in adulthood.

Basically in the programming, the child will be put typically on a gurney. They will have an IV in one hand or arm. They'll be strapped down, typically naked. There'll be wires attached to their head to monitor electroencephalograph patterns. They will see a pulsing light, most often described as red, occasionally white or blue. They'll be given, most commonly I believe, Demerol. Sometimes it'll be other drugs as well depending on the kind of programming. They have it, I think, down to a science where they've learned you give so much every twenty-five minutes until the programming is done.

They then will describe a pain on one ear, their right ear generally, where it appears a needle has been placed, and they will hear weird, disorienting sounds in that ear while they see photic stimulation to drive the brain into a brainwave pattern with a pulsing light at a certain frequency not unlike the goggles that are now available through Sharper Image and some of those kinds of stores.

Then, after a suitable period when they're in a certain brainwave state, they will begin programming, programming oriented to self-destruction and debasement of the person.

In a patient, at this point in time about eight years old, who has gone through a great deal, early programming took place on a military installation. That's not uncommon. I've treated and been involved with cases who are part of this original mind-control project as well as having their programming on military reservations in many cases. We find a lot of connections with the CIA.

This patient now was in a Cult school, a private Cult school where several of these sessions occurred a week. She would go into a room, get all hooked up. They would do all of these sorts of things. When she was in the proper altered state, now they were no longer having to monitor it with electroencephalographs, she also had already had placed on her electrodes, one in the vagina, for example, four on the head. Sometimes they'll be on other parts of the body.

---

[31] This actually sounds like some of the Dr. Spock babycare nonsense that was quite popular in the 50s. Dr. Spock later renounced these ideas. My guess is that he was used as a dupe to "prepare the ground" for other, more nefarious activities. Nevertheless, an entire generation of American babies were treated rather badly. Those babies are middle aged now, and many of them are in positions of power. A scary thought, indeed.

They will then begin and they would say to her, "You are angry with someone in the group." She'd say, "No, I'm not" and they'd violently shock her. They would say the same thing until she complied and didn't make any negative response. Then they would continue. "And because you are angry with someone in the group," or "When you are angry with someone in the group, you will hurt yourself. Do you understand?" She said, "No" and they shocked her. They repeated again, "Do you understand?" "Well, yes, but I don't want to." Shock her again until they get compliance. Then they keep adding to it. "And you will hurt yourself by cutting yourself. Do you understand?" Maybe she'd say yes, but they might say, "We don't believe you" and shock her anyway. "Go back and go over it again."

They would continue in this sort of fashion. She said typically it seemed as though they'd go about thirty minutes, take a break for a smoke or something, come back. They may review what they'd done and stopped or they might review what they'd done and go on to new material. She said the sessions might go half an hour, they might go three hours. She estimated three times a week.

Programming under the influence of drugs in a certain brainwave state and with these noises in one ear and them speaking in the other ear, usually the left ear, associated with right hemisphere non-dominant brain functioning, and with them talking, therefore, and requiring intense concentration, intense focusing. Because often they'll have to memorize and say certain things back, word-perfect, to avoid punishment, shock, and other kinds of things that are occurring.

This is basically how a lot of programming goes on. Some of it'll also use other typical brainwashing kinds of techniques. There will be very standardized types of hypnotic things done at times. There'll be sensory deprivation which we know increases suggestibility in anyone. Total sensory deprivation, suggestibility has significantly increased, from the research. It's not uncommon for them to use a great deal of that, including formal sensory-deprivation chambers before they do certain of these things.

[Pause]

Now let me give you, because we don't have a lot of time, as much practical information as I can.

The way that I would inquire as to whether or not some of this might be there would be with ideomotor finger-signals.[32]

After you've set them up I would say, "I want the central inner core of you to take control of the finger-signals." Don't ask the unconscious mind. The case where you're inquiring about ritual abuse, that's for the central inner core. The core is a *Cult-created part.* "And I want that central inner core of you to take control of this hand of these finger-signals and what it has for the yes-finger to float up. I want to ask the inner core of you is there any part of you, any part of Mary," that's the host's name, "who knows anything about Alpha, Beta, Delta, or Theta."

If you get a Yes, it should raise a red flag that you might have someone with formal intensive brainwashing and programming in place.

---

[32] IMR is an exploratory method of uncovering repressed material used extensively by many hypnotherapists. On a subconscious level, an individual generally remembers everything, even if it is too traumatic to bring up to awareness. The suggestion is given that the fingers can be used to signal the answer, bypassing the mind, and yes or no questions are asked.

I would then ask and say, "I want a part inside who knows something about Alpha, Beta, Delta, and Theta to come up to a level where you can speak to me and when you're here say, 'I'm here'."

I would not ask if a part was willing to. No one's going to particularly want to talk about this. I would just say, "I want some part who can tell me about this to come out."

Without leading them ask them what these things are.

I've had consults where I've come in... Sometimes I've gotten a Yes to that, but as I've done exploration it appeared to be some kind of compliance response or somebody wanting, in two or three cases, to appear maybe that they were ritually abused and maybe they were in some way, but with careful inquiry and looking it was obvious that they did not have what we were looking for.

Let me tell you what these are. Let's suppose that this whole front row here are multiples and that she has an alter named Helen and she has one named Mary, she has one named Gertrude, she has one named Elizabeth, and she has one named Monica. Every one of those alters may have put on it a program, perhaps designated alpha-zero-zero-nine. A Cult person could say, "Alpha-zero-zero-nine" or make some kind of hand gesture to indicate this and get the same part out in any one of them even though they had different names that they may be known by to you.

Alphas appear to represent general programming, the first kind of things put in. Betas appear to be sexual programs. For example, how to perform oral sex in a certain way, how to perform sex in rituals, having to do with producing child pornography, directing child pornography, prostitution. Deltas are killers trained in how to kill in ceremonies.

There'll also be some self-harm stuff mixed in with that, assassination and killing. Thetas are called psychic killers.

You know, I had never in my life heard those two terms paired together. I'd never heard the words "psychic killers" put together, but when you have people in different states, including therapists inquiring and asking, "What is Theta," and patients say to them, "Psychic killers," it tends to make one a believer that certain things are very systematic and very widespread.

This comes from their belief in psychic sorts of abilities and powers, including their ability to psychically communicate with "mother," including their ability to psychically cause somebody to develop a brain aneurysm and die.

It also is a more future-oriented kind of programming.

Then there's Omega. I usually don't include that word when I say my first question about this or any part inside that knows about Alpha, Beta, Delta, Theta because Omega will shake them even more.

Omega has to do with self-destruct programming. Alpha and Omega, the beginning and the end. This can include self-mutilation as well as killing-themselves programming.

Gamma appears to be system-protection and deception programming which will provide misinformation to you, try to misdirect you, tell you half-truths, protect different things inside. There can also be other Greek letters.

I'd recommend that you go and get your entire Greek alphabet and if you have verified that some of this stuff is present and they have given you some of the right answers about what some of this material is, and I can't underline enough: DO NOT LEAD THEM. Do not say, "Is this killers?" Get the answer from them, please. When you've done this and it appears to be present, I would take your entire Greek alphabet and, with ideomotor signals, go through the alphabet and say, "Is there any programming inside associated with epsilon, omicron," and go on through.

There may be some systematic-ness to some of the other letter, but I'm not aware of it. I've found, for example, in one case that Zeta had to do with the production of snuff films that this person was involved with. With another person, Omicron had to do with their linkage and associations with drug smuggling and with the Mafia and with big business and government leaders. So there's going to be some individualism, I think, in some of those.

Some of those are come-home programs, "come back to the Cult", "return to the Cult" program.

Here's the flaw in the system. They have built in shut-down and erasure codes so if they got into trouble they could shut something down and they could also erase something. These codes will sometimes be idiosyncratic phrases, or ditties. Sometimes they will be numbers maybe followed by a word. There's some real individuality to that. At first I had hoped if we can get some of these maybe they'll work with different people. No such luck. It's very unlikely unless they were programmed at about the same point in time as part of the same little group. Stuff that I've seen suggests that they carry laptop computers, the programmers, which still include everything that they did twenty, thirty years ago in them in terms of the names of alters, the programs, the codes, and so on.

Now what you can do is get erasure codes, and I always ask, "If I say this code, what will happen?" Double-check. "Is there any part inside who has different information?" Watch your ideomotor signals and what I've found is you can erase programs by giving the appropriate codes, but then you must abreact the feelings.

So if you erase Omega, which is often where I've started because it's the most high risk. Afterwards I will get all the Omega, what were formerly Omega alters, together so that we will abreact and give back to the host the memories associated with all the programming that was done with Omega and anything any Omega part ever had to do in a fractionated abreaction.

They use the metaphor – and it is their metaphor – of robots and it is like a robot shell comes down over the child alter to make them act in robotic fashion. Once in a while internally you'll confront robots.

What I found from earlier work, and so I speed the process up now because I confirmed it enough times, is that you can say to the core, "Core, I want you to look – there's this robot blocking the way in some way, blocking the progress. Go around and look at the back of the head and tell me what you notice on the back of the head or the neck." I just ask it very non-leading like that and what's commonly said to me is that there were wires or a switch.

So I'll tell them, "Hold the wires or flip the switch and it will immobilize the robot and give me a yes-signal when you've done it."

Pretty soon you get a yes-signal.

"Great. Now that the robot is immobilized, I want you to look inside the robot and tell me what you see." It's generally one or several children. I have them remove the children. I do a little hypnotic magic and ask the core to use a laser and vaporize the robot so nothing is left. They're usually quite amazed that this works, as have been a number of therapists.

[Pause]

Now that there are many different layers of this stuff is the problem. Let me come over to the overhead and give some ideas about them.

What we have up here are innumerable alters. I'll tell you one of the fascinating things I've seen. I remember a little over a year ago coming in to see some cases, some of the tough cases at a dissociative-disorders unit of a couple of the finest of the MPD therapists in this country, who are always part of all the international meetings, have lectured internationally. We worked and I look at some of their patients. They were amazed at certain things because they had not been aware of this before.

As we worked with some of the patients and confirmed it, I remember one woman who'd been inpatient for three years, still was inpatient. Another who had one intensive year of inpatient work with all the finest MPD therapy you can imagine – abreactions, integrations, facilitating cooperation, art therapy, on and on and on, journaling, intensively for one inpatient year followed by an intensive year of outpatient therapy two, three hours a week.

In both patients we found out that all of this great work had done nothing but deal with the alters up here and had not touched the mind-control programming. In fact it was not only intact, but we found that the one who was outpatient was having her therapy monitored every session by her mother, out-of-state, over the telephone, and that she still had intact suggestions that had been give to her at a certain future time to kill her therapist.

Now one of the things that I would very carefully check is, I would suggest that you ask the core, not just the unconscious mind, ask the core, "Is there any part inside that continues to have contact with people associated with the Cult? Is there any part inside who goes to Cult rituals or meetings? Is there a recording device inside of Mary," if that's the host's name, "a recording device inside so that someone can find out the things that are said in sessions?"

This doesn't mean they're monitored. Many of them just simply have it.

"Is there someone who debriefs some part inside for what happens in our therapy sessions?"

I have the very uncomfortable feeling from some past experience that when you look at this you will find the large proportion of ritual-abuse victims in this country are having their ongoing therapy monitored.

I remember a woman who came in about twenty-four years old, claimed her father was a Satanist. Her parents divorced when she was six. After that when her father had visitation, he would take her to rituals sometimes up until age fifteen. She said, "I haven't gone to anything since I was fifteen."

Her therapist believed this at face value. We sat in my office. We did a two-hour inquiry using hypnosis. We found the programming present. In addition to that we found that every therapy session was debriefed and in fact they had told her to get sick and not come to the appointment with me. Another one had been told that I was Cult and that if she came I would know that she'd been told not to come and I would punish her.

If anything meaningful comes out in a patient who's being monitored like that – from what I've learned thus far, they're tortured with electric shocks – my belief is if they're in that situation you can't do meaningful therapy other than being supportive and caring and letting them know you care a lot and you'll be there to support them. But I wouldn't try to work with any kind of deep material or deprogramming with them because I think it can do nothing but get them tortured and hurt unless they can get into a safe, secure inpatient unit for an extended period of time to do some of the work required.

I have a feeling that when you make inquiries you're going to find that probably greater than fifty percent of these patients, if they're bloodline, meaning mother or dad or both involved, will be monitored on some ongoing basis.

[Pause]

Now when you come below the alters, you then have Alpha, Beta, Delta, Theta, so and so forth, the Greek-letter programming and they will then have backup programs. There will typically be an erasure code for the backups. There may be one code that combines all the backups into one and then an erasure code for them, simply one code that erases all the backups. So I will get the code for, let's say, Omega and for all the Omega backups at the same time. After I've asked "What will happen if I give this," I will give the code and then I will say, "What are you experiencing?" They often describe computer whirring, things erasing, explosions inside, all sorts of interesting things.

I've had some therapists come back and say, "My Lord, I had never said anything about robots; she said something about robots vaporizing."

I remember one therapist who'd been with me in several hypnosis workshops and consulted with me about a crisis MPD situation. I told her to inquire about Alpha, Beta, Delta, Theta. She did. She got back to me saying, "Yeah, I got an indication it's there. What is it?" I said, "I'm not going to tell you. Go back and inquire about some of this."

We set an appointment for a week or so hence. She got back with me and said, "I asked what Theta was and she said, 'psychic killers'. I asked her what Delta was and she said 'killers'." Okay.

So I told her about some of this stuff for a two-hour consult. She called back and she said, "This seemed too fantastic. I heard this and I thought, 'Has Cory been working too hard?'" she said, I'm embarrassed to admit it, but she said, "I held you in high professional regard, but this just sounded so off in the twilight zone that I really thought, 'Is he having a nervous breakdown or something?'" She said, "But I respected you enough to ask about this." She said, "I asked another MPD patient and she didn't have any of this."

So in this patient she started describing things and how she worked, for example, with an erasure and she was describing things like robots vaporizing and kinds of things. She said, "I hadn't told her about any of these things."

Well, here's the problem. There are different layers and I think some of them are designed to keep us going in circles forever. They figured we probably, in most cases, wouldn't get below the alters which they purposefully created.

The way you create Manchurian Candidates is you divide the mind. It's part of what the Intelligence Community wanted to look at. If you're going to get an assassin, you're going to get somebody to go do something, you divide the mind.

It fascinates me about cases like the assassination of Robert Kennedy, where Bernard Diamond, on examining Sirhan Sirhan found that he had total amnesia of the killing of Robert Kennedy, but under hypnosis could remember it. But despite suggestions he would be able to consciously remember, could not remember a thing after was out of hypnosis. I'd love to examine Sirhan Sirhan.

It appears that below this we've got some other layers. One is called "Green Programming" it appears. Isn't it interesting that the doctor's name is Dr. Green?

One of the questions in a way that does not contaminate is after I've identified some of this stuff is there and they've given me a few right answers about what some of it is, "If there were a doctor associated with this programming and his name were a color, you know, like Dr. Chartreuse or something, if his name were a color, what color would the color be?"

Now once in a while I've had some other colors mentioned in about three or four patients that I felt were trying to dissimulate in some way and I don't really believe had this. In one case I got another color and I found out later it was a doctor whose name was a color who was being trained by Dr. Green almost thirty years ago and he supervised part of the programming of this woman under this doctor.

I remember one woman couldn't come up with anything. No alter would speak up with anything. I said, "Okay," and we went on to some other material. About two minutes later she said, "Green. Do you mean Dr. Green?"

We found this all over. There appears to be some Green Programming below that and I suspect that you get down to fewer and more central programs the deeper you go.

Well, all Green Programming is Ultra-Green and the Green Tree. Cabalistic mysticism is mixed all into this. If you're going to work with this you need to pick up a couple of books on the Cabala. One is by a man named Dion Fortune called "Qabala" with a "q," Dion Fortune. Another is by Ann Williams-Heller and it's called "The Kabbalah".

I knew nothing about the Cabala.[33] It was interesting. A patient had sat in my waiting area, got there considerably early and drew a detailed multicolored Cabalistic Tree over two years ago. It took me two months to figure out what it was. Finally, showing it to somebody else who said, "You know? That looks an awful lot like the Cabala Tree" and that rang a bell with some esoterica in an old book and I dug it out. That was the background of Dr. Green.

Now the interesting thing about the Green Tree is his original name was Greenbaum. What does "greenbaum" mean in German? Green Tree, Ultra-Tree and the Green Tree.

I've also had patients who didn't appear to know that his original name was Greenbaum, volunteered that there were parts inside named Mr. Greenbaum.

Now let me give you some information about parts inside that may be helpful to you if you're going to inquire about these things, because my experience is one part will give you some information and either run dry or get defensive or scared and stop. and so you punt and you make an end run and you come around the other direction, you find another part. I'll tell you several parts to ask for and ask if there's a part by this name.

And, by the way, when I'm screening patients and fiddling around with this, I throw in a bunch of spurious ones and ask, "Is there a part inside by this name and by that name" as a check on whether or not it appears genuine. For example,

---

[33] It is interesting that the new "cult" of choice among many media personalities is called "Kaballah." This group sells courses that offer "total fulfillment in life" plus "control over the physical laws of nature." The founder of the sect, Philip Berg, who changed his name from Feivel Gruberger, was a Brooklyn insurance agent before turning kabbalistic teacher and author. It is said that their "business model" has been adapted from Scientology – i.e. hard sell. I think it is more sinister than that, based on the information in the Greenbaum Lecture.

"In addition to the core," I ask, "is there a part inside named Wisdom?" Wisdom is a part of the Cabalistic Tree. Wisdom, I've often found, will be helpful and give you a lot of information. "Is there a part inside named Diana?" I mean I may throw in all sorts of things. "Is there a part inside named Zelda?" I've never encountered one yet! Just to see what kind of answers we get. I try to do this carefully. Diana is a part that, in the Cabalistic system, is associated with a part called the Foundation. You will be fascinated to know that.

Remember the Process Church? Roman Polanski's wife, Sharon Tate, was killed by the Manson Family who were associated with the Process Church? A lot of prominent people in Hollywood were associated and then they went underground, the books say, in about seventy-eight and vanished?

Well, they're alive and well in southern Utah. We have a thick file in the Utah Department of Public Safety documenting that they moved to southern Utah, north of Monument Valley, bought a movie ranch in the desert, renovated it, expanded it, built a bunch of buildings there, carefully monitored so that very few people go out of there and no one can get in and changed their name. A key word in their name is "Foundation". The Foundation. There are some other words.

The Foundation is part of the Tree. So you can ask, "Is there something inside known as The Foundation?" I might ask other things to throw people off. "Is there something known as the Sub-Basement?" Well, maybe they'll conceive of something. Or "Is there something known as the Walls?" There are a variety of questions you can come up with, to sort of screen some things.

I've also found that there will often be a part called "Black Master," a part called "Master Programmer," and that there will be computer operators inside.

How many of you have come into computer things in patients? There will typically be computer operators: Computer Operator Black, Computer Operator Green, Computer Operator Purple. Sometimes they'll have numbers instead, sometimes they'll be called Systems Information Directors. You can find out the head one of those. There'll be a source of some information for you. I will ask inside, "Is there a part inside named Dr. Green?" You'll find that there are, if they have this kind of programming, in my experience.

Usually with a little work and reframing, you can turn them and help them to realize that they were really a child-part who's playing a role and they had no choice then, but they do now. You know, they played their role very, very well, but they don't have to continue to play it with you because they're safe here and in fact, "If the Cult simply found out that you talked to me, that you had shared information with me, you tell me what would they do to you?"

Emphasize that the only way out is through you and that they need to cooperate and share information and help you and that you'll help them.

So all these parts can give you various information. Now they have tried to protect this very carefully. Let me give you an example with Ultra-Green.

I used to think this programming was only in bloodline people. I've discovered it in non-bloodline people, but it's a bit different. They don't want it to be just the same. I don't think you'll find deep things like Ultra-Green and probably not even Green Programming with non-bloodline people. But let me tell you something that I discovered first in a non-bloodline and then in a bloodline.

We were going along and a patient was close to getting well, approaching final integration in a non-bloodline and she suddenly started hallucinating and her fingers were becoming hammers and other things like that. So I used an affect-

bridge and we went back and we found that what happened was that they gave suggestions, that if she ever got well to a certain point she would go crazy.

The way they did this was they strapped her down and they gave her LSD when she was eight years old. When she began hallucinating they inquired about the nature of the hallucinations so they could utilize them in good Ericsonian fashion and build on them and then combine the drug-effect with powerful suggestions. "If you ever get to this point you will go crazy. If you ever get fully integrated and get well you will go crazy like this and will be locked up in an institution for the rest of your life."

They gave those suggestions vigorously and repetitively. Finally they introduced other suggestions that, "Rather than have this happen, it would be easier to just kill yourself."

In a bloodline patient then, as I began inquiring about deep material, the patient started to experience similar symptoms. We went back and we found the identical things were done to her.

This was called the "Green Bomb". B-O-M-B. Lots of interesting internal consistencies like that play on words with Dr. Greenbaum, his original name.

Now in this case it was done to her at age nine for the first time and then only hers was different. Hers was a suggestion for amnesia. "If you ever remember anything about Ultra-Green and the Green Tree you will go crazy. You will become a vegetable and be locked up forever." Then finally the suggestions added, "And it'll be easier to just kill yourself than have that happen to you, if you ever remember it."

At age twelve then, three years later, they used what sounds like a [Sodium] Amytol interview to try to breach the amnesia and find out if they could. They couldn't. So then they strapped her down again, and gave her something to kind of paralyze her body, gave her LSD, an even bigger dose and reinforced all the suggestions.

Did a similar thing at the age of sixteen.

So these are some of the kind of booby traps you run into. There are a number of cases where they combined powerful drug effects like this with suggestions to keep us from discovering some of this deeper level stuff.

What's the bottom?

Your guess is as good as mine but I can tell you that I've had a lot of therapists who were stymied with these cases who were going nowhere. In fact someone here that I told some basic information about this to in Ohio a couple of months ago said it opened all sorts of things up in a patient who'd been going nowhere. That's a common thing.

I think that we can move down to deeper levels and if we deal with some of the deeper level stuff it may destroy all the stuff above it. But we don't even know that yet.

In some of the patients I'm working with we have pretty much dealt with a lot of the top-level stuff. I'll tell you how we've done some of that.

We'll take and erase one system like Omega. Then we will have a huge abreaction of all the memories and feelings in a fractionated abreaction associated with those parts. I typically find I'll say to them, "Now that we've done this are there any other memories and feelings that any parts that were Omega still have?" The answer's usually "No". At that point I will say, "I usually find at this point in time the majority, if not all, of those parts that used to be Omega no longer feel a desire or need to be different, realizing that you split off originally by them and want to go home to Mary and become one with her again." I use the concept often now – which came from a patient – of going home and becoming one with her. "Going back from whence you came" is another phrase I'll use with them. "Are there any Omega parts inside who do not feel comfortable with that or have reservations or concerns about that?" If there are we talk to them. We deal with them. A few may not integrate. My experience is most of the time they'll integrate and we may integrate twenty-five parts at once in a polyfragmented complex MPD.

I think it is vitally important to abreact the feelings before you go on. Also for many patients it hasn't seemed to matter the order we go in but I've found a couple where it has. If it doesn't seem to matter I'll typically go Omega, then Delta because they have more violence potential, then Gamma to get rid of the self-deception stuff. What I will do before I just assume anything and do that, is once we've done Omega and showed them that success can occur and something can happen and they feel relief after, I will say to them, "I want to ask the core – through the fingers – is there a specific order in which programs must be erased?" You know maybe it doesn't matter but most of the time I found "No". There are cases where we found "Yes".

I recommend doing one or two or three of those because they'll produce relief and a sense of optimism in the patient. But then I would recommend starting to probe for the deeper level things and getting their input and recommendations about the order in which we go. Question?

Q: What has been the typical age and typical gender of this type of person?

Dr. H: I know of this being found in men and women. Most of the patients I know with MPD ritual abuse that are being treated are women, however. I know of some men being treated where we've found this.

Awhile back I was talking to a small group of therapists somewhere. I told them about some of this. In the middle of talking about it all the color drained out of one social worker's face and she obviously had a reaction and I asked her about and she said, "I'm working with a five-year-old boy," and she said, "Just in the last few weeks he was saying something about a Dr. Green." I went on a little further and I mentioned some of these things and she just shook her head again. I said, "What's going on?" She said, "He's been spontaneously telling me about robots and about Omega."

I think you will find variations of this and that they've changed it, probably every few years and maybe somewhat regionally to throw us off in various ways but that certain basics and fundamentals will probably be there.

I have seen this in people up into their forties including people whose parents were very, very high in the CIA, other sorts of things like that. I've had some that were originally part of the Monarch Project which is the name of the government Intelligence project. Question in the back?

Q: I'm still not grasping how one starts, how you find out how to erase. How do you get that information?

Dr. H: I would say, "I want the core, if necessary, using the telepathic communication ability you have to read minds," because they believe in that kind of stuff, so I'll use it... I was trained in Ericsonian stuff, "...to obtain for me the erasure code of all Omega programs. When you've done so, I want the yes-finger to float up." Then I ask them to tell it to me. "Are there backups for

Omega programs?" "Yes." "Okay? How many backups are there?" "Six," they say, let's say. It's different numbers. "Is there an erasure code for all the backup programs?" "No." "Is there an erasure code that combines all the backups into one?" "Yes." "Obtain that code for me and when you've go it give me the yes-signal again." It can move almost that fast in some cases where there's not massive resistance. Question?

Q: Yes, can you tell me what you know about the risks to the therapist? (Laughter.)

Dr. H: You would have to ask.

Q: Yeah, I'd like to know that. What kind of data do you have given that you've had contact with large numbers of people. Not just threats but also any injury, any family problems that have arisen. That's one question. A second one is are you aware of anybody that you've treated – or others – with this level of dissociation and trauma that have recovered? Integrated? Whole and happy?

Dr. H: Okay, I have one non-bloodline multiple, complex multiple who had this kind of programming where they have a lot of access to the patient as neighbors and where the doctor, by the way, you'll find physicians heavily involved. They've encouraged their own to go to medical school, to prescribe drugs to take care of their own, to get access to medical technology and be above suspicion. There have been a couple, in fact, in Utah who've been nailed now. We now in Utah have two full time ritual-abuse investigators with state-wide jurisdiction under the Attorney General's Office to do nothing but investigate this.

[Applause]

In a poll done in the State of Utah in January by the major newspaper and television station, they found that ninety percent of Utahans believe that ritual abuse is genuine and real. Not all of them believe it's a frequent occurrence but some of that was imparted from two years of work by the Governor Commission on Ritual Abuse, interviewing, talking, meeting people, gathering data.

Now when people say, by the way, "There's no evidence. They've never found a body," that's baloney. They found a body in Idaho of a child.

They've had a case last summer that was convicted on first-degree murder charges, two people that the summer before that were arrested where the teen-aged girl's finger and head were in the refrigerator and they were convicted of first-degree murder in Detroit.

There have been cases and bodies.

Back to risk. I know of no therapist who's been harmed. But patients inform us that *there will come a future time* where we could be at risk of being assassinated by patients who've been programmed to kill at a certain time anyone that they've told and any member of their own family who's not active. If that would come about is speculative. Who knows for sure? Maybe, but I don't think it's entirely without risk. A question in the back?

Q: It seems to me that there seems to be some similarity between these kinds of programming and those people who claim that they've been abducted by spaceships and have had themselves physically probed and reprogrammed and all of that sort of thing. Since Cape Canaveral is across the Florida peninsula from me and I don't think that they've reported any spaceships lately, I was just wondering is there any sort of relationship between this and that?

Dr. H: I'll share my speculation, that comes from others really. I've not dealt with any of those people. However, I know a therapist that I know and trust and respect who I've informed about all this a couple of years ago and has found it in a lot of patients and so on, who is firmly of the belief that those people are in fact ritual-abuse victims who have been programmed with that sort of thing to destroy all their credibility.

If somebody's coming in and reporting abduction by a flying saucer who's going to believe them on anything else in the future?

Also as a kind of thing that can be pointed to and said, "This is as ridiculous as that."

All I know is that I recently had a consult, a telephone consult, with a therapist where I had been instructing her about some of this kind of stuff. When we were consulting at one point in the fifth or sixth interview she said, "By the way, do you know anything about this topic?" I said, "Well, not really" and shared with her what I shared with you. I said, "If it were me being with this guy…" that she'd been seeing for a couple of months, I said, "I would ask inside for the core to take control of finger-signals and inquire about Alpha, Beta, Delta, Theta." She proceeded to do all that, got back to me a week later and said, "Boy, were you on target. There is a part inside named Dr. Green. There's this kind of programming."

Q: What's the difference between this kind of program and cult-type abuse and Satanic abuse in the kind of cults with the candles and the…

Dr. H: This type of programming will be done in the cults with the candles and all the rest. My impression is this is simply done in people where they have great access to them or they're bloodline and their parents are in it and they can be raised in it from an early age. If they are bloodline they are the chosen generation. If not, they're expendable and they are expected to die and not get well.

There will be booby traps in your way if they aren't bloodline people that when they get well they will kill themselves. I'll tell you just a little about that.

My belief is that some people that have ritual abuse and don't have this have been ritually abused but they may be may be part of a non-mainstream group. The Satanism comes in the overall philosophy overriding all of this.

People say, "What's the purpose of it?" My best guess is that the purpose of it is that they want *an army of Manchurian Candidates*, tens of thousands of mental robots who will do prostitution, do child pornography, smuggle drugs, engage in international arms smuggling, do snuff films, all sorts of very lucrative things and do their bidding and eventually the megalomaniacs at the top believe they'll create a Satanic Order that will rule the world.

One last question. Then I'll give you couple of details and we need to shift gears.

Q: You have suggested and implied that at some point at a *high level of the U.S. Government there was support* of this kind of thing. I know we're short of time, but could you just say a few words about the documentation that may exist for that suggestion?

Dr. H: There isn't great documentation of it. It comes from victims who are imperiled witnesses.

The interesting thing is how many people have described the same scenario and how many people that we have worked with who have had relatives in NASA, in the CIA and in the Military, including very high-ups in the Military.

I can tell you that a friend and colleague of mine who has probably the equivalent of half the table space on that far side of the room filled with boxes with declassified documents from mind-control research done in the past which has been able to be declassified over a considerable – couple of decades – period and has read more government documents about mind control than anyone else, has a brief that has literally been sent in the past week and a half asking for all information to be declassified about the Monarch Project for us to try to find out more.

Now let me just mention something about some of the stuff that my experience is in several patients now that you may run into late in the process. I know I'm throwing a lot at you in a hurry. Some of it is completely foreign and some of you may think, "Gosh, could any of this be true?" Just ask. Find out in your patients and you may be lucky and there isn't any of this. Somewhere at a deep level you may run into some things like this. Let me describe to you, if I can find my pen, the system in one patient. One patient I had treated for quite a while, a non-bloodline person.

We had done what appeared to be successful work and reached final integration. She came back to me early last year and said she was symptomatic with some things. I started inquiring. I found a part there we'd integrated. The part basically said, "There was other stuff that I couldn't tell you about and you integrated me and so I had to split off."

I had done some inquiring about things like Alpha, Beta as a routine part of it and found they were there and I said to this part, "Why didn't you tell me about this stuff?" She said, "Well, we gave you some hints but they went right over your head." Says, "I'm sorry, but we know that you didn't know enough to help us but now we know you can."

So the stuff started coming out. It was interesting. She described the overall system – if I can remember it now – as being like this. The circle represented harm to the body, a system of alters whose primary purpose was to hurt her including symptoms like Munchhausen's, self-mutilation, other kinds of things. Each of the triangles represented still another different system. She said, "With the exception of me," this one part, "you dealt with the whole circle with the work that we did before but you didn't touch the rest of the stuff."

Okay. In the middle of all this was still another system consisting of the Cabalistic Tree, which some of you are aware, looks approximately like this with lines in between and so on and so forth. There's a rough approximation. That represented another system.

Then once we got past that she implied that this entire thing was somehow encompassed by, what do you call it, an hourglass. I kept thinking we were at final integration then I'd find some other parts.

This person had an eagle-eye husband that was watching for certain things that we found to be reliable indicators. So often I would get evidence of dissociation within a few days. It would suddenly be picked up. You know, what we found was I continued to find evidence of dissociation and I'd find parts. Finally this part, as I got angry with him and said, "Why when I give these ideomotor inquiries am I getting lied to?" This part said, "Because you don't understand. You're going to get us all killed."

We started talking and then she basically said, "It's been programmed so that if you succeed and think you've succeeded, you will fail. They build it in as a way to laugh at you, that if you ever get us integrated, we will die."

Here's what she said, this part said, "I'm one of twelve disciples," and I've seen this in others, twelve disciples within this hourglass each of whom had to memorize a disciple-lesson which were basic Satanic kind of premises, philosophies of life like "be good to those who hurt you, hate those who are nice to you," on and on and on. There may be two or three sentences like that associated with each that they had to memorize them. They said, "We are like grains of sand falling and when the last grain of sand falls, there's Death." I said, "Is Death a part?" "Yes. When the last grain of sand falls the Sleeping Giant awakens." The Sleeping Giant was Death, who was then to kill them on Day-One or Day-Six after awakening unless certain things were followed and we did some of those.

Well we also found Death had a sister as a backup, used with mirrors to create the sister part. We had to get past and deal with that too.

Death had certain things that they said had to be done to integrate. I started to say, "Oh, come on, they lied to you before." She said, "Wait a minute. This what they said you'd say. They said that no doctor would ever believe that they had to go these extremes to get us well and that's part of the reason they'd fail." I said, "Well, tell me, tell me again." She said, "I have to be dressed all in red. I have to have Demerol onboard, have taken Demerol. A code has to be given and it has to be in a room that's totally dark. It has to happen on Day-One or Day-Six after this part's been awakened."

I said what I'd have to lose? I had a psychiatrist give her a little Demerol. We used the code. My office didn't have any windows anyway. It was pretty easy. Oh, and there had to be four, I think, candles lit. Well, fine. So we did it and everything went well. Maybe it would have gone well if we hadn't done it, but I decided not to take the chance and to trust the patient maybe.

Well, so we go on and then we find another part. There's Death And Destruction, another backup also with a sister that we had to get through. In fact, I think there were two backups there.

Interestingly, the very last part was an extremely nice part, made especially that way so that they wouldn't want to lose them because they would be so adorable and so loving and so sweet that they wouldn't want to maybe get rid of them. Then we found that she continued to have these feelings with this last part left now of darkness and blackness inside.

What did we find? A curtain. She said, "They assumed that if you ever got to this point, you would," and along the way, by the way, we had encountered this stuff about the LSD stuff, the Green Bomb programming. The message was that she said, "There is a curtain behind which are the remaining feelings and memories, but it can't be opened from the middle. It's like a stage curtain. It has to opened this way," that it can't be opened. They assumed that you would try to deal with all the feelings. That can't be opened until you've dealt with that last part and they've integrated. So far it looks like we've got integration that's holding.

So I found Death And Destruction and the Hourglass in non-bloodline. "The Tree and the Hourglass," this patient informed me, "were made of sand because we were meant to die. We're expendable. We're the unchosen generation."

I've heard variously that it's crystals or blood that fills the Hourglass in bloodline people.

By the way, you can do real simple things like turn the Hourglass on its side so nothing can fall out, so time stands still to be able to do certain kinds of work. Spread the grains of sand on the seashore so that they can't be numbered and the time will not be counted. Got that idea from a ritual-abuse victim who had seen some of this kind of programming done that another therapist was seeing.

So those would be just a few other hints about things that may be helpful or meaningful. We're talking about very intensive things and at deep levels to me this give us two things.

One thing it gives to me is hope because it gets to material and it makes progress like nothing else we've ever seen with these people who have it.

The second thing it does for me is it demoralizes me, too, because although three years ago I had a pretty good idea about the extent and breadth of what they'd done to these victims, I had no real appreciation for the depth and breadth and intensity of what they'd done.

I want to come back to the other question over here now. The other question is how many of them can get well?

We don't know. In most things in the mental health profession we accept two-thirds of the patients are going to improve, maybe seventy percent. There's very little we can get everybody well. I think one of the sad things we have to face is that many of these patients will probably never be well.

My personal belief is that if they are being messed with their only hope of getting well is if they can somehow get out of contact.

Now I know patients who've gone to other states and simply had deep-level alters pick up the phone and call and said, "This is our new address and phone number" so that they could be picked up locally. I mean in an inpatient unit for an extended period of time. If they are in a Cult from their area and they are still being monitored and messed with, my own personal opinion is we can't get them well and can't offer more than humanitarian caring and supportiveness.

Lots of therapists do not like to hear that. That's my opinion. I believe that if somehow they're lucky enough to be wealthy enough to have protection, to have somehow gotten away in some way and we can work with them without being messed with, that they have a chance to reach some semblance of normality and livability with enough intensive work.

My own personal belief is I don't think anybody with this kind of programming is well in this country yet. There are some who are well along the way. I've got a couple who are well along in their work and have done a tremendous amount, but they're clearly not well yet.

Q: Could you speculate on the relationship between this stuff and the fantasy games that have been proliferating, Dungeons and Dragons and that sort of thing?

Dr. H: Well, there are a lot of things out there to cue people. You want to see a great movie, interesting movie, to cue people? Go see "Trancers II." You can rent it in your video shop. Came out last fall.

One night in sheer desperation for something at the video store, you know? Nine o'clock on Friday night. Everything's gone. I rented a couple of movies and one of them is that. Fascinating. They're talking about Green World Order. Yes, "Trancers II." And who is the production company? Full Moon Productions. I couldn't see much cuing in "Trancers I," but who's the production company in "Trancers I"? Alter Productions. There are lots of things around that are cuing.

There's an interesting person in the late sixties who talked about the Illuminati. Have any of you ever heard of the Illuminati with regard to the Cult? Had a patient bring that up to me just about exactly two years ago. We've now had other stuff come out from other patients. Appears to be the name of the international world leadership. There appear to be Illuminatic Councils (?) in several parts of the world and one internationally. The name of the international leadership of the Cult supposedly. Is this true? Well, I don't know. It's interesting we're getting some people who are trying to work without cuing who are saying some very similar things.

There was an old guy in Hollywood in the late sixties who talked about the infiltration of Hollywood by the Illuminati. Certainly what some patients have said is all of this spook stuff, horror stuff, possession and everything else that's been popularized in the last twenty years in Hollywood is in order to soften up the public so that when a Satanic world order takes over, everyone will have been desensitized to so many of these things, plus to continually cue lots of people out there. Is that true? Well, I can't definitely tell you that it is.

What I can say is I now believe that ritual-abuse programming is widespread, is systematic, is very organized from highly esoteric information which is published nowhere, has not been on any book or talk show, that we have found all around this country and at least one foreign country. Let's take a couple of quick questions and we need to get on to other material. Yes?

Q: Do you have any techniques for decreasing your level of uncertainty that a patient is or is not being still tampered with, "messed with," as you said?

Dr. H: Just that I would ask several of the parts I've inquired about, Core, Diana, Wisdom, Master Programmer, several parts inside I would ask about these sorts of things and I will keep asking it. As you do additional work and get a bit further, I would ask again to find out. In the back?

Q: I wonder if you've heard or you know of the Martin Luther Bloodline?

Dr. H: The what?

Q: Martin Luther Bloodline?

Dr. H: I know nothing about Martin Luther Bloodline. I'll give you one other quick tip. Ask him about an identification code. There's an identification code that people have. It will involve their birth date. It may involve places where they were programmed and it will usually involve a number in there that will be their birth order, like zero-two if they were second-born. It will usually involve a number that represents the number of generations in the Cult, if they are bloodlines. I've seen up to twelve now, twelve generations.

Q: I have seen a lot of the things you've been describing today in several patients. I wanted to ask you a question about the Seven Systems. You mentioned something about systems here. Are there Seven Systems?

Dr. H: There has been that described in some patients, yes, the Seven Systems.

Q: Could you say what that is or a little diagram?

Dr. H: I don't think we know enough to know what it is, honestly. I think it may have to do with Seven Cabalistic Trees.

Q: Have you ever had any evidence where any of these people have been tagged and there have been anything of their body-parts that might be related to this, private parts in particular?

Dr. H: Well, there are certainly people that have had tattoos, that have had a variety of other kinds of things, some of which have been, you know, documented in cases, but I mean to say, well, maybe they did that to themselves or had it done consciously to really prove something, not that occurs to right off the bat. Let me just take this one last question back and we need to go on to other material because we're never going to get through it all. I'll just ask you to hold your question.

Q: It's not a question but I wanted to say for myself, personally, and perhaps for others here as well, I wanted to thank you very sincerely for taking this time to come forward.

[Applause]

Dr. H: A dear friend who's one of the top people in the field, who I know has had death threats, but I know struggled for professional credibility in believing in MPD and was harshly criticized for even believing in that ten and fifteen years ago, and struggled to a point of professional credibility. I think in his heart of hearts he knows it's true, but he will say things like, "I wouldn't be surprised to find tomorrow it was an international conspiracy and I wouldn't be surprised to find tomorrow that it is an urban myth and rumor."

He tries to stay right on the fence and the reason is because it's controversial, because there is a campaign underway saying these [are] all false memories induced by, along with incest and everything else, by "Oprah" and by books like "The Courage to Heal" and by naive therapists using hypnosis. It's controversial.

My personal opinion has come to be if they're going to kill me, they're going to kill me. There's going to be an awful lot of information that's been put away that'll go to investigative reporters and multiple investigative agencies, if it happens, and an awful lot of people like you, I hope, that if I ever have an accident, will be pushing for a very large-scale investigation.

I think we have to stand up as some kind of moral conscience at some point and I tried to wait until we had gotten enough verification from independent places to have some real confidence that this was widespread.

I know we've gone like a house afire to try to pack as much as I could in for you. I hope it's given you some things to think about and some new ideas and I appreciate being with you.

[Long sustained applause]

Now, let's go back to just a couple of things from the Greenbaum lecture that I would like to highlight for the reader. The first is the following remark made by Dr. Hammond:

> I have seen this in people up into their forties including people whose parents were very, very high in the CIA, other sorts of things like that. I've had some that were originally part of the Monarch Project which is the name of the government Intelligence project.

While there are a number of CIA mind control research projects that have been confirmed in Senate Hearings, I haven't been able to find similar confirmation of the alleged "Monarch Project". However, there is circumstantial evidence for the existence of this type of work.

New Orleans therapist Valerie Wolf brought two of her patients before the President's Committee on Human Radiation Experiments on March 15, 1995 in Washington D.C. The astonishing testimony made by these two women included accounts of German doctors, torture, drugs, electroshock, hypnosis and rape, besides being exposed to an undetermined amount of radiation. Both Wolf and her patients stated they recovered the memories of this CIA program without regression or hypnosis techniques.

The most incriminating statement to date made by a government official as to the possible existence of Project MONARCH was extracted by Anton Chaitkin, a writer for the publication, *The New Federalist*. When former CIA Director William Colby was asked directly, "What about monarch?" he replied angrily and ambiguously, "We stopped that between the late 1960's and the early 1970's." Suffice it to say that society, in its apparent state of cognitive dissonance, is generally in denial of the overwhelming evidence of this widespread, nefarious conspiracy to experiment upon literally thousands of human beings, undoubtedly, mostly American. This, of course, brings us to ask a few questions about the goals of such a project. Let's look at another thing mentioned by Dr. Hammond:

> Back to risk. I know of no therapist who's been harmed. But patients inform us that *there will come a future time* where we could be at risk of being assassinated by patients who've been programmed to kill at a certain time anyone that they've told and any member of their own family who's not active. If that would come about is speculative. Who knows for sure? Maybe, but I don't think it's entirely without risk.

"There will come a future time..." At the present point in time, as I am editing this book for hardcopy publication, having spent the past several years publishing our *Signs of the Times* (http://sott.net) news report on the fascist takeover of America, I wonder if we are not already living in that "future time"? If so, perhaps we ought to carefully examine some of the details Dr. Hammond has elicited from his patients:

> Alphas appear to represent general programming, the first kind of things put in.
>
> Betas appear to be sexual programs. For example, how to perform oral sex in a certain way, how to perform sex in rituals, having to do with producing child pornography, directing child pornography, prostitution.
>
> Deltas are killers trained in how to kill in ceremonies.
>
> There'll also be some self-harm stuff mixed in with that, assassination and killing. Thetas are called psychic killers.
>
> You know, I had never in my life heard those two terms paired together. I'd never heard the words "psychic killers" put together, but when you have people in different states, including therapists inquiring and asking, "What is Theta," and patients say to them, "Psychic killers," it tends to make one a believer that certain things are very systematic and very widespread.
>
> This comes from their belief in psychic sorts of abilities and powers, including their ability to psychically communicate with "mother" including their ability to psychically cause somebody to develop a brain aneurysm and die.
>
> It also is a more future-oriented kind of programming.

Then there's Omega. I usually don't include that word when I say my first question about this or any part inside that knows about Alpha, Beta, Delta, Theta because Omega will shake them even more.

Omega has to do with self-destruct programming. Alpha and Omega, the beginning and the end. This can include self-mutilation as well as killing-themselves programming.

The Cassiopaeans had a few things to say about Greenbaum programming.

August 17, 1996

Q: (T) Are you aware of the Greenbaum effect? Dr. Greenbaum and his mind control experiments, that we've been looking at lately?

A: Yes.

Q: (L) Is what's said there factual? I won't say true, but is it factual? Most of it?

A: Close.

Q: (T) Okay, the question is, is the fellow that just shot three professors in San Diego, I think it was, at a University, before they read his thesis, because he was afraid they would throw his thesis away, and make it look bad, and flunk him. Was he a Greenbaum-type subject?

A: Yes.

Q: (T) Why did they turn him "on" at that point?

A: Not correct concept. What if: those programmed in the so called "Greenbaum" projects are preprogrammed to "go off" all at once, and some "malfunction," and go off early?

July 31, 1999

Q: (L) Okay, various folks are now saying that Dr. Mengele of Nazi fame is the same person as Dr. Green of Greenbaum programming fame.

A: No.

Q: (L) Did Mengele go to South America and die there as reported?

A: Yes.

Q: (L) The Greenbaum material says that there was a Jewish boy brought to America and trained as a doctor who became this infamous Dr. Greenbaum. Is that true?

A: No. "Green" is an alias, or more accurately, a pseudonym for multiple persons engaged in mind control efforts.

July 22, 2000

Q: (L) I had a call from Vincent Bridges[34] who informed me that *The Wave Series* was really creating a stir. It seems that he [claims that he] has had a connection to this Dr. Hammond of the Greenbaum lecture fame, and also had a

---

[34] A self-proclaimed "Enochian Magician" who advertises himself as "author, lecturer and general pagan gadfly, is one of the pioneers of psycho-acoustic therapy, a trauma abreaction technique using light and sound entrainment of brain frequencies." The story of our interaction with Bridges is told in *Petty Tyrants* and *Facing the Unknown*. Mr. Bridges may very well be a Greenbaum victim whose job is to trigger programs in other victims.

number of exchanges with Andrija Puharich, and it is Vincent's contention that the UFO phenomenon, the alien abduction phenomenon, and the many and varied other things we talk about and study and discuss, are a product of super advanced technological, human controlled mind-programming projects using the technology of Puharich and Tesla. Yes, it is supposed to be so advanced that they can not only read minds and can control minds, but that it is, in the end, merely human engineered programming. Is he, even in part, correct?

A: Well, there are elements of the phenomenon which may be connected to human, 3rd density STS engineering, but by and large, this is not the case.

Q: (L) He also said that it was his opinion, that the center of the web of all of this mind programming conspiracy, is in Tyler, Texas. Is that correct?[35]

A: The what?!?

Q: (L) Well, what about the center of the human branch of the programming conspiracy?

A: We feel that Vincent needs to recharge his batteries a bit.[36]

Q: (L) He also said that the area we are living is the center of a particular programming experiment, something like Nazi/Black magick cultists or something like that.

A: Better not to get too carried away. Remember, the root of all "negative" energies directed at 3rd density STS subjects, coming from 4th density, is essentially the same. [...]

Suggest a review of the transcripts relating to the situation in Nazi Germany for better understanding here. [...]

The concept of a "master race" put forward by the Nazis was merely a 4th density STS effort to create a physical vehicle with the correct frequency resonance vibration for 4th density STS souls to occupy in 3rd density. It was also a "trial run" for planned events in what you perceive to be your future.

Q: (L) You mean with a strong STS frequency so they can have a "vehicle" in third density, so to speak?

A: Correct. Frequency resonance vibration! Very important.

Q: (L) So, that is why they are programming and experimenting? And all these folks running around who some think are "programmed", could be individuals who are raising their nastiness levels high enough to accommodate the truly negative STS fourth density – sort of like walk-ins or something, only not nice ones?

A: You do not have very many of those present yet, but that was, and still is, the plan of some of the 4th density STS types.

With that pleasant though, let us continue.

---

[35] The "Tyler Texas" connection was a theory cooked up by murderer Ira Einhorn, who did, in fact, work with Andrija Puharich. Before Ira's recapture, after being on the run for many years, Vincent Bridges frequently identified with him, claiming that Andrija Puharich told him "you remind me of Ira." It seems that Bridges modeled his life on that of Ira Einhorn. I discuss the Einhorn case in detail in *Almost Human*.

[36] This remark was particularly interesting in that it almost suggested that Bridges was "mechanical" in some way. Later events proved this to be correct.

HE HIDETH MY SOUL IN THE CLEFT OF THE ROCK

He hideth my soul in the cleft of the rock
that shadows a dry thirsty land...
He hideth my life in the depths of His love,
and covers me there with His hand.[37]

Writing this segment as background for the events that follow has been extremely difficult; but it is necessary. In my other writings, when I have talked about my personal experiences, I have generally avoided some of these details for obvious reasons – it is painful to remember.

Additionally, I am always concerned that the reader will be either bored or turned off by personal data, and I have tried to cover only the salient points that will come up again later in a general discussion, while also making them as brief as possible. However, my experience has shown me that many of the things that are recounted herein are not unique to me.

As we left me in the last episode, I had decided that maybe having a brain was not such a bad thing even if the "faith trip" frowns on using it to any great extent, other than offering it up as a sacrifice to be hypnotized so it can be twisted like a pretzel and used to justify theological nonsense by acts of cerebral derring-do.

I remember visiting a friend of mine at her office one day, and there was a sign posted on her desk saying: *God doesn't create junk.* That really struck me in a funny way since I was right at the point of struggling to be free of the hypnosis that says the human being is incapable of using his brain to discover or understand God, and must therefore use only faith and, of course, the Scriptures – whatever they may be in the varying faith trips.

How many times had I heard sermons on the subject of the brain – the mind – being solely the instrument of Satan? Of course, when talking about the "Predator's Mind", we see how this is one side of the coin. But, nevertheless, it was pretty clear to me that whatever existed, existed within the mind of God – whoever or whatever he/she/it might be – and therefore the human mind, as a ray of the Divine Mind, certainly must have a function in finding him/her/it.

Reading that little sign brought me face to face with the realization that I had bought so completely into the faith trip that I had actually become afraid to think. I had become embarrassed by my own tendency to ask questions, and had been made to feel extraordinary guilt for my capacity to use logical analysis.

---

[37] Christian hymn by Fanny J. Crosby. It was always a favorite of mine, and though I have learned that Christianity – as it has been promulgated for 2000 years – is not the original Christianity, I still find some useful concepts buried there like little gems in the mud.

One of the standard hypnotic suggestions of the Way of the Monk is that no thinking is allowed. Thinking leads to questions, and the unwritten 11th commandment is "Thou Shalt Not Question!"

With sudden clarity it dawned on me that obviously part of our creation exists in the fact that we *do* have brains – amazing instruments – for a reason. (I know that the reader must be pretty sure by now that I am the slowest learner of all time!) But, anyway, this self-evident fact that God had given us brains *for a reason* gave birth to the next thought: shouldn't we be using them to *discover* God, rather than to justify obvious nonsense about God that has been passed down as tradition by folks who clearly didn't do much to improve the state of the world and could, in fact, be cited as the creators of the system that has gotten us into the mess we are in today by *not* using *their* brains?

About this same time, something very strange happened. I didn't think of it as abduction at the time. It is only in retrospect that I see the clues for what they might be. On the other hand, there could be other explanations.

As I said, we lived in a cabin. A very tiny cabin. Most of it was taken up with our beds, storage and a tiny galley type kitchen. (If I learned anything from this experience, it was how to design the perfect kitchen!)

My bed was a standard double size pushed into a corner with one side flush against a wall. There was a very narrow space at the foot of the bed between it and the baby's crib. I slept on the inside, against the wall. The only way to get in and out of bed was either to scoot out backwards, or get my ex-husband up so I could get out on the side. In the condition of physical disability I was in at the time, the "scooting" option was difficult, if not impossible. Once I was in the bed, I was pretty much stuck there for the night without waking up my ex-husband and asking him to help me get up.

One night, something woke me up, though I don't know exactly what. It was like a low roar, if you could call it that. I was *very* sleepy – feeling almost drugged, so it was difficult to open my eyes. But, I thought that I ought to check out this disturbance, and I forced my eyes open and lifted my head up off the pillow to just look around. I noticed the strangest effect I had ever seen up to that point in my life, and I still cannot explain it precisely.

What I saw was light, but it wasn't an ordinary kind of light. It was more like a solid thing. It was actually penetrating the walls of the house through what seemed to be cracks and pinpoint openings all over the walls. Of course it came in the windows, but the needle like beams that came through the walls really were strange. They were almost solid, like icicles or even crystalline shards.

When I saw this, I was, of course, a bit puzzled. I couldn't think of what would be so powerful a light that it would shoot through cracks in the walls from all directions at once, considering that the cracks were, for all intents and purposes, almost microscopic. The sunlight didn't even do that, though I knew that the cabin structure surely had such fine cracks. The whole room seemed to be crisscrossed with these beams of light.[38]

Seeing this very strange light, what did I tell myself? I rationalized that it must be a group of my ex-husband's friends playing a joke on him by driving up to the house in a whole convoy of mud bogging trucks with the hunting lights mounted on the cabs all turned on and pointed at the house! Of course, that meant that there must be trucks on all sides of the house, facing the house, as well as one above, with lights shining down. At that moment of true delusion, it seemed like a reasonable explanation for something totally inexplicable to me.

The only problem was: my ex-husband didn't *have* any friends with mud boggers equipped with hunting lights! But, not to let that little detail bother me, I decided that it was *his* friends playing a joke and I was too tired to laugh, so let *him* get up and chase them off! How dare they come in the middle of the night, playing games, when he had to get up early and go to work! What's more, I needed my sleep! I was a sick person after all!

And that is what I did. I just pulled the covers over my head and went back to sleep!

The next thing I knew I was in pain. Not any specific place, but I was still so fragile from the many months of convalescence from having the baby (in which, as I have written in *Amazing Grace*, I was bedridden for most of six months due to pelvic injuries sustained in delivery); any sort of activity could make me hurt and ache all over. The pain seemed to have a central point in the abdominal area that penetrated to my back, almost like the early signs of labor.

So, it was pain that woke me up. But, what is so bizarre is that when I woke up I found my face pressed against my ex-husband's feet! I was completely reversed in the bed. In addition, my nightgown was *wet* from the knees down. It was a very painful operation to get myself into a sitting position against the wall, and pick my legs up one at a time, and swing them around to the foot of the bed so I could pull myself to my feet to find out what was the problem, but I managed.

I just stood there with the wet nightgown clinging coldly to my legs and tried to think how my gown got wet. I remember feeling almost hysterical in the very act of thinking about it, so I had to quickly stop thinking about it! I struck a match and lit a lamp so I could find something dry to put on. As I took off the wet gown, I noticed that it was covered with little black specks – the seeds and pollen from the Bahia grass outside that was about knee-high at the back of the property.

How did I explain this to myself? My immediate reaction to it was a rising feeling of hysteria, and so, again, I suppressed it. I told myself that I must have gotten up during the night and gone to the bathroom and dipped my gown in the

---

[38] In the years since I wrote the above description, I have seen something that conveys a bit of the impression I had of this light. There is a movie with Sean Connery and Catherine Zeta-Jones, *Entrapment*, that has a scene of the actress navigating a field of laser light. If you just make the beams of light blindingly brilliant, you may have some idea of what I was seeing.

buckets of water kept on hand to flush the toilet in the night. (I had insisted on the installation of fixtures, even if we had to operate them by hand.) But somehow, I had forgotten that I had done this. I didn't even *try* to explain how I had gotten into bed backwards.

That was my explanation *to myself*. It made absolutely no sense because I have never in my life, before or since, gotten up in the night and not remembered it or been unaware of what I was doing. I remember putting the gown in the hamper in a ball so I wouldn't have to look at it, and when I finally came to wash it, I did it hurriedly as if to cover something up; to hide it from myself.

Now, of course, that explanation, considering my physical condition and the logistics of getting myself out of bed at all, just didn't fly. But, that didn't matter to me. I created it and accepted it. The part of it that I couldn't explain, I shoved "under the rug" and avoided thinking about it at all. I had to. What else could I do? If I even approached the problem with any rational thinking, there was no rational explanation that was part of my world view and it only produced a sensation of inner panic and something akin to what a deer must feel when it is frozen in the headlights of an oncoming vehicle.

I wonder how many other people have similar experiences that they explain in such ways?

At this point in time, the heart condition began to worsen, and I began to suffer from more than the back flush, or fibrillation. I began to have angina attacks every week or so with involvement of both arms, though it was mostly concentrated on the left side. I also began to have a recurrence of a former problem, endometriosis, which caused almost constant pain. (I ended up having a D&C and laparoscopy done which revealed that I had a severe case of adenomyosis.)

And then there were the headaches: pain so monstrous that the very act of breathing was agony. Nothing touched this pain – no drug, no therapy, no solution. The pain began in a strange way with a swelling of my head right at the occipital ridge where the back of the skull sits on the neck. It would sometimes swell as big as a golf ball and it was from there the pain radiated in ever increasing waves of pulsating torment, until it gripped me like a steel helmet squeezing my head, until I felt it must shatter, for how else could such a convulsion of agony end? The only way to cope – forgetting entirely about getting relief – was to lie perfectly still in darkness and to breathe as shallowly as possible so as to minimize movement. This would continue for up to a week at a time with only snatches of sleep, until finally I would fall into a deep sleep of utter exhaustion from holding my sanity in the face of this wracking torment, from which I would awaken free of pain at last, though living in terror of the next, inevitable attack.

As if all of that were not enough, there was also the constant struggle with ear infections that were so massive that the affected side of my head would swell until the ear itself closed completely, obstructing the draining of fluids that poured when the eardrum would finally rupture in a blinding burst of pain that, had I been able to stand, would have dropped me to my knees to beg for mercy!

The curious thing about these chronic, regular "blowups" in my ear was that I had no warning. There was no slow building of a sensation of something being wrong – I would simply wake up with the side of my head swollen, in pain, and it would develop, in the course of a single day, to a critical situation that required a trip to the emergency room.

I have to laugh in retrospect (though it is *not* a funny subject for those who have experienced it!) when I think about one doctor who proposed to obtain a specimen of the fluid leaking from my swollen ear. She just came up beside me with a cotton swab and was going to insert it into the tumescent ear canal for a gentle swipe. The instant she touched it, the explosion of pain immediately transmitted itself to my arm and the reflexive blow nearly knocked her across the room! She understood immediately that when I said it was *very* painful, I wasn't joking in the least! And just for those who think I am a whiner here, let me point out that I had four children by this time, and one of them required the separation of my pelvis to deliver – utter agony – and I never once raised my voice, uttered a single cry, or did anything more than groan discreetly. In my family, pain was endured with dignity, not complaint. One certainly didn't physically assault a doctor tending to the problem!

My solution to this was to meditate even more in conjunction with my reading and endless note taking. I had not entirely given up my quest for subsuming all emotion into the Love of God; so meditating on this was a daily activity – sometimes more than once a day. Meditation, taken in proper doses, along with "tuning the reading instrument", can certainly accelerate one's progress.

For me, meditation is a dual process. I later learned that some paths refer to my method as "meditation with seed". The process really begins as an exercise in contemplation, or a focus upon an idea or image. It's pretty standard, I believe.

My meditation practice rapidly progressed, as I later learned when I read some advanced texts on the subject. Of course, at the time, I really had no guide and had never actually studied it *in method* except to read books *about* meditation pathways per se.

There are two basic ways to meditate: with seed and without seed. That is, to have something to focus on, or to attempt to completely empty the mind. It is generally more productive to meditate with seed in the beginning. Depending on your type the seed will be different. If you are a visual person, holding a visual image in the mind works. If you are an auditory person, holding a phrase and "hearing" it in your mind works. If you are kinesthetic, holding a feeling or trying to achieve that feeling, works best.

Also, at the point when you begin to have some success in stilling the chatter, you can experiment with changing the seed or combining. You might have a visual and auditory, or feeling and visual, or auditory and feeling, or all of them at once.

My personal preference is a phrase that I can also "see" as letters forming words that appear and dissolve. With this, I have both thought content as well as visual image and can easily add feeling and sound at will. I can also discard visual, auditory and feeling elements and simply concentrate on the content.

Breathing is very important for a number of reasons. Very slow, controlled breathing with counting to start the process works very effectively. Breathe in through the nose and out through the mouth. Once the breathing (that your are counting in order to regulate) becomes deep, slow and regular, then introduce either your phrase, visual image, or whatever you have selected as seed. The breathing ought to continue as you have set it.

The object, in the beginning, is to set several tasks for your mind to focus on intently and to hold that focus for as long as you can. If your mind wanders and other thoughts come along, as soon as you realize that you have lost focus, just bring your mind back to the focus and don't get irritated that you have lost your concentration. Most people can't focus on a single thing for longer than two or three minutes. That is why it is useful to begin with concentrating on the breathing and counting the breaths with the intention of setting up a specific depth and frequency. If you breath in for a count of 6, hold for a count of 3, breath out for a count of 9, and do this for at least 25 breaths in a row, you have achieved a respectable first step.

Another very useful technique is to find a poem or more lengthy quote to use as your breathing template *and* content. For example, the so-called "Lord's Prayer" is very useful in this way.

Recite in your mind, "Our Father Who art in Heaven," on the in-breath while holding in mind that the "kingdom of heaven, the "heavenly father" is the higher intellect. "Hallowed be thy Name," on the out-breath while holding in mind that this is the part of you that is holy and which you desire to manifest through your self. "Thy Kingdom Come, Thy will be done," on the in-breath while considering the fact that you wish to establish a link with your higher self – the *real* you. "On Earth as it is in heaven," on the out-breath, contemplating the fact that once the lower self is balanced and integrated, that the will of the spirit, the "heavenly kingdom" can be brought into your life.

You don't have to do the whole prayer; the above is sufficient seed, but if you want to do the whole thing, I think you have the idea. You can visualize the words, consider the content, feel them, all the while the words themselves are acting as the counter for your breathing.

Some people can achieve very good results with very simple seed, other people require more complexity. Again, the point is to have something that you can focus on and to hold that focus intently. It is more or less an exercising of the Will and Intent, building a sort of "psychic muscle." You may be surprised at the tenacity of the chatter and its resistance to this one-pointed focus.

Nevertheless, the result of this activity was that, after only a few months of practice, I found myself "zoning out" for up to three hours at a time, coming to myself feeling as though no time at all had passed. The only problem was: I never seemed to bring anything back with me. I had no idea what had been going on, where my mind had been, what my consciousness had been doing or anything. I did note that I was far more peaceful and able to cope with the difficulties of my life, but it was still frustrating to not be able to obtain something a bit more concrete from this entire endeavor. The C's recently commented on this "zoning":

> August 5, 2009
> Q: (L) What is this [zoning] phenomenon?
> A: See previous answer ["Humans should remember the hermetic maxim can go both ways in some respects. Those who are destined to "meet" themselves in the future can now do so with greater facility due to these efforts. We once said that "you in the future" could "rewrite" cosmic programs... that goes for others too. They are now learning the programming language."] and think of it as spending "time" with the higher self/teacher instead of wasting the ability to dissociate on futile illusions. Also remember that "time" spent in this process utilizes this "soul ability" as it was originally intended. It taxes the soul greatly to be embodied.

This recalls something from Gurdjieff:

> [T]he only right way to objective consciousness is through the development of self-consciousness. If an ordinary man is artificially brought into a state of objective consciousness and afterwards brought back to his usual state *he will remember nothing and he will think that for a time he had lost consciousness.* But in the state of self-consciousness a man can have flashes of objective consciousness and remember them. [...]
>
> If we could connect the centers of our ordinary consciousness with the higher thinking center deliberately and at will, it would be of no use to us whatever in our present general state. In most cases where accidental contact with the higher thinking center takes place a man becomes unconscious. *The mind refuses to take in the flood of thoughts, emotions, images, and ideas which suddenly burst into it. And instead of a vivid thought, or a vivid emotion, there results, on the contrary, a complete blank, a state of unconsciousness.* The memory retains only the first moment when the flood rushed in on the mind and the last moment when the flood was receding and consciousness returned. But even these moments are so full of unusual shades and colors that there is nothing with which to compare them among the ordinary sensations of life. This is usually all that remains from so-called 'mystical' and 'ecstatic' experiences, which represent a temporary connection with a higher center. Only very seldom does it happen that a mind which has been better prepared succeeds in grasping and remembering something of what was felt and understood at the moment of ecstasy. But even in these cases the thinking, the moving, and the emotional centers remember and transmit everything in their own way, translate absolutely new and never previously experienced sensations into the language of usual everyday sensations, transmit in worldly three-dimensional forms things which pass completely beyond the limits of worldly measurements; in this way, of course, they entirely distort every trace of what remains in the memory of these unusual experiences. Our ordinary centers, in transmitting the impressions of the higher centers, may be compared to a blind man speaking of colors, or to a deaf man speaking of music. [...]
>
> The existence of these higher centers in us is a greater riddle than the hidden treasure which men who believe in the existence of the mysterious and the miraculous have sought since the remotest times.

All mystical and occult systems recognize the existence of higher forces and capacities in man although, in many cases, they admit the existence of these forces and capacities only in the form of possibilities, and speak of the necessity for developing the hidden forces in man. This present teaching differs from many others by the fact that it affirms that the higher centers exist in man and are fully developed.

It is the lower centers that are undeveloped. And it is precisely this lack of development, or the incomplete functioning, of the lower centers that prevents us from making use of the work of the higher centers.[39] (Emphasis added)

As a matter of practicality, I generally meditated lying on the bed. Some people cannot do this because they tend to fall asleep, but that was never a problem for me. I could "zone out" in meditation, "come to" some time later, and *then* go to sleep if I was doing it at night. I was generally so uncomfortable in any position that getting to sleep was problematical if I *didn't* meditate first.

One night, after a particularly trying day of struggle with the situation (I don't really remember why I felt so extremely unhappy at that moment in time; probably just a combination of the constant pain, the struggles to make ends meet, anxieties for the children, and feeling completely alone in my marriage), it was standard practice for me to use any unpleasantness or unhappiness as the fuel for the meditative fires. Being able to achieve the sensation of love and peace in the face of some great difficulty was part of the challenge – and the purpose.

So, I went to bed and waited for my ex-husband to go to sleep. His attitude about the direction I was going was, on the surface, tolerant, but he always managed to say or do something to put some monkey wrench in the works if he was aware of what I was doing. If he thought I wanted things to be quiet for meditation, he would manage to just "have to" make some sort of noise or disruption, for which he would apologize profusely, and then go on to do it again and again.

After he was asleep, I began my breathing exercises. This part of the process I had borrowed from my hypnotherapy training. It was extremely useful. Of course, I later learned that it had been "borrowed" for hypnotherapy from certain meditation systems.[40]

At this point, I don't know *what* happened. All I remember is starting the breathing phase, which came before going into the contemplative phase of the exercise. But, what happened seems to be that I sort of made some kind of big "skip" or something.

The next thing I knew, I was jerked back into consciousness by a sensation that can only be described as a roiling turbulence in my abdominal area. It was so powerful that, at first, it felt actually physical – like there was a boiling agitation in my organs that was going to erupt upward in some way. I could

---

[39] Ouspensky, *The Fourth Way*, pp. 149, 201, 202.
[40] We have now made this breathing/meditation technique available for free on our website. The full program is also available in a 3-CD/DVD set, also available on our website. We call the program Éiriú Eolas, which is Celtic for "Growth of Knowledge". See: http://www.cassiopaea.org/Eiriu-Eolas/

distinctly sense that it *was* building and *was* going to travel upward, and I was frightened that something crazy and strange was happening with my body with which I was completely unfamiliar. I knew I had to get out of that bed and get outside before "it" happened, though I had *no* idea what it was.

I was frantically holding my throat, because I could feel a tightening of the muscles in the throat area, as wave after wave of energy blew upward like the precursors of steam blasts from a volcano before it erupts. I struggled out of the bed, holding the wall with one hand and my throat with the other, all the while clenching my teeth so whatever it was would not come gushing out of me and disturb either my ex-husband or the children. For all I knew, I was just going to be violently sick! There certainly was a certain similarity between that feeling and the feeling that you are going to throw up!

I rushed outside to the porch where there was a lawn sofa and collapsed onto it just as the outpouring began.

I wish I could describe this in better words, but there are simply none that apply other than to use ordinary descriptions that don't come close to the essence and intensity of the event. What erupted from me was a shattering series of sobs and cries that were utterly primeval and coming from some soul-deep place that defies explanation.

Accompanying these cries, or actually, embedded in them, were images – visions – complete scenes with all attendant emotional content and implied context conveyed in an instant. Again, it was like the idea of your life "passing before your eyes". But, in this case, it was not scenes from this life. It was lifetime after lifetime. I knew that I was there in every scene, that the scenes I was seeing were vignettes of other lives, and I was experiencing myself as all these people.

And the tears! My god! The tears that flowed. I had no idea that the human physiology was capable of producing such copious amounts of liquid so rapidly! Where was all that liquid coming from?

Now, if this had been just an hour-long crying jag or something like that, it would have to pass into history as "just one of those things," maybe like PMS. But, this activity had a life of its own! It went on, without slowing or stopping, for over five hours!

I had absolutely no control over any of it at all. If I attempted to slow it down, stop it, or switch my mind in another direction, the inner sensation of explosive eruption rapidly took over, all the muscles in my body would begin to clench up and I was no longer in control. I could only sit there as a sort of instrument of grief and lamentation, and literally sob my heart out for every horror of history in which I had seemingly participated or to which I had possibly been a witness. I think that there were even some that I was simply aware of and in which there had been no participation. And some of them were truly horrible scenes.

Plague and pestilence and death and destruction. Scene after scene. Loved ones standing one moment, crushed or laying in bloody heaps the next. Rapaciousness, pillaging, plundering; rivers of blood and gore; slaughter, carnage and butchery in all its many manifestations passed before my eyes; holocaust and hell. Rage and hot anger, bloodlust and fury, murder and mayhem, all around me, everywhere I looked. Evil heaped on evil like twisted, dismembered bodies. And the grief of centuries, the unshed tears of millennia, the guilt, remorse and penitence, flooded through me; melting, thawing and dissolving the burdensome shell of stone that encased my petrified heart; washing away the pain with my tears – an ocean of tears.

At the same time as this release of the worlds of accumulated guilt and grief of many lifetimes was going on, there was the voice in the background, ever soothing, ever calming, intoning over and over again: "It's not your fault. There is no blame. It's not your fault. You didn't know." And I came to understand something very deep.

I understood that there is no "original sin". I understood that the terrors and suffering mankind experiences here in life on earth are *not* the result of some sort of mistake or error or aberration. They are not punishments. They are not something that one can be saved from, for I understood that every scene of terrible suffering and heart-rending cruelty was the *result of ignorance*.

It is easier to see this idea when you think about something such as the Crusades or the Inquisition. You can trace the path of twisted reason that led from the idea of the Love of God, to the idea of imposing that view of the Love of God on others "for their own good". And, taken to an extreme, it even can result in ideas of torture and murder in the mind of a person who *truly loves*! Forget for a moment about those psychopaths who just viciously used such philosophies for their own gain and political maneuvers.[41] Think for a moment about the sincerity of the followers of such philosophies. This following of evil disguised as good was based on *ignorance*. Even beyond that, those who were seemingly out for gain and self-aggrandizement were operating out of ignorance – fear and hunger of the soul that cannot be satisfied. It is only a matter of degrees, but in the end, it is only ignorance.

When the flow of energy, images and tears finally began to subside, there appeared the sensation of warm, balmy liquid that was almost airy in its lightness, and so sweet that to this day, I can still remember the piercing quickening of the fire of love for all of creation. It was ecstatic, rapturous and exultant all at the same time. I was lost in wonder, amazed and at the same time bewildered at this vision of the world.

The C's also recently commented on this meditation:

June 20, 2009

Q: (L) Alright then. Is there anything that we could do?

---

[41] See Andrew Lobaczewski's *Political Ponerology*, which Red Pill Press published in 2006, for the best analysis evil in our world. It painfully describes the psychopaths who come to rule nations, and the psychological processes that lead to atrocities like the Holocaust. His book covers the spectrum of human behaviors: what is evil, and how even good people can get swept up in its influence.

ALL THERE IS IS LESSONS

A: Perhaps if you could share the technique that you used to achieve emotional cleansing, a lot of people would benefit including the two individuals in question.

Q: (L) What technique is that?

A: Remember an entire night of cleansing tears?!

Q: (L) Yeah. Well, that was just a meditation technique I developed. I would breathe a certain way and repeat certain things in my mind as I breathed, and I did it every night. Strange things started happening.

A: Strange indeed! You stumbled instinctively on an ancient method that is unsurpassed in its efficacy. So why not share?

Q: (Joe) Spill the beans, Laura! (L) Well I just never thought it was anything particularly special - it just worked for me! I mean how does something like that compare to this Art of Living Kriya thing [a popular Indian breathing program]?

A: AoL is for beginners and robots!

Q: (laughter) (L) Well then why were you so enthusiastic when C*** proposed teaching us? I mean, he asked if he should teach us, and you said yes with seven exclamation points!

A: Got you to do it and jump started your thinking didn't we?!

Q: (L) So the point wasn't that this method was "the best" or the only one or so great. It was to draw our attention to the idea of breathing, or control of breath, as a means of effecting emotional healing. Is that it?

A: Absolutely!X7

Q: (laughter) (L) Shorthand. Um...

A: Remember that your method employed a powerful "seed".

Q: (DD) Seed? (L) Yeah, that's a reference to meditating with or without seed. (Joe) What was the seed? (L) Phrases that I used in my mind. (Allen) Were those phrases particular to you though, like something that someone has to come up with for themselves? (L) Well, I dunno, were those phrases particular for me?

A: They were super powerful!

Q: (C) Where they like prayers? (L) Yeah, and it's really funny because I started out using the Lord's Prayer. Then I decided that I wasn't happy with it because it wasn't open enough. It had associations with specific religious things, and so I rewrote it. I'll have to... It was something like... (DD) Did you use those words as a template? (L) Yeah. (Joe) I used to say a Lord's Prayer that was modified. At night, like a mantra, I used to just go over and over... (L) Did you do it in concert with breathing? (Joe) Not consciously. (L) Yeah, well you see, I did. It was very deliberate controlled breathing. I did this every night for months. (DD) How were you breathing? (L) Very similar to what C*** teaches, what they call this Victory Breath. (Joe) Was it both in and out through the nose? (L) In through the nose, out through the mouth. (Joe) Because I thought Victory Breath was weird when we did the course since it was all through the nose. (A**) Yeah, that's what was missing. (L) Yeah, I did it in through the nose, out through the mouth. It was in and count, hold and count, out and count. And it was very controlled... it was very similar to what they call this Ujjai breath, or Victory Breath. That was kind of familiar to me, because I'd done that for years. (C) And while you were doing it, you were saying... (L) I was repeating these phrases, and each phrase was created so that the in or out breath fit the phrase exactly. So for the first phrase, I would

170

breathe in, and then out for the second phrase, etc. And my objective was to do it twenty times. I don't think I ever did it twenty times, because I would get to about ten or twelve, and then I would just leave the body or something, just zone. And after a certain number of times of doing that, then I had this... I dunno, I came back to myself with this... I dunno whether I want to call it a kundalini experience or not, but I felt there was this tremendous cleansing event that went on for hours and hours and hours. I've described it before. Something happened. But anyway, that was the story. So I found that to be very effective. I dunno what to ask now. (Joe) Is what you just described the idea?

A: Yes and another excellent technique though for other purposes is what you call "power breathing".

Q: (L) Oh, my Power Breathing. (C) What is that? (L) For me, that's just energizing. The fast pace on the treadmill accompanied by a very particular kind and pace of breathing. This is the one that it's not the head, it's matched to the body. The one is like intellect and heart, and Power Breathing is like moving center and heart... You let the movement of your body take you where you need to go.

A: Remember what that technique did?

Q: (L) Oh yeah! (Joe) What did it do? Did you fly? Superpowers? (A**) That was the past life thing, wasn't it? (L) Yeah, I went into a past life memory in the gym. (Joe) Where, here? (L) No, in Florida. Geez... But I guess if people do that, they need to have somebody there. So, there are a couple of ways to tap into these emotional issues that you're talking about that are actually somewhat different from this Art of Living thing?

A: Yes and probably more effective if utilized faithfully. AoL is like the "Diet Coke" of breathing techniques... Just one calorie.

The prayer I used is called the "Prayer of the Soul", which goes as follows:

Oh Divine Cosmic Mind
Holy Awareness in All Creation
Carried in the heart
Ruler of the mind
Savior of the Soul
Live in me today
Be my Daily Bread
As I give bread to others
Help me grow in knowledge
Of All Creation
Clear my eyes
That I may See
Clear my ears
That I may hear
Cleanse my heart
That I may know and love
The Holiness of True Existence
Divine Cosmic Mind

Well, the result of this event was a state of prolonged elevation, or loving peace that persisted for a very long time. You could even say that the effects reverberate to the present time because never again was I ever able to pass judgment on another no matter how wicked their deeds. I could see that all so-called evil and wickedness was a manifestation of ignorance and that there is no person, no matter how holy and elevated they may think they are in this life, who has not reveled in the shedding of another's blood in some other time and place. The original denial of responsibility by Cain when he cried out "Am I my brother's keeper?!" belongs to all.

But there was another significant point. Ignorance is a *choice*, and it is a choice that is made for a reason – to learn and grow.

And that realization led to another – to learn how to truly choose – to be able to learn, at this level of reality, what is and isn't of ignorance – what is of truth and beauty and love and cleanliness. Of course I understood that it was like the saying of Jesus that some things are bright and shining on the outside, but inside they are filthy and full of decay. And I don't mean that I was seeing this negativity as something to be judged – I clearly understood its reason and place as modes of learning – but I was deeply inspired to seek out all I could learn about this world so as to best manifest what was of light.

I was so excited by this revelation that I wanted to go straight back to the church and tell everybody. At that point, the only people with whom we had any contact were members of the church we had attended. They were coming by occasionally to find out why we had sort of dropped out, and these visits gave me the opportunity to talk about some of my branching out in terms of my spiritual experiences. In every single case, I was literally rebuked as having been duped by Satan. Boy, was I ever naive!

I thought about that a lot. I wondered if it could be so, if the whole drama of the visions, the actions of the minister who had been a wolf in sheep's clothing, could have been set up and dramatized just to deceive me. I was truly on the horns of a dilemma. On the one hand, if they were right and I had been deceived, then perhaps my soul was in peril. But, if they were wrong and I was right then what did that make of the whole basis of Christianity? If they were wrong, if they *could* be wrong in such a fundamental thing, how could anything about what they had built on this basic error be right?

This distressed me because, while I was ready to "adjust" my Christian position, I was not quite prepared to toss the whole thing out the window. I mean, after all, through all the years of study and investigation, it had been there in the background. When I took the position that I was questioning the existence of a god at all, that was altogether different. There I was asking a question. But, in *deciding* that Christianity was just simply wrong, foundationally wrong because if there was no original sin from which to be saved, there was no necessity for a savior, then that was an altogether different thing. *It amounted to making a choice.*

It was a matter that took a number of years to resolve. So, we will leave it there. What is important is that, from this experience forward, I was never again able to see sin in quite the same light. When I read about murderers and deeds of mayhem, I knew that these were things in which I had participated in times past, in my ignorance.

When anyone did something that hurt me, I knew that I had done such things as well. I could no longer feel any judgment or criticism of anything or anybody because I knew that, at some place and time, *it was myself I was judging.* It had been a learning process, and I grew from each experience. I learned what *not* to do by doing it. And, in a very real sense, this is the reason for pain and suffering. It is like an automatic guidance system that keeps a person on the path of learning. But the trick is to be able to discern the difference between choosing a path that gives immediate physical comfort, and then leads to great psychic or soul pain, and a path that may be physically uncomfortable temporarily, that then leads to peace of the heart.

I suppose that you could say, in a sense, that I had accomplished a good part of the objective of the "love path", but it was not that simple. I was still a very ordinary human being trying to function in the real world with real children and real events to contend with and some sort of balance had to be achieved between knowing that everyone is at some stage of learning and avoiding being part of their lesson. That was something that took some time. Had I not had children, I might have simply withdrawn from the world to spend the rest of my life in studious contemplation and repetition of ecstatic exercises. But I couldn't. I had responsibilities. I was *in* the world, and it was my classroom.

What actually happened in the real world of practical affairs at this point, was a series of events that could be considered more or less ordinary, but in light of the previous trend of events in conjunction with my inner state and activities, can be looked at in a more miraculous light. We might even say that they were a direct reflection of the shift in my perspective.

Suddenly, my ex-husband was offered a congenial job. This actually happened because the man who offered it found himself needing help operating his business because he had suddenly decided to expand and found it to be too much to handle. He actually thought of my ex-husband specifically, asked around to find where we had moved to, and drove out in the boondocks to make this offer. At the time, I didn't relate these external events directly to the shift in my state, but I was certainly grateful. So, the main worries about being able to live from one day to the next were solved.

Then, a friend who owned a business that included a fleet of trucks decided that it was time to get new ones, perhaps to be able to write it off on his income tax, and offered to sell us one (with very low mileage) for less than a fifth of its market value.

We added onto the cabin, doubling our living space, installed electricity and plumbing, and basically returned to the real world. Of course, by this time I had already had to sell my piano and all the jewelry that had been given to me over the years by friends and family before my marriage. If I hadn't, there might have been no food to eat or no Christmas for the children.

I resumed doing hypnotherapy, which had been abandoned during the faith trip, and began to learn Spirit Release techniques.

It was at this point, also, that my mother woke up from her spell and realized how horribly she had behaved. It was too late to salvage the business or the real estate that had been sold to keep her friend happy, but she did sign back over to me the house I had inherited from my grandparents, from which she had evicted us several years earlier when my grandmother died. In the meantime, she had mortgaged it heavily, so I don't think her motives were entirely selfless because the only thing I could do was sell it. I was able to utilize what funds were left after the mortgage was satisfied to buy a house that was big enough for our growing family.

But even before the move, something else happened. About three years after the birth of my fourth child, a longtime friend of mine who had observed the events of my life from the sidelines without judgment or comment, decided that I needed to get away from it all for a little break. I had never been away from my children for more than a few days – generally in the hospital – and I was not very comfortable with the idea of it, but the particular vacation being proposed was one that was hard to resist.

My friend and her husband owned a vacation home in North Carolina, and we had long followed the work of Al Miner who channels an entity calling itself "Lama Sing". There was to be a meeting of the many people interested in this work in Maggie Valley, organized by a physician and his wife who were close friends of Al. There were going to be lectures, group meditations, dinners and so on. It sounded like not only a lot of fun, but also a path to something, though I was not sure what. I agreed to go.

At the symposium, everything was going along as might be expected at such an affair. People were claiming to see auras; folks were wandering around with ecstatic expressions on their faces pronouncing sagely on the "wonderful energy present", and the talks were both lively and interesting.

Then, the doctor's wife – the couple who had sponsored and organized the event – who was, I believe, a psychotherapist or counselor in some capacity – gave a talk about the many people who were coming forward at the time with "reincarnational memories" of the holocaust. This had the most unusual effect on me of producing an uncontrollable spell of crying. I had to leave the room and hide in a stall in the ladies lavatory until this particular talk was finished. I really thought I was losing my grip because *nothing* had ever affected me that way in public! Heck, not only do I *not* wear my heart on my sleeve in the presence of others, I don't even dance in public because I have always felt that, for me, it was undignified!

But then, on the last day of the symposium the headache came. When my friend left to go to a group meditation, I stayed behind in the darkened motel room with cold towels and ice on my head trying to reduce the swelling. Fortunately this time, by the next morning when we were to all meet for a farewell breakfast, the pain had subsided sufficiently for me to be able to pack and otherwise function normally.

At breakfast, one of the ladies at our table remarked to me that the dress I had been wearing at the meditation the previous day was *very* lovely. I looked at her in surprise and said that I hadn't gone because I had been ill. She looked back at me and said, "But I saw you clearly and I am *not* mistaken!"

My friend assured her that I had been in bed, so we all looked at one another and, after an awkward silence, the chatter began again. But I was pretty puzzled by this.

At the symposium, we had met two ladies who were elderly, but very spry and hugely entertaining and funny to talk with. One of them had had some training in hypnosis and advanced meditative techniques, and my friend and I discussed inviting them back to her vacation home where we planned to go for a few days before setting out for home. They agreed that we would have some fun, go digging for rocks at one of the local public mines, and just generally have a "hen party".

After driving all day into the mountains, we arrived at the house, which was quite isolated and located at the end of an old logging road on the edge of a National Forest. It was completely peaceful and delightful and perfect for our experimental meditations.

Our new friend (let's call her June) was going to direct a guided meditation accompanied by musical tones on tape. We all found comfortable places, and the instructions began. I remember following the breathing part, and tuning in to the musical tones, but from that point, it seems my inner consciousness had plans of its own.

I felt myself lift out of my body and "shoooop!" I was suddenly sort of hovering before a rock face on the side of a tall mountain. There was a sort of crack, or cleft in the rock. I knew that only very few people could pass through this narrow opening, and attempting it without being "one of those who can", would result in a sort of shock, but I decided to try. I sort of aimed for it with volitional intent, and the next thing I knew I was emerging on the other side at the edge of a beautiful valley.

There were meadows of green grass and wildflowers of incredible luminescence and liveliness. The grasses were waving back and forth in the breeze, so it would seem, though this breeze was a sort of conscious caressing of the grass and the waving of the grass was a sort of conscious response to the caress much like a cat purrs when stroked.

I found myself in a sort of body, and began to walk through this grass, which received my steps, caressing my feet and legs as I merged with it at every step. It sort of passed me along, rather than me walking through it. There was a striped tent a short distance before me with banners flying from the posts in the consciously caressing breeze, but it was on the other side of a small river. I knew that this tent was where I was going, though there was no sensation of "supposed to go". I was curious as to how it was going to feel when I stepped into the water of the river.

I looked at the water that was crystal clear and sparkling in the bright sunlight, though there did not seem to be a sun in the sky, exactly. You could say that the jumping and dancing light on the water was a sort of conscious interplay between this ambient, intense light and the water itself.

I stepped into the water, noticing that my feet were bare and that I seemed to be wearing some sort of white under-robe with a striped over-robe, which I hoisted out of the water with my hands. I was surprised to feel the current moving so swiftly, yet giving the sensation of a merging with my feet. The sensation can only be described as "delicious" to my feet!

The glittering, jewel-like stones at the bottom of the river fascinated me. They were smooth, yet constantly flashing with the movement of the water across them. I walked across the river aware that this was an intense experience that had some deep significance. When I reached the other side, I was both glad that I had passed some sort of test, as well as regretful that the experience was over.

I approached the tent and there were two men sitting under an outer tent that was open-sided like a porch, on a carpet spread on the grass in front of the tent. They were also dressed as I was. The tent was striped in the same pattern as the stripes of the over robes, and the colors of the stripes were red, white and black with a constantly repeating thin border to each stripe of lapis blue.

One of the men spoke to me saying: "We have been waiting for a long time. There is joy in seeing you again."

For some reason, this didn't strike me as unusual. I had the feeling that this meeting had been arranged a very long "time" ago. I bowed and acknowledged the greeting. Then, the other one said, "He is inside." That, too, was not unexpected. I ducked my head to enter the tent and there was a man, an old man with young skin like iridescent porcelain, standing inside. His expression upon seeing me was absolute happiness and satisfaction. He embraced me strongly and kissed me on both cheeks, tears coming to his eyes. "We will break bread first." He said. Again, this was not a surprise and there was no question in my mind as to what "first" might mean, though I didn't know!

We sat down on the carpeted ground inside the tent around a small table. The two men outside came in with bowls of bread and milk. There was a golden goblet on the table already filled with something like wine. A large loaf of bread was broken into equal pieces by the old man and each of us was handed a piece. We dipped it in the milk and ate. Then the goblet was taken up by the old man, who passed his hands over it, blew on it, drank from it, and passed it to me. At that moment, I became aware that they were all watching me and I knew that drinking was another test. I drank and expressions of happiness were evident on all their faces.

Then the old man stood up and went through a door into an inner room in the tent, and I knew that I was also supposed to follow. I did. In this room was a golden chest about the size of a large breadbox. He went to it and opened it taking out a large necklace. Now, this necklace was about the strangest thing I have ever seen. It was made up of a series of balls of gold that were graduated like a strand of pearls would be, only the smallest was about the size of a playing marble and the largest, in the center, was about the size of a Ping-Pong ball. Suspended at the center was a figured gold object set with a large stone. The figure of the piece consisted of two spiraling horns similar to Ram's horns mounted to the side of the flat surface on which the stone was fixed. The flat surface was strange in that it was both circular yet triangular. How it could be both, I cannot say, but it was. The circular part of it seemed to be a function of the stone that was rounded like a Ping-Pong ball cut in half. But it was the characteristics of the stone that fascinated me. Imagine a combination between a diamond and an opal and you have some idea of what it was like. It was milky yet crystalline, flashing fire and colors like an opal, yet brilliant and transparent like a diamond. The living nature of this stone was apparent, and I was in awe of it.

The old man turned to me and looked at me long and carefully – searching my eyes for something. He held the necklace in both hands, suspended in air as he did so, and finally said, "You understand?" I replied, "Yes." And the understanding that was instantly opened to my mind was that, if I accepted the stone, there were consequences. The consequences were that any manifestations of falseness in me would turn on me and destroy the instrument in which I was operating, i.e., the physical body of my present incarnation. It didn't matter if they were unintended. I was being charged to seek out and speak only truth with no latitude for subjective wishful thinking.

With this understanding passed to me the enormous responsibility and risk I was accepting. It was sobering, awe inspiring and even a little frightening. But the fear passed quickly. "You accept?" the old man asked. "I do." I replied and bent my head to receive the stone. He placed it carefully around my neck, adjusting the fit at the shoulders so that the stone should rest exactly at the base of my breastbone.

I was embraced again, and passed out of the inner room to the outer where the two other men were waiting. When they saw the stone, their faces lit up with joy and they clasped their hands together and bowed as I passed. I signaled them with my eyes as I did so, knowing that I could no longer speak in that realm.

The next thing I knew, I could hear June's voice calling my name over and over again at a great distance. Like a rocket, I shot through the cleft in the rock and found myself over the mountain where the house was that held my mortal body, and then I was in the body, coming back as though emerging from a dark tunnel into the light of this world. I opened my eyes and my friends were looking at me and laughing that I had "gone to sleep"!

I tried to say that something very extraordinary had happened, but words failed me. I found that I could not really describe this experience in anything but the most prosaic terms and they were making great fun of it, so I decided that I shouldn't talk about it and kept most of it to myself. They did ask what the stone was when I tried to describe it, and the only thing that came to my mind was that it was called The Speaking Stone.

I should mention that, shortly after beginning meditation practice, I had begun to experience a strange anomaly. Things would break in my presence with no apparent cause, things like drinking glasses, lamp chimneys (remember, we were living for some time with no electricity), and so forth. I had attempted to try to explain this as rapid shifts in temperature such as occurs when you pour boiling water into a glass, but that didn't really work in the summer time, when there was nothing in the glass, and the lamp chimney had been sitting unused all day. Another thing to shove under the rug.

But, on the trip down from the mountains on the way home, I was thinking about the stone and how I was going to cope with this condition on my existence in my relations with my ex-husband, and at that very instant, the back window in my friend's new car exploded with a loud noise like the shot from a cannon. We were both so startled that she slammed on the brakes and we quickly looked around. She looked in the mirror and I turned my head and we both saw the window this way at the same time. It was all milky with the fractures of tempered glass that breaks into little "balls". And just at that moment, it began to rain. We looked in directions and there wasn't another car in sight and no apparent place that a missile could have come from. And, in fact, there didn't seem to be any impact point. The whole window was still in one piece, but completely covered with those lines of fracture. It was thus impossible to see through.

Swell! There we are, driving along with about 400 miles to go, with a shattered rear window and a pile of luggage and souvenirs in the back seat! But, the window seemed to be holding, and we kept moving, though slowly. At some point we wanted to check the situation out, so when we came to a place to pull off, a closed gas station, we turned in. The instant we hit the bump of the end of the pavement, the whole window fell in on the seat in a pile of thousands of little glass balls!

Well, there wasn't much to do except find a place to stay, cover the car until morning, and then go from there. We found a motel where the owner very kindly allowed us to put the car in his own garage and the next day we drove to the nearest city with a car dealer affiliated with the maker of the car.

The car was repaired, but the mechanics were completely baffled. They could come up with absolutely no explanation as to why the window would suddenly shatter.

A related incident occurred not long after I was back home. By this time, we had a new bedroom built onto our cabin, which had now become a house, and the room was lined on two sides with large plate glass windows that measured four feet by six. The house was in the middle of a grove of trees and it was like having the outdoors "inside". The head of the bed was against one of the walls of glass and I really enjoyed this room, especially when it rained.

I was meditating on the bed, and my ex-husband came into the house forgetting to catch the screen door to prevent it from slamming shut with the spring attached to it. When it slammed, I felt an internal "jerk" and the next thing I knew, the window at the head of the bed exploded exactly as the window at the back of the car had done some months before. Again, it was tempered glass, and it was a moment before the balls began to start falling, slowly at first, then all at once, collapsing in a pile on top of me.

Needless to say, at that point, my ex-husband became just a bit more cautious in his actions designed to "jerk my chain". He was already wary of the dozen or so shattered glasses and lamp chimneys that had gone before, but this was taking the thing to a new level. Heck, who knows? Maybe he was thinking I was some kind of witch! But it was creating a great distance between us because it frightened him.

I have to admit that I was sometimes a bit frightened also. I didn't know what was happening to me and around me. I only knew that I was on some sort of path and I could only do as I did because to do otherwise was in a strange way, impossible. I thought of it as a sort of "walking on water". In my mind, I was out in the middle of a vast ocean and there was a certain path for me, but each step was an act of both faith as well as judicious consideration of probabilities. I had a pretty good idea of where the supports that were hidden just under the surface of the water were, but I was not allowed to see them before I put my foot forward for the next step. I knew that, at any moment, I might find that my step was *not* met by the support structure, and I would plunge into the waves.

So much for strange experiences while meditating. Now let's jump over a few years to the time of the Flying Black Boomerangs chronicled in *High Strangeness* – another great inner shift. The reader will notice that no single experience was the last word. Things happened in stages and by degrees over years of time. And that, of course, implies that the process is ongoing. As I noted in *Amazing Grace,* it was at this point that my physical system broke down completely. My state of functionality had been precarious for years, and now it became a primary issue.

I continued to force myself to function by sheer will (the way of the fakir?) but I could see that the trend was definitely downhill and I knew that if something didn't change I was going to die. I knew I would die because the will in me was gradually being eroded away by constant pain. I couldn't stand on my feet for more than a few minutes at a time because the pelvic and lower back pain would make all my muscles go into a spasm that would end in spastic release because the muscles refused to support me at all. The muscles that are used to erect the body, assist in transitioning from sitting to standing, and lifting the legs to walk, were involved; and all of those activities – ordinary as they are – were greatly hindered. I needed assistance in and out of chairs, in and out of bed, in the bathroom, in and out of the tub and so on.

However, as long as I was sitting still and didn't try to move, I was fine. And my brain hadn't died, so I continued to read and study to divert my mind, and schedule hypnosis sessions. My ex-husband saw this as malingering. He complained that I could do what I liked to do, i.e., read or do hypnosis sessions for other people, but I wasn't doing anything for *him*, i.e., attend to his physical needs. I was stung and deeply hurt by this because if it hadn't been for reading and my work, I would have felt completely useless; I would have been a vegetable.

There were times when I wished that I had no family who would be damaged or hurt if I just ended it all. The angina was so constant a condition that I actually had fantasies of a madman with an ax breaking into the house and chopping my arm off thereby giving me relief. The doctor was baffled by it, and finally suggested that it might just be nerve damage and that doing carpal tunnel surgery was an option that might clear it up. Naturally, he didn't really explain why the pain was in the upper arm and chest area, but go figure. I was desperate and went to have it done.

When I woke up after surgery that was supposed to have been on my *left* wrist, *both* wrists were bandaged up like boxing gloves. I was completely horrified! How was I going to do anything with both hands like that?

The pain was close to the worst I have ever experienced. It was worse than having a baby. It was in the same category as the headaches and ear infections. I was not prepared for that. And it didn't go away as the doctor said it would.

The surgery also hadn't done anything to relieve the arm pain. So I was worse than before, and now I was almost completely helpless. I didn't even have the strength in my hands to turn a doorknob or take the lid off a jar or hold a potato to peel it. I couldn't lift a pot from the stove; I couldn't even hold a pen or pencil for longer than a minute without being gripped by an agonizing spasm, which resulted in my hand turning into a quivering, spastic claw right out of a horror movie. Forget playing the piano; wasn't ever going to happen again!

That was pretty depressing. And, for some reason, my ex-husband took some sort of perverse pleasure in torturing me with the situation. I was constantly reminded that if I wanted anything done that *I* wanted, I would just have to figure out how to do it myself.

So we find that the situation had improved in many ways, reflective of a change in the inner state, but obviously, there was more that needed to be done. I had no idea what, and was not even able to articulate in my mind that this was what was happening. I was aware of the fact that our bodies reflect some state of the soul, the condition of the Speaking Stone, but try as I would, I could not find the door to heal my own soul so that my body would begin to heal as well. The only thing I could figure was that there must be something more, something deeper, something I wasn't seeing. I knew that somehow my ignorance was playing a part, but of what was I ignorant? What, in the name of God, was I doing wrong?

I had seemingly achieved a state of love and acceptance for all people, for all paths, for all who struggled in ignorance. I was working as hard as I could (and even in my state of physical deterioration, which was considerable) to fix things for those who asked. I never turned down a request for help from anyone whether they could pay anything or not. I was not in it for the money. I was, in a certain sense, in as bad a situation as I had been when the voice had told me that I must "learn" about evil.

Well, I was trying. I was trying to learn how to identify it. What I didn't know and was about to learn was that very often, that which manifests as light and truth is *not*; it is a deception to folly. This was the still unlearned part of the "love lesson". I had already had the lesson that large religious organizations could be a pathway to destruction. For millennia, different sources, different teachers, have provided versions of a blueprint of the underlying forces of the reality in which we live – generally with very little, if any success. My observations over many years – compared with the observations of many other people – have led me to think that most of the expositions on the underlying forces of our reality have been, to put it bluntly, bogus. That is not to say that they have not had good intentions, and maybe even some "keys." But, it seems to be a fact of our reality that we are "in the soup" and some forces really wish to keep us there. Thus there has been a concerted effort to promulgate versions of the deeper reality that are not only misleading, but obviously designed to keep people asleep. However, what I didn't know at the time was just how subtle and torturous this deception could be and how it manifested on an individual, personal basis.

In early 1994, I had a conversation with Frank in which he enumerated for me the string of strange, synchronistic and even quite miraculous events that had brought me to the place where I now was. He cited point after point down through my entire life story, with which he was familiar, right up to the past few years when the bizarreness and synchronicities had increased to the point that I felt like I was living in a madhouse where normal reality no longer held sway, and the formerly solid earth of my reference system was crumbling beneath my feet. With each point he made, I felt like another wave was washing over my foundation of sand, and I was sinking into the mire of complete lunacy.

How can you deal with a life that has gone completely over the edge in terms of strangeness that you neither wish to experience, nor do you wish to perpetuate?

After going over most of my life, Frank came to the more recent times and pointed out how the UFOs had come with the first abduction session I had done, and that clearly this was an unusual phenomenon. Not everyone who might be an abductee under hypnosis attracts a whole flap of UFOs. The question was: was it the abductee, or the therapist in whom the denizens of UFO land were interested?

Then he pointed out the obvious (to him) connection between my deteriorating physical state and my own UFO encounter. When I protested that there might be no relation at all, he pointed out how my dog had suffered and died within a very short time after this exposure and how my symptoms always seemed to peak at exactly the time of night that the UFO had come along. What was my explanation for that little item?

I had none.

Frank's theory was that the whole drama of recent times that was spread across several counties and included dozens of people, most of whom I didn't even know, was staged to get my attention – to wake me up.

I did *not* like the direction the conversation was taking. Like the wet nightgown and the strange lights, I was really struggling to shove this one under the rug.

"Why meeee?" I wailed. I felt a huge pressure on my chest (the "Speaking Stone?") at the very thought. "What am I supposed to DO?!"

At that point, Frank had run out of theories. "I have no idea," he said. "I am just pointing out the obvious. I guess you have to figure the rest out on your own."

I clearly remember sitting on my bed that night, thinking about these strange hints that there was something deeper to our reality than I might have supposed in my years of research and work. The only problem was, as I pointed out smugly to God, I was too sick to do anything. "You blew it, Buckwheat!" I told the Universe. "If there was ever anything you wanted me to do, you let me suffer too much for too long! So there!" I mentally stuck out my tongue in defiance and resentment.

There I was, as nonfunctioning as a human being can be and still appear to be functional. But an overwhelming sensation of purposefulness behind it all swept over me and I immediately regretted my childish resistance. So I resigned to it, accepted it, and declared to the Universe that if all of these things were being orchestrated to get my attention, it had surely worked, but I was too far-gone to pick up the ball and run with it. "If I am supposed to *do* anything about it, you gotta fix me up here," I said. "As I am, I can do nothing."

Within two weeks – actually more like ten days – I found Reiki. Or Reiki found me. And so did Dr. Greenbaum.

LAURA FINDS REIKI AND ENDS UP IN THE SOUP... PEA SOUP, THAT IS

Remember what I said above:

> I had seemingly achieved a state of love and acceptance for all people, for all paths, for all who struggled in ignorance. I was working as hard as I could (and even in my state of physical deterioration, it was considerable) to fix things for those who asked. I never turned down a request for help from anyone whether they could pay anything or not. I was not in it for the money. I was, in a certain sense, in as bad a situation as I had been when the voice had told me that I must "learn" about evil. Well, I was trying. I was trying to learn how to identify it. What I didn't know, and was about to learn was that very often, that which

manifests as light and truth is NOT: it is a deception to folly. This was the still unlearned part of the "love lesson". I had already had the lesson that large religious organizations could be a pathway to destruction, what I didn't know was just how subtle and torturous this deception could be and how it manifested on an individual, personal basis.

What this meant, in practical terms, was that I had expanded my concepts to the more or less standard New Age version of "Unconditional Love" – that one loves everyone and everything and surrounds the self with love and light in meditation or affirmation on a daily basis, and just sort of sails along through life in the belief that if you *believe* in love and light and that everything is *love* and is to be *loved*, then that is what you will experience.

It also means forgiveness in wider terms: a constant "canceling out of the other person's weaknesses" because, in the grander scheme of things, no one *has* weaknesses! They are simply who and what they are and it is *our* job to love them and get along – go with the flow; accept everything and everybody as they are and hang out together in one grand orgy of love and light! What else are you going to do with the realization that there is no original sin, that all are one?

That sort of does sound like what my experiences were teaching me, yes?

Yes and no.

But, again, to give a practical example of how the next lesson transpired, we go back to the events of the "school," i.e., my life.

The day after my little "talk with God", a letter arrived in my mother's mail, and she called me to come and have a look at it. It was from a local retiree organization which was offering a course in home health nursing to retired people who were physically fit and able, and who wanted a new career that would get them out of the house, make them useful, end their boredom, and pay them money to boot! What a deal! To my mother, it sounded too good to be true. It was entirely free to retirees, all supplies, including uniforms, provided; even transportation to and from the site of the course was to be provided. Those who were interested were supposed to call right away and reserve a place in the class.

Mother was pretty excited about this opportunity for action and involvement in the world again. I agreed that if she wanted to have a new career that she ought to do so. So, she called and discovered that she was among the last few to be accepted since there had been such overwhelming response to the offer. Not a surprise.

About a week into this course Mother told me that a lady in her class had invited her to an open-house on the following Wednesday evening and she felt obligated to attend since this lady had sought her out in the class to share their lunch breaks, and had spent so much time being friendly and agreeable. The thing was that she needed me to drive her to this evening affair. I was happy to see her "get a life", so to speak, so I was all for helping her in her new pursuits. No problem.

At that point in time, after the UFO experience, which had brought all my health issues to a crisis state, I had to be very careful to budget my energy so that I could get done in any given day what was essential. Still, even with taking such care, I often had little energy for anything. I had been forced to cut way back on doing hypnosis sessions, using the in-between days to recover. And every night I was plagued with almost constant angina and the swelling of the eyes and mucous membranes of the throat, which I interpreted as allergy overload; I was living on Benadryl, which worked to alleviate some of the symptoms, but had the side effect of knocking me out. Not a very nice way to be living. I was about as minimally functional as a human being could be and still appear to be functioning normally! It was certain that no one could look at me and see anything wrong, but I was trapped in a body that seemed to be like a machine with one circuit after another shorting out or burning up. (Of course, it never occurred to me that new circuits were being formed, but that was a realization that would only come later.)

So, mother had this invitation, and I planned for it so as to be able to provide her with transportation. But, on the day it was supposed to happen, I was in so much pain and I was so exhausted that I just didn't see how I was going to be able to do it. Mother knew the state I was in and didn't push it. Somewhere around the middle of the afternoon, I collapsed on the bed and fell right to sleep. I awakened a couple of hours later – amazingly – feeling almost normal! I remembered that I was supposed to do something and I looked at the clock and saw that I had just enough time to collect mother and take her to her open house. I called her and told her that I was feeling better and she should get ready, as I would be there in a few minutes.

When we arrived at this open-house affair, I was not quite sure what was going on. There were about fifteen people standing around with their hands resting on individuals who were lying on three massage tables. There was incense burning and New Age music playing in the background, and some of the folks were standing with their eyes closed in meditative tranquility. I wasn't sure if I had stepped into a new version of the fundamentalist "laying on of hands" deal or what!

Being a person who tries to find a balance between good manners and my curiosity (which sometimes makes for funny situations I can tell you!), I settled in a chair after the introductions were made and asked something to the effect of, "What exactly, are y'all doing here, and what is the idea behind it and the precise procedure being followed?" No reason to beat around the bush! I expected something like, "We are praying," or, "We are meditating on wellness," or something like that. But instead, the answer was "we are channeling Reiki."

Okay. "What is Reiki?"

The various participants recounted the whole story of Dr. Usui to me as they stood there with their hands on the patients. Every movement and placement of the hands was explained to me, and as it went on, I became more and more skeptical. I mean, out of all the healing methods I had heard or read about or tried, this was truly the most nebulous and least likely! It seemed patently ridiculous to me that someone could "initiate" or "attune" another person in some way so that they had new powers to channel energy to another person that was supposed to be so amazing and miraculous! I expected them to say next that Reiki could help you walk on water! When that one came, I was gonna be outta there! I was urged to give it a try, but managed to decline almost gracefully. I would have felt perfectly silly on that table with five people laying their hands on me for 45 minutes or so. Wasn't gonna happen!

But I was working at being polite and gentle in my skepticism and soon the conversation turned to astrology – safe ground for me – and I mentioned in passing that I had a computer program that did pretty good charts, so the woman who was holding the Reiki open house offered me a trade: three Reiki treatments in exchange for an astrological chart.

How dense can you be? I was wondering how bright this gal was since she was offering me several hours of her time and effort in exchange for a few minutes of data entry and printing! Didn't seem too fair to me but I figured if she was silly enough to be convinced that she could "channel healing energy" to me through her hands, and was willing to go to that length to do it, I was game for the test. I was convinced that it would be another flop, but I also had the thought that maybe it was her way of getting a chart done that she otherwise could not afford. So, to "save face" for her, I agreed. An appointment was made for the following day, and sure enough, she showed up.

So, there I was, in such lousy condition that I actually had to be assisted to lie down on the massage table that was set up in my living room. And more embarrassing, I fell asleep during the treatment! When she had put her hands on me all I could really feel, (and I was paying close attention with a *lot* of skepticism), was warmth that didn't seem to be much more than the normal heat that would be evident when one person puts their hands on another. But the real surprise was to come when I got *off* the massage table at the end of the treatment. I could barely stand! I was so dizzy it was quite literally like being drunk! When I tried to walk I had to hold onto the furniture and walls to keep from falling down. I had to be helped to my bed where I collapsed and closed my eyes. But that didn't help because I had the exact same sick, spinning sensation that comes with having had a bit too much to drink! When I opened my eyes and tried to focus on the ceiling and walls, they spun dizzyingly as though I had been a child spinning in circles and then fallen to the ground to watch the sky and clouds keep moving. I was really concerned that something was going completely berserk with my system and I hoped it would pass. I was nauseated and felt a creeping tingling just exactly like being drunk! I just tried to breathe deeply and stop the spinning into the void in my head and soon fell asleep.

That night I slept better than I had in over 18 years. But it wasn't until well into the next day as I was unloading the dryer when I suddenly realized that my back didn't hurt. Not only that, but I realized that I had already done a lot more of my housework than I had been capable of doing in a very long time! I had just started tackling one chore after another, moving from one to the next, without noticing anything unusual. It wasn't until I had been working for several hours that I realized that something was different. There was something missing here. It was the long familiar pain.

Now, for someone who has gotten used to functioning with pain; who has developed ways to maneuver through life accommodating this pain; and who is *never* out of pain, this was so startling a realization that I actually sat down and began to mentally go over my body to discover if I didn't feel some little familiar twinge here or there. There was *no pain*. I was sure that, at any moment, I was going to get slammed with it again so I got up carefully and continued with my work, constantly monitoring myself for the return of the pain. Actually, I think I even wanted the pain to return because otherwise, I would have to think that Reiki had worked! And we certainly could not believe that sort of nonsense! What a dilemma!

Now, the clear thing here is this: I did *not* expect the Reiki to work. Further, I expected the pain to return. But something objective was going on that I didn't understand. I had become pretty convinced that what you think about or expect was what you experienced and that faith was an integral part of healing and I was working on digging up whatever might be buried in my own subconscious that was responsible for my suffering; which prevented me from having the faith to effect a healing; but, here I was, experiencing an effect in which I had had *no* faith of any kind. What is more, my skepticism about Reiki was rather deep rooted, yet it seemed that the Reiki had worked anyway. Or so we might think. What other explanation could there be? I actually began to cry with gratitude. Only those who have suffered long and constant pain can understand how I felt to *not* be in pain.

But, I was still on guard. Even though I had momentary relief, I expected the pain to return.

I had to go pick my daughter up and while we were driving home I told her about the pain being gone and that I thought the Reiki had done it. She laughed at me and said it only worked because I believed it would work. I pointed out to her that my belief had been exactly the opposite. And since that was the case, I was wondering now exactly what this Reiki business was.

Needless to say, it only got better. After two more treatments and the passing of a week, I was convinced that whatever was happening was working. I went to the open-houses regularly after this, not only was I healed of the back pain, the angina attacks lessened almost to non-existence, the swelling of the eyes and throat stopped entirely, my energy level soared and I was able to see more clients and be more active, which suited me fine! But still I was thinking that it wasn't the Reiki itself, but was merely transference of energy that anyone could accomplish if they just stood around for 40 minutes with their hands on another person. So, even though I was receiving benefits, I had my own theory about what it was. Surely it was an absurdity to think that someone could confer this almost magical ability on another in some way! And, to make this point, I was anxious for the Reiki Master who had initiated my new friends to come to town for a scheduled class – which seemed to be the point of the open-house – to attract new students. I was going to bring all my powers of observation and skepticism to this new investigation. If there *was* anything to this Reiki business, I was going to find out. I had no intention of believing it unless there was more or less objective proof.

When the day arrived for the first initiation, I was there, "loaded for bear", as they say, actively looking for some sort of hocus pocus or mumbo jumbo that would reveal the truth: that people were being charged large sums of money to be made to think they could channel Reiki, when the real effect was merely a natural energy flow that was available to all who had the patience to stand around with their hands on another person. The only thing I can say I felt during the attunement process was what seemed to be a sort of generalized rush of heat from my abdomen up through my head and a little popping sound in my head. But it was so nebulous that I considered it to be discountable as a subjective observation.

What happened later that night *was* surprising. We were told that, after the attunements, the body would experience some symptoms of adjustment such as excessive thirst and urination or even diarrhea. But what I *wasn't* expecting was the fact that when I put my hands *near* any of my children I felt a clear and distinct rush of heat against my palms exactly like the sensation of a blow dryer. This rush would be felt *before* the hand was close enough to be able to detect the normal heat exchange between bodies. I would say that it occurred at about 6 inches. There was a distinct magnetic feeling to this heat; a feeling that was similar to the pulling you feel when you hold two magnets close enough together that they begin to act on one another. The first time it happened, I jerked my hand back as though I had been burned. And then I began to experiment with it. I would start moving my hand closer and closer until I could distinctly identify the point at which the sensation occurred, the attraction was felt, and then I would deliberately move my hand closer by very small degrees in order to feel the effect at every stage of nearness. It was definitely there. No question about it. And the kids could feel it also.

Later that evening I was sitting on the sofa and my son came to sit on the floor in front of me and leaned back against my legs. As soon as he did, I could feel the heat begin to pass from my *legs* to his body exactly like the blow dryer effect. Apparently this was not just restricted to the hands! It was a whole body thing going on here! We soon became so hot from this contact, in an air-conditioned room, that he complained, "Mom! It's hot in here!" and moved away. By this time, we were both dripping with perspiration. It proved to be several months before this effect dissipated where the children were concerned. It continues to this day when I touch anyone who has an energy deficit. But I suspect that, after a time, the children became "energized", and so no longer pulled energy as strongly. Of course, if one of them is ill, there is a drawing of energy, but nothing like there was at the time of the Reiki initiation. (Some time later when I took the Master Level attunements, my palms actually blistered and peeled for several weeks.)

So, the end result was that I realized that there seem to be *objective* realities in which no belief is necessary or required. If you know about, or have access to, these objective levels, you can discover those principles with which to align your actions for subjective results.

But, talking about Reiki per se is not the point here. It was the people involved and the lessons obtained from them. But it seems that the healing I obtained via Reiki was the "set up" in which the lesson played itself out.

This Reiki group was a pretty funny collection of people. The general outline of their affiliation, as far as I could determine, was that they all attended a local Metaphysical/Spiritualist church that had brought the Reiki Master in as part of their many program presentations. Apparently, they also arranged seminars of other teachings and were involved in promulgating many popular modalities such as Hawaiian Huna teachings, psychic surgery, Kabballah, Tarot classes, meditation classes, channeling classes, Native American shamanism classes, Sweat Lodges, and on and on and on. It was a veritable supermarket of New Age Goodies!

Now, having had my personal evidence of the usefulness of Reiki, I was pretty excited to see what else was on the menu! Heck, if that worked, who knows what things I had been passing by in the years that I had been a student and not a participant! A whole new world opened up for me here and I was ready to dive in! I had never been much of a joiner or a group person, but this Reiki crowd that met every Wednesday night was so wonderful and fun and had had such a profound effect on me in terms of healing that I knew that it was time to get over this little loner glitch in my personality. After all, I had found "my group", or so it seemed.

I shared a little bit about my Spirit Release work with the group and they all nodded sagely that they knew all about such problems and their minister down at the Metaphysical Church had talked about such things, telling them that they had only to surround themselves with love and light and they were okay. I pointed out that some serious clinical research did not support this, but they assured me it was true. People only had attachments if they were not sufficiently adept at this "surrounding oneself with love and light," and the only way to do that was, of course, to learn the proper techniques from such a teacher as the Great Reverend Ruth down at the church. Reverend Ruth also seemed to be an expert on about everything else, so I was pretty interested in meeting such a paragon. Not only that, but the Reiki attunements were supposed to "set the direction of energy flow" so that no negative energy could enter a person's "auric field". So, I no longer had to worry about attachments and so forth. I had become a veritable "light being" and any problems in my deep psyche or any idea of darkness in the outer world could not survive in such light! Wow! What a deal! I even had the idea that all future clients who came to me for spirit release should have the Reiki attunements to keep them protected from that point on. Heck, I wanted to give the whole planet Reiki! Having such a healing sure does get a person all fired up!

So, I was invited to the Church. Reverend Ruth, the "Maven of Mystery" was introduced to me by one of the Reiki group. I was a bit surprised at the adoring devotee manner that all of the Reiki people took on once they had entered the environs of the Church. And, I didn't quite know what to make of Reverend Ruth sitting there in her wheelchair. But I felt a frisson of something cold when I looked in her eyes, and it almost seemed that there was something else in there for a moment looking back at me before it quickly retreated. And again, I doubted my perception. Surely the teacher of all these wonderful, loving people with whom I was now associated could not be less than holy! After all, hadn't she been the wellspring from which Reiki, my salvation, had been drawn?

Just as in an ordinary church, the service included singing hymns. Well, that's fine! I'm a hymn singer from way back – always my favorite part of going to church. The problem here was that the selection was a song that no one had ever heard before. Not only that, it was evident that the organist who selected it had never heard it either! To make the matter worse, the organist had only the most rudimentary skills with the instrument, and took so long to place her fingers on the keys in response to reading the notes, that the tempo was something akin to a funeral dirge mired in quicksand. The congregation – mostly women – was all waiting for each note to be able to follow. The note would come, obscured in a bass chord that was a lot like the bellowing of a rutting elephant, and the voices would all tremble into action trying to match the identified pitch… only to have the organist suddenly decide she had hit the wrong key, fumble to the right one, and then all the congregation would jerk their voices in mid-warble to the amended note. At least nobody was going to be hypnotized by *this*, I thought!

Fortunately, my sense of humor did not desert me, even though my aesthetic sensibilities were being savaged to the point that it was actually painful! Since I could not only read music, but could sing as well, I decided to help the situation out a bit by singing the correct notes, at the correct tempo, just loud enough so that the people around me could catch on and follow. I was hoping that this would help both the organist and the congregation to make it through this performance, bringing it to an earlier conclusion than the next ice age.

That part worked well enough, and soon everyone was getting it and singing along. The only problem was the organist was still lagging behind, and the singers were leaving her in the dust. The song was finished with grace and aplomb; but still the organist kept plodding along to her ill-timed and tardy finish. By this time, the entire congregation was struggling to suppress giggles and there was a lot of coughing into handkerchiefs to cover the outright laughter. The final chord was tortured out of the poor instrument, (the rutting elephant "scored"), and everyone sat down in relief wiping tears of laughter out of their eyes, in the perfect mood to get in the spirit. I sat down and glanced around to find Reverend Ruth glaring at me with all the friendliness of a coiled rattlesnake. So much for humor! She obviously had none.

The sermon was being delivered by a woman we will call "Hillary", who channeled somebody or other who was supposed to be something like an Ascended Master or a dead dude (I have forgotten which). Hillary was a very sweet elderly lady with blue hair and wearing a print silk dress, looking for the entire world like anyone's grandma. She just radiated grandmotherly comfort as she talked. She started off in a silvery tremulous voice talking about love and opening the "heart center" and so on. There were overtones of Helena Blavatsky and Alice Bailey in her descriptions of "planes and bodies" of the individual soul. As she got warmed up, her eyes began to glow with subtle power. Her voice became stronger and more urgent and the message turned to saving the world with this love that was supposed to manifest when one's heart center was opened and connected via these "planes and bodies" which were to be activated through certain activities that were not clearly defined as yet. As she talked, she began to walk back and forth in an animated way. Every part of her body was being involved in the action – the words – the message. She was talking with her whole body.

Now the strange thing happened... as she was walking across the little dais in this animated delivery of love and light, she suddenly stopped, frozen for a moment, and sort of trembled slightly and then snapped to attention. She looked around the room at all the breathless, expectant faces – a cool-eyed assessment in the midst of the feverish anticipation of the audience. Her head suddenly snapped back and her "control" was in *full* control. Hoo, boy! Time to rock and roll!

I don't know who this guy she was channeling was, but I can say that he was really good! He must have been a Pentecostal preacher in his last life. It was like being at an old time Southern Revival at its best. There was hooting and hollering and drama. Strutting and stomping and pounding on the podium. The only thing was, the message had changed ever so subtly. Most of the people in the room were hypnotized at this point by the drama they had been drawn into and didn't realize what was going on, but I was remembering the Church I had attended with my ex-husband where I had been exposed to so many preachers of this type. I had already learned about this showmanship and the old "Wolf in Sheep's Clothing" syndrome and I could see that here we were dealing with the same hypnotic factors that were at work in most Christian churches.

The message had gone from love and light and opening the heart, to guilt and chastisement for not being successful in giving enough love and light or opening the heart sufficiently, and this was to be rectified, of course, by more attendance of classes and meditation sessions, more giving of time, resources and most especially money. *Attend church, give money, take classes, and get salvation.* Simple formula. Nothing terribly unusual. Same song, different verse.

After the sermon was over, a couple of the people who were in Reverend Ruth's channeling classes were going to demonstrate their "powers". One of these was Trudy. I was watching with great interest to see how effective these classes might be.

Trudy put her hand to her head and tried to tune in. "There is someone here who has just received unhappy news..." she began. And, of course, in any group that is a pretty good guess; so the person who had just received an "unhappy" phone call raised her hand excitedly and said, "Yes, yes! Me! Me!" So, Trudy tuned in to her further and made a series of pronouncements that either evinced a nod or a puzzled look.

It was a pretty poor performance of cold-reading. Years ago I spent a lot of money checking out various readers and psychics in the area. I had quickly learned their form of reading cues in the face or response of the person in order to gradually weed out what did not apply, and then they were able to make a final, definite and "amazing" pronouncement of the facts that were bothering the individual at the end of this exercise in subtle probing.

Of course I had noticed that many times, things *were* "received" which were clearly out of the cold-reading loop, and quite accurate, but it was statistically no more or less amazing than two friends who have the same thought at the same time. No special rating as a psychic is needed. And my estimation was that *everyone* was psychic, to one extent or another, so "no cigar".

The problem arises when the subject of a reading gives away the anticipated answer in their voice or the phrasing of the question. This enables the reader to know what the client *wants* to hear, and they feed this wishful thinking.

There were dozens of instances, when I was younger and playing with this sort of thing, that the reader would make "predictions" based on what the client wanted to hear, and because it was the desired thing, the person seeking the information felt *en rapport* with the reader and then ascribed to them all sorts of powers and abilities that simply were not there. Then later, when the prediction did *not* transpire as described, the individual was so invested in their belief of the powers of their chosen reader that they would go to all kinds of ridiculous extremes to excuse the failed prediction.

This is a very common situation. These failures are the clues we are given in these kinds of things, they are little alerts to the larger picture, but we tend to ignore them; to cover them up; to excuse them; to continue to believe what we *like* rather than what is *true* – simply because it matches our preconceived notions of how things would be if we *were* creating our own reality!

After Trudy was done with her rather embarrassing demonstration, another student that I did not know got up to do readings. For some reason, she picked me – probably because I was a new and unfamiliar face.

I had long ago schooled myself to be able to keep a poker face and a flat voice when checking out readers, so I kept my face a blank while at the same time providing ambiguous feedback such as "maybe", or "it could be described that way," and so on. At the same time, I was inwardly open to contact so that if there *was* a real talent going on here, there would be no deliberate blocking. I was trying to neither hinder the tuning in nor give anything away externally.

To make a long story short, the reading was worse than would have been accomplished by just random guessing. I was not impressed by the graduates of Reverend Ruth's classes.

After this non-event, a healing circle was formed where everyone gathered around Reverend Ruth and her assistant, laying on hands, praying and giving "love and light" and energy. It was pretty much like any laying on of hands in a Pentecostal church. The only difference was, Reverend Ruth seemed to sort of swell from the contact. I wasn't sure if my eyes were deceiving me, but everyone else was perfectly exhausted after the service, so *something* was draining them.

Again I was wondering why a service that was supposed to "feed" and "energize" a given flock, was actually doing the opposite.

On the drive home, I heard nothing but the praises of Reverend Ruth and her "great works". And, now, since I was considered to be more a part of the group, it being assumed, I guess, that I had been taken in by the recent performance, a new thing was revealed to me. Apparently Reverend Ruth had a secret circle which admitted only those who had proven worthy or had passed certain tests administered in her many classes. The members of this inner group were promised that Reverend Ruth was going to give them many great secrets. My hostess had already signed up for the next series of lessons and sessions with the Great One in hopes that she would be able to pass the tests and be admitted to the inner group.

I said nothing, but I knew I didn't want to go back to that church because it made me feel ill at ease and was clearly a waste of time. I couldn't understand how the members of the Reiki group, which seemed to be so much more advanced than other groups I had encountered in past, could be so taken in by that drivel. But, on the other hand, maybe it was *me* who had the problem because it was clear to me that everyone involved in the Reiki group was certainly full of love and benevolence and good intentions.

The Reiki group was a gathering of people of many ages and backgrounds. "Louise", the woman who had approached my mother with the initial invitations, was an older lady, of retirement age (otherwise she would not have been in the class) but she physically appeared *much* younger. She didn't look a day over 35. She had a knockout figure and such a charming and feminine presence that you just had to be in awe of her ability to control by seeming *not* to do so! She had an almost breathy voice like Marilyn Monroe, gorgeous red hair and alabaster skin. She was also the one who had brought the idea of the original Reiki class to Reverend Ruth, having lived in Virginia Beach and spent some time with the A.R.E.[42] crowd up there, and that was where she had learned about Reiki and had taken her attunements. (It was impressed upon us that we were so fortunate to have our initiations from one of Takata's original students

---

[42] The Association for Research and Enlightenment, Inc. is a foundation associated with the writings of Edgar Cayce (1877-1945), who is considered the best documented psychic of the twentieth century. A.R.E. headquarters are located in Virginia Beach, VA.

since Reiki had later split and been corrupted after Takata's death, but that's another story.) Louise had spent most of her life working as a domestic on wealthy estates in the Northeast.

Then there was "Trudy" and her husband "George" who were also past retirement age. Trudy was a tall, rangy woman, more like a man in many of her characteristics than a woman. In the beginning, I thought she was very funny and engaging with her snappy comebacks and wry humor. But, as time went by, I began to see that there was a certain element of cruelty in her remarks, especially when addressing or talking about her husband. I wrote it off as great familiarity of people long married. And who was I to say that he hadn't done things to invite such remarks? Maybe that was their way of showing affection? George was a retired businessman – owner of several patents and former owner of several factories. Trudy had been his secretary when they met, divorced their respective mates, and married each other. They were considered to be the wealthiest members of the group, and thus had some status.

There were several others of this older group who remain in the background, so need not be mentioned specifically – about 4 or 5 who were regulars. Two of them were nurses, and I can't remember much about the others.

Then there was the younger contingent – some my age or a little younger – the most active being "Candy" and "Sandy". In case the reader has not already guessed, "Candy" is the same as "Maryann" in the first section of *High Strangeness*. At the time I began writing these pages, I had no idea that I would end up talking about Candy in any terms other than to introduce the subject. I did not intend to get into the further details involved which include the name clues. Thus, she was given a pseudonym there that was simply a name pulled out of the air. In the present instance, since the name was part of the clue system, I have had to get more creative and select names that are more functional so to speak.

Sandy was an ex-bartender who had been "awakened" to spiritual issues by the death of her fiancé. After that, she decided to go to school to become a massage therapist and get out of the bar environment. Until much later, I didn't know any more about her.

And last, there were the *very* young members, which included "Tim". Tim was a very young fellow who seemed to be very advanced in the spiritual sense. It was unusual to see someone so young who was so devoted to helping others. He stated his religious affiliation as Wiccan, and this later proved to have some interesting effects.

As we continued to meet on Wednesday nights for Reiki sessions, a lot of conversation took place over the tables. Since Reiki really doesn't require meditative focus or any kind of "Mumbo Jumbo" type concentration, we were all basically free to do two things at once – Reiki and talk. These conversations really ran the gamut when the topic was about our various experiences with spiritual development. I was a bit reluctant to talk about my own; but after awhile, I felt more comfortable sharing some of it with the others, and we were able to begin to form a real bond of closeness.

I very quickly brought the Reiki group up to date on my ideas about channeling and the experiment that was going on with Frank. One of the ladies from the older group pronounced balefully upon our selection of the board as an instrument, citing the movie *The Exorcist* as proof of its direful consequences.

I countered with the facts of the real case on which the movie was based which did *not* indicate that a board was the main player in the demonic possession, and further cited the fact that most of the greatest material in the history of channeling has either come through a board type instrument, or began with one.

Everyone began asking more and more questions about the experiment, so I told them all I could and also talked more about my hypnosis work. The subject of hypnosis led to my recent revelations about UFOs and abductions which had sort of set me up to be led to the Reiki crowd to begin with, and everyone had a really good laugh that I had to be chased by aliens before I found Reiki.

All were having a good time, and there was a lot of laughter and fun and playing around. Before I went home that night, I mentioned that if anyone wanted to participate in our experiment, they were welcome to come on Saturday nights when we sat for contact. Four or five of them were excited and agreed that they wanted to try it out so it was planned that they would come.

The next day, Candy called me and was very mysterious sounding when she said, "There is something I have to tell you and I don't really know how, but you had better beware of Trudy."

"What?" I said. "What do you mean?" A serpent in Reiki Eden?

Candy explained: it seemed that the previous night after I had left that Trudy had made very nasty remarks about me being a "know it all" and that anybody who participated in anything I suggested was definitely being taken in and led down the primrose path to destruction; words to that effect, anyway. I was terribly hurt because I don't preach, but tend to share by describing my experiences and the research of others who are far more qualified than I am to give opinions.

"But you have to understand," Candy continued. "Trudy is like a mother to the rest of us. She's just being protective. She means well, but she's from the old school. She grew up with Cayce and all that. She likes the robes and rituals and things. Reverend Ruth is even saying that she is sort of preparing Trudy to take over the Church, so of course she feels responsible for all of us like we were her own children."

The upshot of the whole conversation was that Candy wanted me to be careful what I talked about to Trudy and the others because they were old fashioned and narrow minded, even if they meant well. It was a maneuver designed to spare their feelings. This, of course, was deemed proper in my mind because it was part of the "love and light" philosophy of acceptance. At the same time, Candy wanted to participate in our experiment and also to have some hypnosis sessions done to speed up her spiritual advancement, since she had in mind that she was destined to be the next Jeane Dixon. Apparently Reverend Ruth had told her that she was showing promise to be admitted to the deeper lessons, but not yet. And Candy was sure that she was ready and that it was just more of the old fashioned, narrow mindedness of the older crowd who weren't part of the New Paradigm of very advanced souls in young bodies. They just didn't understand how fast people were able to progress in the present urgent time.

I wasn't sure that I agreed with her all the way on her ideas that she was supposed to move so rapidly, but I reserved judgment until I could make a better assessment. But at least there was a reasonable explanation for the funny undercurrent that I had sensed at the church – the old fashioned attitude of the older folks as opposed to the younger ones. It made perfect sense. I could finally get some rest from the worrisome little glitches. And I also knew that Trudy was deeply involved there with the church itself. I didn't know what to make of the "robes and rituals" remark, because I hadn't really seen anything of that specific nature there, but I let it pass. Another thing that was clear from this conversation was that Candy wanted to be my friend and have a much closer friendship than just the once weekly Reiki meeting.

Candy was a lot of fun! She was always laughing and joking and mimicking other people's little foibles in the most hilarious way. She could tell a story so that you were reduced to holding your sides from laughing so hard while the tears would stream down your face with glee at her portrayal of everyone's little egotistical hang ups. It was always prefaced by, "You know I *love* so-and-so, but..." It was "all in good fun", and she didn't mean any harm!

But I wondered. If she was saying all these things about other people, was she saying similar things about me to them?

Of course not! Candy was my friend. We had a special rapport which was in evidence from all the many, daily, synchronous events that occurred when we were in contact. I would be talking to someone about something, or thinking about something, and Candy would call and start talking about the same exact things. When we talked on the phone, there were strange clicks and buzzes on the line and after we had begun to investigate the parameters of her alien abductions via hypnosis, we joked that the government was eavesdropping on the line. I laughed at the thought of anybody tapping my line to see what we knew about aliens, because it was a certainty that we knew very little. But Candy was convinced that she had something they were after, that the objective of any surveillance was herself. She was even convinced that a man with whom she had interacted in a seeming abduction at about the same time I had been led to the Reiki group was a government agent sent to keep an eye on her. On the other hand, she felt that he was her soul mate and that he was being used to lure her into some kind of government conspiracy and it was her job to rescue him in some way.

The next Reiki night, I noticed a distinct tightness in Trudy's face when I walked in the room and said hello. She was distant and cool in her manner. Because I had been primed by Candy to be more patient and understanding, I tried to be especially nice to her and defer to her ideas and opinions and keep my own to myself.

Meanwhile, Trudy and George seemed to be having problems. George stopped coming to the Reiki sessions. Trudy would spend the entire session telling us all how dreadfully George tortured her and how he played control games with finances and how tired she was of living in this hell. She needed to get away, so she went away to visit a friend.

One night shortly thereafter, Louise called me, asking if I could accompany her and Candy on a visit to George, who had called her for someone to talk to since he had been "abandoned" by his wife. Louise told us (on the way to his house) that she felt as if George had shown too much interest in her over the phone, so Louise didn't want to upset Trudy by having a private visit with her husband, and that was why we were coming along.

At this little pizza and talk gathering, George broke down and began to cry and tell us a terrible tale of how abused by Trudy he had been for the past few years... how she had turned from a sweet, devoted wife to an abusive monster who had even physically threatened him and since he was now getting sick and old, he feared for his life. He was afraid she would kill him to have access to his money.

We listened in horror at the recitation of events and proofs that all was not well in that household. With every incident he recounted, one or the other of the three of us would suggest that perhaps there was just simply misunderstanding. He insisted that his life was in danger; that it was *not* just a misunderstanding.

With every complaint he made, one of the three of us offered something in the way of a solution, but every idea was turned aside by the fact that it was clear in his mind that she had some sort of "power" and he was helpless in the face of it; he even suspected she might try to poison him! But, in all, he seemed to be so afraid of her that he could do nothing but sit back and be killed by chemicals or mayhem! I was pretty disgusted with *that* attitude. I couldn't grasp a person sitting there saying their life was in danger and being unable or unwilling to do anything about it but weep. So, I simply told him that if he *really believed* that he was in physical danger, he ought to just see an attorney and change the locks while Trudy was gone! That certainly seemed like a reasonable solution to me, *if what he was saying was true.* And he assured us in every breath that it was!

So, George had a good cry and finally was so encouraged that he said he was going to see an attorney the next morning. Everybody gave him sympathy and hugs, we all went home, and that was that. Crisis solved.

The next Reiki night, I walked in the room and Trudy saw me coming and stopped what she was doing and headed right for me. She stopped in front of me and denounced me for the vile serpent I was, and how dare I tell her husband to divorce her and lock her out of her own house! And then she said she couldn't stand to be in the same room with such a horrible person as I was, and stormed out!

Everybody stood around looking stupid for a minute. I looked at Louise and Candy who were both there when I said what I said to George (which certainly had been repeated by him to Trudy, though it was not repeated as I said it nor was it in the context in which I had said it).

Neither of them said a word in my defense!

Later, in private, they were sympathetic and told me not to worry, and that Trudy was just going through a difficult time, but I was a little confused that they would stand there and *not* say something to straighten the matter out immediately, which could have happened if they had pointed out what George had said to provoke my advice!

If Trudy was innocent, as they were suggesting, didn't she need to be warned that her husband was spreading such lies about her? I was pretty confused, and Louise and Candy were entirely insouciant about the whole thing.

The next day, Louise called me and said that a meeting had been set up at a local restaurant so that we could all get together with Trudy and iron this problem out. Was I willing to come?

Of course, I was. I detested discord and misunderstanding and I *never* intended to hurt Trudy. I was simply responding to George's claims that he was afraid for his life. If what he had been saying was true, he should certainly have taken my advice. But obviously, there was some kind of game going on there and both of them were sucking everybody else into it.

I arrived at the restaurant with Louise and Candy. Trudy and several others (who were apparently on her side) were already there at a large, round table. Louise informed us that she had also invited another lady that no one else there had ever met except Louise, and who was reputed to be a *very* good psychic. She just thought it was a good opportunity for all of us to meet this lady, *if* she came, and it was doubtful she would, because she was very reclusive. Louise met her while working as a home health aide, and she raved about this unknown lady's abilities as a "seer".

Trudy was tightlipped and obviously not happy to be present. I was not terribly happy with the situation myself (having made an innocent honest remark that sort of exploded in my face) but I was determined to make the effort for everything to return to normal with the group, and to assure Trudy that if anybody was playing games, it wasn't me. I was pretty upset that Louise and Candy hadn't just talked to Trudy to explain the exact circumstances of the remark that was the cause of all this brouhaha. Had they done so, I felt, the upset would have just evaporated.

Just then, the expected/unexpected guest arrived – Jeanie – and that is her real name, but she has passed over now so it doesn't matter any longer whether I use her real name or not. She was like a rare tropical bird that sort of fluttered about for a moment and then chose to land in the chair right next to me. But just as she started to sit, the chair (on wheels) actually *shot across the room behind her*! I had to literally catch her to prevent her from sitting on the floor with a thud! Being elderly and rather fragile in appearance, such a fall could have been completely disastrous. She was startled and confused for a moment, and Candy jumped up and retrieved the chair. We got Jeanie seated and settled, concerned that she would be just overwhelmed by such a thing and go off on some sort of old lady whining and complaining about chairs and so forth.

But Jeanie didn't miss a beat! She looked at me and said, "Ohhhh! I see all kinds of good spirits around you! You are gonna do *big* things! Yes. Big things! Oh, my! We have to talk, you and I! But later. Let's order now; I'm starved."

Well, that certainly made a shift in the atmosphere and lightened things up a bit. If it hadn't been for Trudy brooding on the other side of the table, looking daggers at me, and dabbing a tear away from time to time, a good time would have been had by all.

We did finally get to discussion of the matter, and Trudy was just obstinately predisposed to think that no matter what I said, I was an evil person. That was the bottom line. I explained the whole incident from start to finish, and while I was doing so, I looked to Louise and Candy for confirmation of the salient points, of which they were witnesses, and the most they would say was, "Yes, it seemed to be that way," or, "I think it was that way too, but I can't remember exactly." All the sympathy was going to "poor Trudy!" It was maddening! I never in my life was in the presence of such mealy-mouthed people who, claiming to be friends, were unable to offer an opinion of their own much less to simply recount the events as they occurred!

But Jeanie, sitting beside me, piped up with, "You better believe what this girl is saying because I can *see* the light in her! There are a *lot* of good spirits around her, and if she says that's the way it happened, then that's the way it happened!" So, everybody sort of looked at her in surprise and got quiet. It had to have been one of the strangest luncheons I ever attended in my life!

Well, Trudy was eventually grudgingly mollified and agreed to "let bygones be bygones," and we all exited to the parking lot to go home. Jeanie asked for my arm to walk her to her car, and on the way gave me her phone number and said I should call her as soon as I got home.

So, I did. What she told me was about the most bizarre thing I had ever heard! She said to me, "Did you see that Trudy make my chair shoot across the floor? She didn't want me there, I can tell you! She was furious that I came. And I almost didn't. I could feel her hate when I was getting dressed! But spirit told me that there was a reason for me to go, and I *had* to do it. That reason was that you needed an ally. And she hates you, too! And she's messed up with all kinds of dark things. That group at that church – I'd stay away from them if I were you! That Reverend Ruth – she's at the middle of some evil things, you mark my words!" and so on. When I asked her what was going on with this whole misunderstanding we had just been through she said, "You have the light in you. Those people hate you for that. When the light comes into the middle of darkness, it exposes things. They can't stand the light. They will do anything to get you away from them. You have to be careful. There are things out there that can really hurt you. I know! They've been trying to kill me all my life. Now they are trying to kill you! And beware of Louise! Did you see how she didn't say a *word* in your defense? Well, that's because she's one of them! And Candy, too. You need to be on your guard."

By this time I was *sure* that Jeanie was like "Aunt Clara" on the old TV show, *Bewitched*. What she was saying just did *not* make sense. It was crazy talk. But she was so sweet and sincere and urgently concerned that I assured her I would take the greatest care. I promised to keep in touch. I told Candy what she had said and we agreed that the poor dear may have been a good psychic (as Louise assured us) but she was obviously over the hill now!

By this time, Candy and I were on the phone every day. When not on the phone, she would drop by and I would stop what I was doing to sit and chat. I really enjoyed her company, and she seemed to enjoy mine and we both had a voracious curiosity about the alien abduction research, so we spent a lot of time talking about it and comparing it to the different teachings that Reverend Ruth was sponsoring at the church, as well as anything and everything we heard about from any other source. When I could get out of the house once in awhile, we would go to rock shops and metaphysical stores and look at all the stuff that was available, occasionally buying a rock or sage or some other such "energy enhancing" thing.

A few weeks went by and we continued with our Reiki nights, and things were better, but there was still an undercurrent of dis-ease. I was doing my best to put as much love and light around the situation as I could, and to also keep myself in a "bubble" of love and light so that all my words and actions would issue from a deep place of love and understanding in my heart. I was terribly grieved that Trudy had been so hurt by me, and I did all I could to make it up to her. But she began to change in some way; even her appearance changed and she began to get heavier. At the same time, her husband just seemed to be wasting away to nothing. He whined and complained and Trudy rolled her eyes in exasperation.

Meanwhile, Candy and several of the others were coming to the experimental channeling sessions on Saturday nights, and even if all we did was chat with dead dudes, we still had fun with it. And all of them wanted to experiment with the Spirit Release process, so there was a lot of experimenting and investigating going on off to the side of the regular Reiki group. Two events stand out at this point as needing to be included here.

The first one was a phone call I received one night from Tim, the young kid who had been participating in the local Wicca group. He was in a complete panic. He had been trying one of the rituals that he had been taught in the coven. I don't know if the exact procedure he was given was what he had followed, or if he was improvising, but the gist of it was that he had run hot water in his tiny bathroom to make it like a sauna, and then had been doing some sort of calling forth ritual while staring in the mirror. (Seems to me that he would have had to be constantly wiping the steam off the glass to even do this!) Well, the upshot of it was that a horrible demonic face had appeared in the mirror and had told him that it was his companion and was now going to have fun tormenting him or "feeding" on him or something. He had the feeling of pressure and his heart started beating like crazy and he thought he was going to die.

He was actually calling from the hospital where they had given him some sort of sedative and had told him that nothing was essentially wrong with him except some sort of stress reaction. He was terrified to go home because the demon was there, and what should he do?

Well, I was a little shocked that such a thing could happen to a Reiki initiate, especially since he and Candy had taken their Second Level initiations. But, I tried to calm him down and told him to come right over – I would fix him up pretty quick.

I called Candy and explained the situation to her, and she was pretty excited at the thought of seeing a real exorcism. She agreed to come right away.

It was a long wait before Tim arrived, and when he did, he was in a *terrible* state. He told us that on his way over, he had actually been in an accident – another car had sideswiped him and spun his car around and into a ditch. He was certain that it was the demon doing it, and his terror had practically gone through the roof!

We got him on Candy's massage table, which had been set up, and started giving him Reiki just to calm him down. As we did, there were all kinds of strange things going on with his body. Muscles would jump and jerk in a way that was definitely *not* normal, and he said he could actually *feel* something "slithery" moving around in him!

Well, we were sort of freaking out too, but my experience with similar things during many hypnosis sessions had schooled me to remain calm and in control of the situation. I asked Tim to recount exactly everything that was done and said, and as he did, he began to breathe more normally and calmed down.

Soon I was able to put him under hypnosis and address the entity directly. It was a new level of Spirit Release – rather bizarre to say the least. As I addressed what was clearly *not* a dead dude, nor an elemental spirit, but something altogether more powerful, devious, and nasty, poor Tim alternately swelled and expelled the most horrible gas imaginable. This was definitely not a case of finding a poor lost, departed individual who needed to be counseled to "go into the light", thereby releasing the victim. This critter had no intention of going anywhere! He had been "invited", and he liked his new "home", and there was not going to be an eviction!

Well, I had a different opinion of the matter and was equally determined that he was going to depart rather quickly, so it was pretty much a matter of who was going to prove to be the strongest in the dispute.

I did the usual calling on the "guides" and "light workers" of the astral planes to come and assist in the freeing of the victim, followed standard procedures and so forth. No dice. I did the "in the name of Jesus" routine, which can work depending on the religious affiliation of the victim. Didn't work. The entity was making poor Tim jerk and jump on the table, constantly swelling with gas and expelling it in quantities that were simply abnormal by any pathological criteria. When I directed Tim to join with Candy and me in generating light and heat to encapsulate the entity, it began to complain that it was "hot" and "burned" and for us to just stop and leave it alone. It started to whine and moan that we ought to have sympathy and compassion for him because that *was* the philosophy we were espousing in the "love and light" New Age trend. It was actually a caricature of the recent machinations of both Trudy and George and I was not fooled one bit.

Finally, I just simply told the entity that I was *not* going to leave him alone, I was not going to stop harassing him with heat and light, that if I had to, we would stay there all night and all the next day and however many days it took. That seemed to have an effect, and I demanded that the entity leave in no uncertain terms, and with a last "blow up" of Tim's abdomen, followed by a particularly noisy expulsion of the most horrible sulfurous stench, the entity left and Tim was finally peaceful.

I brought him out of the hypnosis and we discussed the matter. One of the things that the entity had said was that he had been initially attracted to Tim at one of the coven meetings where a whole host of such entities commonly congregated, selecting their prey, and then hanging around, waiting for the opportunity to "connect" in a more permanent way. They would influence the individual to perform certain acts that would facilitate entry, and even though the individual thought that these ideas were their own, they were not. Apparently enough mind contact can be made to plant thoughts and ideas that will lead to fuller possession.

Well, Tim was certainly cured of his interest in Wicca. After such a horrible experience, he was not going to risk going back into that environment and getting another "hanger on" of that sort!

We agreed between us to keep this quiet because of Tim's obvious embarrassment as well as the fact that we were trying to "protect" Trudy in her "less advanced" beliefs. Candy said that she just could not handle the idea that "love and light" was not the be-all and end-all of all answers.

But I was concerned about the implication that Reiki was *not* as all-powerful and protective as was being taught. I felt that we needed to convey this to the others in some way. Candy agreed, but urged that I let *her* do it in her own way and time. I agreed.

The second event of concern was directly stimulated by this incident with Tim. Candy wanted me to do the Spirit Release process on her "just to see". She had been on a terrible emotional roller coaster for some time, and she was now thinking that much of this could be directly attributed to attachments of one sort or another. I agreed and we scheduled it for the next day.

For some reason Candy wanted to bring Louise in on the action, and with reservation, I agreed. Candy was, after all, the subject and whatever was necessary for the comfort of the subject was to be considered desirable. So, Louise was informed, and after expressing interest in being a witness she invited us to do the session at her house, which was okay with me.

During this session, an attached entity identified himself as "Thomas". His story was that he had been a practitioner of Voodoo in Haiti and had been killed by a rival Voodoo doctor in 1945. The *real* shocker was when he claimed that he had been induced or commanded by a "magician" to attach to Candy as a "control conduit".

A "Magician"? Who, where, when? And all that.

He would *not* identify the "who", and it was clear that he was terrified of punishment if he betrayed his "master", but he did say that this had occurred in the previous few weeks and that Candy *did* know this individual.

There was another entity that had attached to Candy via marital relations with her husband, but that one was rather glad to be sent to the light, and gave no trouble.

There were two suicides who had attached to the first frequency available host, i.e., Candy, in their fear of having violated a religious taboo in killing themselves. This is not uncommon. One of the biggest reasons for spirit attachment is the ignorance of the individual about what *really* happens after death. A strong religious belief can be as detrimental as no belief in an afterlife at all. There was also an automobile accident victim, as well as a victim of a shooting. I never found out if that particular entity was involved in a crime or if it was just an accident, because he/she left almost immediately to go into the light, after having followed the process with the previous entities, learning from what was being exchanged with them. This is also not uncommon. If there are multiple attachments, they seem to be influenced by the actions of each other in their "shared host/home".

Both Candy and I were beginning to get the idea that there was something fishy going on here, and she was somewhat upset to think that even *she* had been attached in this way by "someone" trying to control her. She was also angry and determined to find out *who* it was.

Louise, as usual, expressed no opinion. She kept saying, "Isn't that amazing!" over and over again with her eyes wide and innocent.

Now, what happened next was surrounded by several weeks of bizarre synchronicities that are just simply too numerous to recount. I am also sorry that I didn't keep a daily journal of events because trying to remember everything in the proper order is surely not easy.

For some time – almost exactly two years – I had been trying to obtain a second copy of Velikovsky's *Worlds in Collision* without success. I had been to every book store, had called book distributors; had even contacted the publisher who told me it was out of print with no plans for another press run. So, I had gone around to all the used bookstores and filled out little cards for them to look for it and call me if it became available.

Another event that converged at this moment in time was a funny thing that had to do with the murder investigation I had been involved in peripherally back in 1993 which I should divert to recount as briefly as possible since it certainly was a sort of a "doorway" to the later UFO/Alien awakening in my own life.

As our experiment in channeling had proceeded, we discussed the many possible ways that a true higher source might be identified or validated. We both thought that a higher source, by virtue of greater and more inclusive Cosmic Perspective, would be able to make absolutely stunning predictions that would hit the mark every time. But, in a short term feedback loop of testing, how to validate such a hypothesis?

As recounted in *High Strangeness*, Frank came up with a solution to play the Lottery and even though we did have a few hits in that regard, they usually came up on a different day than predicted.

In January of 1993, my old friend Keith died.[43] I had driven up to see him some months earlier and he looked terrible. It had been 20 years – almost to the day – since I had sat in his house and watched him brandish a gun with the ostensible purpose of putting a period to his existence.

During my last visit with him, Keith seemed tired and broken. He told me that if he had a switch on the wall to turn out the lights of his life the same way he could bring darkness to his room before sleeping, he wasn't sure he'd have the courage to do it. "I realize at long last what a coward I have always been," he said. The bitterness in his voice nearly undid me. Whether it was a new manipulation or just a sad statement of fact, borne of great struggle in his life, I will never know.

When his secretary called to tell me he had passed away during the night of the 23rd of January, I felt as though a door had closed on an entire episode of my life. In his honor, I put on a tape of Puccini. It actually wasn't too bad.

A few weeks later, a local 12 year old girl was reported missing. I was very shaken by it because, when her photo was displayed on the television, she looked so much like my number two daughter that I almost began to cry! I was surprised by my emotional reaction! And, even more surprised when, watching the news report, I "saw" in my mind's eye that the girl was dead, naked, wrapped in what looked like saran wrap, lying in a stand of pine trees. I even had a sensation of the general location.

The vision came to me as if remembering an intense experience from my own past. In my mind, the heat shimmered at the edges of the shade in a pine woods. Mottled shadows moved slightly as the rising air softly rushed between the pine needles. I could actually smell the pine sap. The body lay nearly face down with an arm tucked under the side. Flies droned sickeningly as they reconnoitered the rapidly putrefying flesh. I didn't know exactly where this place was, but I knew I was seeing the missing girl.

I forced my normal awareness back into place, much like pulling a shade down over a window, and continued to listen to the details about the child. She had only been missing since the day before, and, under normal circumstances, no investigation of any kind would be launched for at least twenty-four hours. But, in this case, the family was close to a high ranking member of the sheriff's

---

[43] See *Amazing Grace* for details.

department. From his personal knowledge of the situation and the persons involved, he determined that foul play must be strongly suspected. A full scale investigation had been launched within just a couple of hours after she was due home.

The name of the "high ranking sheriff's department official" was given in the report as Henry Smith (a pseudonym). Good old Henry. Son of a friend and former employer of my mother; two years ahead of me in high school. As I watched the newscast, I wanted to tell them there was no point in looking for a living child. The child was already dead.

There had been a number of occasions in my life when I just "knew" things about crimes I would read or hear about. It's always an initial flash of insight which, if I try to push it further, sort of disappears. It actually became a sort of side hobby to make predictions about who may have done a crime just to test myself. On the occasions when I did get an initial impression, I was always right. But I never had an opportunity to provide the information to anyone who could do anything about it. In fact, I probably would not have told anyone if I had the chance, because I had no taste for being labeled a "psychic freak".

The point is, I keep score with *myself*. It's a game I play and I win only if I am right on every point and it is certain that I could have no way of knowing what I know by normal means. When I get the information, it is good, but there are times when I get nothing at all. It is as though some people and some situations are simply on another channel.

But this case was one I could tune in to more clearly than others. I had a twelve-year-old daughter of my own who was so similar in appearance. The newscaster described a child very much like my own.

It seems that the missing girl, the perfect child, had gotten off the school bus and disappeared. No physical evidence of any kind was found. She disappeared with books, purse and clarinet. No one saw anything at all unusual, except that the other kids on the school bus seemed to remember a blue truck in the vicinity. The details on the blue truck were vague and there seemed to be nothing else to go on. So, I watched the case with interest.

On the following day Marcia Matthews (another pseudonym) called. Marcia is a local self-proclaimed psychic, hypnotherapist, western dancer and general wise woman. She didn't waste any time getting to the point.

"Have you heard anything about the little girl that's missing?"

I acknowledged that I had.

"Well, I just came from over there and I just want to run some things by you to get your reaction."

"What do you mean you just came from over there?" I asked.

"Well, not exactly *there*. We were at the fair, you know, and it seems the girl's parents have been working with some group over there. The cops were all over the place. So I decided to see if I could get some feelings... There's a van they were checking out... and I tell you, when I got near that van, my flesh just crawled! I mean, there is some nasty stuff there! And I just know she's alive but she doesn't have much time. I *have* to find her! She's cold and in a dark place and she's hanging on for dear life... and I'll tell you, if some of these bastards don't listen to me they're going to have that girl's death on their hands."

"Slow down, Marcia!" I was used to Marcia getting all wound up. I knew if I was going to make any sense of the conversation I was going to have to make her stop and start at the beginning.

"You and Bennie (Marcia's husband) went to the fair, right? How did you get involved with the cops? Did they just come up to you and ask you if you knew anything?"

"Well, not exactly. We saw the posters they were putting up all over, you know, the pictures of the little girl, and I went up and introduced myself and offered to help. I told them I'm a psychic and, I was surprised, they didn't seem turned off at all! In fact, they invited me over to see if I could pick up anything from a van parked behind the fair. They think that maybe one of the fair people had something to do with it."

"Why do they think that?" I asked patiently.

"Because the girl's parents belong to some civic organization doing something here at the fair and the kid has spent a lot of time in the past few days hanging out here. The cops think that maybe one of the carnies found out where she lived and abducted her."

"So tell me about this van," I prompted.

"Well, I wanted you to tell me what you get."

"It's white, full of junk, and has something blue on the engine cover," I replied promptly. I have no idea where it came from, but then, I never do.

"Yes," she urged, "but what is the blue thing."

"I have no idea." I was getting impatient. I knew the van had nothing to do with the missing girl and I could feel another one of Marcia's wild goose chases coming on.

"It's a Bible," she announced breathlessly. "A Bible! Can you figure that! And I can just see the girl on the floor in the front curled into a ball with rags thrown over her and this son of a bitch driving her down the road. He raped her, man, he tortured her... she's a mess and I've got to find her before its too late!" Marcia was starting to wind up again, so I stopped her with a question.

"Where do you think she is?"

"I'm not sure, but I know it is near her house. I get a well house – a shed, something to do with water. Oh man, she's in pain!" I could see the conversation was going nowhere so I decided to tell her the truth.

"She's dead, Marcia. She's been dead since yesterday."

"No, I don't agree. She's out there calling to me. I'm going to look. This cop named J.D. gave me her card and I am going to go and look. There's a road I noticed on our way in here. I had a funny feeling about that road and I just know she's down there. If I can't get them to look, I'll do it myself. I have to find her! When I find the spot, I'll call this J.D. and get her to get some men out there. I gotta go, I'll talk to you later."

"Sure, keep me posted." I hung up the phone wondering just what kind of cosmic drama was being played out with this event.

Marcia had probably called every psychic person she knew, gotten their impressions and was now unable to distinguish between true intuition and all the interference she was picking up. The only problem was that most of the so-called psychics around town were shrewd cold-readers with very little true ability. Oh, they had an occasional flash now and then, but generally they failed miserably. Because of psychics like that, I don't want to be numbered as part of their group.

Over the next few days I kept my own counsel. Marcia called with frequent updates of her wild goose chase. She told me that another friend of ours, Danielle, worked with the missing girl's stepfather at the local resource recovery plant.

I called Danielle to pick up any information I could. All she could tell me was a reprise of Marcia's insistence that the girl was alive and that, as far as she could see, the family was a normal happy one. Obviously, she had been talking to Marcia.

I told Danielle I was sure that the child was dead. She totally rejected the idea. But she did say that the child's stepfather was *at the plant at the time of the girl's disappearance*.

The media appealed for information on the missing child, keeping up an onslaught of endless stories about the family and how "normal" and "upstanding" they were. For some reason, I had no further insights. On the night the family appeared before the TV cameras to beg for the return of their daughter, I watched in horrified fascination. I couldn't help but put myself in their shoes. They asked for every resident of the county to search every building they owned, every shed, every pump house – again I could see Marcia's hand at work – to leave no trail un-walked and no stone unturned.

There was something odd about the interview, though. I just couldn't put my finger on it. The stepfather did all the talking while the mother sat stony faced and silent. It made me wonder. But it's easy to criticize. What I would be doing myself, I couldn't know. I couldn't go that far in my imagination. It was too terrible.

I called my friend Sandra, who was a bigwig at the state social services agency where I had also been employed so many years ago. Sandra was also extremely intuitive. In fact, she was more psychic than those people who hang out their shingle and "practice" at being psychic. As I expected, she had already done a little poking around through the files in the agency to see if there was anything on that particular family. There was.

The scuttlebutt within the agency was that the family had some problems with the girl. There were signs of rivalry between the new stepfather and the girl's natural father. There were whispers that the child had tried to run away before to go to her father. Sandra was putting her money on the stepfather as the culprit. She was convinced from what was in the social services files that sexual abuse was rampant in that house and that a confrontation on the subject had led to the child's death.

Like me, Sandra also knew the girl was dead. I pointed out that the stepfather could not have been a party to the fact the child was missing because he was at work with a lot of witnesses at the time as Danielle had asserted. We both pondered the matter in light of this information, but nothing else came up. It was most definitely a curious case.

I wondered about what was in the Social Services files. It was likely that the sheriff's department was already privy to the information that there had been problems in the home. So why had they launched a full scale crime investigation into what must have looked, at first glance, like a simple runaway?

Something wasn't adding up.

That night, I tried to meditate and clear my mind of all conflicting ideas and information. I knew the torture I would feel not knowing where my child was or if she was dead or alive, certain that every moment I would be thinking the worst and that the burden of those thoughts would drive me mad. Just thinking about it was more than I could bear. I began to cry. I silently sent a summons to the universe to bring that little girl home! Over and over I repeated it, "Just bring her home". Suddenly, I felt a flood of peace wash through me and knew that events would soon begin to move.

The following day, I was as tense as if my own daughter was missing. It seemed as if the whole county was holding its breath. The missing girl had become everyone's child. I was still frustrated because I had no further impressions. But I continually "asked the question". The only thing I could see was an old road I used to drive as a teenager – a road with hills and curves and fields of hay and cattle. I knew she was there, somewhere in the vicinity of that road.

I picked up the children from school. They were excited with news that the missing girl had been found. Their source seemed to be a school teacher whose daughter worked for a local newspaper. The kids' story was confirmed by a bulletin on television almost as soon as we arrived home. A body had been found off the very road I had been seeing in my mind. No positive identification of the body had been made, but everyone knew who it was.

The evening news confirmed the rumors. The missing child had been positively identified but no further details would be forthcoming until an autopsy was performed. We could all breathe again but we did so with tears and trepidation. There was obviously a killer on the loose.

The appeals to apprehend the killer intensified. Everyone was now looking for a blue truck that some of the children on the school bus thought they remembered seeing. I paced the floor in anguish, realizing that the only way I would be able to get the answer would be if someone connected to the case "asked me the question".

This was another thing I had noticed about my abilities. Just as the process of channeling *Noah* had occurred only in response to mental questions, very often I have no insight into what is not my business until someone *whose business it is* asks me about it. When they do, the answer simply comes to me.

Finally, unable to just close my mind to the affair, I sat down to write a letter. I addressed the letter to Henry Smith and asked him to please not share with anyone what I was going to say. You just never know who else might work down at the sheriff's office and, of all things, I didn't want to get a reputation as a weirdo.

I told Henry what I had seen so far, which had been accurate, and I felt I might be able to see more if only I were asked. I intended to use astrological charts on the subject as the method of focusing. I had the idea that it was possible, in this way, to identify the killer, or at least some things about him to produce a rather specific profile. What I was offering, however, might not be any better than nothing and I said so. But, I was willing to have a go at it.

I really did not expect a response except a polite "thank you, but we have all the leads we can handle". I certainly did not expect Henry himself to call me the very next day after I mailed the letter! But he did. He told me that he had consulted the family and, on their behalf, and *as a friend of the family and not as a public official*, he was asking me to look into the matter.

The type of chart I was going to do as my focusing device is called a horary chart. Horary means "of the hour". The idea is that when a question is asked in seriousness and sincerity, the answer is inherent *in the moment of asking*. I recorded the time of the question as well as the birth data he gave me for the astrological charts.

During the course of the conversation, he confirmed my vision: the body had been stripped, had been hosed to remove all traces of evidence, and was *wrapped in plastic sheeting*. I pointed out that this indicated someone who was familiar with forensic procedures and who intended, most definitely, to remove all traces of fibers or other microscopic elements that might have served to at least identify where the murder occurred. Not only had all evidence been thoroughly removed, the body was left *just over the line in the adjacent county* which most definitely confused investigative issues. Henry agreed with this assessment.

"Would you go out to the site and see if you could sense anything else?" he asked me.

"Henry, this really is not my forte!"

"We need your help, Laura. Isn't that standard psychic procedure to go to the scene and..."

"But I probably only had the original insight because of my emotional reaction to seeing her face," I told him. "It was just so similar to my own daughter's. I'm sure I would get better results by working on the astrological charts."

"I understand. But for the family's sake, could you just give it a try?"

It was about 20 miles to the location where the body was found. That's not a great distance, but it included a lot of driving around the area where the girl lived.

HACKING THE SOUL

I don't know what made me think of doing it the way I did, but that's what I did. My objective was to see everything *through the mind of the killer* and get into his thought processes.

Well, that was a big mistake. Yes, I got impressions. Yes, I later did all the charts. Yes, I believe I solved the crime, and insiders on the subject are also convinced that my solution is the correct one. But there is not one single, solitary shred of real evidence on which to justify an accusation, much less an arrest. It is also very unlikely that the individual will ever kill again.

But if he does, someone is watching.

As a result of all this traipsing around and putting on that "mind of the killer", the stress nearly killed me. My whole body swelled with what the doctor called ascites, speculating that I had damaged my liver by taking nine Tylenol a day for the past seven years or so. My heart was backflushing constantly, my kidneys had shut down, and I was as close to death as I have ever been.

The doctor wanted to admit me to the hospital, but I refused. I remembered the horror of my grandmother's death, which could have been peaceful with me at her side. I remembered how the hospital personnel deprived me of those last few moments with their absurd resuscitation efforts. If I was going to die, I wanted to do it at home.

My doctor shook his head in near despair at my stubbornness, ordered me to bed for complete rest for two weeks or longer, and prescribed medication. He was sure I would give in and he would see me at the hospital by the next day at the latest. I was just as sure he wouldn't. I had my ex get me home to bed. I almost couldn't walk.

After a few days of feeling on the verge of death, declining all medicine, drinking only distilled water, I began to feel just a tiny bit better. My thought processes had almost completely stopped working from the build-up of toxins in my body, but I soon began to feel the need for new activity. It was at this moment that Frank brought me the pile of UFO books that I have discussed elsewhere.

I hadn't had any involvement with the murder case for many months, so I was surprised when the phone rang one day, and it was the Private Investigator friend of mine who had acted as liaison between me and certain law enforcement officials at a later stage in that murder investigation. He had a question about something unrelated to that, but then asked me about a conversation between me and a certain detective in the homicide unit of the local law enforcement agency.

Well, this conversation had never happened, so I asked him what he was talking about. He said, "I called you back in October when he was here in the office with me, and one of your kids said you were in the hospital, so I left his number and a message that you should call him. I was sure you had by now."

I never got the message. The kids must have forgotten. So, I took the name and number down again and called and left a message on the detective's answering machine. I was curious to find out what he wanted to talk to me about.

His name was "Marion Thomas". (Not the real name, but the "made up name" relationships are similar here because they were part of the "clue system" as I later figured out.) I knew that "Marion" was often used as a man's name in the past, but it wasn't too common in the present time so I thought it odd. Also, Thomas is my brother's name, and his best friend's name when we were kids was "Thomas Marion".[44] My brother had been named after my grandfather. All those little thoughts ran through my head at that moment.

I was getting ready to take my mother home since she had been at my house most of the morning. As we started out the door, the phone rang again. I answered it and it was "Marion Thompson", the owner of a local used bookstore calling to tell me that she had a copy of Velikovsky's *Worlds in Collision* that I could have for seven dollars. I was so excited that I told her to put a "sold" tag on it and I would be right down. It wasn't until I hung up that I said to myself, "Marion Thompson? Marion Thomas? What is going *on* here?!"

But, I brushed it aside as I headed for the door. Mother was standing there waiting.

The phone rang again before I was out the door the second time. I almost *didn't* answer it, but decided I had better. It was my cousin – the one I had met for the first time at the first MUFON meeting I had attended after the UFO sighting over the pool.[45] He was my grandfather's cousin, being the son of the younger brother of my grandfather's mother. He, too, was calling to announce that he had just found a copy of Velikovsky's *Worlds in Collision* in a box of books in his garage. He knew I had been looking for it, and it was mine if I wanted it!

Well, that was just *too* much! Two "Marions", two books, two years of searching for the book was at an end, and all within about 30 minutes of time! I mean, what were the chances of two people named "Marion", for God's sake!, calling me within a few minutes of each other? What were the odds of having two people offer me a specific book within a few minutes of each other after two years of no results? Additionally, there was the Thomas/Thompson connection that occurred as a triplet. But, by this time I was used to that sort of thing. It just meant that things were *really* getting weird. I just didn't know how weird they were going to get!

It was Wednesday, Reiki night.

When I arrived for the Reiki session, I noticed that there were several people sitting on the patio outside. As I got closer, I was surprised to see that one of them was Reverend Ruth. There was also a big redheaded woman, and a man dressed all in white – white shorts, white shirt, white socks, and even white shoes – with heavy gold jewelry dangling from his neck to disappear inside his partly unbuttoned shirt, and heavy gold chains on his wrists. I spoke to them

---

[44] I am mostly using pseudonyms here for the sake of the privacy of the individuals involved, but I am being a bit creative so as to preserve the "name relationships" that were part of the series of synchronicities.

[45] See *High Strangeness* for the details.

cordially as I went in the house, but their responses seemed to be somewhat less than friendly. But, I just mentally sent love in their direction and closed the door.

The woman who was up, when I found my place at one of the tables, was a hospice nurse who had been suffering from a lot of physical problems that were probably related to the stress of her job. I was given the head position and when I put my hands on her, it was like the two powerful magnets suddenly connecting – BAM! – in a way and with a strength that I had not experienced before. And the energy began to pour.

Now, the only way I have ever been able to describe my personal sensation of channeling Reiki energy is that it really feels like nursing a baby. The instant contact is made, it feels like the milk "lets down", only it is in the arms and not the chest. But it is a distinct sensation. I can feel and monitor the flow constantly, exactly like I could feel and monitor my own milk flowing while nursing my children through the years.

This particular woman, the hospice nurse, was pulling energy so hard that it was actually painful! My wrists began to ache like an abscess that needed to be lanced. I knew that this might relate to the surgery I had on my wrists, and that there were obviously some "short circuits" or something, but I had hitherto been able to deal with this discomfort. In this instance, I could hardly stand the pain. I disconnected for a few minutes and shook my hands and rested them, and then put them back. Same thing. This poor woman was sure exhausted of all reserves and I was glad to be able to help her in this way, even if it was somewhat uncomfortable. But soon, the flow began to slow down, the pain eased, the magnetic sensation released, and I knew that she was finished for that treatment.

I was going to take a break and have some punch and let somebody else have my spot, but just then the man in white from outside came in and said, "Don't go yet!" Louise introduced him as a friend of Reverend Ruth's who had come to try out the Reiki since he had a phlebitis problem. He hopped onto the table with such spryness – I could hardly believe he had any problems at all! I went back to my position at the head as requested.

There was nothing unusual about this man in terms of energy consumption. In fact, he didn't seem to be drawing at all. I *did* smell whiskey on his breath and it had been my experience that alcohol and Reiki do *not* mix. I have seen people get violently sick if they drank too soon after a Reiki treatment. I thought I would mention this to him as he got off the table, that it might be better if he refrained for a few hours, but I never got the chance.

As soon as we took our hands away (there were five of us per table), the man sat up and jumped to his feet swinging around to face me in the same motion. "This is for you," he said as he reached out his hand and traced some sort of figure on my forehead with his finger.

That is what he did, described in just a couple of words, but the way it happened was strange. It was as though everyone in the room froze for a few almost imperceptible moments. And everyone *remained frozen* until he had walked out the door and we were startled back to awareness by the sound of car doors slamming, a motor starting, and a car driving away. Everyone was staring at me and everyone began to talk at once. "What was *that* all about?" or "What *did* he *do*?" or "Who is that man?" or "How *dare* he touch you without your permission."

The last was the main issue. It was pretty standard in Reiki classes that no one touches anyone without his or her permission. It was repeated over and over again to us, and we took it seriously.

I asked Louise who the guy was, and she claimed not to know any more than the fact that Reverend Ruth and her friend had brought him. Candy and the others were all exclaiming in outrage and examining the smudge on my forehead to see if they could make out what had been drawn there. Nobody knew who the man was. Nobody knew the meaning of his actions. Nobody knew what was going on with the sudden visit of Reverend Ruth and her friends. That was the consensus.

After the hubbub died down, we all settled back to our work, and I was surrounding myself with love and light, certain that whoever the man was and whatever the purpose of his strange behavior, it couldn't penetrate my shield.

That night, at about midnight, I woke up in so much pain that I *knew* I was having a heart attack. There was not only an elephant sitting on my chest, there was a fence post driven through my breastbone and I was encased in an iron maiden that was slowly squeezing the breath out of me. I woke my ex-husband and he took me to the emergency room.

As soon as we arrived at the hospital, the pressure and pain began to subside, but with the symptoms I described, they took me in right away. Since I seemed to be stabilizing, there wasn't a *huge* rush (you know, like grabbing the little electric paddles and the "jump start" machine) but they were still working rather quickly to get me prepped. The doctor said I would have to be admitted for tests and kept under observation for a few days, so that was fine with me. I was pretty terrified at this sudden activation of a condition that I believed to have been long cured. But, when the nurse wheeled in the cart with the IV setup and started the preparations to insert same, a voice as clear and powerful as anything I can ever remember spoke in my head telling me that if I let them put that needle in my arm, it would be used to kill me.

My rational conscious mind immediately countered with, "That is *utter nonsense*! You are paranoid! You've been reading too much weird stuff for too long and it has affected your judgment."

Then a wave of heat washed over me and the "knowing" that I would die if I stayed in the hospital surged forward again drowning out the conscious argument. I felt totally schizoid for a moment. And, not only that, there was the problem of how to get *out* of the situation I was now in. How do you say, "Thanks for trying to save my life, but no thanks!"? I was between a rock and a hard place of overwhelming proportion, and there seemed to be no way out.

I tried to convince the nurse that an IV wasn't necessary. She simply brushed my objections away and said it was "standard procedure" and had to be done. There was no option.

I then told her quite simply, "No, I don't *want* the IV." It was clear she was going to ignore me.

I quickly calculated in my mind the possibilities. Yes, I could have been having a heart attack, and it could have been a precursor to the "big one"; but, on the other hand, it could also have been something that had to do with that man at the Reiki meeting. I was acutely aware of the information extracted from both Tim and Candy in their spirit release sessions. But how reliable was that sort of thing? It was one thing to work with it in others, when no definite act of a physical nature had to be made, and another to have to consider it as *real*, and base a crucial decision on such knowledge. *If* it *was* knowledge, and not just another layer of the onion, so to speak; if it was accurate information of how things could work at psychic or unseen levels, then maybe what was happening to me *was* designed to get me in the hospital. And maybe it *was* done so that somebody at the hospital could then be activated to "get to me" and "accidentally" do something stupid that would result in my death.

At the same time I was thinking all this, I remembered Frank's recitation of the events of my life, pointing out that some of it was, indeed, a bit unusual and his idea that there was a reason for it. If that *was* so (and remember, there was *no proof* of this except for the uncertain proof that, as soon as I asked for help with my health, I was led to Reiki) then there also might be a reason for some people or groups of people to want me "out of the picture".

But, no matter what, it was still a choice I had to make without visible *proof!* I could either go with the surface or standard interpretation of the events – which was that I needed to be in the hospital because I might be having a heart attack, which entailed taking the risk of dying either naturally or unnaturally; or on the other hand being "saved" by the medical profession.

The other choice was that I could go with the subtle, spiritual interpretation, take the responsibility for my life into my own hands, do something significant based on knowledge *without proof,* and, if I was wrong, I would die. But if I was right, I would not. And if that were the right interpretation, then I would certainly die if I stayed.

Talk about the horns of a dilemma! And every single thing in my enculturation and social programming tended toward the normal interpretation – I had a health issue and needed to be hospitalized to be saved.

My learning to this point, my experimentation, and my expanding awareness could all be brushed under the rug as subjective or even crazy. Heck, I thought it was crazy too, at that moment! What was I *thinking*?

But some sort of crazy courage swept over me. Right or wrong, for once in my life, I *had* to listen to my inner impressions. If I was wrong and I died, so be it. It would not be for lack of courage!

I decided.

A great calmness descended over me and I told the nurse firmly that she could put the kit away; I was not going to be admitted. At first, I don't think she believed me, but when I got off the gurney and began to put my clothes on, she said, "Let me get the doctor."

The doctor came in and gave me the "you are making a big mistake here!" talk and said I would have to sign release of liability forms and all that. "I'll sign," I said. "I have nothing against the hospital or you or anything, but I am *not* going to stay here and I am *not* going to have needles and drugs pumped into my system." And, just for good measure, I said, "It's against my religion."

Well, that must have been the right thing to say, because they had the forms ready by the time I got to the desk. I signed, went out to the waiting room and told my ex-husband to take me home.

He thought I had completely lost my mind. So did I! But I just simply could *not* argue with the force that was compelling me to leave that place.

I went home, went to bed and began to shake like a leaf with the implications of what I had done. I had opposed and defied all normal convention. I had gone against all the programming of my life to be under one kind of control or another – to be a "good girl" and let "the doctor", or whoever make the decisions about what happened to me. After the fact, I was assailed by so many doubts that it is a wonder I didn't have the "Big One" there and then!

The next day I was feeling very bad. I was weak and felt on the edge of something deep and dark. The "fence post" effect was mild, but constant, the pressure was present, but less severe, and the elephant on my chest had lost weight. When I went to the kitchen to get a drink of water, I looked out and saw that the pool was green. It had turned into "pea soup" overnight.

This distressed me even more and I asked my husband to have the water tested and fix it. He did. About a hundred dollars worth of chemicals and procedures later, it was still pea soup.

Somehow I knew that this condition of the water in the pool represented my space and my self. There was an invasion of psychic "slime". And clearly, judging by the fact that it was not responding to ordinary treatment, it was going to take some additional work to handle.

At that point, Candy called and I told her briefly what had happened. She seemed to be distressed and sympathetic and said she was going to try to find out something about the man who had been at the Reiki session. She would call me back later to report.

Meanwhile, Tim called me and wanted to talk about the incident at the Reiki session. He was as distressed about it as I was.

Nevertheless, Tim had many suggestions for cleaning my psychic environment and offered to come over and do so. He also wanted to see the pool situation for himself. I was open to having a little help here, so said "sure, come on over." Tim came and had a look at the pool and then did some ritual type activities that were supposed to clear things up.

Nothing happened. I continued to have the iron maiden sensation of being compressed. It was much like the way you would feel in a pressure chamber, I guess.

Candy called again. She said she had been *very* clever in getting information out of Reverend Ruth's assistant, and it seems that our gentleman of the Reiki open house was a man who was reputed to be an adept in ritual magick, and was, supposedly, the "Big Banana" of metaphysical Mumbo Jumbo in the whole state.

Swell. That didn't make me feel any better. In fact, I was downright depressed thinking about people who would do something so nasty and hurtful when I hadn't ever done anything to them. *What*, precisely, had I done to these people to make them hate me so much? Not only that, there was a *lot* of confusion in my mind about how such a thing could even happen when I was "surrounded with love and light" and always thinking loving thoughts and sending love, etc.

Candy said that she had the perfect answers to how to clear things up and offered to come over and do her thing. Again, I was open to about anything that might work, so I agreed.

She came over armed with sage and candles and salt and crystals and a whole raft of metaphysical accoutrements.[46] Just like Tim had done, she set to work. She cleared a place in the study and set up an altar with candles, bowls of herbs, stones that had been "charged" and all sorts of things. She went around the house with burning sage, opened all the doors and windows to air the place out, and so on and so forth. She had me stand in a loose gown while she "saged" my entire body, and then waved incense all around (incense guaranteed to get rid of any negative energies or your money back!). Nothing happened. As much as I was relying on these rituals to be able to "fight fire with fire", I still felt the elephant on my chest, and the sensation of depression and constant pressure was still there.

The next day, the pool was still pea soup. I sent my ex-husband down to get *more* chemicals. We dosed the 15,000-gallon pool with enough chlorine and algae killer to clean an Olympic sized pool, or four or five times as big. We ran the pump constantly, cleaned the filter over and over again, ran it again, and cleaned it, and so on for another 24 hours.

Pea soup. The pool guy said it looked like we were going to have to drain the pool and start over with fresh water.

Day after day I struggled to function against the horrible oppression in my mind. It was like I was wounded and there was a pack of wolves slowly circling, getting closer and closer, sniffing and testing, waiting for the weakness to take away all powers of resistance, at which point they would spring forward and destroy me.

---

[46] In American Indian and Neo-Pagan religions, the burning of sage is used to "clear" the area of unpleasant or discordant energies. This can be used both within an enclosed space, such as a room or outdoor grove, or alternatively a person's body, essentially creating a "sacred space".

Day after day there was pea soup in the pool. We put chemicals in the pool, performed rituals, prayed, and "cleansed" the house. Hours were spent erecting psychic barriers of love and light around the house, around me, etc. We tried psychic mirrors. Cutting psychic connections. You name it, we tried it. Nothing was working.

We discussed it up one side and down the other. I had some clues from the spirit release work that the problem might be an etheric cord of some sort that was kept in place by association with certain people. I knew from discussing with various entities where and how they had attached, that very often it is from simply being around certain people and that these people usually didn't even realize that they were "carriers" or "instruments" of connection. It was rather like the idea of a psychic Typhoid Mary. So, I decided that if this might be the case, and since I couldn't exactly *see* who the carrier was, I would simply have to break with all the crowd at the Reiki sessions until I was strong enough to individually experiment to see *who* was the conduit of attack.

This was a hard decision to make because I really liked these people and we had a very good time together. Of course, the incident with Trudy made me inclined to think that she was the one who was the conduit of attack, but that meant that anyone who associated with her and then with me could "carry" the "infection" by proxy.

Candy and Tim agreed with this assessment and we all decided to stop association with the group until we could make some tests. We had all three experienced problems of one sort or another by associating with people who were not as they seem, but there was still the problem in my mind as to whether it was deliberate or not. Apparently, as the evidence seemed to show, it didn't even have to be conscious!

But that was another decision that went against the "love and light" philosophy of acceptance and "unconditional love". It also went against all the social and enculturated teaching about compromise and working to get along, and so on. But, I had to do something, to have time to sort and figure things out, and this seemed to be the safest course at the moment. So, the decision was made. I mentally closed off all those people, determined to not even talk to them until I could find out more about what was going on.

That night I had a dream.

In the dream there was the pool. Somebody had driven a car into the pool and I was distraught trying to figure out how I was going to get it out. A woman came who seemed to be a relative, though the exact relationship was not clear. She called a wrecker truck to come and pull the car out, and then she helped me drain the pool, scrub the mud and oil and gas out of it, and a wave came from the nearby ocean and refilled the pool with sparkling water.

I woke up and wondered what the dream might mean. It had given me a positive feeling and I got out of bed feeling much better. The pressure was gone, and my breathing was much easier. I went to the kitchen, looked out the window, and the pool was clear. I stood there staring at it in disbelief. We had put such a fortune in chemicals into it, and in the past few days, had given up, thinking that we were going to have drain it, and there it was just as clear and sparkling as the pool in my dream.

At that moment, Tim knocked at the door and I let him in telling him that the pool was now clear. He became very excited and went to look. He stood there staring at it, shaking his head and saying over and over again, "I can't believe it!" He had been helping with the chemical applications, the filter cleaning, and so on at the same time he had been making himself available for his little spiritual cleansing activities, so he knew everything that had been done with no effect and that we had given up on it. He was as amazed as I was at the sudden turnaround. So, I told him about the dream, but I was uncertain as to the exact meaning of it or even who the woman relative was that had come to help me.

At this point Candy called with news. It seems that she had just received a call from one of the members of the Metaphysical church who had informed her that Reverend Ruth's assistant and the Big Banana guy had been in an automobile accident during the night. They were both in the hospital and Reverend Ruth was requesting prayers for them. I told Candy how bizarre this accident news was because of my dream about a *car* being driven into my pool, and that now the pool was clear. What was more, the elephant had finally gotten off my chest. Was there a connection between the dream, the clearing of the pool, and the relief from the attack, and my decision to terminate contact with the group or any particular member?

It was possible. But it forced me to consider ideas that were just totally bizarre. It seemed that surrounding oneself with love and light was just not as effective as was touted, especially in certain circumstances. Could it be that the "bubble of love and light" was some sort of inhibitor of knowledge, of growth, of progression?

It was pretty clear to me now that people who were living in such cocoons of belief were as likely attached to, and used by, dark forces or dead dudes as anyone else. Maybe even *more* likely. The reason being that they did not *believe* it was possible, and therefore had no impetus to learn that it not only *was* possible, but that it was *happening* to *them*! It was like the famous saying: "The only thing necessary for the triumph of evil is for good men to do nothing." Here we had a perfect example of this statement. When a person is locked in a belief system, they cannot *see* what is *really* happening in an *objective* way. They do not question their observations or experiences in an open way, but rather interpret them according to their belief system with no options for other explanations. Square pegs that don't fit in the round holes are ignored or swept under the rug.

It also seemed that a lot of people were presenting themselves as "light workers" who were not, in fact, of such a nature. Maybe they *were* in their conscious minds, but at some deep level, something was going on that really required some astute observation to discern and I was as baffled as I could be as to what to make of the whole thing. Not only that, but it seemed that at every step I was being required to make choices as to what I would or would not do based on a very subtle level of understanding. But this seemed to relate to the fact that I was constantly *questioning* everything. I was *not* stuck in *belief.*

There was still a worrisome matter: the issue of Candy. How could it be that she could sit on the fence? How was it that she had such easy access to and contact with these people? I tried to brush those questions aside, but they demanded answers eventually. In a certain sense, at that point, I erected a mental shield against her and no longer confided in her so freely.

I continued my interaction with Candy for some more months, through the early period of the Cassiopaean contact, constantly assured by her that she had everything under control. The Cassiopaeans were saying otherwise, but at that point, I didn't know what to believe.

She was spending a lot of time interacting with a purported UFO investigator who was going to write a book about her case and, (it was implied) make her famous. I checked up on this guy through my P.I. friend and found his credentials to not only be lacking, but that legitimate researchers would have nothing to do with him. When I told Candy this, she apparently went and told him what I had said, and he was able to persuade her that I was the one she should be avoiding because obviously, I wanted to use her case to make myself famous as a "UFO investigator". He, on the other hand, just "wanted to help". Of course, he also wanted to have an intimate relationship with Candy.

Led by this man, Candy withdrew into a circle of people whose belief in the Billy Meier "Pleiadians" was so fanatical that it had become almost like a cult. And, at this point, her actions became so bizarre that I was felt obliged to warn her about this group. She became angry that I even questioned their intentions. It was clear that there was a constant effort on their part to convince her that I was her enemy. Nothing could have been further from the truth.

At one point, Candy had discovered that the dress she was wearing at the time of her major abduction had been thrown into a corner of her closet and left untouched for many months. She said that she had just been unable to deal with it because of the emotional turmoil that the event had produced. I told her to put it in a plastic bag and set it aside until I could find out how to get it properly examined for any kind of traces.

I called my P.I. friend and told him about the whole affair. He was very interested in this piece of physical evidence since it could be scientifically tested. He decided to use his connections in law enforcement to get it to a proper lab, but he was going to do it without telling them that it was possibly UFO connected. We thought that this would be the best way to prevent the disappearance of the evidence, if any.

I called Candy and told her that I had managed to arrange this, and she was pretty excited and agreed to bring the dress over so I could take it to the P.I. A few hours after she had dropped the dress off, she called and asked me if I had taken it down to the guy yet, and I said, "No, not yet." I was just getting ready to, though. She insisted that I *not* do this, because her UFO investigator/paramour had told her that he had the "right resources" to examine and test the dress, a chemist friend of his with his own lab. I already knew that this guy was a complete fraud, and I warned her that she was making a terrible mistake, that her evidence would be completely compromised if she allowed him to take it.

But, she was convinced. It was rather like the choices I had been making; only she was doing it with her eyes closed to the objective facts. She came and took the dress back.

My cousin was in touch with a lot of people in MUFON and he called me one day to tell me that there was a lot of scuttlebutt about this incident. It seems that after Candy had turned the dress over to her new "guru" of UFOlogy, he had then turned it over to a the fellow who claimed to be a scientist whom my cousin happened to know quite well. My cousin said he thought that this guy might have taken some chemistry courses in college, but that he was definitely *not* a scientist – in fact, he was only a technician at the sewage treatment plant. *That* was his laboratory!

Effectively, Candy had chosen a tech at a county water treatment facility to perform the *very scientific* analysis of whatever got shaken out over a shower curtain (!), over a legitimate scientific evaluation in a high tech forensics lab. Go figure. It was her choice.

I was completely disgusted with the whole lot of them and their UFO games and one-upmanship.

Right around this time, I was supposed to give a well advertised talk about the Cassiopaeans at a book store down in Indian Rocks Beach and a couple of days before this event was to take place, I received a phone call from the woman who owned the shop. She was very upset and said that she had received an anonymous phone call from a person who was obviously using some sort of electronic device to disguise his voice saying that if she did not cancel my talk, that she had better be prepared for "bad publicity" because I was on a list to be "eliminated", and did she want that to happen in her store.

Fortunately, she was outraged at being threatened and was willing to take the chance, but I wasn't taking *any* chances. I called my private investigator friend and told him the situation. His partner volunteered to act as my bodyguard, and drove me to the place, inspected every person who entered the room, and was armed and prepared for action.

I realized that things had gotten completely out of hand when I had to have an armed bodyguard in order to talk about the Cassiopaean material!

Not only that, but exactly what *was* going on here? Why was it that the whole process of experimentation with the channeling, once it had passed a certain point, had been fraught with attack after attack? One could say that such actions probably did not come from the "good guys". So, they must come from the "bad guys". And if so, why? The only logical answer was that there must be some reason they did not *want* us to proceed with the experiment. And once the contact had been made, they definitely did not want the information we were receiving to be shared with anyone. Again, I had to ask why? The only logical answer for why it would be desirable to shut me up was because what we were receiving was the *truth* – or very uncomfortably close to it!

It also brought up the question of why so many other channeled sources are *not* attacked in such a way? Logic tells us that they are not attacked because nothing they are saying is significant enough or correct enough to warrant suppression.

At this point, one day when Candy visited, I brought up the issue and she admitted that she had continued to interact with the metaphysical church group and the Reiki group. I told her that my opinion was that it wasn't such a good idea. Hadn't we learned something from all these experiences? She then went in a direction that surprised me. She began to talk about how silly it was to cut people off just because of such trifles as the games that were being played obviously were. I pointed out that *she* had not been the one whose life was threatened in this last series of incidents. She agreed, and then said that she just felt that she was "protected" and that she was able to navigate the treacherous waters of hanging out with the "other side". I tried to persuade her that she might be falling into the trap, but she insisted that this was not the case, so I let it go for the moment.

The next day one of my daughters was sick with a fever and rash that was terrifying to look at. I took her to the doctor immediately. The diagnosis was severe systemic Candidiasis.

I didn't need any more clues. When Candy called later that day to talk, I regretfully told her that as long as she continued to interact with the group, we would have to terminate contact. I couldn't take any more risks – especially when my children were now involved.

Needless to say, she thought I was crazy and judgmental and all that, but it was a decision I had to make and it later proved to be right. Now, remember what I said at the beginning:

> I had seemingly achieved a state of love and acceptance for all people, for all paths, for all who struggled in ignorance... I was, in a certain sense, in as bad a situation as I had been when the "voice" had told me that I must "learn" about evil... What I didn't know was just how subtle and torturous deception could be and how it manifested on an individual, personal basis.

Now, what conclusions can we draw from all of this?

I have recently asked several friends to have a look at this particular narrative in order to discover if their analyses of the events is anywhere similar to my own. I was very grateful at the clarity of their responses, which are so astute I would like to quote them in part. "C" writes:

> What comes up for me is:
>
> 1. The hierarchy of the attack system may or may not be known consciously to the conduits, especially those at the lower rungs of the hierarchy.

2. Compromise can be fractional or great; attacks come through integrity breaches of the chosen relay, and spread by contagion or artifice through to any weak spot of the end person.

3. One can observe strings, little nagging ideas or "small faults" which can be explained away or overridden by other more positive or engaging attributes of the person in question.

4. On the other hand, "weirdness" or "personality quirks" are not necessarily indicators of contamination at all.

5. The obvious "love and light" fallacy brings up a point of interest for me personally, and this relates to 3 above. [i.e., Forgiveness.]

On the topic of forgiveness: this is something that can easily go on automatic, and appears to be a point where one can easily go blind to these little strings.

When one is faced with attack, one needs to be very clear on the dynamics of a situation, and where one has consciously or unconsciously overlooked/forgiven someone for some wrong or fault, it creates weakness in one's own integrity. And by integrity I am not limiting my definition to moral integrity. I mean this as more of a generic "wholeness".

When you go down the path of forgiveness, you also *open up the realm of not-forgiveness.* I think that the subject does warrant some new inspection/reworking of thoughts. I think that forgiveness as [an] automatic mental process is a Christian program. There is also the question of how can students truly forgive each other when every action/counteraction is part of a lesson?

I'm not advocating the holding of a grudge either by this.

True forgiveness implies a canceling out of the other person's weak spot, an acknowledgment that the damage has been ended in the Forgiver.

Forgiveness can be viewed in a mundane way as a judgment (just as a refusal to forgive can be judgment). *It does not guarantee that the underlying weakness in the forgiven person has now been addressed and resolved.* It also implies to the forgiven one that the forgiver has resolved his own lesson. Are we as humans really qualified to do this?

Seemingly to me, in a similar way, when we make allowances for others' weak spots by reason of judging that their other good qualities "cancel out these weak spots", we agree to overlook, *we can also close the door to receiving information about our own more unconscious aspects from our true friends. Integral to this type of scene of course would be the ability and means with which to make effective corrections and improvements.* And of course each member would have the right and responsibility to maintain his/her own integrity. *Any organization would be subject to contamination, and would be as strong as its weakest link.*

Therefore, the individuals in the group would really have to be completely responsible as individuals for their participation in the group. Each of us has weak spots and points where we can be "used", just as others' weak spots can be used to wreak havoc on us. The question is to what length am I going to shore up my own weak spots and to assist others who are willing to do the same?

What are our strengths and our weaknesses? What do we nurture? What do we watch for in our own ranks? Are we willing to kindly give and receive help in this direction? What can we do to mutually assist in strengthening our union and each other? Seems there should be an astral immune system, parallel to a physical immune system. If there were such a system, I would expect that integrity would be a measure of the health of that system. Knowledge protects, not forgiveness.

[There are] no guarantees that one won't get attacked, but one can minimize the duration or severity of the attack and adverse effects as one goes through life. "Forgiveness" can be a blinder to knowledge... I know also that I have swept correct original impressions under the rug of "forgiveness" and have regretted this later.

[In terms of Forgiveness and Love and Light] the forgiven party now "knows" he is not responsible, and if it ends there without further inspection, the source can use the same or similar modes for future feeding.

To the degree that the target of attack employs a simple "turning of the other cheek," he is marked for further attack, for as long as his energy can be siphoned off.

On the other hand, if both the attacker and the attacked can honestly and openly inspect the mechanics of the attack, and be willing to take steps to repair the holes in the integrity of the relationship, there is a formidable strength, i.e., turning the petty tyrant around.

[In any relationship where such attack transpires] if a person can observe and realize on his own steam and without judgment or blame that he is being used in this way, there is hope. But no guarantee... One has to be able to also commit to knowing one's own limitations, be ready for other varied and sundry modes of attack and betrayal coming through the weaker party, and also take responsibility for his part in the other's evolution and growth – *even if the correct next action is to withdraw for one's own sanity and so as to not disrupt the lesson of the other.*

Another friend then gave a very good analogy of what is described above:

> We all have on our "spiritual" armor, our shield and sword. I picture us standing in a line. The warrior standing next to you has to be outfitted in the same gear; you can't take off your breast plate and give it to the warrior next to you because he woke up late and forgot to bring his; your chance of getting pierced through the heart would be ten fold; nor could you be fighting with a warrior standing next to you that didn't do any training – he just decided to wake up and put on some armor that day.
>
> In other words you have to be on equal footing [with those with whom you associate closely.]
>
> But also like a warrior, you don't leave your injured behind and if you see them being attacked from all sides you charge in swinging your sword. These people are your *comrades*, they are closer than family at times of battle.
>
> This reminds me of something I read in Carlos Castaneda's books: Don Juan said, "A warrior loses compassion because he no longer feels self pity." In many ways this is true. I think of forgiveness as just a "letting go", knowing that some things have to happen in order to fulfill a lesson; that everyone has their role to play.

And that is the point: everyone has their "role" to play in the lessons we are all learning. And we can use these lessons to get better at who we are and what we do, or we can retreat into the cocoons of our belief systems, closing our eyes to the marvelous wonder of the universe and the great Cosmic Drama.

Yes, in a real sense we *are* all one, but we seem to be under a mandate to discover our true options, *choose* our role, and act it to the hilt, bringing down the house with applause and cascades of flowers when the final curtain comes down.

When the play is over and we all meet "backstage", we may clap each other on the back, shake each other's hands, and congratulate each other for a fine performance! But that is a different level. There seem to be many more acts in the play before we reach 7th density. And if we are *not* playing our part well, we can very likely be "pulled from the play" and "recycled" as an extra! We are in the middle of the play. And we cannot become playwrights or directors until we prove that we can act. And this "acting" seems to involve very specific choices and behaviors so that the play will be successful.

So, back to practical terms in the cosmic drama: a very difficult situation had been survived, and a very interesting lesson had been learned. But, that was not the end of it. Not by a long shot! Whoever or *what*ever it was that wanted to kill me had *not* given up. I was about to learn that when you block it from one direction, it sneaks around and tries to find another way to get in. And sometimes, the way in is through your own mind!

WANDERING AROUND IN 3RD DENSITY CAN BE HAZARDOUS TO YOUR HEALTH!

We're going to back up a bit here and focus on another line of events that were occurring parallel to the events of the previous section, involving some of the same people and occurring just prior to my decision to distance myself from the Reiki/Metaphysical Church crowd. This series of "lessons" involved the fact that Louise took her Master Level Reiki initiation. This happened in a funny way.

As I said, the Reiki Master who had initiated all of us was one of Takata's students – an elderly lady who was quite well known among the Virginia Beach metaphysical crowd. She traveled to Florida for these Reiki seminars as soon as Louise would assemble enough eager students, and would spend three days teaching and doing the attunements. She was careful, thorough, and a veritable encyclopedia of Reiki knowledge. She had in her possession copies of Takata's diaries and personal writings, as well as books that have since been written about Reiki that were annotated by several of Takata's actual students. It seemed, from this information, that there had been a definite split in the Reiki teachings with certain persons taking it upon themselves to alter or add to the original work (claiming "inspiration" from God or some channeled source, as far as I have been able to determine).

Louise was very anxious to have her Master Level initiation, but for some reason our Reiki Master was unwilling to give it to her. I have no idea on what she based this decision, but it was apparent that Takata was also very choosy about who she gave the Master Level initiations to. Having been taken into

Takata's confidence, our Reiki Master told us that after Takata died, a couple of her students, to whom she had *denied* the Master Level attunements, had persuaded Takata's heir to issue an "Official List" of Reiki Masters personally initiated by Takata, but that this list was doctored to include them. It was suggested that money changed hands but further than that I cannot say because it is, after all, hearsay and not hard evidence. But, I listened to many things about this matter told to us by our Reiki Master, and I had no reason to think that she would make this story up.

The upshot of the whole affair was that there were people claiming to have received not only their Master Level initiations directly from Takata, but also certain secret teachings who had not, in fact, done so. Our Reiki Master stopped short of calling these people liars and frauds, but her meaning along that line was pretty clear. She told us that these same people were the ones who had changed and added to the original material and techniques even adding new levels of initiation so as to have more initiations for which more money could be charged. Further, many people were apparently giving Reiki seminars wherein a person could become a Reiki Master in three days or less! Our Reiki Master was very clear on this: the initiations must be given over a period of years or they would not "take" properly. Each level had to be observed by the Master to determine when and if the next level could be assimilated.

So, there it was: Louise wanted the Master Level and had been told she was not ready yet. She was working as hard as she could to gather students and arrange seminars for Reiki classes, and felt somewhat put out because the Reiki Master would not respond to all her hard work by giving her the Master Level initiation. So, she decided to take matters into her own hands.

There was a Reiki Master down in Clearwater who had been initiated into the lineage of one of the persons who was reputed to have altered and added to the Reiki teachings. (In fact, as I understand it, due to extreme promotional efforts and books, etc., this person's teachings are the most widely known version of Reiki in the country today.) So Louise became resentful at the refusal of our Reiki Master and decided to go to this other Reiki Master of the altered line for her Master Level.

After she had obtained her Master Initiation, she offered to give me, Candy and Tim the Second Level attunements at a tremendous discount. Okay. Sounded like a good deal to me. I couldn't imagine how there could be anything wrong with it because I wasn't even sure what was done or how. I agreed.

Along with the Second Level initiation, a little booklet was provided which included the symbols that the Second Level student was now "empowered" to use. I was reading through this book when I came to a page that was headed "Power Exercises". It began:

> The Reiki Alliance form of teaching involves using the body as an energy channel to pass the attunements. Usui Traditional Reiki does not use this method, or

the power exercises given here. The advantage of these exercises is that with them you need to pass the attunement only once to transmit the Reiki degree.[47]

I didn't really notice the distinction between "The Reiki Alliance" and "Usui Traditional Reiki" as I was reading this the first time, so I continued on. The instructions for the "power exercise" for women began: "Sit with legs open, so that you can press the heel of one foot against your vagina and clitoris. Use a firm, steady pressure... You may experience sexual stimulation or orgasm."

I have to admit that warning bells went off in my head with this one. Believe me, I am *not* unaware of Tantra and certain Kundalini stimulating practices, nor the benefits to be gained from them, but after studying these things in some detail, I *knew* that in such ancient traditions, the student is carefully led through many stages of instruction and preparation before being introduced to such a practice as was being described in this Reiki manual; and "sexual stimulation or orgasm" is *not* encouraged in these traditions; at least not in the early stages of training, which can take *years*! This kind of exercise can actually be quite dangerous if you don't *really* know what you are doing!

But, I continued to read. A page was included that showed the method for using the Reiki symbols to basically "bomb the Earth with love and light." Well, at that point in my education, it didn't seem like a bad idea. I had even considered doing remote Spirit Release on all the members of Congress!

But *then* I reached the back of the book where there was a page headed "Alternate Reiki Symbols (Usui Traditional Method.)" I had a look at them and then I went back to the symbols that the "Reiki Alliance" was teaching and compared them. Not only were they *very* different, one of them, the "Power symbol", was completely *reversed*.

Now *that* disturbed me in a *big* way! I had a sort of visceral understanding of these symbols as being a Cosmic or interdimensional language, or electromagnetic circuit diagram, and here I was seeing that somebody had not only altered them, but also had even reversed one of them.

If these symbols are, as I was understanding it, a sort of cosmic microchip that can be installed in the body to enable a flow of energy from other dimensions; if they are a language that tells the body something in a deep, objective way, and then somebody changes them, *what* are they now "programming"? What is being said to the body? What are the circuits being routed to *do?*

I called Louise immediately and pointed out to her that she had apparently "gone over" to the group that our Reiki Master had been talking about, though none of them had ever been named by her. Louise was not only dismissive of my concerns; she was actually contemptuous of my idea that there could be a real problem here. As I remember her saying, "If you believe they will work, they will! It's all a matter of what you believe. If you don't believe they will

---

[47] Diane Stein, *Essential Reiki* (Ten Speed, 1991).

work, they won't. If your spiritual development is weak or backward, of course, nothing will work for you."

MIAOU!

Wow! What a cut! Now I was spiritually retarded because I had a problem with people altering symbols and maybe corrupting information. Hmmm... How often has this manipulation been used to jerk questioners back in line?

I didn't buy it. My experience with Reiki had been that it was something that was truly objective – it did *not* require "faith" or "belief". That was the truly unique and amazing thing about it. At that moment, I decided that Louise simply wasn't getting it. But I figured that my initiation from her was still good even if she didn't know what she was dealing with. Surely the method of transmission was still the same and worked? I decided that I would just use the Usui Traditional Symbols and maybe experiment with the others to see what they were really doing.

There was already a problem though, even if it took awhile for it to repeat often enough for me to take notice: the heat that generally would manifest so powerfully when I touched people seemed to have dissipated and now, instead, I was actually feeling an iciness that was of the kind that can be felt as heat unless you have been used to real heat. I commented on this to Candy and she said that this was normal. She said that our Reiki Master had told her that the body knows what kind of energy it needs and when you have the Reiki attunements the body will naturally send the right energy to whatever person you are channeling it to. That seemed like a reasonable explanation.

But to give an example of what I mean about the changes made in the symbols, take a look at the following examples:

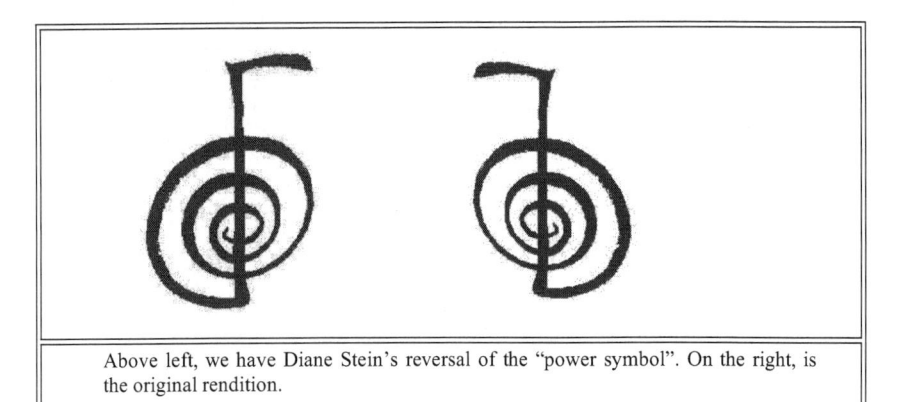

Above left, we have Diane Stein's reversal of the "power symbol". On the right, is the original rendition.

Hon-Sha-Ze-Sho-Nen
Healen op afstand, het Akashi-archief,
verleden-heden-toekomst

On the left, above, we have Diane Stein's "adjustments" to the "etheric connection" symbol, that she called the "distance healing" symbol. On the right is the more traditional version.

As time went by, I noticed that my energy was really low and I had some occasional aches and pains that would pop up and force me to slow down. It was nothing really severe, just annoying. I wrote it off to needing to relax a bit. And that is where the matter stood through the time period in which the Cassiopaean contact was finally established.

I thought the whole idea of these symbols and their use was fascinating and, for some reason, it made perfect sense to me. In order to make this clear, I have to talk about Reiki a little bit more so that the reader can follow my thinking as the events unfolded. The following is an amalgamation of my notes for a Reiki manual I have been meaning to write for some time:

> Have you ever watched a Martial Arts demonstration where the Master decimates an entire stack of boards, bricks or blocks with a single blow? If you have witnessed enough of them you know that there is no fakery involved. But, how is it done?
>
> For more than 5,000 years the Chinese have practiced Martial Arts. Secrets of retention of vital energies to develop internal power were passed from father to chosen son. The first stage of the practice was to get the warm current of en-

ergy to open the channels of circulation so that the internal power could be circulated freely. One then had to learn how to strengthen one's vital organs and to "pack" the energy for use when needed. The Martial Arts fighting styles were not effective without this internal power. [...]

During the present century the West has witnessed a phenomenal growth of interest in "Wholistic/holistic" health disciplines. At the same time science is finding that deeper realities bear a striking resemblance to the classical worldview of the major oriental religions and Martial Arts practices. The increased interest has manifested in multitudes taking classes in Yoga, Martial Arts, Macrobiotics, Tai Chi Chu Chuan, and a host of other variations on these themes. We have become comfortable with meditation and yoga and Buddhism. But, what do we really know about these traditions other than a few fragments of the wisdom of the I-Ching, the *Tao Te Ching* and a few other pieces of disconnected knowledge?

In the sixth century BC, Lao-Tse began his classic essay, the *Tao Te Ching*, with this admonition: "The Tao which can be spoken of is not the Tao." In early Chinese writings, the Tao implied an understanding of life, which stressed individual harmony with the forces of nature. The practice of Reiki is rooted in the same way with the forces of nature. *This energy works independently of any particular belief or scientific concept.* It is not related to any religious practice that has grown up around it. It is, in brief, a subtle but verifiable life energy, "chi," flowing through the body in a specific pattern. This "Chi," as it is known in Chinese, or "Ki," as it is known in Japanese, was known by the ancients, and its secrets have been attainable throughout all ages by those who were willing to put a great deal of time into the prescribed practices. The limitation has always been the fact that it was only available to those who were willing to train for long hours daily for many years to alter the flow so that the body could make active use of this energy.

The applications of Ki/Chi in daily life are virtually limitless. It is the most important building block of transformation. If a person can master the circulation of the healing energy, everything else proceeds more quickly. Opening this energy channel is like being given the tools to do all other things. Without the flow of the Ki/Chi, the individual will find it difficult to advance to higher levels in other disciplines. You could spend years in other disciplines with less direct methods in order to achieve the same end, or, even a lifetime. However, a person could study hundreds of volumes in a dozen languages without ever learning how to awaken the much-poeticized healing power of the Tao. There are those who have read the thousands of volumes and received the valuable oral teachings, which have been shrouded in secrecy the same way medieval alchemy was hidden in Europe, who still have not achieved the mastery of this energy and the power to direct it. What many today do not know is that there is a method of awakening and utilizing the Ki/Chi by initiation. That is, it is like starting a car with a battery rather than a hand crank!

This secret is rooted in the "language" of the body. The body comes into being by virtue of the Electromagnetic pattern that is determined at another dimensional level. *These patterns are expressed on the other dimensions as symbolic figures.* It is an entire language of its own, the language of the cosmos which is expressed in the body via the axiom: As above, so below. Without a language, one cannot create words, sentences, paragraphs, or develop simple or complex ideas. These symbolic figures *convey* knowledge, *alter* energy with this knowledge, and are essential *conduits* between our reality and higher realities.

The symbolic figures of Reiki manifest knowledge that speaks to the "soul".

The Reiki Master makes use of higher energies expressed through symbols to clear the routes and raise the level of chi production. The current of the Reiki initiation or "attunement" is like installing a new circuit board or computer chip into the system.

The important thing is that, as soon as I saw the Reiki symbols, I *knew* that they were a language – a soul language, so to speak. We began to utilize them in our channeling experiment, inscribing them in the air over the board, or drawing them on sheets of paper and putting the paper under the board. It was within a few weeks of this implementation, after two long years of sitting with intent, that the Cassiopaeans came through as described elsewhere, with a series of very loud thunderclaps over my house, so strong that they literally shook the house like an earthquake.

So we can see that all of the previously described interactions had a positive side and a negative side. And, in the end, they were pretty well balanced. Not only was my health restored in a miraculous way, but we received a tool thereby that assisted in our contact with the Cassiopaeans. On the negative side, I nearly got myself killed and certainly suffered some really unpleasant experiences. These experiences were what we came to call "attacks". But, in a very real sense, these "attacks" are both Lessons *and* initiations! If the universe is balanced, as we are told, and which seems to be self-evident upon deep reflection, then it is almost necessary to experience both aspects in any learning experience. It is what you *do* with the "attacks" that makes them either lessons from which you learn, or troubles from which you suffer. And it is in this sense that awareness plays the major role of transforming attacks into lessons; awareness being the thing that you acquire with knowledge, which then enables you to see the realities behind the Symbol System, so that you can choose the most harmonious option of those offered to you in the Masked reality in which we live. There is also a further consideration as was brought up by a member of our discussion group, DD, who commented:

> I am wondering if the problem with Reiki is that the attunements that give the healing power work regardless of the level of spiritual development of the person in question, and that the attunements not only give us the ability to facilitate healing, but give other psychic powers as well, powers that can be used either for good or for ill. Reiki in the hands of a really negatively oriented person might be a dangerous thing.

I agree. And the energy can certainly be used negatively. That is probably why Takata was so choosy about who she initiated as Masters and why my Reiki Master would not give the attunements to Louise. She clearly saw something there that was not obvious to others.

Naturally, the conditions surrounding us at the time the Cassiopaeans came through became the main subject of our questions. We were awash in a sea of conflicting information about UFOs, aliens, contradictory New Age teachings, and a whole host of confusing elements. But what we haven't talked about very much is what we call the "Attack Syndrome", which is really at the crux of the control system of our reality.

These questions were asked not particularly for the sake of getting the right answer, but more in the line of tests. They were part of the challenge process that I felt was the right and proper way to deal with any source claiming to have knowledge to share. I wanted to ask many questions on many subjects so as to assemble a body of information that could be tested and examined for accuracy, perspective, consistency, and so forth. Before I was going to decide whether I believed the Cassiopaeans were who they said they were, I was going to "put them through their paces."

In one respect this was a useful thing, but in another it led to later problems in assembling the material in any useful order. I would jump from subject to subject trying deliberately to confuse or disorient them. I would stick trick questions in and ask them rapid fire to see if I could trip them up. I had enough experience chatting with dead dudes and elementals and even demonic type entities that I was using all the tricks I had learned in exposing such types to see if there was anything of that orientation in the Cassiopaean responses. I'm just glad that they had a good sense of humor, were patient and understanding throughout this period!

So, we come to some of the personal issues of "attack" with which we challenged the Cassiopaeans. Things happen for a reason, and this information was to prove to be invaluable to us as we proceeded with the project. At the very first solidly identifiable Cassiopaean session, I tossed in some questions about abduction as it related to us personally. Candy was present at this session. Keep in mind that the early sessions were reconstructed from the notebooks. At that point we had not begun to tape the sessions so they seem to be a bit choppy and brief.

July 16, 1994

Q: (L) Have any of us been abducted?

A: All.

Q: (L) How many times?

A: Frank-57; Candy-56; Laura-5.

Q: (L) Why has Laura not been abducted as much? (Laura laughs.)

A: You fight it. It is not over. (Candy laughs.) Candy was abducted last month.

Q: (L) Who is abducting us?

A: The other. [Referring to the Consortium of STS aliens and humans which was identified at the beginning of the session.]

Q: (L) What is the name of the specific group?

A: Different names.

Q: (L) Are we all abducted by the same group?
A: Mostly.
Q: (L) What did they do to us?
A: Gave false memories. Made you inhibited as children. Caused headaches and sickness at school.
Q: (L) Do we have implants?
A: Yes.
Q: (L) Where?
A: In the head.
Q: (L) What are the implants for?
A: Study device.
Q: (L) To study what?
A: Soul composition.
Q: (L) Do any of the rituals we perform provide protection against further abduction?
A: Maybe some Crystals with energy fields. Don't need protection if you have knowledge.
Q: (L) How do we get this knowledge?
A: It is deep in the subconscious.
Q: (L) When did we get it?
A: Before birth.
Q: (L) Is there anything else we can do for protection?
A: Learn, meditate, read.
Q: (L) Are we doing what we need to be doing at the present?
A: So far. Need to awaken.

In the following week, Candy, Louise and I had gone to visit another Reiki Master in Tampa who lived just north of the airport and who had shown us what she claimed to be the "real" Reiki symbols which were still *another* variation! She also regaled us with a story about the individual who had instituted the "New Reiki".

The tale was that this woman was part of a metaphysical/New Age group touring Egypt and she had actually stolen an item from a shop in a bazaar because she felt the price was outrageous. She was later "taken for questioning" by the Egyptian police. Extraordinary efforts were exerted in her behalf to get her out of this dangerous situation, (in Egypt, they cut off the hands of convicted thieves!), and baksheesh was liberally applied to ensure that no formal charges were lodged against her. The story was funny and well told, and if true, really made you wonder about the energy behind this Reiki faction.

As we were driving home, we spotted a triangular arrangement of lights hovering in the airspace of the flight path of the landing airplanes. Since there was a *lot* of aerial activity going on, we were unsure if it was anything strange at all. Candy was driving and decided to accelerate so that we could "catch up" to where this object was. As we got closer, we could clearly see that it *was* staying in the same place because several planes passed by it rather closely in their landing approach, and the object remained stationary. It had a big, bright light on each corner of the triangle, and a series of smaller lights inside the triangle shape on the bottom of the craft in some kind of circular arrangement. I was certain that it must be a helicopter, but I couldn't figure out why it would just sit there in that rather busy and dangerous airspace! Dumb pilot, I figured.

So, we got to close to it, almost directly under it (it was right over a busy 6 lane road) and as we did this, it moved a little to our right and hovered over an apartment complex. At that point, I could distinctly see it doing the "falling leaf" maneuver. Candy screeched around the corner of the driveway into the parking lot of the complex and slammed on the brakes while I stuck my head all the way out of the window to look directly up at the object. I was puzzled because I couldn't hear any noise such as you would expect being right underneath a helicopter that was only about 300 feet up; there was no sound at all but the passing cars. I only had a few seconds to look directly up at it before it shot away – whoosh! There one instant, gone the next. I did manage to see that it was definitely a triangular, black object. I would guess the size to be about 30 feet per side, with a *very* bright light on each corner, which was strange because it did not illuminate the parking lot!

We turned around and continued home, but we were very interested in seeing what the new source had to say about *that*! (Keeping in mind that we are still in the early phase and did not consider the session worth recording.)

July 30, 1994

Q: (L) Do you have messages for us?

A: Be careful.

Q: (L) Of what?

A: Aliens.

Q: (L) Which Ones?

A: Orions.

Q: (L) What do they do?

A: Follow you.

Q: (L) Did Louise, Candy and Laura see an alien craft last night?

A: You better believe it.

Q: (L) Whose craft was it?

A: Orion.

Q: (L) Was it there because of us specifically?

A: No.

Q: (L) Do they know we saw them?

A: Yes.

Q: (L) Did they leave because we saw them?

A: Yes.

Q: (L) Were they planning to abduct somebody?
A: Maybe. You are next.
Q: (L) What?
A: To be abducted.
Q: (L) Who?
A: LK
Q: (L) By whom?
A: Orion.
Q: (L) When?
A: Open.
Q: (L) Why?
A: For Knowledge monitoring. Craft above now.
Q: (L) Above the house?
A: Absolutely.
Q: (L) Is it good for me to be abducted?
[There was a lot of confusion in my mind about this subject since so much material is being promulgated by "experiencers" who claim that the aliens are here "to help us" and we just don't understand it, nor can we because they are so much more advanced than we are.]
A: Neutral.
Q: (L) Will I be abducted because I saw them last night?
A: Partly. MF and K*** have reported you.
[This was certainly a shocking answer! MF was the "hotshot" UFO investigator that Candy was becoming very "attached" to during this time, and K*** was, of all people I knew, so *anti*-alien that I could not imagine him being abducted! He was, in fact, a follower of the works of Zecharia Sitchin.]
Q: (L) What? Are they in cahoots with the aliens?
A: Not knowingly.
Q: (L) How, then?
A: Subconscious. Implants.
Q: (L) Do we have implants?
[A small "trick" question since this had already been asked.]
A: Two implants; one monitor.
Q: (L) What is the difference between a monitor and an implant?
A: All are monitors. Implant is permanent. Frank and Laura have permanent implants. Candy got monitor three months ago. Next is implant.
Q: (L) Why?
A: To watch and observe you.
Q: (L) Why?
A: You are all higher-level beings. Frank implant: 4 years old. Laura implant: 5 years old. [...]
Q: (L) Are we chosen?

A: What is chosen? Only you can choose. The choice comes by nature and free will and looking and listening. Where you are is not important. Who you are is and also what you see.

Even if I didn't like some of the things the Cassiopaeans were telling us, I was at least satisfied that they weren't using our egos to capture our allegiance. So many cases that I had looked at had been led into corruption because of that very factor. A source will tell their channel that he/she is "special" or "chosen" or whatever. The Cassiopaeans were definitely *not* playing the "ego stroking" game here nor were they telling us what we *wanted* to hear!

What was most interesting to me, in the above excerpt, aside from the unverifiable claims about aliens and implants and all that, was that people's minds could be manipulated, tapped or utilized in some way *subconsciously*, regardless of their conscious attitude toward the "alien reality". The two people mentioned had almost nothing in common whatsoever except, actually, a certain form of fanaticism. One was a Billy Meier devotee and the other was certain that Sitchin was the only one who had a clue. But the remark that they had "reported" us was puzzling in the extreme! What, exactly, could be going on here? Did human beings live on more than one level and did this conscious level of which we are most aware, constitute some sort of completely programmed fantasy?

At about this point in time we discovered *The Ra Material* and I was pretty interested to see that Ra's "take" on the situation was quite similar to what the Cassiopaeans were saying even if it was couched in cumbersome terminology. The upcoming quotes from Ra are from *The Ra Material* by Elkins, Rueckert and McCarty. I have removed some of the convoluted multiple words and replaced them with single words that represent conventional usage, keeping (I believe) the meaning intact. I have also combined the question that was being asked with the answer so as to simplify the excerpts for the present purpose. Those who have not read the Ra books are urged to do so as they are an invaluable source – one of the few available on the planet – for information about the true nature of our reality.

One of the comparable points of *The Ra Material* was the statement that the motivation of the "aliens" who abduct and probe and examine humans, and, for the most part, are those sighted by many people the world over, is to conquer the Earth and enslave its people. Ra said that the aliens sought out, specifically, people who were influential in some way so as to subvert them for their own use – this use being to enslave even more people.

> [The purpose of the Orion STS] is conquest... their objective is to locate certain [individuals] which vibrate in resonance with their own [frequencies], then to [use these contactees to] enslave the [masses].

The obvious inference is, of course, that our political leaders, the heads of state, industry, finance, and so forth are likely targets for this contact. What Ra did not say, but which I also inferred from the above, was that many, if not most, of the "experiencers" and "contactees" who have come forward with their versions of the alien reality are being cleverly used as "Pied Pipers" to lead humanity into enslavement. Just exactly how this is done was described:

> [The Orion STS who come to this planet for mind control purposes] follow the Law of One observing free will. *Contact is made with those who call.* Those then act to disseminate the attitudes and philosophy of Service to Self. These become the elite. Through these, the attempt begins to create a condition whereby the remainder of the planetary entities are enslaved *by their free will.*

What I think Ra is saying here is that the Orion STS are the ones most generally contacted by those who attempt to channel, he says "contact is made with those who call", and that teachings are being promulgated that seem to be of "love and light" and a positive nature so that people will willingly follow them, not realizing that, at some point, a trap will snap shut on them because they have not, as the parable of the Wise and Foolish Virgins describes, "filled their lamps with oil (knowledge)." These "contactees" then publish books, conduct seminars, promote the alien agenda, and just generally become popular and garner huge followings of devotees. As Ra said: "people are enslaved by their Free Will!" They choose it! And you don't think they would choose it if they knew that was what they were choosing, do you?!

Of course, Don Elkins wanted to know *who* these people were, (including the obvious category of social and political leaders) but neither Ra nor the Cassiopaeans will tell. This is one where we have to make choices, it seems.

> To name those involved is to infringe Free Will. We request your contemplation of the fruits of the actions. In this way you may discern for yourself this information.

Of course, there are those who do *not* seek contact, who just sort of end up getting messages inside their heads. Ra discusses this as well:

> Many of those seen in your skies are of the [Orion STS] group. They send out messages. Some are received by those who are oriented toward Service to Others. *These messages then are altered to be acceptable to those entities while warning of difficulties ahead.* This is the most that self-serving entities can do when faced with those whose wish is to serve others... If the entity is oriented toward Service to Others, [he/she] will begin to receive messages of doom. If the entity is oriented towards service to self, the [Orions STS] do not find it necessary to lie, and will simply begin to give the philosophy they are here to give.

So it seems that this "broadcast" is pretty widely disseminated and can be picked up by many people, including those who are internally oriented toward Service to Others. What then happens, as Ra states, is that *after* reception of the information from the STS faction, the individual's mind will alter the information so as to make it acceptable while "warning of difficulties ahead." I sort of infer that this means much of the information about coming cataclysms is merely the re-forming of the information about alien conquest and domination into more general, global/geological concepts. It may also mean that a lot of psychics who are not "into" the "alien scene", are getting information from these beings that are then being transformed in their brain circuits to be of a different nature. The last category however, those who are oriented to Service to Self, will be *the ones presenting the aliens as our "saviors" or "helpers" or "brothers"*.

So we seem to have a number of general categories of disinformation being described here. Two of them are worth particular focus for the deviousness of the propaganda. The first is the "cataclysmic" school from those who are STO, yet still sleeping; and the "alien rapture theorists" from those who are STS and part of the enslavement machine. Ra goes a bit further into this last category:

> The contacts which the [Orion STS] group finds most helpful to their cause are those contacts made with entities whose orientation is towards Service to Self... Through telepathy the philosophy of... Service to Self is promulgated. In advanced groups there are rituals and exercises given and these have been written down just as the Service to Others oriented entities have written down the promulgated philosophy of their teachers.

Don Elkins had the idea that this must refer specifically to practitioners of magick, and Ra affirmed that this was a part of this mode. But he suggested that there was a lot more to it and that the observer must use his/her own judgment. The one thing that comes to my mind as being the closest to what Ra is describing as a "written body of material" with advanced groups with rituals and exercises, are the books and higher methods of processing employed by the followers of ritual magick. But then, of course, the whole gamut of formalized religion falls entirely within this category as well. Enough said. Let those who have eyes to see, see; let those who have ears to hear, hear.

Ra did give additional clues as to the specific processes involved:

> The philosophy [of Service to Self] concerns... Manipulating others that they may [serve another through manipulation or trickery, i.e., enslavement] thus through this experience becoming able to appreciate Service to Self. These entities would become oriented towards Service to Self and in turn manipulate yet others so that they in turn might experience the service towards the other self [via enslavement].

What Ra seems to be saying is that by this, is that by engaging an individual, through manipulation or deception, to "follow" or "serve" a "master", whether it be Jesus, Buddha, Lord Sananda, or being saved via a copyrighted and patented "technology", the person is being conditioned to accept the Service to Self pathway and to think that it is Service to Others! It becomes like a hierarchy where one is encouraged to deeply desire advancement in the levels so that they, too, can someday achieve the proffered carrot of "salvation" which they can then offer to others "below" them. This is reflected in the beliefs of many Christians that they will be among the "chosen" who will "stand at the right hand of God" and "judge the quick and the dead" along with their "elder brother, Christ." The same sort of thing is going on in other religions. There is a saying, "The oppressed become the oppressors," that applies here and it is a rather transparent psychological ploy.

Upon initial inspection, one might have the idea that the serving of others that is being called forth in the STS manipulation is little different from serving others in the STO paradigm; but there is a key difference – *manipulation*. Manipulation implies that the service is induced or coerced by *deceptive* tactics; that the individual is serving something or someone that is a lie or an illusion. This "serving of a lie or an illusion" is the dynamic that locks the person's energy flow into the implosive, contractile mode of a draining of energy rather than an exchange where something real, i.e., truth or reciprocity, is being exchanged for the service.

A very simple way to explain it would be that it is like an investment scam where many people are tricked to give their money to a con artist who has convinced them that he is a representative for a legitimate investing firm or plan. They give their life savings; the con artist puts it in his pocket, and then moves on to the next sucker. The thing that occurs with the STS mode of investment scams is that they take place over a person's entire life and it is generally only after many lifetimes, or at least, at the end of any given life, that the person being scammed realizes that they have been "taken for a ride". They die with their soul energy depleted, entrapped by the STS faction, unable to progress in any significant way. The old saying, "If it sounds too good to be true it probably is", applies here. Salvation as is taught by Christianity; the Alien Rapture theory where aliens are going to "airlift" their true believers off the planet during coming cataclysms; ascension by application of simplistic "rituals" or "initiatory meditative exercises" that can be done if you just attend the seminar, buy the book, (a bargain at $29.95!), or wander around in muddy mazes with a blindfold on, all fall into this category. *Caveat Emptor!*

But, in the case of the Orion STS, we have a special problem. They have capabilities of control and deception that we cannot even imagine! Ra tells us:

> You must plumb the depths of fourth-density negative understanding. This is difficult for you. Once having reached third density space-time continuum through your so-called windows, [the Orion STS] *may plunder as they will*, the results completely a function of the polarity of the, shall we say, witness/subject/victim. That is due to the sincere belief of 4th density STS that to love self is to love all. *Each other-self, which is thus either taught or enslaved, thus has a teacher that teaches love of self.* Exposed to this teaching, it is intended there be brought to fruition an harvest of 4th density negative or self-serving beings.

As if it weren't enough that they can deceive us via time and space manipulation, they can also mislead us through the teachings that come to us from the "astral planes"! This information was particularly interesting to me in light of the attachment that had been discovered hanging with Candy who had been "sent by a magician"!

The Orion STS have aided many negatively oriented entities... and there are many upon your so-called inner planes which are negatively oriented and thus available as inner teachers or guides and so-called possessors of certain souls.

Then there is the problem of people channeling without "tuning". An individual of completely pure intent and STO nature can produce material that is deceptive disinformation due to their lack of ability to discern which is a result of lack of knowledge.

It is entirely possible for untuned channels to receive both positive and negative communications.

Another problem in being able to figure out the machinations of beings with space-time manipulation capabilities is that of proof. Over and over again we read about miracles and apparitions that are taken as proof of some sort of divine contact. People don't seem to get the very simple fact that *if you believe because you have proof, you are not* choosing *from Free Will*! You believe because you have no choice *not* to believe. What sort of energy could be behind such a thing, despite the lovely appearances, the miraculous healings, the celestial harmonies, or deeply emotional responses of the witnesses? Borrowing from the discussion of Ann Haywood in *High Strangeness*?

"One night the Lady took me back in time. We were in a foreign country and the people wore old-fashioned clothes. *The Lady took on the appearance of a beautiful woman in a blue robe. She performed miracles for them...*"

Ann Haywood, the human host of the above-described entity (many aspects of this case are startlingly similar to the Betty Andreasson Luca case[48]), apparently was punished for this revelation to the media.

Suddenly Ann's face turned ashen and she asked to be excused. Her scream of pain was heard from the bathroom where she had taken refuge. When Ann came out, she was sniffling and holding her abdomen. The Lady had savagely attacked her for revealing that down through history, creatures like the Lady have taken the form of saints. They then use the gullibility of humankind to misguide and misinform people so that they believe they are seeing miracles performed. Ann begged the newsman to delete that portion of the interview."[49]

Hmmmm? We are beginning to get a picture of a contrived reality that is positively Machiavellian in its manipulations and deceptions. Ra says about it:

Many of your so-called contacts among your people have been confused and self-destructive because the channels were oriented towards Service to Others but, *in the desire for proof, were open to the lying information of the Orion STS* who then were able to neutralize the effectiveness of the channel.

---

[48] See Raymond Fowler's The Andreasson Affair, The Andreasson Affair Phase Two, and The Watchers.

[49] Nancy Osborn, *The Demon Syndrome* (New York: Bantam Books, 1983).

I was recently reading a book that is devoted to miracles down through the ages, most particularly apparitions of the Virgin including the "miracle at Fatima", and so on. The one thing I noted over and over again was the "bidding process". Such entities will ask for something to be done – prayers, build a church, repentance, or whatever – and the witnesses, being overcome by the miraculous nature of the appearance, immediately set about complying with these wishes. In some cases, there is a deal whereby the entity (usually the Virgin and assorted saints or members of the "Holy Family") offers some sort of compensation for the required observances. In one case it was victory in battle, in another it was a good harvest or rain.

What so many people don't realize is that to respond to a command of any kind, the "bidding", whether it is to pray or build a church or paint a sign on your shield or even to erect a monument by piling three stones on the side of the road, one has accepted domination! One has tacitly agreed to serve the one who has made the request or issued the command. A psychic bond is immediately established, and the dance begins. The tricky part comes in when the requests or commands are either couched in terms that make them seem useful or good, or they come by way of pity or manipulation.

June 9, 1996

Q: (L) My question is: is the information we are receiving similar to what Al-'Arabi calls an "opening"?

A: Yes.

Q: (L) You say that you are unified thought forms in the realm of knowledge.

A: Yes.

Q: (L) Al-'Arabi describes unified thought forms as being the "names of God". His explication seems to be so identical to things you tell us that I wonder...

A: We are all the names of God. Remember, this is a conduit. This means that both termination/origination points are of equal value, importance.

Q: (L) What do you mean? Does this mean that *we* are a part of this?

A: Yes. Don't deify us. And, be sure all others with which you communicate understand this too!

Q: (L) What quality in us, what thing, enabled us to make contact. Because, obviously a lot of people try and get garbage.

A: You asked.

Q: (L) A lot of people ask!

A: No they don't, they command.

Q: (L) Well, a lot of people do ask or beg or plead, but they get all discombobulated with the answers.

A: No, they command. Think about it. You did not beg or plead... that is commanding.

That "begging and pleading" or maneuvers designed to evoke pity are "commanding" is made a bit more clear in the following from the Cassiopaeans:

August 5, 1995

A: Remember, for quite some period of time now, as you measure time, we have tried to inform you to the effect that your third density environment has been completely controlled and will be controlled by forces that seek only to serve themselves for a period, as you would measure time, exceeding 309,000 years.

And, many, many times in your current life existence, you have reflected upon the questions involving the beneficial or otherwise existence of individuals or an individual IN this environment, the pros and cons of continuing such existence, and what is involved with it. And, you have correctly perceived the conclusion that this is, primarily, a negative experience.

But, not that good things do not come from a negative experience, but that the basic indicator that it is a negative experience, should also indicate to you that it is an experience related to *a chain of command* involving Service to Self. And, therefore, *Service to Self is a manipulative action rather than an openly beneficial action. It is a withdrawing and taking motion rather than an expanding motion.* And these statements can answer for you, not only simple questions, but the very nature of your existence to begin with as well.

Q: (L) This leads to a couple of our other questions. What are the criteria to be a fourth density candidate?

A: There are no criteria. A criterion implies a judgment system, which implies that an individual or individuals are watching over the progress of other individuals. It is merely part of the natural process of learning, which you are in total control of from beginning to end, in one sense.

In that sense, you choose to be in the environment you are in, which does not indicate any recommendation of the environment by any higher source, or, conversely, any condemnation of the environment by any higher source, but merely the existence of the environment and your choice to exist within it.

Therefore, being a candidate merely means that you have chosen to be a candidate for ANY level of density, be it first, second, etc. It is a choice of the self to continue that learning pathway.

So we have a clue here: one of the indicators that something is of an STS orientation is the presence or evidence of a Chain of Command!

Now I would like to bring up the subject of those individuals Ra has designated as Wanderers. Ra describes them as follows:

> When a [soul] has achieved its complete understanding of its desire, it may conclude that its desire is Service to Others [in the form of] reaching their hand [figuratively speaking] to any entities who call for aid. These entities whom you may call the Brothers and Sisters of Sorrow move toward this calling of Sorrow. These entities are from all reaches of the infinite creation and are bound together by the desire to serve in this way.
>
> ...The number [of Wanderers incarnated on Earth at this time] due to an intensive need to lighten the planetary vibration and thus aid in harvest... approaches sixty-five million... The largest number of Wanderers... are of the sixth density.

The desire to serve must be [of] a great deal of purity of mind and what you may call foolhardiness or bravery. The challenge/danger of the Wanderer is that it will forget its mission, become karmically involved, and thus be swept into the maelstrom of which it had incarnated to avert (the destruction).

...Due to the extreme variance between the vibratory distortions of third density and those of the more dense densities, if you will, Wanderers have as a general rule some form of handicap, difficulty, or feeling of alienation that is severe. The most common of these difficulties are alienation, the reaction against the planetary vibration by personality disorders, as you would call them, and [physical] ailments indicating difficulty in adjustment to the planetary vibrations such as allergies, as you would call them.

...The energies of the Wanderers, your teachers and adepts at this time are all bent upon increasing the harvest. However, there are few to harvest.

The problem seems to be that of "waking up" to the nature of the mission and this presents special problems. Ra gives us several more clues:

Wanderers become completely the creatures of third density in mind/body complex. There is just as much chance of [them being subjected to Orion STS mind programming attempts] as to a mind/body complex of [strictly third density]. The only difference occurs in the spirit complex which, if it wishes, has an armor of light, if you will, which enables it to recognize more clearly that which is not be desired by the mind/body/spirit complex. This is not more than a bias and cannot be called an understanding.

So we begin to understand that even the purest of the pure are subject to corruption and deception. They *do* seem to have a bit of help in separating the wheat from the chaff, but Ra describes it as "not more than a bias and cannot be called an understanding."

The problem is, the "bias" often comes into direct conflict with the mind programming efforts of the Orion STS and a lot of suffering and torture can result. And there is also a special weakness of those who are configured to STO – since they don't have meanness and deception in their own hearts, it can take almost forever for them to see it in others who are being used to keep them from awakening! Ra remarks on this as well:

Furthermore, the Wanderer is less inclined to the deviousness of third density and therefore does not recognize as easily as a more negative individual would, the negative nature of thoughts or beings... [If the Wanderer is successfully co-opted by the Orion STS it would be] caught into the planetary vibration and, when harvested, possibly repeat again the master cycle of third density as a planetary entity.

Ra also confirmed Don's remark that those with missions, Wanderers, are "high priority targets" of the Orion STS faction. That's a scary thought!

What it means is that *if* a person comes into incarnation from a higher density with a mission to serve, not only are they enveloped in the "veil of forgetting", they become special targets for a bunch of Intergalactic rapists and murderers who are only restrained in their actions by some sort of vague Law of Free Will which still allows every imaginable trick and deception to be perpetrated on them so that they will engage in relationships, beliefs, actions or reactions designed to "bring them down a few densities," so to speak!

And they only get a "bias" toward what is Truth, and not a clear understanding!

So with all of this information we are trying to put together about what is out there just waiting to trap and deceive us, how in the world are we supposed to have a clue as to what is going on? Just *who* are the Good Guys here?!

> [In terms of STO contacts from the higher densities] the infringement upon free will is greatly undesired. Therefore, those entities, which are Wanderers upon your plane of illusion, *will be the only subjects for the thought projections that make up the so-called "Close Encounters" and meetings...*

Ra seems to be saying that only the "Wanderers" have any hope of being in contact with the higher level "Good Guys" because they are, *ipso facto*, already of STO configuration and therefore, contact is not an infringement upon their free will as it would be if the STO contact came to a third density being who has not yet graduated to the higher densities.

Of course, they all look alike here on the Big Blue Marble, and they are all mostly engaged in living relatively normal lives side by side with one another. And they *do* have to be "awakened"! Also, there is a special condition under which Wanderers may be contacted, it seems, that pretty much eliminates your "weekend seminar" in channeling. It seems that there is an almost mathematical law involved in being able to communicate with higher density beings:

> The calling of a *group* of people whose square overcame the integrated resistance of those unwilling to search or learn...

If we just stop and think for a moment about the nature of most people on the planet who do *not* want to search or learn; they do not want to think or do the necessary work that prepares a "vessel" for the inflow of higher knowledge; they want to be "saved" with as little effort as possible, then you begin to understand the odds against contact with truly higher density STO beings. That is the operation of the Law of Free Will.

The majority of beings of third density *are* STS – they would not be in this density otherwise. By this choice, they have also chosen the illusions that are part of this "con job". Yes, at a very deep level, it is a choice to experience in order to learn, but let's not get ahead of ourselves here.

By the very fact that this is the choice of the majority, the few who might truly wish to perceive the truth are overruled by the mass choice according to the law of Free Will!

Even if the being is a fourth or sixth density "Wanderer", by entering this density, they have chosen to "play by the rules" and cannot abridge them!

Thus, in order to penetrate this "veil of forgetting", *extreme* effort is required *in a mathematical ratio*. A consistent "call" by a *group*, must go out. And the energy required to penetrate the veil must be built up over a period of time in order to meet this requirement. This principle is expressed in two of the purported sayings of Jesus: "Wherever two or more are gathered in my name..." and you must "ask and *keep on* asking, knock and *keep on* knocking, and it will be opened to you."

So, just by thinking about this very simple Law of Free Will and its implications, we come to an understanding that the likelihood of the many "sources" of information that purport to have "serendipitously" contacted this or that channel who was just humming along one day and – ZAP! – along came Swami Whosits or Koot Hoot or Lord Sandyando or whoever, are very likely victims of the deception – possibly even Wanderers being "neutralized" by STS forces, or simply those who are "agents" of the STS forces, including those programmed a la Greenbaum.

Ra did give us a figure: 65 million Wanderers on the planet at the time he was speaking. That amounts to about one person out of every hundred on the planet. But how many of them survive the attacks? How many of them actually do, can, or will wake up? Particularly when we must expect them to be objects of special "attention" in terms of "attack"?

But, apparently all is not lost! Those Wanderers who have struggled and worked or survived the attack/lessons to the point that something inside them is ready *can* awaken via subtle "contacts" or inner urgings:

> The feeling of being awakened or activated is the goal of this type of contact... The methods used to awaken Wanderers are varied. The center of each approach is the entrance into the conscious and subconscious in such a way as to avoid causing fear and to maximize the potential for an understandable subjective experience that has meaning for the entity. Many such occur in sleep, others in the midst of many activities during the waking hours. The approach is flexible and does not necessarily include the "Close Encounter" syndrome.

So we are given to understand that such "wake up" experiences can be varied. Considering the deceptions and manipulations of the Orion STS that have already been described, we also must consider that there will be many efforts to block, obfuscate, or *mimic* such awakenings. Again, only knowledge can give us the tools with which to discriminate. Again Ra brings up a special class of attack that can occur to those who are on a destined mission, as the Cassiopaeans call it:

> Wanderers *do* have "Close Encounters" with Orion STS, though it is rare. [Such] occurs either due to the Orion entities' lack of perception of the depth of positivity to be encountered or due to the Orion entities' desire to, shall we say, *attempt to remove this positivity from this plane of existence*. ...A mistaken Orion STS contact with highly polarized positive entities can wreak havoc with Orion troops unless [they] are able to depolarize the entity mistakenly contacted.

This occurrence is almost unheard of. Therefore, the Orion group prefers to make physical contact only with the weaker-minded entity... The most typical approach of Orion entities is to choose what you might call the weaker minded entity that it might suggest a greater amount of Orion STS philosophy to be disseminated.

So now we begin to understand the special traps set up for these Wanderers wherein *human agents* are used to manipulate and control them. If they cannot be corrupted directly, the strategy is to corrupt those around them – including family, friends, spouses and associates of all kinds. While I would never claim to be one of these "Wanderers", even if the profile does fit (since I am not inclined to "true believership" in anything), there was a curious exchange with the Cassiopaeans at one session which included another individual who also fits this profile that gives some clues as to how this occurs:

May 3, 1997

Q: (L) Reading through the session of May 23, last year, when TK was also here, and the issue of his living in isolation from the rest of the world was addressed, you asked who had begged him to stay there even though he wanted to move to a place where he could have more contact with other people and more opportunities for growth and stimulation. The answer to this question was that it was his wife who insisted on remaining even though it was clear that he was unhappy in the environment. Then you made a remark about an EM [Electromagnetic] vector. The way I understood it is that you were saying that a person can be an EM vector. Is that possible?

A: Vector means focuser of direction.

Q: (L) So his wife is the one who controls the focus of his direction. But how? Could that mean that a human being can vector EM waves simply by their presence and that these EM waves are part of the control system that manipulates people? Can it be that such "agents" are used as EM vectors in the sense that they emanate a special frequency that literally affects the mind in terms of shutting down clarity, or even actually transmitting pre-coded thought loops?

A: Precisely.

Q: (L) I also noticed that several of us have been involved with persons and relationships that seem designed to confuse, defuse, and otherwise distort our learning, as well as drain our energy. Basically, keeping us so stressed that we cannot fulfill our potential. Is there some significance to this observation?

A: That is elementary, my dear Knight! [...]

Q: (L) Were the individuals in our lives selected for the extremely subtle nature of their abilities to evoke pity, or were we programmed to respond to pity so that we were blind to something that was obvious to other people?

A: Neither. You were selected to interact with those who would trigger a hypnotic response that would ultimately lead to a drain of energy.

Q: (T) Well, it is a fact, because my energy is sure drained. (L) What is the purpose of this draining of energy?

A: What do you think?

Q: (T) So you can't concentrate or do anything. You can't get anywhere with anything.
A: Or, at least not the important things.
Q: (T) Is that why my concentration is so low?
A: Yes. You are dealing with a no-win situation!! As you know.
Q: (T) So, if I don't get out, I will just keep going down. Is it the area or the person?
A: Both. One is wrapped within the other. [...]
Q: (L) Is it true that being in the presence of such people, that one is under the influence of an energy, an emanation from them physically, that befuddles the mind and makes it almost impossible to think one's way out of the situation?
A: It is the draining of energy that befuddles the mind.
Q: (L) Where does this energy drain?
A: 4th density STS.
Q: (L) These people we are associated with drain our energy from us and fourth density STS harvests it from them?
A: "They" do nothing!!!! 4th density STS does it all through them! [...]

Lesson number 1: Always expect attack.

Lesson number 2: Know the modes of same.

Lesson number 3: Know how to counteract same.

When you are under attack, expect the unexpected, if it is going to cause problems... But, if you expect it, you learn how to "head it off," thus neutralizing it. This is called vigilance, which is rooted in knowledge. And, what does knowledge do?

Q: (L) Protects! I guess that a person just has to come to the full realization that virtually everything that happens on the planet – no exceptions – is a symbol of some interaction of STS vs. STO energy at higher levels.
A: Yes, and for most, that is not as of yet realized. It must be part of a natural learning process.
Q: (L) Well, I guess that all of us tend to keep one or another area sacrosanct and think that it is not subject to attack, or that we can use logic and third density thinking to explain it. Until a person realizes that attack can come through even one's self, wives and husbands, children and parents, friends – virtually *anybody – nobody* is exempt.
A: The block is a lack of faith in the concept. Remember, when one has been indoctrinated by religion, culture and/or science, they are predisposed to view all things in the sense of the measurable physical reality exclusively. One must be cured of lack of faith in the reality of nonphysical attack.

One major thing we see from the above is that our associations can be crucial. Of course, if we are *aware* that anyone and everyone can be used as an "EM vector" to modulate our frequency or behavior or thinking, then we have some protection. But to be unaware of it, to be in close association with those who are unaware themselves, and therefore subject to this manipulation, is to be firmly "in the trap".

But suppose one person in a relationship begins to "wake up", and becomes aware (even if only vaguely), that all is not as it seems. They will have continual glimpses of the reality, mostly when not in the presence of the other individual. They may clearly see that something is not working, that it is not right, and may even make decisions to change it or to leave. But the instant the other person is physically present with their EM vectoring capabilities, the glimpses of truth are "damped" or even shut down and the waking person begins to feel schizophrenic or crazy in some way for having such conflicting and opposing thoughts. Add to this the social and religious enculturation to "turn the other cheek" or "suffer because it's noble and holy," and you have the recipe for cooking the Wanderer's goose!

Another of the factors in the control system is the "self-destruct" program. Obviously the aliens have no problem abducting and killing and eating many people who are still lost in the initial choice for STS/third density. But there are the special cases of the Wanderers who, obviously, the STS invaders don't want to tangle with at that level, as described above by Ra, so they have a rather clever way *around* this little stumbling block to their machinations: the suicide game.

This is a very cunning setup, I can tell you! It can follow a variety of lines in the lives of different people, and it seems that the STS Orions take some sort of fiendish delight in designing variations for their entertainment pleasure, but the gist of it is this: a Wanderer is born. Obviously they have to be born somewhere, to some family, with certain genetics. It is also equally obvious that the choices probably *don't* include having Wanderers for parents or siblings, (though there are exceptions). There they are, innocent little babies, volunteers for a great mission, surrounded by potential EM vectors and Lizzie agents! And the game begins!

Abuse – physical, sexual, and psychological – comes into play to "set them up" for a later fall – if in fact they are not just simply killed by same right at the beginning. But the special characteristic of the Wanderer type is that they continue to "shine" with a sort of "inner purity" of the questing spirit even in the face of such treatment. As a result of this abuse, they can be attached by any number of "dead dudes" or elementals or even demonic-type entities that enter in through wounds in the psychological/psychic shield like cosmic bacteria.

The usual next stage in this drama is to cause the Wanderer to be attracted to a particular type of person who is a sort of "false image" of STO. This can be what researcher Eve Lorgen calls a *Love Bite* relationship where a great "cosmic love" is simulated, only to fall flat as soon as the EM vector is turned off.[50] The intended result of this betrayal is to induce suicidal feelings or to set the Wanderer up for the *next* variation of the game.

---

[50] Cf. Eve Lorgen, The Love Bite: Alien Interference in Human Love Relationships (Bonsall, CA: ELogos & HHC Press, 2001).

What happens now is that the Wanderer is set up by the previous dramas to seek out marriage or love partners who are also abusive either overtly or covertly. And, of course, the Wanderer's special characteristics of being unable to really understand negative thinking because it is not a part of their own make-up, prevents them from seeing exactly what is going on. They always seem to attribute the same high motives and ideals to others that are in themselves. They endlessly excuse abuse and hurt to themselves and others with the idea that if they just love the other long enough, hard enough, pure enough or stand by them through thick and thin, that the abuser will overcome *their* hurts/wounds which are the cause of their abusive behavior, and they will then be able to be whole, which, of course, the Wanderer believes to be a person similar to themselves!

Gee, sounds like the Way of the Monk, doesn't it? Perhaps that "way" was created just to trap such positive individuals and to use them as energy food for STS.

Then there is the constant projection of the suicide program by the many EM vectors that the Wanderer finds in their environment. It takes careful observation to determine who these individuals may be, but it can be done! The natural feelings of being lost and alone and alienated from this environment are intensified and twisted so that the Wanderer begins to focus solely upon the idea of getting out from under this enormous psychic pressure. Spirit attachments can also be used in this respect, attacking the Wanderer from the "inside", so to speak.

April 15, 1995

Q: (L) [You have mentioned attack.] Is this physical danger or just harassment danger?

A: Mind attack for purpose of self-destruction.

Q: (L) Is there anything that can be done to shield against this kind of attack?

A: Yes. Knowledge input on a continuous basis.

Q: (L) And what form should this knowledge take? Does this mean channeled information, books, videos, what?

A: All and other. Networking of information now, warning!!! All others will very soon experience great increase of same type of attack, two of you have had episodes in past from same source for similar reasons, but now your association puts you in different category!! Remember all channels and those of similar make-up are identified, tracked, and "dealt with". Suicidal thoughts?

Q: (T) So, we have the knowledge and that's all we need to do to prevent the attacks from being nasty?

A: You do not have all the awareness you need! Not by any means! Remember, all there is is lessons. Daily prayer helps.

Through it all, the Wanderer never whines or complains that others are "doing it to" them; they always tend, first of all, to seek *in themselves* the cause of the events or the treatment they receive. They react with the idea that somehow they are not giving enough or in the right way, though they are entirely naive about what "giving" really is because, as mentioned, they have been brainwashed by the erroneous ideals of the third density STS environment which are manipulations to induce service to an illusion.

With this enculturation, the most difficult thing that the Wanderer has to face and do is to learn to *not* give in some instances, because this *not* giving is actually a form of *giving* at the soul level. Ra exemplifies this in a curious series of comments:

> For many of your centuries, both the [STO group] and the [STS group] busied themselves with each other upon planes above your own, shall we say, planes in time/space whereby machinations were conceived and the armor of light girded. Battles have been and are continuing to be fought upon these levels.
> ...Picture [your mind] in total unity with all other minds of your society. You are then single-minded and that which is a weak electrical charge in your physical illusion is now an enormously powerful machine whereby thoughts may be projected as things.
> ...In this endeavor the [STS group] charges or attacks the [STO group] armed with light. The result, a standoff, as you would call it, both energies being somewhat depleted by this and needing to regroup; the negative depleted through failure to manipulate, the positive depleted through failure to accept that which is given.
> ...[To explain "failure to accept that which is given"]: At the level of time/space which this takes place in the form of what you may call thought-war, the most accepting and loving energy would be to so love those who wished to manipulate that those entities were surrounded and engulfed, transformed by positive energies.
> ...This, however, being a battle of equals, the [STO group] is aware that it cannot, on equal footing, allow itself to be manipulated in order to remain purely positive, for then though pure it would not be of any consequence, having been placed by the so-called powers of darkness under the heel, as you may say. It is thus that *those who deal with this thought war must be defensive rather than accepting in order to preserve their usefulness in service to others*. Thusly, they cannot accept fully *what the [STS group] wishes to give, that being enslavement*.
> ...The only consequence which has been helpful is a balancing of the energies available to this planet so that these energies have less necessity to be balanced in this time/space, thus lessening the chances of planetary annihilation.

So we see here a guiding principle of balance. For those who believe that it is Love to "accept enslavement" – which is to respond to manipulation and thereby serve the STS faction, it becomes clear that to do so is to neutralize their effectiveness as an STO candidate because they are then no longer "purely positive"! *By accepting the manipulations, they become part of the other side!*

The bottom line here is this: if you are duped or sucked into the illusions of the machinations of STS, you are effectively "one of them", no matter what your intentions, and you thus further contribute to the unbalanced energies. This neutralizes the true nature of Service to Others.

Getting back to our story now, we remember that I was beginning to wonder if human beings live on more than one level and our conscious level of existence was sort of "mini-drama" that caricatured the *real* action at some other level of existence. We continued to probe for answers.

The very next session, at that point, was almost entirely taken up by Candy's personal concerns with her divorce proceedings and how best to maneuver financially since she was sure her soon-to-be ex-husband was stashing money in offshore accounts. But, even these personal issues of hers brought out some interesting information about the attack/lesson syndrome.

Candy was certain that aliens were manipulating her life (with a tendency to think that it was for her *benefit,* and who is to say that it ultimately wasn't?), and her questions pushed those issues. I will include only the parts of the session that are useful to our subject here:

August 8, 1994

Q: (L) Is this situation involving [Candy's divorce] engineered or caused by the aliens?

A: Not entirely.

Q: (L) Did aliens do anything to create emotional turmoil here?

A: They always do.

Q: (L) Is there anything that can be done to help this situation?

A: All is learning. [...]

Q: (L) Why has [Candy's husband] gotten himself into this situation with the accident, the divorce and everything else?

A: Karmic lessons for him. And you think about it Candy. Did you not value moneymen too much once before? Remember your first husband, where did love of money lead him? [Candy's first husband was involved with the "Mob" and was murdered in jail leaving her a rich widow at a very young age. Candy was *very* indignant at this remark.]

Q: (C) I married for love! It wasn't very pleasant to have your husband die at that age and I sure had a struggle after he died.

A: Lesson is for Candy. Karmic destiny.

Q: (L) Is this because she may have loved money too much in another life?

A: Extending into this one.

[Candy was actually reluctant to address questions directly to the Cassiopaeans and would whisper to me what she wanted to know and I was obliged to ask for her.]

Q: (L) Candy thinks she has learned this lesson by now.

A: Not yet.

Q: (L) Candy wants to know what she can do to end this pattern and stop these awful things from happening in her life?

A: Up to you. Stop loving money so much.

[Candy kept insisting that what the Cassiopaeans were saying about this was *not* true.]

A: It is subconscious. And what about the first time?

Q: (L) She insists that she married for love.

A: Thought you did.

Q: (L) But what about her present husband? He didn't have money when she married him like the first one did.

A: [Candy's husband] was recognizably money oriented. You knew this subconsciously. [Candy used her money to set her second husband up as a stockbroker. He did very well until he became involved with fast cars, faster women, and drugs. These things were the crux of the divorce battle.]

Q: (L) Well, if all this is subconscious, what can she do about it?

A: Learn to change. Candy must come out about her previous relationships. She must open up and be honest with herself and others to begin to clear the karma. She must soul search. Come to your senses. Find that out yourself.

Q: (L) We don't understand what you mean that Candy must come to her senses.

A: It is complicated. All is part of lesson.

[At this point I brought up the subject of the "hot shot" UFO investigator that Candy was dallying with since her husband had moved out.]

Q: (L) Well, I have warned her about MF. I think she is playing with fire there.

A: Of course. MF thinks any woman will come under his spell.

Q: (L) Is he trying to manipulate Candy as I suspect?

A: What do you think? It's working.

[Candy was, of course, getting more and more irate with the way this discussion was going.]

Q: (L) Well, Candy thinks she can handle the situation and there is a lot she thinks she can learn from MF.

A: He is not telling the truth.

Q: (C) But he seems to have so much knowledge. He says he can help me!

A: That is part of the spell. He knows how to visualize. Powerful man.

Q: (L) Well, is this power something he gets from attachments or alien help?

A: Both.

Candy continued to insist that what the Cassiopaeans were saying about her marriage, her affair, and her attitudes in general were *not* correct. It was pretty much at this point that she made the decision to believe her UFO investigator paramour against what the Cassiopaeans were telling her and against my advice that she ought to check his background and use reason and not emotion to make her choices. The bottom line was that she was being told that she needed to do some real work to clean out her subconscious, face her issues, and overcome her "programming" in order to bring her attacks/lessons to an end. She chose *not* to do so. And shortly thereafter, the incident of the Candidiasis of my daughter occurred and I terminated contact.

Frank and I continued to pursue some of the attack issues of our own in between the many universal type questions and my passion for historical subjects. One night, we had been asking a series of questions about Jesus and I had read earlier, when preparing the questions, that there was an incident in the Bible where Jesus is depicted as blowing on his disciples to "transmit the Holy Ghost" to them. Since this blowing is part of the Reiki initiations, I had the idea that Reiki was connected to the healing miracles of Jesus which the Cassiopaeans said were real events, even if the person they identified as being "Jesus of Nazareth" was someone quite different from the usual tradition or even some of the modified traditions.

September 30, 1994

Q: (L) Was [Jesus] able to literally heal with the touch of his hand?

A: Yes.

Q: (L) Is Reiki the method he used to heal, or something similar?

A: Yes.

Q: (L) Is there any way to enhance the Reiki energy to make it powerful enough that one could do in a very short time what now takes quite a while?

A: Yes.

Q: (L) What can one do to enhance the Reiki energy?

A: Attain lofty spiritual purity.

Q: (L) I have here two sets of Reiki symbols; which set is the correct or most powerful set: the first set or the second? [Holds up two sets of symbols.]

A: The second set.

Q: (L) It says here that the ones you have identified are the Usui Traditional symbols. Are these the original Reiki symbols as given to Dr. Usui?

A: Close.

Q: (L) Are the Reiki symbols in the possession of [the Reiki Master in Tampa] the correct symbols?

A: No.

Q: (L) Are the symbols that Louise is using correct?

A: No.

Q: (L) Is Louise able to transmit the initiation in a full and powerful way as she claims?

A: No. V*** has strongest ability.

[This was an of off-the-wall comment about one of the other Reiki students of Louise. It sort of surprised me.]

Q: (L) Does this mean that V*** has the strongest Reiki ability of us all?

A: Yes. Candy has no ability. Crosses yours out.

Q: (L) Are you saying that Candy has been giving me Reiki that has canceled my own Reiki out?

A: Precisely.

Q: (L) Is there someone I could go to for the correct initiation?

A: Yes.

Q: (L) Do I know that person?

A: No.

Q: (L) Whom do I know that may know that person?
A: H*** D***.

That was pretty upsetting, to say the least! Not only to know that I had taken my Second Level attunements from a Reiki Master who had no ability to transmit them, but also that there was the possibility that the corrupted form of Reiki could cancel out the beneficial Reiki! What's more, the person named as knowing someone who *did* have the proper Reiki lineage was so unlikely that I was completely incredulous! HD was an elderly psychic reader down in St. Petersburg who was a friend of a friend of mine and I had only been to see her once out of curiosity. She had made something of an impression on me because of her ranting *against* Reiki as being a completely useless "New Age Scam" because she believed that anybody who had "the gift" could heal without paying big bucks to somebody to do "hocus pocus" on them. So having the Cassiopaeans specify her in particular as a path to the "right" Reiki initiation was bizarre in the extreme!

But, the whole point of all this "testing" was to see if the Cassiopaeans really "had a clue" about anything, so I called HD the next day, feeling completely stupid, to inquire if she, by some miracle, knew a Reiki Master.

Her reply was funny. She said, "Well, you *know* I don't put any stock in all that nonsense – waste of money if you ask me! – But, yes, I *do* know a couple of gals who swear by it. They are both Reiki Masters, so let me look up their numbers and call you back."

A little bit later she called me back with one name, SB. The second Reiki Master had moved away, so it ended up that she only had a connection to one. I took down the name and number and called to see what I could find out.

As it turned out, the Cassiopaeans were right! This lady had the same lineage as the Reiki Master who had given me my First Level initiation, with only one added "descendant" between her and Takata. And, she also had the same material passed to this line from Takata and knew my original Reiki Master. She knew the same stories and inside information that is held by this lineage, and so on. So, the Cassiopaeans had a "hit". I made arrangements with her to retake the Second Level attunements to correct the damage done by Louise, in her ignorance, and a year later I took the Master Level attunements from SB. I can guarantee that when she did the job, the sweat broke out again, and my "Reiki heater" was turned back on! What's more, we had still *another* set of Reiki symbols, different from the previous three I had seen. I presented them to the Cassiopaeans:

November 19, 1994

Q: (L) Now, we went to the recommended person to take the Reiki initiation, do we now, at this point in time, have the true Reiki initiation?

A: Getting there. Must allow energy to solidify. Do you understand the concept of imprinting?

Q: (L) Yes.

A: Then you know.

Q: (L) Practicing Reiki is the thing that will solidify the force?
A: Partly.
Q: (L) Are there symbols for Reiki that are even older and stronger than the ones we have been given?
A: Yes.
Q: (L) Are the original symbols in Sanskrit?
A: Yes.
Q: (L) Where are we going to find them?
A: You are not.
Q: (L) And the Reiki Symbols we learned from SB are the closest we can get?
A: Yes. Good enough.

Later, a funny incident occurred in which I was made aware of the potential for the Cassiopaeans to "draw" things if there were a pencil attached to the planchette. I had made a statement that I "understood" something and they responded:

December 3, 1994
A: You do??? [Inscribed giant question mark on board.]
Q: (L) Do what?
A: You said you understood concept. Really? Learn.
Q: (L) Well, since you guys can do that, why can't you teach us power symbols that will enhance our Reiki?
A: You are not ready.
Q: (L) But if we work on the Reiki will you teach us more power symbols?
A: Okay, we'll give you one. [Pencil is attached to planchette that draws symbol.]
Q: (L) What is this symbol called?
A: Anuki. Pronounced: AH – NEW – KEY.
Q: (V) And, as it applies to Reiki, what does it do? What does it represent?
A: Retention of energy at location most in need. All Reiki you have as yet learned involves passage of healing energy, this one involves prolonged retention for strengthened power, thus results.
Q: (L) Where are you getting this?
A: Access is Universal.
Q: (L) Did Dr. Usui also receive this and then not remember it? I mean, the story is that he received a *lot* of symbols, but as far as I know, there are only half a dozen or so being passed down in the teachings.
A: Usui did not reveal all to Takata.
Q: (L) Why?
A: He was told that the knowledge was priceless and must not be wasted by too much dissemination particularly to those who do not have the burning desire for truth. Those who did, as you do, would find some way of accessing knowledge.

It was not lost on me how similar to some crop circles the Reiki symbols are, so I brought this up:

> Q: (L) Is it true that crop circles are a kind of grand Reiki being given to the planet?
> A: But also messages and lessons.
> Q: (L) Well, could it also be said that Reiki symbols as applied to the body are etheric messages to the etheric body?
> A: Yes.
> Q: (L) Do they communicate information into our field, so to speak?
> A: Everything that exists at all levels is just lessons.
> Q: (L) Well, in the case of Reiki, what I specifically want to know is if, say an individual is psychically, spiritually, karmically, or otherwise wounded or discombobulated, does the application of Reiki symbols give messages to the electromagnetic field to re-form or rearrange the pattern in the perfect pattern intended?
> A: Yes.
> Q: (L) And can repeated application of this, can not only physical things, but also etheric things, be healed? That is karma and so forth?
> A: Yes.
> Q: (L) So that our continual use of Reiki and application to each other and ourselves literally would cleanse us from our karmic burdens, memories or scars of the soul?
> A: Yes.

No wonder Reiki fell under corruption almost at its inception in this country!

A TRIP TO "ALLIGATOR ALLEY"!

This now brings us to a most interesting thing. I am jumping over about a year here to get to this incident, but it is directly related and *crucial* to the understanding of what is going on "out there" in the world of attack/lessons. It will be rather graphic and there are some pictures in this section that are *not* for the squeamish, so be warned!

First, I would like to remind the reader of the remark made by Terry, a long time member of our group, when he was addressing the MUFON crowd at which we gave the Cassiopaeans a little "test drive" in public:

> March 11, 1995
>
> What we have been told on that is that this universe was created as a Free Will Universe. It was created specifically to allow all souls to do whatever they wish to do; they have complete choice about what they wish to do. The Grays, the Lizards – whomever they are who abduct and put implants in people, have the right to do that because it's their free will to come here and do that to us. And, they have the right to tell us whatever they want to tell us to rationalize their behavior.

Our right is to *not* believe what abducting entities tell us. We have free will to believe or not believe them.

If they tell us in one lifetime that they have the right to do this to us, and we choose to believe them then, and then, in this lifetime, they try the same tricks and we choose *not* to believe them, in each case, we are exercising our free will and so are they. This is a Free Will Universe. We can change our mind. *They* are trying to convince us that we have no choice in that. Whether we believe them or not is *our* choice.

And that seems to be the crux of the matter. A Free Will Universe. We are being challenged in every moment to *choose*.

Very early in the Cassiopaean contact, there were suggestions that I connect to the Internet – that some "great opportunity" would transpire after I did.

November 19, 1994

Q: (T) Are different people receiving different pieces of information or are some people receiving as much as they can handle and then it moves to another person to receive more of the information in varying amounts? ... Is this information being given out in pieces to different people to be put together?

A: Close.

Q: (T) The information I have would not then be whole unto itself?

A: Network! Use computer net. There are others communicating and piecing together in this way.

Q: (T) How do I retrieve the information?

A: Ask.

Q: (L) Start taking the melatonin?

A: No. On computer Network!

Q: (T) Ask on the computer network how to retrieve the information?

A: No. Others ask.

Q: (L) Ask if others are having dreams of a similar nature?

A: Open dialogue.

November 24, 1994

Q: (L) Is there anything in a few words that you want to tell us before we end tonight?

A: Network but be careful with whom.

December 5, 1994

Q: (L) I had a dream last night, I dreamed about large mechanical flying "V's" that had flapping wings like metal bat boxes. They scared me. Then, I was with my family and we were going to see my cousin who is deceased and she had just had a baby. The baby was walking and talking and quoting Shakespeare. My Aunt got very upset and said it was unseemly because the baby was illegitimate and she walked out. The baby was only 10 days old. My aunt ran out the door and said it was evil.

A: Suggestion, get on computer net ASAP.

Q: (L) In other words, I really need to take my computer down and get the A: drive fixed, etc., and log onto the network?

A: Yes.

Q: (V) What does that have to do with the dream? (L) I think it relates back to when Terry and Jan were here and we were talking about dreams and the suggestion was given to hook up to the network and discuss and share dreams. Like a dream forum kind of thing. Is there any significance to the ten days in this dream?

A: When you network, your entire life will dramatically improve immediately! See, sometimes we do advise when appropriate.

December 17, 1994

Q: (L) How do we find a horticulturist? Network?

A: Always "Network". Networking is 4th Density STO concept seeping into 3rd density with upcoming realm border crossing.

Q: (DM) Networking is the way to get things done from third level into fourth level?

A: Coming from 4th level into 3rd because of influence of wave.

Q: (DM) So, each of us has a skill that we develop and help each other. (L) We are all part of a body.

A: This is the way to live in STO!

December 23, 1994

Q: (L) We got the program loaded for the computer net, which you told us once we got online our lives would change suddenly and dramatically. (D) Are we not quite ready for this?

A: Discover. [...]

Q: (D) Is there something we can do to help other people?

A: Access instincts, network.

Q: (D) Are you talking about the computer network?

A: In general.

December 27, 1994

Q: (L) You did say that once we got on the network, things would happen suddenly and dramatically.

Now, as you must know, I did have an automobile accident the day after I got hooked up to the network. As you can see. I am put back together now with screws and tape!!![51] I'm sure I look charming!

---

[51] I suffered a concussion, a cracked vertebra, and my left arm was nearly torn out of the socket. All the rotator muscles and ligaments in my left shoulder had been torn, and even though I had been released to go home, I was in a brace and was soon to suffer many problems due to having been released too soon. The neck injury was the most serious, and over the next weeks, swelling of the cervical disks caused paralysis on the

Now, oddly, as I was driving, just a few minutes prior to the accident, I was thinking very strongly of the fact that you Cassiopaeans were with me and I was saying to you in my mind that I wished you would also go and help my friend, Sandra, who was in the hospital. I was planning on rushing through my Christmas Eve and going to the hospital to give her Reiki. And then, Kowabonga! I got the smasho-smacko in the rear.

Why did this happen? What did I do wrong? Is this what you meant by "sudden and dramatic [change to my life]?"

A: All happens for a reason.

Q: (L) Was there something I was supposed to learn from this smash-up?

A: If so, learn by meditating.

Q: (L) Is there something about our state of being that we can be sitting there thinking loving thoughts about others and then we get smashed?

A: Meditate.

Q: (V) Is her accident directly connected with getting online? (L) Well, they didn't kill me, though they tried! (V) Back to my question...

A: Not necessary to answer.

Q: (L) Is that because I know the answer?

A: Okay.

Q: (L) And my answer is that there is a definite connection between the accident and getting hooked up to the computer network, is that correct?

A: You explore well.

Q: (L) I think... now, my whole spinal column snapped like a whip on impact and I did have a concussion... and my shoulder is in *really* bad shape... I am really surprised that they didn't keep me in the hospital longer...

A: You must be a "Whippersnapper".

Q: (L) Are there going to be some really positive results from the computer net? I mean, this is a rather painful beginning.

A: What have we told you?

So, there it was: I was just going along in my "love and light bubble" and nearly got killed by an old guy in an Oldsmobile who hit me in the rear at full speed while I was stopped and waiting to make a left turn. The reader might want to go back to the last part of the first section, "The Truth Is Out There", for a review of the accident itself.

As a result of the injuries sustained in the accident, I was subjected to all kinds of medical procedures that I knew were *not* going to help me get any better and were, in fact, making me worse. In desperation, I thought of Sandy, the member of the Reiki group who did not seem to be "connected" to the Metaphysical Church in any way, so I felt safe in calling on her skills as a massage therapist for pain relief work during my long recovery.

---

left side of my body. Nevertheless, I took pain pills and participated in a session, as I was to continue to do through the two years of intense physical therapy that was needed to restore mobility to my arm and leg.

Sandy knew about our channeling work and was very curious about it all, so just to sort of check her out further (I was getting more cautious now!) I invited her to our New Year's party where we had a sort of "Party Session" with the Cassiopaeans. I hadn't seen her in about five months, after having cut off any contact with that crowd, and she seemed very happy to attend.

Sandy was so interested in the session we had that night that she asked for any material we had received thus far that she could read, and I gave her a long printout of what had been typed up to that point. She called me a couple of days later just absolutely enthralled with it! It was highly gratifying to have someone who was so enthusiastic about it! (Here comes the downfall through ego!)

As a result of her enthusiastic reception and her willingness to help with the work of getting the material transcribed and printed, Sandy became *very* close. Not only did she undertake my therapy, she also wanted to attend all the sessions. Whenever I was short of money for computer supplies, she offered money, and often came over with reams of paper and printer cartridges for my computer. I felt that I had a wonderful helper practically sent by God!

Now let's recap this chain of people: through my mother I met Louise, through Louise I met Candy and Sandy and that whole crew, through Candy I met Marti, a woman who owned a metaphysical book store, who introduced me to Roxane, and who sent *Lilly* to me. I am just putting this in here to note the connections between all of them.

As soon as I was disconnected from Louise and Candy, Sandy came into the picture seemingly out of both necessity and serendipity and Marti became active and connected me to Roxane.

Now, Roxane had an astrology magazine she wanted to get out from under, having decided to move to Sedona or somewhere out west, and Marti knew I was interested in putting a magazine together as a sort of "organ" for the Cassiopaean Material. She thought that I ought to get together with Roxane and find an agreement that would allow me to take over her magazine subscription list. So, she put us together and we began to work on the transfer of this "abstract entity" which I began to think of as my "Aurora Journal".

Meanwhile, the work on this magazine idea was producing other interesting effects.

There had been a little print shop a few miles down the road that I had frequented on a number of occasions for various copying needs, and I thought that I might talk to them about printing the magazine since their prices were very reasonable.

I walked in and started to talk to the girl behind the counter about what I wanted to do, and after a minute or two, a woman came out from the back of the shop, stood there and stared at me in amazement. It was Pat of the flying black boomerangs![52]

I nearly dropped my teeth!

---

[52] See *High Strangeness* for details.

As it turned out, Pat had recently bought the print shop as a business venture for her kids. She invited me into the back of the shop for coffee and we brought each other up to date on what had been happening in our lives since the "incident" of the UFOs. That event had upset her so badly that she completely retreated into denial and the "normal life" routine.

I told her how that event had done just the opposite for me – I had been catapulted into a series of learning experiences that had completely shattered my previous world, and made it seem like I was on a continual roller coaster ride. I told her about the Cassiopaeans and all that they were saying about aliens. She was very intrigued. She wanted to attend a session.

In the meantime, my communications on the Internet were opening doors of access to the information of other researchers, and one of them sent me the "Greenbaum Speech" and something entitled "Elaine and the Sisters of Light" which was drawn from a book entitled *They Came to Set the Captives Free* by a "Dr. Rebecca Brown".

I was pretty upset at the Greenbaum material because it just exemplified how low human beings can go, but my opinion of the Elaine piece was a bit different. I had read a few other things of that type – sworn to and attested by the doctors who worked with the patient recovering the memories, and I had never quite been able to accept that it was anything more than some kind of confabulation. It was just *too* crazy – even for me – to consider as factual in the real world.

As it turned out, I made a good call on that one: Dr. Brown was discovered to be a fraud, though she certainly was a real doctor. Reading her case was very troubling, however, because what seemed to emerge from it was exactly what was described in the Greenbaum Speech. The poor woman struck me as exactly the kind of victim that the C's had described as "malfunctioning".

August 17, 1996

Q: (T) Okay, the question is, is the fellow that just shot three professors in San Diego, I think it was, the University, before they read his thesis, because he was afraid they would throw his thesis away, and make it look bad, and flunk him. Was he a Greenbaum?

A: Yes.

Q: (T) Why did they turn him "on" at that point?

A: Not correct concept. What if: those programmed in the so called "Greenbaum" projects are preprogrammed to "go off" all at once, and some "malfunction," and go off early?

Scarier still was the following answer to a question asked by Sandy:

May 25, 1996

Q: (S) I don't want to sound paranoid, but all the reports about mind programming… is it as widespread as we have been lead to believe? That it could be the guy next door, and a certain color, or word or sound could set them off?

A: Vague.

Q: (L) That's not exactly vague. What is the percentage of programmed people?

A: 2 out of every 100.

Q: (L) How many are programmed by human means?

A: 12 per cent of the .02 per cent. [This should probably read 2 per cent.]

Q: (L) So, out of every 1,000 people, there are 20 that are programmed, and 2.4 of these are programmed by humans and 17.6 are programmed by aliens, as in fourth density STS?

A: Understand that 4th density is physical, indeed. You are drifting further and further toward an ethereal only perception/theoretical position.

Q: (L) You are saying that the humans working on these kinds of things... and...

A: No, Laura, we are saying that there is really a very strong "nuts and bolts" reality to this phenomenon, and don't ignore it!

So, of course, the Greenbaum material offered a partial explanation for many strange things. What if the descriptions of satanic ritual abuse that emerged in the memories of various patients was really an implanted memory engineered by the Greenbaum method for the purposes of hiding the real source of the Greenbaum programming?

Another question was: what if alien abductions and all that were also engineered memories just like the Elaine and other ritual abuse material? Engineered, that is, via the Greenbaum program.

Then, there was another way of thinking about it: what if the Greenbaum program and the Elaine program, both, are "screen memories" of alien abductions?

In any event, I thought that the Greenbaum text deserved wider distribution and I planned to publish it in the first issue of the Aurora Journal along with a commentary giving my ideas as above.

At the time I was putting the first issue together, Marti referred "Lilly" to me. Lilly wanted to talk to me about placing an ad in the magazine.

This woman claimed to be a somewhat well known New Age teacher of many subjects including Reiki, meditation, aura-reading, create your own reality, and a slew of other interesting things. She is quite attractive, and a real "ball of fire" at getting things organized and "on track" for her many classes and seminars. She claims that her lectures draw a big crowd, that she receives great reviews for her work, and is generally quite popular in the New Age communities around the country.

I learned that she also travels to many New Age or UFO Seminars, Expositions and Conferences, making new contacts and connections, and spreading the word. I was also aware that she was occasionally invited to appear on television and radio as a paranormal expert, and the last I heard, she claimed she had gotten a Ph.D. in metaphysics by mail and published a book, though I have never been able to find it at any bookstore or on the Internet.

Lilly called me about placing an ad in our magazine. She wanted a quarter page, which we were selling for $350.00. However, she didn't have the money to pay for it, so she asked me if I would be willing to do an exchange. I asked her what she had in mind, and she said that she would come to one of our sessions with her Polaroid aura camera and take photos of all the participants as well as the process itself. That sounded completely cool, so I agreed. It also happened to be the same session that Pat was going to attend.

Early on the evening of the session, Lilly arrived early to haul in and set up her equipment. I examined it all as she did so and realized that it was a pretty simple concept. It was pretty much just an ordinary Polaroid camera mounted on a tripod. The truth is that they don't really photograph your aura. The so-called aura photos are the result of photomontage technique where an illusion of an aura is created. There is a light source inside the camera that illuminates the film directly based on the measured electrical skin resistance. At the same time, the camera is photographing you in an ordinary way. That is why I was so amazed at the "aura photographs" of myself and the board, which pretty much went against the rules of how this setup should work.[53] There is absolutely no explanation for why I had disappeared from my photograph, and the presence of the light figure on the board has no precedent either, as far as I can tell.

Sandy arrived late and came in while we were in the middle of all this photography. She was very quiet and soon complained of a headache and declined to participate in the aura photography.

We were soon done with all the pictures and Lilly suddenly announced that, except for my photo and the photos of the process, she expected to be paid for her "services". She quoted exorbitant prices that she claimed she received for this work, as well as a special "fee" for having brought the equipment to us.

I was, needless to say, a bit surprised with this "bait and switch" routine, but not wanting to engage in a dispute over it, I decided that I would just pay for all the participants since I was the one who had told them that Lilly was bringing the camera as an exchange, and they had all participated believing that there was no additional charge. However, the group, seeing the situation for what it really was, came to my rescue and paid for their photos. In the end, my aura photo and the aura photo of the board were quite expensive: about $175.00 apiece!

After what seemed to be a fleecing of my guests, Lilly declined to stay for the rest of the session. This puzzled me because I thought she had said she wanted to ask specific questions. She packed up her equipment and left.

After Lilly was gone, we resumed our session. Pat was very interested in some health related questions so nothing of a particularly significant nature came through.

The next day Lilly called and hemmed and hawed a bit before saying, "I have a question that I just have to ask you. Where did you meet Sandy? How well do you know her?"

---

[53] The pictures are reproduced in color in *Secret History*.

I was a little taken aback by this question, and, of course, I was still a bit put out by her behavior the night before, but told her that I knew Sandy from a Reiki group and that, due to the accident, she had been one of my therapists for almost a year now.

"Are you guys connected with that coven up there in Hernando County?" Lilly next asked.

"What?!" I was flabbergasted. "What coven? Do you mean Wicca or something like that? Absolutely not! I don't mess with that Mumbo Jumbo stuff! What in the world made you think that?"

Lilly explained that she recognized Sandy and she *knew* that she was involved in some sort of group that was deeply into ritual magick.

I was absolutely stunned. I was also a little angry. How dare she say things like that about Sandy!

But, I wanted to understand why this woman would just call me on the phone and tell me that a member of a close knit group like ours was a member of some cultic coven-type thing.

Lilly launched into a history of having been in a healing class of some kind with Sandy. After the class graduated, they all went on a trip to the Yucatan to visit the Mayan ruins. I vaguely remembered Sandy being absent from the Reiki group at one point and that when she reappeared, she talked about her trip to the Yucatan. So, I knew that Lilly must know something since that was a fact.

She went on. Apparently, she had been the one who shared the cabin with Sandy on the cruise and had also been assigned to her on their "buddy system" while they were sightseeing. She explained how Sandy had tried to convert some of the members of this class to some of the ideas of this cult/coven saying that they were able to "really get results" with their rituals and so forth. She had approached Lilly with an invitation, but Lilly had declined, sensing that there was something unsavory about it.

She went on with some more details, many of which coincided with things I did know to be true and as she talked I became sicker and sicker. I realized now that there was an explanation for a lot of strange "absences" and funny behaviors of Sandy's that I had just "shoved under the rug". It also explained her quietness the previous evening when Lilly was there – and maybe even why she didn't want her aura photo taken.

I was completely devastated. I just didn't see how Sandy could have a whole secret life like that! Yet Lilly cited details about her that I *knew* were true! And at the same time, all the missing pieces of Sandy's own puzzle were falling into place.

My mind was racing for an answer. I knew that a well-to-do older couple – pillars of the community – had adopted Sandy in the same area of the country that was the setting for the Elaine story; but that was just *too* crazy!

I also knew that Sandy had spent many of her early years as a Motorcycle Mama with the Outlaws motorcycle gang. Frank and I had discussed what a great epiphany Sandy must have had to leave that life to go into massage therapy and metaphysical studies. We knew, from things that she had said, that there were some very dark things in her past. Frank had questioned her closely on one occasion and she had admitted to having been involved in covering up a murder, though she made it explicit that she had not participated in the actual murder.

But she was so soft-hearted toward animals, and refused to even kill roaches, that I was assured that her attitudes were certainly from the heart, and whatever reason had driven her out of her home to live with known criminals, she must have been horribly abused! I had nothing but sympathy for her.

So, I explained to Lilly that, even if that was the case a few years ago, Sandy was definitely a reformed person now! There was just no way she could participate in something like that on one night of the week and then sit in on our sessions on another. She had been so devoted to me in helping me to recover from my accident that I simply could not believe that she was still connected to any of those people.

I then told Lilly about the Metaphysical church folks and all that had transpired there, that Sandy knew all about it and was definitely *not* involved with those people anymore.

Lilly was reassured and asked if she might now attend a session in the future. She had some very definite issues she wanted to deal with involving the many strange things that had been happening to her.

She claimed she was in an abusive marriage, her son had been hospitalized for a minor illness but was nearly killed by the anesthesiologist, and she had recently met a man who demonstrated signs that he might be her "soul mate" and she was desperate to know what to do. All kinds of "synchronous events" were happening between her and this man, she said, and I had just been through that scenario, so I tried to warn her that it can be as much a warning as an indicator that one is going in the right direction.

I was wary of this individual because she had already demonstrated that what she said at one time, could not be relied upon in a consistent way. Nevertheless, against my better judgment, I agreed reluctantly. She then asked if she might bring a friend! I was beginning to think that there was just simply no end to this woman's presumptuousness, but I made excuses for her in my mind that, perhaps, she just simply was brought up in a family where good manners were not exampled or taught. And, to my way of thinking, just because people don't know how to conduct themselves socially according to what most people consider etiquette, it does not detract from their souls' value. Thus, I let another warning go by.

Lilly came to the next session and it was one of the strangest we have ever had. (I have no idea why I describe *any* of them as being "the strangest"! The whole thing is bizarre as all get-out!) But, anyway, it was a perfect example of what we have been talking about.

January 11, 1997

Q: (L) We have "Lilly" here with us this evening, as well as the usual crew. V is absent. Her parents are visiting. We have been discussing...

A: Discuss prophecy, maybe?

Q: (L) No, we weren't discussing prophecy... (T) Well, no, maybe they want us to discuss prophecy...

A: Sure, why not?

Q: (T) Well, since they brought it up... Give us a point to start on the subject of prophecy...

A: Well, it is important, you know. You have one here tonight who has been badly misled, controlled and programmed. In grave, grave danger. Another who attempted contact today... likewise. Must change at once!!!!

Q: (L) Change what?

A: Directions

Q: (L) Change directions in what?

A: Studies, life situations, etc. This is one who was recognized as having great potential for ultimate 4th density STO change over at a very early stage, thus attack was instituted then, and has slowly and steadily increased, with ultimate goal of total elimination. Sadly, that goal is on verge of realization.

Q: (T) Is this guy she has just met and is asking about involved?

A: No! What is important is the subject has been programmed to lead a life designed to "open the wrong doors". And when this transpires, with one of these target subjects, if they don't get help, or more importantly, do not listen to the guidelines, they are destroyed as part of a grand plan.

[We stopped at this point to discuss Lilly's husband, marriage partners that can be chosen because of spirit attachment, and close relations, including children, that can drain one's energy, be used as agents of attack, and so on. I am excluding that part of the discussion due to its personal nature.]

Q: (L) Is this what we are talking about?

A: Close. Those are not the only dangers. You asked about the "visitor". Well, what about that?? And what about your son's illness? What about the woman from across the street? What about W___, and her son? And the possible connection between him and your husband? And what if your husband worked for the "secret government?" And what about your father, and whom he worked for? What does it all mean? [Discussion about Lilly's father and his role in the military.]

Q: (T) Anything more for Lilly?

A: Only if she asks.

But Lilly didn't want to ask anymore. It was pretty evident that, like Candy had been, she was highly indignant that the Cassiopaeans would suggest that her "spirituality", her cocoon of love and light, was not sufficient protection. Never mind that she claimed that her son nearly died, her husband, who she claimed was a "trained government assassin", had recently, while enraged, driven the car through the side of the house, pulled a gun and threatened to kill her; her daughter had been arrested for shoplifting, as well as the fact that she was being "lured" by a stranger she had just met in one of her classes whose primary objective seemed to be to get her alone with him for purposes unknown, but hardly likely to be benevolent!

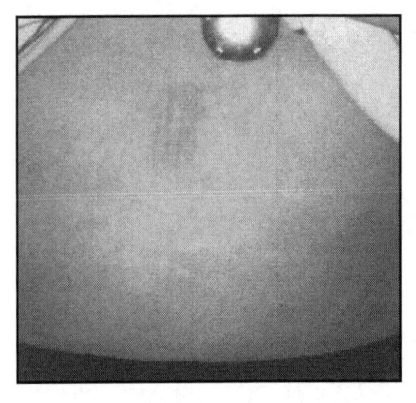

She did not want to acknowledge the symbolic nature of the Universe and how the events of our lives are mirrors of what is inside us. She was, in fact, just another case of a self-made New Age "teacher", promulgating the new religion of "you create your own reality" who was unable to demonstrate in any aspect of her personal life that she "walked the walk" she was talking.

Well, all that would have been that except for the next event involving Lilly. She called early one morning shortly after that last session. She was in a panic and quite obviously on the verge of collapse. Apparently she had suffered a terrible nightmare in which a Lizard type being raped her. That was bad enough, but what really sent her plunging over the edge was when she woke up, she was covered with welts and a rash exactly as if she had been exposed to something violently allergenic.

In the dream, she said, the Reptoid had nipped her on the solar plexus, telling her that it was a "love bite" so she would remember him. When she looked at the area after awakening, there were scratches that corresponded exactly to the teeth she remembered in the dream.

She also had another puncture on her leg added to a long series of them that had appeared at various points in her life, and assorted other marks and scratches all over her body.

I was pretty skeptical. It was my thought that the woman had just gone hysterical and maybe had done something to herself for attention. After all, from her own description, she was in a horrible marriage, may have been sexually abused as a child, and had a whole host of issues just waiting to erupt in her life. Her public persona was one thing; her private life was a disaster waiting to happen!

It would not have been at all unusual for a woman in her situation to deliberately manufacture such an event to get attention, create drama and excitement, or to use it as a platform from which to launch other difficulties for those around her. I thought it was a "cry for help".

I figured that if she was making it up or over-dramatizing it, I would be able to catch it eventually, and gradually she would be able to look at her life in more realistic terms. It was a bit inconvenient to deal with her at that moment, but she was so desperate and insisted over and over again that she needed help *now*. She didn't have the money to pay for the hypnosis, but I have never let that be a factor in whom I accepted to work with, so even though I was very pressed for time, I decided to rearrange my schedule to accommodate this sudden eruption of something into her life. She came to my house and I took pictures first, because she wanted proof that she wasn't just imagining things.

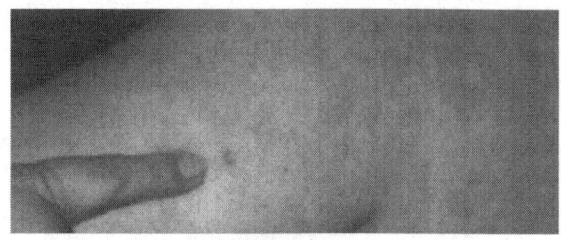

Out of a dozen or more photos, the ones displayed here are the only ones that really show anything of any significance – assuming it wasn't a hysterical overreaction to a nightmare, nor an attention getting ploy of a frustrated housewife trapped in an unhappy marriage.

The photo above shows the scratches that Lilly claims were made by the Reptoid being with his teeth after he raped her – a sort of "parting gift", as he said. Again, these marks could easily have been made by Lilly herself in any number of ways. Note also the rash, or hives, all over the abdominal area. It was particularly bad going down toward the groin.

In the photo right, I am pointing to one of over a dozen or so small, semicircular puncture wounds that were present in areas where Lilly claimed the Reptoid beings held her with their hands.

In the photo on the next page, there is the new puncture mark at the bottom, and a series of overlapping scars of similar puncture marks that Lilly said she had had for a long time. She was unclear as to when the first of them appeared, or even any of the subsequent ones. My thoughts upon examining them were that they were similar to the kind of scars that many women get on their legs from careless shaving. If there is an area that is easily scraped, it gets scraped over and over again, so that would account for multiple scars. But, clearly, this last puncture is *not* a shaving cut. It appeared to be rather deep, and already starting to close, as would be natural if it had occurred several hours earlier.

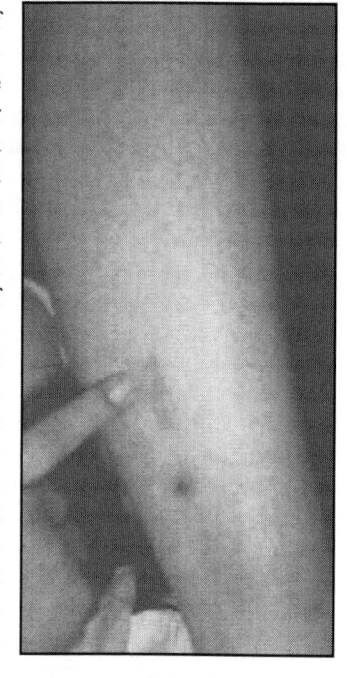

Shortly after making the pictures, we settled down to do the hypnosis that Lilly requested. She seemed genuinely at a loss to explain what had happened to her, and I was at a loss to explain it either. I had never heard of a Reptilian being raping anyone. In fact, I knew little about so-called "Reptilian aliens" at all other than what the Cassiopaeans had said, and that didn't tend to make me think that they went around raping women. How does a hyperdimensional being, who is somewhat ephemeral by definition, have the physical solidity necessary to perform rape?

But, Lilly was hyperventilating, having palpitations that terrified her, and every time she tried to talk about the event she would start shaking uncontrollably to the point that her teeth chattered loudly. Serious Post Traumatic Stress indications, for sure.

It took a little while to get her terror under control, to get her to relax, and finally, to get her under hypnosis. As it turned out, she was an excellent subject. When she did go, she went *deep*. After setting up a safe environment in which to view the event, I asked Lilly to describe what had happened that night.

Apparently, she had had an argument with her husband and Lilly decided to sleep in the living room on the sofa. She went immediately to sleep as though she were drugged. The next thing she was aware of was some sort of disturbance, like a noise or a sudden bump. She was awake, but paralyzed. She could see a glow in the corner of the room she was facing, and saw a shimmering "opening" in the ceiling. This opening of shimmering light began to expand in a columnar way so that it became like a shaft of light coming through the ceiling to the floor. As she watched, she struggled unsuccessfully against the paralysis and her heart started pounding so hard she thought the blood would burst out of her ears.

The light began to have "sparkles" in it – like swirling dust motes in a sunbeam – and these sparkles began to coalesce into a figure. And it was a figure out of a nightmare, for sure! A huge, muscular Lizard man who was soon joined by two others. She was too distressed when trying to describe them accurately, but she did manage to say that they had scales, claws, and lips that were vaguely fish-like.

The beings didn't talk to her, but simply came over, one took hold of her arms and the other took hold of her legs so as to position her for the third that immediately leaned over her and began to copulate.

I stopped her at this point and backed her up. I wanted to get certain details that might give me an idea if Lilly was making this whole thing up.

Q: When these beings entered your room, were they dressed?
A: I don't think so.
Q: When this being appeared in the room, did you notice his genitalia?
A: No. He didn't have any.
Q: If he didn't have genitalia, how did he have sex with you?
A: It was strange... umm... he started to kneel over me, and it sort of emerged out of his body. It like came out of a slit...
Q: Before he began copulation, as his genitalia emerged, did you have a chance to see what it looked like?
A: That's strange... I see it very sharp and pointed... you know, like a devil's tail in a cartoon.
Q: Very sharp and pointed? Was it painful?

A: It burned. It was like so cold that it was burning me.

Q: At any point did you have the feeling that this being was raping you because he lusted for you, in particular? Was he attracted to you or did he feel kindness toward you?

A: No. That's another funny thing. He was telling me sort of telepathically that he was "changing the program". I don't know what that means, but it has something to do with my DNA.

Now, that was a pretty bizarre remark. Her DNA programming was being changed by this act of rape? Hang on to that thought, as we will come back to it in the next section.

Now, as I have been putting these pages together and going over some of this past material, I have been trying to confirm or explain as much as I can. In this particular case, aside from the photographs of the subject which certainly showed something going on, though it is impossible to tell what, the only thing she said that could be used as a point of validation was her description of the Reptoid genitals. Otherwise, her tale falls into the category of a wild fantasy of another New Ager who has gone too far into fantasy, occurring in response to an unhappy marriage, triggered by an argument with her husband. Was she confabulating, or did something really happen to her?

I tried to find another case of reptilian interaction with humans where the genitals were described by other witnesses somewhere on the Internet, but I failed completely. Maybe nobody else has asked this question.

I first thought in terms of snake genitals since the Reptoids are also known as the "serpent race". But then, I remembered that the Cassiopaeans had described them as biologically like "upright alligators". So, I thought that I should be looking for alligator genitals to compare to Lilly's description. I figured that there was always the chance that Lilly had seen a picture of them in a book somewhere and was describing what she remembered. If so, I could just go to the library and have a look myself.

Nope. No book at the library had a picture of alligator genitals. Not even snake genitals! What about the bookstore?

Nope. Nothing at Booksamillion.

How about on the Internet?

Ark and I spent almost an entire day trying to track down a photograph of alligator genitals so that I could satisfy my curiosity as to whether Lilly had described them accurately.

Nothing.

Finally, Ark, using his status as a university professor, wrote to a professor of herpetology and inquired about obtaining a photograph of alligator genitals for my article.

Well, such a photo *does* exist, but is not generally available to the public. It is for specialists only. But, since inquiring minds want to know, here it is. You be the judge.

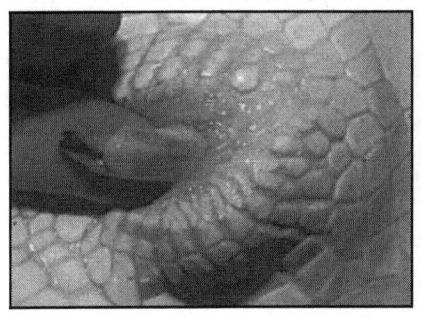

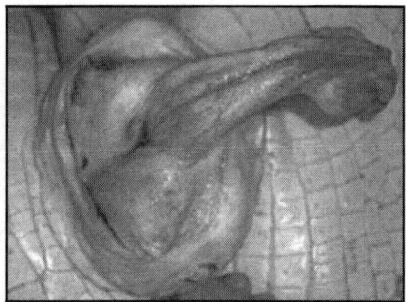

The image above is the genitalia of a male alligator, partly everted from the slit opening behind which they are concealed when not in use. Remember how Lilly described it: "That's strange... I see it very sharp and pointed... you know, like a devil's tail in a cartoon."

The image below shows the genitalia fully everted. The large white globular objects at the base of the organ are the muscles used to erect the organ to the outside of the body.

DR. GREENBAUM AND THE SOUL HACKERS...

Now, aside from the bizarre way in which it was depicted (i.e., being raped by a Reptoid) this "changing the program" was something I had heard before. To be more specific, in one of Candy's numerous sessions focused on regression to the time of purported alien abductions, such a remark was made, though the description of the event was quite different. It almost seemed that this "changing of the program" was a direct response to the interaction of these individuals with yours truly!

I presented Candy's case in *High Strangeness*, and in case the reader does not have a copy to refer to, here's what I wrote about her:

The subject was about 35 years old; the wife of a stockbroker, owner of her own jewelry business, and mother to two girls. She had been born and raised in Colorado in a Mormon family, but had left at an early age and traveled to California to stay with a brother who worked in a jewelry store. There, she also obtained employment in the same business and ended up marrying the owner who subsequently died leaving her with a small child and a large inheritance.

She moved with her second husband, the stockbroker, her child from her first marriage, and a new baby to Florida. The object was to get away from the unhappy memories of the loss of her first husband and start a new life. The jewelry business she left in the care of her brother in California.

After her youngest child started school, the subject, (and we can call her Candy, though that is not her real name), became bored and decided to go to work for the large brokerage that employed her husband. She took an administrative position and settled into her corporate role with ease, being very intelligent, charming and attractive.

At the same time, she began to attend a Metaphysical/Spiritualist church, probably more out of curiosity than anything else, but soon became deeply involved in the spiritualist beliefs and practices. At this point, strange things began to happen, though she claimed that strange things had happened to her all her life, she just had managed to suppress most of it.

The first thing was that she kept encountering a man in the building where she worked. He was employed by a firm on a different floor, so she only saw him in the elevators, the parking lot, and the local eateries. But, every time she did encounter him, she was conscious of a strange electricity between them and it was not long before they were exchanging brief pleasantries.

One night when she was leaving the building, her husband being away on company business, she encountered the man and engaged in a short, casual conversation. That would have been that except for the fact that he walked her to her car and she discovered that her keys were locked inside. The man "rescued" her by spending an hour or more getting the door open, and then suggested that they needed to have a drink to celebrate success. Not having to go home right away, and feeling gratitude for such kindness, Candy agreed to go next door to a pub for a beer before going home.

At the pub they met another of Candy's co-workers, and this lady joined them. At the table, over their glasses of beer, the subject turned to metaphysical things, and then to Indian shamanic beliefs. The man said he knew where there was a local Indian mound (there are a number of them in this area) and that it was a place of great power. He offered to show both ladies where it was. Feeling secure with a lady companion, Candy wanted to see this Indian mound, and they all went together in the man's car. It was late and past dark, and when they arrived at the location, a swampy, wooded area on the Gulf of Mexico, they all got out and proceeded to hike through the underbrush to the purported Indian mound.

At some point, the second woman was left behind and lost and something happened to frighten Candy, but afterward she couldn't say what it was, only that she was very confused and demanded to be taken home. The man cheerfully obliged, they located her friend wandering in the bushes, and he took them back to their cars and off they went home. The only problem was, when Candy got home, it was almost midnight. She had "lost" over three hours.

At that point her life began to fall apart. She was suddenly so emotional and upset all the time that she couldn't stay on an even keel from one minute to the next. She became obsessed with the man in the building, and believed that he was her "soulmate" one minute, and that he was a government spy the next. She felt that somehow she must find ways to be with him. At the same time, her husband was in an auto accident with another woman in the car and her marriage began to disintegrate. The series of events becomes very complicated, and is not relevant to our present subject, but it was at this point that I met her [at a Reiki gathering.]

Now, having some idea of Candy's background, let me explain the circumstances behind the following hypnosis session. This will only touch on certain aspects of the case because it was a long and complicated situation.

The obsession, or "Love Bite" situation, with the man who worked in the office building where Candy's husband was employed, and where she also had a position, was so out of control that Candy was desperate to find out the source of the almost insane fascination she had with this man.

Candy *knew* she was behaving in a crazy way. She also knew that the constant fantasies, urges to seek him out under any pretext, to follow him or call him repeatedly on the phone were absolutely out of character for her. The explanation that she came up with was that it was *destiny* for her to be with him and that could be the only reason for this intense, internal drive she was struggling against. She was sure she *knew* him deeply, and even though she actually had very little interaction with him, she ascribed almost mystical significance to every word they did exchange. Every glance from his eyes was full of fire and cosmic power. Never mind that most of this occurred in the elevator or the halls or parking lot of the office building. She was certain that there was impossibly deep communication in every instant their eyes made contact!

I listened to her talk about it endlessly, thinking it would eventually run out and she would see how irrational it was, but that didn't happen. She insisted that the proof of the destined nature of their inevitable union would be found under hypnosis. I privately thought that, if nothing else, it might cure her of the obsession; so I agreed.

After the first incident when this man had taken Candy and her friend out to look for the Indian mound, she had maneuvered to run into him again. They met at a local pub, including her friend, "Eileen", who was Candy's source for info at the office. They ended up going for a ride to the woods – another act that was just totally out of character for all of them – and Candy was certain that something significant had happened there because, again, she had "missing time".

All she remembered was driving out in a wooded area to look for a swimming hole that one of them had heard of, but when they got there, they found nothing and immediately turned around and left. But a lot more time had passed than would have been required to just drive out there, turn around, and come back. The strange thing about this event was that Candy cried almost constantly for two days after this "drive in the woods", and could not explain to me or anybody why she was crying. All she knew was that she had a "great longing and sadness" for this man who was the object of her unrequited love.

We are going to skip over all the induction process, the setting up of the working environment, and just go right to the first question (and we are going to call this guy Bill).

Q: Now, what is the point in space-time, in this life, that you first met Bill? Where are you and what do you see?

A: I see him walking up the steps at [the brokerage].

Q: Okay. And this is the first involvement, the first meeting between you and Bill in this life?

A: Mmm. It's almost like I see two children playing together.

Q: Is that in this life or another? Physical or spiritual?

A: Mmm. I think it's this life.

Q: Is there anything else you can give on that?

A: Um... [Long pause.]

Q: Tell me what you see, what you feel.

A: It's almost like we're together in a room.

Q: What kind of room?

A: Kind of like a square silvery room.

Q: And what are you doing in the square, silvery room?

A: We're playing.

Q: What are you playing?

A: Games.

Q: You are children?

A: Um-hmm. [This answer had a "childish" lilt to the voice.]

Q: Where is this square, silvery room?

A: Umm— [Sigh.] It's umm— They came and got us.

Q: Who came and got you?

A: I see the, um, they're little white— They kind of look like children. And they play with us. They make us happy. It's like they know when we're sad and they're here— They're like playmates.

Q: How old are you?

A: I think I'm like three or four.

Q: All right, take a real deep breath. I'm going to count to three and on the count of three you are going to be at that point in space-time sometime in the first part of May in this year, when you ran into or met Bill and Eileen at a place called the Player's bar and went for a ride in the woods. Go to the point in space-time when you arrive in the woods and you will be able to easily describe what occurred at that time. On the count of three. [Countdown.] What do you see and what happens?

A: Umm. You know, that's funny! I don't remember getting out of the truck! I see us getting out of the truck. For some reason— I see the lights of the truck on. I see something over the top of the truck. I see a flash of light. I see us getting out of the truck. I see us walking in the woods.

Q: Where are you going in the woods?

A: I don't want to go in there. Umm. [Pause.] I see almost like I'm fighting, like fighting going or something. I'm afraid...

Q: Take a deep breath, let's go deeper. Begin to describe what happened. You said you are fighting and resisting...
A: Um-hmm.
Q: What are you fighting? Who are you fighting?
A: No, I don't— I— It's like I'm— Nobody's around me but we're all three like walking into the woods. I'm afraid— I don't want to go— There's like a fear somewhere— It's like I know there's something there...
Q: Okay, what happens next?
A: It's like I fall— I'm asleep.
Q: Okay, well the subconscious mind continues to record even when you are asleep. What happens next?
A: I'm being carried.
Q: By who or what?
A: Umm. [Pause.] I see this large hairy thing with huge hands...
Q: Okay. Where is it taking you?
A: It's taking us to a place. [Pause.] I don't know how we get there. [Pause.] I don't know how we get there, but I see this place, and I see— What I see is a cave-like thing but I see at the top of the cave are these yellow lights...
Q: Yellow lights?
A: Big yellow lights. [Pause.] It's almost like, um, not bright lights— Like covered yellow lights— Like, huge— As big as, um— like small swimming pools— They're big. [Pause.] And they are up in the ceiling— And they're yellow.
Q: Up in the ceiling and they're yellow?
A: Yeah, they're in the cave. [Pause.] Boy! This is a strange place!
Q: Okay. Describe everything. What do you see?
A: Um, I'm just going to tell you what I see— This is strange. I see a cart— Almost like a little golf cart...
Q: What is the cart doing?
A: Umm. I see it there— I almost see us, umm— This is like a conveyor belt type thing. It's almost like we're put on a silver disk, or like a silver stretcher-type thing...
Q: What happens next and what do you see around you?
A: Umm. I see myself on a table...
Q: Where is Bill and where is Eileen? [Subject shows signs of distress.] What's the matter?
A: I see this face I don't like.
Q: What face don't you like?
A: Umm...
Q: Describe the face.
A: Let me see it— Can't see it— It flashed and then I can't see it...
Q: All right, lets back up. On the count of three whatever is preventing you from seeing that face will fall away and crumble, and you will see it clearly and pho-

tograph it the instant that it appears, with your mind, so that you can describe it in every detail. On the count of three. [Countdown.]

A: It switched— It changed— One face came in and then another face came in and I can't see it...

Q: What feeling do you get from those faces?

A: I don't like them— They are angry.

Q: Why are they angry?

A: Cause somebody's snooping around.

Q: Who's snooping around?

A: They're mad about the hypnosis.

Q: Which hypnosis?

A: The ones you did.

Q: Okay. What do they propose to do about it? How did they find out about it?

A: They know everything.

Q: Okay. What do they propose to do about it?

A: Change things.

Q: What are they going to change and how?

A: It's almost like I'm hearing them say that, um, change the programming.

Q: Whose programming are they going to change?

A: I guess, mine.

Q: What else can you tell from what they are saying?

A: Um, it's almost like they've got to Bill. Umm— They feel like they're safe with Eileen because she'd never believe anything like that.

Q: And what about you?

A: Umm. [Sigh.] I hear, "She's so damn curious!" They are saying: "Too intense, too fast. Knew something like this was gonna happen," then I hear them say that they're behind schedule—running out of time...

Q: Can you tell what they are behind schedule for and what they are running out of time for?

A: Umm. It's funny, I hear them saying that the cleansing time is almost here— Something like that...

Q: Why do they object to the hypnosis? Do they not want you to know what is going on?

A: Umm. They just don't want me to be hurt.

Q: So, you sense that there is concern for you?

A: Um-hmm.

Q: Why don't you like them?

A: They scare me.

Q: Why do they scare you?

A: Umm. [Distress.]

Q: What do you see?

A: It's almost like they're pinching me.

Q: Where are they pinching you?
A: My arm.
Q: What are they doing to your arm?
A: Like they are running a tube up my arm— Like at the crease of my arm they're running a tube— Into my arm.
Q: All right, now what are they doing?
A: I don't know what the hell they're doing with my arm. Umm, what was that?
Q: What was it?
A: I see a flash…
Q: And then what?
A: I don't know, it's really hard to see.
Q: What color flash? Just a flash of light?
A: Like a green light or something.
Q: Now what? What do you feel? What do you sense?
A: I feel like they're putting stuff in my veins.
Q: And what is this stuff doing to you?
A: Changing me.
Q: How is it changing you?
A: I don't know— It's funny— It's almost like they're putting something in my blood. Umm, I'm hearing "ignite the flame." I don't know what that means. Umm— It's almost like— putting receivers on a stereo and then all of a sudden turning the stereo on— Like speakers of a stereo— It's like you spent all this time putting all these speakers all over and then you turn the stereo on, and it's almost like, I see when you turn the stereo on I see the energy go to the receivers to make the music.
Q: How many people on this planet have these speakers?
A: Umm. [Pause.] Lot of 'em.
Q: How many times have you been abducted?
A: I think this is absolutely ridiculous but I'm going to say it anyway. They are saying a few hundred.
Q: Okay, have these abductions all been in the body or out of the body?
A: I'm hearing they're making adjustments all the time.
Q: Did they come because you called for them?
A: No.
Q: [Inaudible.]
A: Umm, I don't know. I see all these lights in front of me.
Q: What are the lights doing?
A: Circling around— Like I'm seeing different colors spiraling— Purple— Yellow— Making me tired.
Q: Makes you tired. Take a deep breath.
A: My body's hot.

Q: Okay, let's go back to your event in the woods; you're in the cave; you're on the table; you saw the face; they're putting something in your veins; they are changing the project; what happens next...

A: Hold on. [Pause.] I feel like there's— They're angry...

Q: Why are they angry and who are they angry at?

A: Umm, you know, it's like they put blocks of fear up, and then I broke through some of those fear blocks that are supposed to keep me from doing things.

Q: And that is why they're angry?

A: Um-hmm. That I'm strong-willed— I'm— Driven...

Q: Do they see me as an interference?

A: [Laughing.] Yes!

Q: What happens next?

A: [Laughs.] Eileen's there.

Q: And what is happening to Eileen?

A: I think she's getting an implant. This is why she hears voices in her head. She thinks it's Tom, then she thinks it's Bill.

Q: What happens next? Go through the experience...

A: I don't know why I'm seeing this— It's almost like I see— I almost see a Sasquatch— And it's like he's turning over a— My nose itches.

Q: Turning over a what?

A: My nose itches. He's umm, I don't know what— (Rubbing nose vigorously.) My nose is itching.

Q: What is happening to your nose?

A: My nose is itching. [Rubbing nose.] I don't know. [Laughing.] I got hair in my nose!

Q: Whose hair is in your nose? Sasquatch?

A: I guess so. It's like— Eww. [Laughing.]

Q: What does it smell like?

A: [Rubbing nose and giggling.]

Q: What does Sasquatch smell like?

A: It almost smells like a burnt ammonia smell. [Pause.] God! I've got hair everywhere— You know— (Brushing herself all over as though trying to brush hair away.)

Q: Now, is Sasquatch carrying you back to the vehicle?

A: Um-hmm.

Q: Okay, now you are back in the vehicle and you are going home...

A: Oh, we, uh— Stopped— I had to go to the bathroom. [Pause.] They turned up my hearing.

Q: They turned up your hearing?

A: Um-hmm. I can hear Eileen talking to Bill inside of the truck and I'm outside...

Q: What's she saying?

A: She was telling him that— that— It's like he got upset with her— or he was running away from her— and she said, I just wanted to be friends, I didn't want— I just wanted to be there— I guess he's like— You know— She's chasing him— You know...

Q: Take a deep breath. Move forward to the point in space-time when you became overwhelmed with grief and sadness. Why did this incident cause you such sadness?

A: [Sighs.]

Q: You cried for two days after this event. What made you cry?

A: [Sighing in distress.] There is something really wrong— I don't know.

Q: Take a deep breath... [Countdown. Suggestions. End of session.]

At this point in time, Candy's interest in Bill pretty much just turned off. She became obsessed with MF, the "UFO investigator" mentioned in the previous section. I could see that, under the guise of "therapy", he was pursuing a physical relationship, and she began to behave completely erratically. One clue to this new obsession was that she more or less abandoned her children. On several occasions, the little one called me and asked if her mother was at my house because she had barely been at home for days and there was no food in the house.

I could see and sense that there was this *huge*, overwhelming, sex thing going on between Candy and MF! (And, we have to remember that he was one of the ones the Cassiopaeans had designated as being a sort of "unconscious mole".)

Soon after the above session, Candy called me in a state of complete hysteria. The previous night she had gone to dinner with MF. That night, after coming home from this date and going to bed in the normal way, she had a dream about some men coming in her house. She then said that she woke up in the morning feeling drugged and that her legs were sore behind the knees. When she looked, she saw that there were bruises on her legs. And, more than that, they were bruises that showed the clear imprint of a four-fingered hand on the back of each leg!

I had previously suggested to her that we talk to my Private Investigator friend, and now she was pretty desperate to get a handle on all of the things that had been happening. So, we met with the PI.

After listening to the whole story and examining the bruises, the PI said that, in his opinion, the proper way to approach the matter was to treat it as a "crime", and look for some material evidence. During his questioning, Candy remembered the dress from the first "abduction" that was possibly still on the floor in her closet. The PI privately told me those bruises such as were on Candy's legs could be "manufactured" by a hysterical woman wanting attention, but it would be hard. He was as puzzled as I was as to what might be the explanation of bruises that clearly depicted a hand that was not human. He was also interested in getting some hard evidence and wanted to be present at the next hypnosis session so as to determine what direction to go with a real investigation. Candy agreed. She wanted it right away and, for some reason, didn't want MF, the hotshot UFO investigator there! Clearly she was at some level aware that her interactions with him might have had something to do with this latest incident. And, we were both feeling some relief that a professional was taking the whole thing seriously and was willing to devote time, talent and resources to the cause of getting to the bottom of this.

Regarding the dress that Candy thought was still in the closet (never having been sent to the cleaners), the PI was going to try to make arrangements to send it to a forensics lab as possible evidence of a rape. He wasn't going to mention anything about "aliens" but would leave it to the lab to do the standard work that would be done when trying to gather evidence to identify such an attacker – including such things as DNA profiling. She agreed to pick it up carefully and place it in a zipper bag and deliver it to me and I would convey it to him.

We then scheduled the session for that evening.

> Q: Okay, take a deep breath. I want you to just move to that point in space-time, specifically the night before last, and I want you to see yourself just as you are getting ready to go to bed. Tell me what you are doing. You went out to dinner, came home and are getting ready for bed. What happens?
>
> A: I have a terrible headache.
>
> Q: Okay. What happens next?
>
> A: I go to sleep.
>
> Q: You are sleeping. What happens?
>
> A: I see these men.
>
> Q: Where are they? Are they in your room?
>
> A: No. [Distress.]
>
> Q: Back up, you are sleeping, what happens? Do you hear something, see something, have a dream?
>
> A: I don't know how this is possible but I see men in army fatigues— They're— They twisted me or something. My back hurts...
>
> Q: Where did they come from? Is this a dream? When did you first become aware of them?
>
> A: [Distress.] I see myself in a truck or something?
>
> Q: How did you get in this truck?
>
> A: [Distress and inability to answer.]
>
> Q: Take a real deep breath and let's go back to when you were sleeping. You are sleeping in your bed. When do you first become aware that something is different? Even while you are sleeping your subconscious is recording everything happening around you. What does your subconscious see and record?
>
> A: I am just going to tell you what I see and I don't know where this is coming from. I see men coming into the house.
>
> Q: How do they get into the house?
>
> A: Through the back door.

Q: Through the back door from the pool?
A: Um-hmm! They just come right in my house go right in my bedroom, grab me, take me right out...
Q: Why doesn't it wake you up?
A: I don't know.
Q: You had the headache before you went to bed...
A: Um-hmm.
Q: Okay, they grab you, they take you out and then what do they do?
A: Umm...
Q: How many of them are there?
A: Two, but they are not nice people.
Q: Are they saying anything while they are grabbing you and taking you out?
A: Uh-uh.
Q: Which door do they take you out, the front door or the back door?
A: The back door.
Q: Where do they take you from the back door? Which way do they walk?
A: It's right outside— This is weird. I wanted to say we got in a black helicopter but it isn't a helicopter.
Q: What is it? You went right out the back. Which way did you go, right or left?
A: Left, out by the lake.
Q: Okay.
A: They just loaded me on a...
Q: On a what?
A: I want to say a spaceship.
Q: A spaceship? What shape is the spaceship? Where is the spaceship parked?
A: It's kind of hovering above the ground, above the lake. It's real quiet.
Q: What shape is it? What color is it?
A: It's round, I can't see it... [Sigh.]
Q: Do they load you on there physically?
A: Um-hmm.
Q: Do they climb in after you or is there somebody already in there?
A: They're in there but my head hurts and my leg hurts.
Q: Are they saying anything?
A: My ears hurt. I feel sick.
Q: Why does your head hurt, your ears hurt and your leg hurt?
A: I don't know, I just don't feel very good.
Q: Do you feel sick?
A: I don't know. I just don't feel very good at all.
Q: Okay, now what's happening.
A: I don't know. I just don't feel very good.

Q: Go with it. Take a deep breath. Take four or five deep breaths. Are you feeling better?
A: No, my body hurts.
Q: Why does your body hurt?
A: I don't know. My back hurts— They hurt my back.
Q: Did they do something to your back?
A: I don't know. [Distress.]
Q: Okay, what's happening now? Are they saying anything?
A: I'm at a table— They're talking to me.
Q: What are they saying to you?
A: They are asking me questions.
Q: What are the questions? When they say it repeat it to me.
A: (Sigh, distress.) What have you been doing?
Q: What else are they asking?
A: I don't know. My head hurts.
Q: What did you tell them when they ask you what have you been doing? Are you giving them answers without your conscious control?
A: Yeah, it's almost— I am just in a lot of pain now.
Q: What is causing the pain?
A: I don't know.
Q: What else are they doing, just asking you questions?
A: Um-hmm.
Q: What kind of questions?
A: I don't know. My head hurts.
Q: Take a deep breath and you won't feel any pain. What kinds of questions are they asking you? Did they do anything to you before they started asking questions?
A: Um-hmm.
Q: What did they do?
A: I don't know, this is going to sound really weird. It is almost like they have their own implants in...
Q: Okay. What kind of questions are they asking you?
A: They are showing me a map and they want me to point to things and show them...
Q: What do they want you to show them? What kinds of questions are they asking you?
A: They ask me what, where is that base...
Q: What base do they want to know about?
A: It's a military base.
Q: What else do they ask you?
A: I don't know... I don't know... My head hurts.
Q: Is your head hurting right now?

A: Um-hmm. My head hurts and my neck hurts, my whole body hurts.
Q: Okay, what happens next?
A: I'm tired. I don't like this. I'm hurting. [Extreme distress.]
Q: Are they hurting you deliberately?
A: Yeah, my whole body is in pain right now. I got to stop this. My head is killing me...
Q: Let's move forward... [Suggestions, end of session.]

The curious thing to me was that this pain response was exactly what had happened with Pat, my first abduction case, the night of the Black Boomerang sightings over the three county area. Whenever I tried to get to the actual event of what happened that night, she began to experience so much pain that it became clear that, in spite of suggestions for comfort, I should not continue.

It was about a week after this session that Candy came and demanded the dress back because MF told her that *he* could get it analyzed by a *real* scientist who was sympathetic to the UFO investigations process. He told her that she shouldn't trust anybody connected to the authorities because if she turned the dress over to them, it would certainly "disappear" and her chances of ever knowing the truth would vanish with it. And, of course, by association, I was implicated as one of those who could not be trusted.

As I mentioned before, it turned out that his "real scientist" was an undergrad chemistry student who worked part-time at the county sewage treatment plant. There was nothing I could do to dissuade her and, by this time, I knew enough about MF to be thoroughly disgusted with the whole thing. It was clear that he was manipulating her and suggesting to her all kinds of negative things about me, and I learned a long time ago that I couldn't fight liars and manipulators. You have to be one to outmaneuver them.

Shortly after this period, I began to hear rumors. A friend who knew MF called me and told me that he was telling people that I wanted to "get famous" writing a book about Candy's case – a "classic abduction with evidence" – and I was thus "using" her and her near psychotic state for my own aggrandizement. He, of course, on the other hand, was only trying to "help her get over the trauma" – never mind that he was seeking personal involvement with a person who was traumatized and, therefore, vulnerable.

Needless to say, I was not only shocked by this, I was hurt. It was pretty clear that MF was the one who had an agenda. Maybe *he* was driven to have a perfect case on which to ride to fame and glory and because that was *his* drama, he naturally thought it was everyone else's. On the other hand, maybe his motivations were inspired from some other source and were a lot more sinister.

At this point, another friend had downloaded some info from a UFO Internet Bulletin board where Candy's case was the hot topic of discussion. In these exchanges between people who I didn't even know, nor had I ever met them, I was being described as a "fraud" and "incompetent" and "using the poor abducted victim for my own gain."

No part of the description of the way the investigation was being handled by me was anywhere near accurate and it was obvious that someone was deliberately lying with the intention of defaming me personally, and thus any work I ever did.

The only one who was in a position to distort the facts in this way was MF. He knew enough about what I was doing to know better, unless of course, Candy was telling him things that were not true.

I couldn't decide which I thought was most likely, but the end result was that I was *furious*! I learned that the person who had posted the info was the wife of the sewage treatment plant worker claiming to be a "chemist" and "scientist" and "professional analyst". My friend told me that Candy had taken up with this woman in much the same way she had taken up with me.

Further information came to me from an authoritative source (a onetime director of a MUFON group) that MF, who Candy was now intimately involved with, had a very bad reputation. He had been a part of a large MUFON organization that, based on his claims to knowledge and expertise (having come to Florida from another state), had placed him in a position of trust and authority in their UFO Field Investigations unit. It soon became clear that he "did not work well with others," and, in fact, brought a great deal of negative publicity and attention to the organization. The MUFON group asked him to resign, but he refused. Having no alternative at that point, the entire group voted to dissolve their organization rather than continue with this man in their midst!

He then attached himself to this couple who were so busily blackening my name in the local Metaphysical/UFO community (without, I must add, having ever met or talked with me!). Not only that, but this same couple were members of the bigger MUFON group in the Clearwater area and later attached themselves to Dr. Santilli as "research assistants".

At this point in time, it is my thought that Dr. Santilli's distancing from our work was a direct result of the influence of this small group of "bad apples", so to speak. It is true that, (as I have recently learned), two of this group of individuals later became heads of the Clearwater MUFON after two others took over the publication of the MUFON newsletter from Terry and Jan. Since that time, it is said that the organization has pretty much declined in terms of being a moving force or any kind of hub of information or help to others in the area who may have experienced sightings or abductions.

A funny incident did occur at the last UFO conference I attended in Pensacola. Ark and I had attended a lecture by Whitley Strieber where he made a heartfelt and anguished plea to the world of science to bring all their minds and tools to bear on solving the problem of "the Visitors", as he coyly refers to them.

Well, since Ark is a scientist with a pretty good reputation in international circles, and many publications in the reputable journals, as well as considered to be an expert in Riemannian Geometry and Kaluza-Klein theories, we thought that he just *might* fit the category of the kind of scientists Whitley was crying for.

So, we stood in a very long line after the lecture to speak to Mr. Strieber and offer help. As we were standing there, I heard a man speaking to someone behind me. He was saying something to the effect that he was a scientist and he *really* needed to speak to Mr. Strieber privately. I turned around to see who it was, and – yup! You guessed it! It was our Sewage Water Treatment Expert!

Oh well. Of course, as it turned out, Mr. Strieber wasn't very interested in real science since he brushed us off with the excuse of how urgent it was to sign the books he was selling, and avoided us for the rest of the conference.

So, there it is. It's nice to make heartfelt appeals when one is at the podium pretending to be really interested in getting the facts of the matter, but when one is actually faced with scientific scrutiny, it seems to be the last thing one wants to have focused on one's self! Better to have Sewage Water experts in the lab – they are far more qualified to analyze the BS that goes on in the UFO community.

In retrospect, it is clear that the changing of the program Candy was sensing had to do with getting her away from me and my process of combining both intuitive *and* scientific analysis. The obvious way to do this was to bring in reinforcements, i.e., MF, and his cohorts. It was also not lost on me that, in both cases, the only information channel about *me*, to both the Metaphysical Church bunch, and this MUFON bunch, was *Candy herself.*

Whether it was conscious or unconscious I will never know. I only know that every interaction with her resulted in attack/lessons, lies and obfuscation, confusion and back stabbing They were all busily talking about me and what a wicked person I was, but in fact, none of them knew me or had ever talked to me directly. Funny how that works!

And, of course, Candy's obsession with Bill just sort of died right then. Remember Bill? The "soul mate"? The "Cosmic Destiny" guy? Ooops! That was yesterday! Today we have a new program to run!

Whether Candy's "abductions" were real, we will never know. Whether her evidence was real, we will never know either. The evidence was so contaminated by all the incompetent hands it passed through and the primitive analysis conditions it was handled under, that no respectable or legitimate analyst would touch it now.

Of course, the question arises: was this whole drama of "changing the program" a direct result of the fact that there *was* something that could be exposed, learned, or uncovered through Candy?

And what about Lilly? Here we find another person who, shortly after interacting with the Cassiopaeans and me and my learning/analysis approach to every situation, gets their "program" changed? Just what is the story here?

Getting back to Lilly's situation. We left her describing the genitalia of her rapist as somewhat resembling the red tail of a cartoon devil. We had a look at the real thing, and saw that it was indeed rather as she described it. We also pretty well know that this information about the nature of alligator genitals would have been hard for her to obtain, but not impossible. So what happened next?

Well, after working through the rape during the hypnosis session, we went through some processing of the emotions. As I was doing this, I had the idea that I should test my hypothesis about the Greenbaum material by asking some of the Greenbaum questions. It was really just an idea and I certainly did *not* expect to get a positive response from my subject!

Following the Greenbaum program, I set up the ideomotor finger-signals and suggested:

> I want the central inner core of you to take control of the finger-signals. And I want that central inner core of you to take control of this hand of these finger-signals and what it has for the yes-finger to float up. I want to ask the inner core of you is there any part of you, any part of Lilly, who knows anything about Alpha, Beta, Delta, or Theta.

I nearly dropped my teeth when I got a "yes" response.

Okay, that was the "red flag". I was sailing in unfamiliar waters here and really wished I hadn't started down this path without more training. But, it was like surgery: the patient was open, so I needed to see what I could find, do no damage, and hopefully, fix something before I closed her back up.

After receiving the "yes" answer I said, "I want a part inside who knows something about Alpha, Beta, Delta, and Theta to come up to a level where you can speak to me, and when you're here say, 'I'm here'."

A voice that was quite different from Lilly's voice said, "I'm here." I asked for the name and the response was "Gatekeeper".

Well, the only thing to do was to press on and identify as much as I could in the time I could do it. I definitely identified seven different programs and one of them was "Delta". Now, remember what Dr. Hammond said about "Delta"? "Deltas are killers trained in how to kill in ceremonies."

I went through the programs asking for the "erasure codes", and was given some of them. On some others, the very mechanical response "Access Denied!" came back.

The freaky thing was, I was getting an almost textbook series of responses from this woman that exactly matched the information in the Greenbaum speech! I was utterly dumbfounded. I mean, what are the odds that a very short time after I became aware of this sort of thing a person would just sort of "enter" my life who had this very situation active in her life? It just boggled the mind.

I went on with my probing, and it was in this process that the most stunning information that I have ever confronted in this work came out.

One of the programs identified itself as "Master Programmer". I began to inquire *what type of program* this was.

"Master Programmer" was designed to turn Lilly into a dynamic New Age/Metaphysical teacher whose job was to travel the country, giving classes and seminars in many and various subjects, in order to *turn on the already installed programs of other Greenbaum-type victims.*

I asked how this could be done. The answer was simple: not only her words, but guided meditations, mantras, tones and symbols incorporated in some of the "Metaphysical jewelry" she carried to sell at her various lectures were used as program triggers. She was also using inaudible frequencies emitted by various gadgets she used in her "healing classes".

Further, the teachings, even though they were ostensibly of "love and light", were designed to use *certain word sequences* that were standard program triggers. Not only that, but some programs were set up in such a way that even if a person were confronted with the logical inconsistency of their belief system, they would be unable to break through the "coded thought loop implant" to understand their own faulty logic! In other words, when a person was confronted with "truth" or obvious factual information, the program would "turn on" and deny them the ability to think anything other than the "pre-coded" thoughts that would go around and around in their head like a "message from God" or their "guides" or whomever.

I asked what would happen if Lilly stopped doing this. The answer was, "Compliance is necessary to the mission; not performing the task is noncompliance."

I asked what would be the result of noncompliance. The answer was, "Termination of subject by activation of self-destruct program."

Well, that was pleasant! Definitely *not* what one would think of as a "loving guide", "angel", or "higher self"!

I asked some questions about where, when and how the programming might have been installed. I wanted to see if she had the same information about "Dr. Greenbaum". It was during this portion of the session that the information was revealed that the real reason Lilly knew Sandy was because they had been in the same "programming set" as children! They had then been brought together in the healing class in Tampa because the teacher of that modality was another such as Lilly: a "Master Programmer".

Well, that was a surprise! And it also made me think of Candy's depiction of her relation with Bill as children playing with a little "alien" guy who was "helping them". Just what is going on here? How many people are talking to "guides" or "angels" who are merely programs?

I was probing to get the code to deactivate some of the programs and suddenly Lilly began to moan and cry, "It hurts! It hurts!" and her hands went to her ears and she was trying to block out a sound that was obviously quite painful. She was twisting and turning in pain.

I kept speaking to her, attempting to get one of the programs or the "core" to come forward when the most horrible voice came out of her repeating over and over, "Access denied! Access denied!"

I was finally able to get the "Gatekeeper" to come back and he stiffly informed me that any further attempts to probe or deactivate would result in immediate destruction of the subject.

Hoo, boy! That was heavy! We were playing with some nasty bullies here!

At this point, Lilly had been under hypnosis for a lot longer than usual for most subjects, so I released the "Gatekeeper" with assurances that no harm would come to Lilly from me, gave her some "feel good" suggestions, and ended the session. There just didn't seem to be any other option.

So, we have three different cases where attempts to probe resulted in activation of "pain blocks" of such a nature that it was dangerous to continue. The first was Pat, the second was Candy, and now Lilly.

After the session, I didn't know *what* to tell Lilly. She obviously didn't remember anything about the latter part of her session, but she felt a lot better and her rash was definitely calmed down by at least half, so I ventured to broach the subject of her program. I wanted to know what, exactly, was she doing in her classes? What kinds of things were being used to "turn on" other people's programs? I had the idea that if it was brought to her conscious attention that she could begin to learn about it and to further evaluate exactly what she was doing. I even had hopes that she would be able to combat the influence and recover from her programming.

The only things I can tell you are that as soon as I began to talk to her about it, there was a definite shift in her personality and a fanatical look began to glow in her eyes.

She began to recite all the standard "love and light" philosophy and how she was a "Lightworker" and it went on for a few minutes with my growing awareness that I was actually listening to a program!

It was eerie beyond imagining hearing this "tape" running. Yes, she was saying all the "right things" to inspire confidence and warm and fuzzy feelings! Yes, she was espousing a philosophy that is more or less standard in the "New Age" theatre. But now, I was hearing it in a different way. It was no longer just the content of the words that was significant – it was something between and behind them – something sinister and lurking in wait to jump out at any moment.

I was fully aware that there were other programs in Lilly that could, at a moment's notice, be turned on and that one of these was a killer. There was nothing to do but agree with her that she was doing a "great work for mankind" and send her home. I remembered what Dr. Hammond said about such individuals being programmed to kill their therapists. I hoped I hadn't been classified as such and marked for death. Seeing the fanatical fire in her eyes, there was no doubt in my mind that she could kill just as she was programmed to do.

The very next day, Lilly called me and began to chat in a normal way. I asked her how she was feeling, and she said fine! She was bright and sunny in her words and manner. I was listening carefully to her to determine if I was hearing the "real Lilly". Everything seemed to be okay, and she didn't sound like she was going to come over and kill me – at least not at that moment – so I relaxed and chatted casually along, staying alert for any signs of a switch to an alternate personality. Nothing was out of line.

I began to think that maybe we had just encountered a particularly crafty entity attached to Lilly who had used all this Greenbaum idea to avoid being sent into the light. Heck, maybe I was imagining things altogether! How could I possibly think that there was anything sinister or bizarre about Lilly?! What a great gal! So bright and easy to talk to! So engaging and funny and charming! Sheesh! This UFO business was really getting to me! I was getting paranoid! I was going off the deep end! That's it! It was *me* who needed a therapist!

But then, just as she was getting ready to hang up, she remarked, "We need to get together soon! There are a lot of things I want to talk about since I saw you last on Saturday night." That was the night of the session with the Cassiopaeans, *not* Lilly's hypnosis the very night before.

I said, "You mean something has happened since last night?"

Lilly said, "Last night? What do you mean?"

I reminded her of the previous night's hypnosis.

Lilly laughed and told me I must be dreaming because she had gone to bed early the previous night – she had been exhausted from her classes that day! She certainly had not been with me doing a hypnosis session!

One of us was missing some time here or one of us was going off the deep end and I was pretty sure it wasn't me! Not positive, just pretty sure!

I assured her that we had, indeed, done a hypnosis session. I reminded her that she had called me about her dream of the Reptoid rape and that she had come to my house covered with a rash and scratches. I told her to look at her abdomen to see the scratches.

At that point, Lilly became quite angry and screamed that I was crazy and slammed the phone down!!! A sort of "cloud of unreality" descended over me and I really wondered for a moment if I was losing *my* mind!

I called Frank and he assured me that I had, indeed, done the hypnosis session, that he had been there manning the recorder, and we had the tape and the notes and the photographs.

Even though I was seeing glimpses of this bizarre reality beneath the surface, my mind really did not want to accept it. Of all the many synchronistic events that had been falling fast and furious upon me, this business of receiving the Greenbaum material and then just sort of having a real subject of it more or less drop into my life was pushing the limits of credulity. Just what in the heck was going on? So, naturally, we brought the subject up at the next session.

March 10, 1996

Q: (L) I have a number of questions that I want to get into tonight. The first thing I would like to ask is: I did a hypnosis session with Lilly and utilized some of the Greenbaum techniques. She responded in the affirmative. I was told that she had several alter personalities: "Master Programmer, Gatekeeper, Alpha, Beta, Theta and Delta, Zero," and others. Were these responses valid?

A: Validity is subjective. Be careful of data, which originates from sources which may mislead.

Q: (L) Which is the misleading source? Lilly or the Greenbaum text?

A: No it's the center of origin. This "subject" appears to be fragmented.

Q: (L) Are her fragments caused by abductions? [I was assuming that the Cassiopaeans meant that Lilly was fragmented. In retrospect, I think they meant that the "subject" of Greenbaum programming was "fragmented".]

A: She has had abductions and the like, but not the issue here. She is "searching," and when one is searching...

At this point, the phone rang. It was a long distance call from a researcher in California who wanted to discuss a case, and we had to continue at a later time.

I was frustrated by the interruption and plagued with the questions in my mind. Did the Cassiopaeans mean that the Greenbaum scenario was possibly a screen for alien programming? Was the imagery of the Reptoid rape also a screen? Or was it completely the other way around? Were the images of alien abductions and Reptoid rapes a product of some sinister human experiment on mankind? Or even elements of both?

That then led me back to the idea that the whole Satanic Ritual abuse scenario could also be either of these things: a screen over Greenbaum-type programming, or a screen over alien programming. Further, many so-called "recovered memories" of sexual abuse within families could even be screens of programming activities by various persons or beings unknown.

I was familiar already with much of the material being produced by the psychological community about these subjects, and I had read many sessions from these books and articles that were supposed to prove the existence of Satanists and their wicked agenda because this or that individual had begun to experience flashbacks or bits and pieces of memories of abuse. They would then rush themselves off to a psychologist, psychiatrist, or hypnotherapist who would engage them in non-directive therapy to assist them in the recovery of both their memories and, by default, the "missing parts" of their "soul".

I would read these accounts and see the clues scattered throughout that the emerging scenarios were, very likely, "created". And that is not to say that the individual was creating them at all! They were more likely "manufactured" just as the scene of the "benevolent Mantids" who were "teaching the children in a loving way" in the session at the beginning of this series was manufactured. When the screen was directively "removed", the revealed activity of Mantids eating human children was exposed.[54] It was clear that in "non-directive" therapy, this would never have occurred.

The problem was that, in the field of hypnotherapy, there had been such an outcry from skeptics in past years about the suggestibility of the client, and the

---

[54] This is described in *High Strangeness*.

purported "agendas" of the therapists, that directed therapy had fallen into disfavor. It was now all client-directed. The therapist was more a "sounding board" who merely gave gentle, non-directive suggestions that the client should give him/herself "permission" to "recover" the memory (whatever it was). In this way, it was believed that the client would "recover *their* truth". In this sense, "their truth" amounted to little more than another illusion.

The problem with this approach is twofold. In the first place, if we consider for even a moment that there is the possibility that there are beings – whether human or otherwise – who are out there engaged in mind programming efforts (and there is some considerable factual evidence to support this) then we have to consider that they would install blocks to recovery of the memories of their activities as a *first line of defense*. They would very likely make these blocks or screens interactive with some installed mechanism of severe discomfort so that the subject would either avoid retrieval or be unable to retrieve such memories without serious pain or stress.

The second problem is that I have experimented with suggestibility of subjects to some considerable extent and have found that they are not as malleable as skeptics might wish us to think. Which leads, of course, to the idea of manipulation of opinion regarding directive therapy so that it falls into disrepute as a therapeutic mode, thus adding a layer of protection over such nefarious activities.

There was an experiment done some years ago by a researcher who selected a random sample of individuals who were, ostensibly, *not* abductees and, under hypnosis or guided imagery techniques, led them into an alien abduction scenario. Because a significant number of them began to describe abductions in the same terms as persons who had claimed to be abductees due to some conscious representations surfacing, it was decided that this proved that the abduction complex of images was more or less archetypal and therefore, false.

It never occurred to the researchers that the non-abducted persons who described accurately the abduction process might really have been abducted, but that their abductions and programming did not have the glitches that cause others to remember or to have clues that lead them to active therapy to recover their memories.

Anyway, this experiment was taken as "proof" that the recovered memories of abductees could very well be suggested to them by literature, movies, and even the therapists. So, "directive therapy" was tossed aside in favor of just allowing the client to let his memories – whatever they might be – sort of "drift to the top".

I can demonstrate hundreds of instances where this idea of suggestibility is false. An example would be when I say to a client under hypnosis who is describing an alien being, that I want them to tell me what kind of nose they have; is it big or little. Now, right there I have suggested that the being *must* have a nose and that it is either big or little. If the client were as suggestible as is proposed, they would naturally tell me one or the other or even that it is a "medium sized nose". But time and again, the answer would come back: "I don't see a nose. There is a little hole or a dimple-like thing, but no nose."

Or, I would say, "What are you smelling?" That is a direct suggestion that they must smell something. But the answer might come back "Nothing at all." Or, if a smell *is* present, they might have their attention directed to that factor and tell me that there is some sort of smell.

Another example would be when I ask the client: "How did you get out of the room? Did you go out the door or the window?" And they would respond "Neither. I sort of 'went through the wall'." On the other hand, if I suggest that they were "carried on a beam of light" as was the case in a different instance they had previously described, they might come back and say "Not this time. I was carried through the door."

Over and over again I have tried these little directive suggestions to get data, and over and over again I have seen that, even with powerful direction, the client will recover whatever is there to recover with very little fabrication, if any.

And that is where we have to begin to deal with the screening process. If there is a screen, that is what the victim will perceive as the actual memory. And it is in probing the screen that other clues must be noted and followed in order to arrive at what is beneath the screen *if possible*!

For example, in one of my early abduction cases, the client had a vivid dream that she was sure was *more* than a dream. She dreamed about our friendly "Mantid beings", as described by the second subject I discussed in *High Strangeness*. The subject described in the earlier chapter in *High Strangeness* was actually a much later case chronologically, and this earlier case that I am now mentioning was the one that had given me the clue that there was something deeper in the situation than was being presented.

This first "Mantid" case was also a description of the beings as kind and loving and friendly – just full of great wisdom and kindness. The subject went through a whole description of how grand and glorious it was to be in their company and care, and after all these glowing praises of the wonderful, consciousness raising experience, I brought the session to an end thinking that it was exactly as presented.

However, the instant the client was awakened, she leaped up from the couch and ran to the bathroom where we could hear her vomiting violently for some minutes. When she returned, she said that her stomach was very upset (obviously!) and that she must have "eaten something" that didn't agree with her earlier.

But that episode bothered me. It kept coming up in my mind as a clue that ought to be followed.

The next time this particular client scheduled a session, I was determined to get to the bottom of this matter, so I utilized the somatic technique where I asked her "body consciousness" to speak to me and tell me why, at the last session, she had become ill after recovering the memory of the "abduction". The somatic technique is, again, the ideomotor signals of the fingers where the index finger rises to indicate a "yes" answer and the little finger rises to indicate a "no" answer.

I asked the body consciousness if the description of the abduction that had been given in the previous session had been what actually happened, and the answer came back "no". I asked if the beings that had been presented as kind and benevolent had, in fact, acted kindly and benevolently toward the subject. Again, the answer was "no". I then asked if they had done harmful and painful things to the subject. The answer was "yes". Next, I asked if the memory of the abduction as presented in the earlier session was a screen that had been created and implanted into the subconscious mind, and the answer was "yes".

So, we had a problem here. The subconscious is not as sacrosanct as we would like to think. The emerging memories that we would all like to think are the "individual truth" of the client could not only be manipulated, they could be entirely false.

How to break through them?

I came up with a little technique that I experimented with and it seemed to work quite effectively – as far as I could tell. I call it the "screen splitter". In order to make it work properly, the client has to be situated in a safe environment while under hypnosis, which means that the events to be reviewed must be placed at a "remove" and the client must have some directed means of accessing via the ideomotor construct that goes beyond just finger signals. This construct becomes a sort of "internal television" which translates the body information into "television signals" which are then projected onto a screen, which the subject controls with a hand held "remote".

A further consideration that must be clear in this type of therapy, is that the hypnotherapist *must* take a more or less dominant role as not only guide, but as a warrior-companion. The therapist must "go in" with the individual and watch for the lurking dangers and defend the client from them so that they can safely make the journey to the truth and back again. It becomes more of a shamanic type of activity than anything else. I was later surprised to learn that what I had developed was pretty close to the techniques of the ancient Siberian shamans who would "journey into the underworld," and do battle with the forces present there that were controlling, obfuscating, and/or using the client for their own purposes via tricks and deception.

Mircea Eliade writes in *Shamanism: Archaic Techniques of Ecstasy*:

> The principal function of the shaman in Central and North Asia is magical healing. Several conceptions of the cause of illness are found in the area, but that of the 'rape of the soul' is by far the most widespread. Disease is attributed to the soul's having strayed away or been stolen, and treatment is in principle reduced to finding it, capturing it, and obliging it to resume its place in the patient's body. In some part of Asia the cause of illness can be the intrusion of a magical object into the patient's body or his 'possession' by evil spirits; in this case, cure consists in extracting the harmful object or expelling the demons. Sometimes disease has a

twofold cause – theft of the soul aggravated by 'possession' by evil spirits – and the shamanic cure includes both searching for the soul and expelling the demons.[55]

These archaic conceptions of the cause of disease and disorder are startlingly reminiscent of the way the Cassiopaeans have described the abduction process.

June 17, 1995

A: These experiences [abductions] must be known in their entirety as to what they really are.

You are not normally removed as a physical third density being from one locator to another.

What happens is very simple. The time frame is normally frozen, and we use the term "frozen" for lack of a better term. What this means is that your perception of time in your physical locator, third density body, ceases to pass during this period of time that is called "zero time" variously by members of your human race.

What happens is that the soul imprint occupying or of that particular host body is removed forcibly, transported to another locator, and remolecularized as a separate physical entity body for purpose of examination, implantation, and other. The soul imprint is used for the purpose of duplication process; it is then demolecularized and the soul imprint is replaced in the original body at the original locator. That is the process that takes place.

On occasion, the fourth density beings doing the abduction make a mistake in the time referencing points of the third density illusion… Normally, however, that is not a problem.

On rare occasions, the host, or the subject of the abduction can actually find himself or herself replaced in the time frame illusion in what could appear to be several hours, day, weeks, or even, sadly, years prior to the beginning of the event, which, of course, could cause side effects such as total insanity and other such things. Fortunately that did not occur in your case, but there was some fracturing of the time frame reference illusion. This is why you thought you saw two ships when in actuality you only saw one. [Referring to the Black Boomerang incident.]

Now, it is most important that you understand that this is not a physical, third density experience in its entirety.

There is the soul imprint that all first density, second density, third density, and fourth density beings possess, as you already know; that is extracted. From that soul imprint, a duplicate copy or cloning, if you will, which appears on fourth density, can then be made and studied and the soul imprint is then replaced into the original body at whatever density it was taken. This is normally how the process is done.

Most often, *if the third density being is removed in total physicality, there is no return of that being to third density.* They are permanently removed to fourth density. Most often that is what takes place although on rare occasions there can be return. However, there is no need for this as complete duplication for all pur-

---

[55] Mircea Eliade, *Shamanism: Archaic Techniques of Ecstasy* (New York: Oxford University Press, 1964).

poses of examination, alteration of sensate, and implanting – need not be done on third density – can be done completely in the fourth density duplication process. Do you understand?

Q: (T) How does the implant come back to the third density body that's originally still here?

A: The process we are describing, which involves the remolecularization. It is very complex to try and describe how the fourth density is translated into third density, except that once the duplicate, the fourth density cloning, or duplicate, is present, all fourth density realities surrounding that fourth density duplicate will be matched in third density whenever and wherever desired. Because, in effect it is the entire density level, which is being exchanged, not just the object contained within.

Q: (L) So, in other words, just as the soul imprint, when it goes into fourth density, can be used as a template to create a carbon copy, so to speak, then anything that is done to the carbon copy then becomes a template that recreates that same manifestation when it is sent back into the third.

A: Precisely. With the only variance there being that technology is used to make sure that implants, or added material that comes from fourth density, is such that it will also translate equally into third density through the remolecularization process.

Q: (L) Is there any method that we could or should know about to remove or deactivate fourth density implants?

A: No, you are not capable of doing that without causing death of the host. And, by the way, please don't believe those who claim that they can do such things, as they cannot. [Apparently those "implants" that are claimed to have been removed are third density "decoys".]

Even though the Cassiopaeans are saying that we cannot remove the fourth density implants, they have said that we can deactivate them by being aware of them and refusing to respond to their machinations.

Nevertheless, over and over again we find this concept expressed in the most archaic shamanic practices: "healing by extraction of the magical object that has brought on the sickness and the search for the soul abducted by evil spirits." Or "[they] attribute sickness to an object introduced into the body by a god or a spirit, or to possession. And treatment consists in extracting the magical object or expelling the spirit." Eliade writes:

> Only the shaman can undertake a cure of this kind. For only he 'sees' the spirits and knows how to exorcise them; only he recognizes that the soul has fled, and is able to overtake it, in ecstasy, and return it to its body. ...Everything that concerns the soul and its adventure, here on earth and in the beyond, is the exclusive province of the shaman. Through his own preinitiatory and initiatory experiences, he knows the drama of the human soul, its instability, and its precariousness; in addition, he knows the forces that threaten it and the regions to which it can be carried away. If shamanic cure involves ecstasy, it is precisely because illness is regarded as a corruption or alienation of the soul.

...The struggle against the evil spirits is dangerous and finally exhausts the shaman. 'We are all destined to fall before the power of the spirits,' the shaman Tusput told Sieroszewski, 'The spirits hate us because we defend men...' And in fact, in order to extract the evil spirits from the patient, the shaman is often obliged to take them into his own body; in doing so, he struggles and suffers more than the patient himself.

...Aside from the rare cases of 'infernal specialization' (confined to descents to the underworld), the Siberian shamans are equally capable of celestial ascents and descents to the nether regions... This two-fold technique derives in a manner from their initiation itself, and for the initiatory dreams of future shamans include both descents (ritual sufferings and death) and ascents (resurrection). In this context we can understand that, after battling the evil spirits or descending to the underworld to recover the patient's soul, the shaman feels the need to re-establish his own spiritual equilibrium by repeating the ascent to the sky.

...The shaman's power and prestige derive exclusively from his capacity for ecstasy. It is to his mystical capacities that the shaman owes his ability to discover and combat the evil spirits that have seized the patient's soul; he does not confine himself to exorcising them, he takes them into his own body, 'possesses' them, tortures and expels them.

[Shamanism today has deteriorated and lost its focus.] We observe a certain decadence of shamanism, a condition attested almost everywhere. The Tungus compare especially the strength and courage of the 'old shamans' with the cowardice of shamans today, who in some districts no longer dare to undertake the dangerous journey to the underworld."[56]

I was still somewhat concerned about Lilly's revelations about Sandy and the remark under hypnosis that she and Sandy had been part of the same "programming set", which I took to be a group. Not only that, but there was the receipt of the "Elaine and the Sisters of Light" material at precisely the time that Lilly made her revelations to me about Sandy.

Was I looking at another aspect of the "hidden control mechanism"? The whole thing was so unlikely and so crazy that I was really stretching my credulity to even deal with it on a rational basis. But heck! When you talk to "sixth density light beings" via a board on Saturday nights, how unlikely and weird can anything be?

It was a few weeks before we had another session because we were busy helping Sandy straighten out a big mess in her life involving her mother in a nursing home. It was taking a huge amount of my time and energy and I really felt that Sandy ought to be able to manage these things herself like anybody else, but she was so pitiful and seemingly grateful for every minute of my time that I felt guilty for resenting the many demands placed on me.

But, after a time, I started to get the idea that something was not quite right with this scenario. Every interaction with Sandy and her mother resulted in a serious draining of energy. Every interaction with Sandy in the group resulted

---

[56] Ibid.

in an argument or misunderstanding. On several occasions, these disagreements almost led to the giving up of the project altogether!

Of course, my mind was working overtime to explain things in a rational way. I did not want to fall into the trap of "believing and thereby making real" in terms of the Greenbaum and Elaine material, and maybe if I hadn't been doing that, I would have noticed things sooner!

I sat down with Sandy one day to talk and worked around to the subject of her current associations. I wasn't going to directly ask her if she was involved with a sort of "coven" up in Hernando County as Lilly had reported, but I was going to try to find out where it was she went several nights a week that she never talked about.

The long and short of it was that she admitted that she had been going up to Trudy and George's house two nights a week to do "therapy" with both of them. She very innocently wondered why it would even be a problem, since they were simply "bodywork clients" and she needed to make money in her profession.

I was absolutely devastated. Sandy *knew* what those people had done to me, she had denied any contact or association with them for a long time, and now she was telling me that she was hanging out with them two nights a week?! And then, after working on them (ostensibly) she was coming to do body work on me, bringing that energy directly into my house, and possibly into my very physical structure?! Clearly she was *not* getting it in regards to the hidden nature of things going on here on the Big Blue Marble.

But, I stayed calm and said nothing to her. I realized, at this point, that it was entirely possible for her to be doing things in an alternate personality of which the Sandy I knew was totally unaware. But Frank and I decided to have a private session to address this issue. The result was quite interesting.

> April 24, 1996
>
> Q: (L) Now, some time ago Lilly called me and told me that Sandy was involved in some sort of coven or group that was into rituals and magic or whatever. I just have a very difficult time believing this. How can Sandy seem so innocent and, at the same time, be a part of such activities? The only reason I am asking is because Lilly knew things about Sandy that "clicked" and could not possibly have been said unless she knew *something*. Is it possible that Sandy could have multiple personalities and one of her other "selves" is doing this? As in Greenbaum?
>
> A: Sure!
>
> Q: (L) If that is the case, then it seems that these "alternate personalities" are so cleverly installed that they can take over, do something, and then "turn off" leaving no trace at all! That makes it possible that *anyone* can have this programming and *no one* would even know! Heck, they wouldn't even know it themselves! We are talking about perfect Manchurian Candidates here! And that brings up the idea that if Sandy can do things *she* isn't aware of, is it possible for either Frank or I to be involved in such and not be aware of it?
>
> A: Yes, but it is not that.

Q: (L) Does that mean that there *is* some other thing that we are involved in, in some other aspects of our selves that we are not aware of?
A: Close.
Q: (L) Is this something that happens in altered states or in sleep states?
A: Not happens, *happened*.
Q: (L) Something that happened in the past?
A: Laura, you need to consult a powerful, practiced, effective hypnotherapist to unlock these questions for you.
Q: (L) Is this something I could do for Frank in the meantime? Obviously Frank could have a big piece of the puzzle locked up in there...
A: Both of you and others. The locks have been installed in such a way that it is literally impossible for you to unlock them, as they were installed with full knowledge of present circumstances.
Q: (L) Who installed these locks?
A: Supremely powerful STS consortium!!
Q: (L) And what circumstances were they aware of, as you have mentioned, when they installed these locks?
A: All. [That implies time travel capabilities.]
Q: (L) You are the Cassiopaeans, correct?
A: Yes.
Q: (L) And you are STO?
A: Yes.
Q: (L) And you are telling us that we have locks on knowledge installed in us, installed by supremely powerful STS consortium. Can we not, in our conscious state, simply reject this programming, and ask you to inform us of this information?
A: Not possible! You cannot unlock, and we cannot tell you the details of what, or why.
Q: (L) Why can you not tell us?
A: Free will violation, and endangerment of you if done thusly.
Q: (L) Is there some way to do it that does not endanger us?
A: We have just told you what you must do.
Q: (L) Is it a danger to us to *not* unlock these things?
A: In a sense.
Q: (L) When you say that things "happened" but are not currently happening, what do you mean? I was abducted or something... Why?
A: To install self-destruct programming.
Q: (L) I find this to be incredible! So, I have a "self-destruct" program. Considering my life, that could be true and a reasonable explanation. And Frank has one also?
A: Similar, but not an exact copy so as to mask.
Q: (L) Was Frank abducted in a similar fashion?
A: Close, but not exactly.

Q: (L) Was Frank's pneumonia when he was a child, which nearly killed him, part of this self-destruct program?

A: Yes.

Q: (L) Was Frank's father also programmed since he was partly responsible for much of Frank's psychological abuse?

A: Semi.

Q: (L) And my mother? She seems to have been the most consistent source of "attack" in my life...

A: Yes.

Q: (L) Well, I think we can safely assume that probably every member of our families have had some sort of program installed, if only to facilitate *our* destruction. This whole situation is beginning to sound inexpressibly grim.

A: Grim?!? You have lived decades after these episodes! How many brethren? Multiples of millions!

Q: (L) That is why I am saying it is pretty damn grim... think of all those who don't survive these programs.

A: And it is part of a natural process, do not forget.

Q: (L) Well, we need some help from the good guys. It sounds so dreadful. We need some help here. I am becoming *very* tired. It is not only the constant battles against forces that we can neither see nor understand, but also even learning about all these things is a *huge* burden!

A: You only need knowledge.

Q: (L) Well, I want to have a little direction here.

A: Concentrate on your insurance settlement. This can be a problem solver if handled wisely, a curse if not so! Use some of the funds to locate a "superhypnotherapist".

Q: (L) Who might this person be? A clue?

A: No.

Q: (L) Is there some progress that we can make on our own?

A: Yes.

Q: (L) Give me a clue... I want something that produces knowledge that will protect me...

A: Won't succeed until locks are blown off in proper way.

Q: (L) Well, I hope I survive until then.

A: Refer to previous answer.

Q: (L) If you guys were here, I'd throw something at you!

A: We'd dodge!

Q: (L) Well, you see my problem here... I guess I just want to know that there is someone out there who cares...

A: You should by now.

Q: (L) Then you guys ought to get behind my lawyer and jack him up...

A: We do, *through* you.

Q: (L) So, we have a *lot* of stuff locked up inside and all we have to do is find the key...
A: Yes, exactly.

That was *not* a pleasant thought. But then, it is because of the fact that the programming has "glitches" and is not foolproof that we know about it at all. Apparently it *is* possible to escape the controls, though whether one has the capacity to really get to the bottom of it and see it for what it truly is remains to be seen. A lot more work needs to be done in this area.

A few days later I received a phone call from Lilly, inquiring how I was doing and I was surprised at the normal, chatty tone of her voice considering the circumstances of the last conversation we had together when she began screaming at me and slammed the phone down. But, by this time, I was accustomed to the idea that some people might have all kinds of "personalities" that can be turned on or off, and perhaps it would only be through constant exposure to the information about these things that could assist in their awakening. I mentioned that I had some material for her to read, and she came by and I gave her a printed copy of the Greenbaum speech. After reading it, she called again and was *very* anxious to attend another session. Tim, from the old Reiki group had also contacted me and was present.

The session began with some questions about our ability to do research in a free and independent way considering the limitations that we were becoming aware of in the world around us. The Cassiopaeans gave a very significant clue to the process of awakening in their reply:

October 5, 1996
A: There are no limits, just controls... The knowledge gives one all the necessary tools to overcome the controls.

The next question was for Lilly who had experienced a strange event during a Reiki class earlier that day.

Q: (L) Lilly took a particular type of initiation today, and she had an event occur during this... [Lilly described the event as leaving her body and going through a "life review" sort of what is described as happening at the time of death.]
A: She should be careful not to "spread herself too thin." One does not need to cram learning, "steady as she goes."
Q: (L) Can you describe what it was that was taking place with her? Or define it?
A: Soul bilocation.
Q: (L) Was this a beneficial event for her?
A: No. She has been ripping open the fabric too much. Each soul has its own patterning, which is held in place by the three main bodies of existence [planchette swirls a few times]... "thought/consciousness center, spirit/etheric center and physical center," remembering, of course, that your physical center has the "interface genetic body" as well. But we are here dealing with the primary patterns. There are specific methodologies for adjusting these, and

traveling into or out of other planes of existence. When one does not properly utilize these, one tears the fabric of their trilateral continuum when they seek to travel. This can be very problematic, and may lead to the soul being unable to reconnect with the body, thus causing the physical center to perish!!!

Q: (L) The man who was facilitating the initiation, was he aware of what was happening, or what he was doing?

A: Aware only of unusual sensates.

Q: (L) Did it have anything to do with the attunement?

A: No. It had to do with previous experiments.

Q: (L) She said that she also experienced a past life review just as if she were in the process of dying.

A: You described it well.

Q: (Lilly) Well, experiments by whom?

A: You. [Meaning Lilly.]

Q: (L) So, what was, what happened with this interaction that caused this to trigger right there and then? At that moment? What was the trigger?

A: Spirit center stimulus. The "initiation".

So there was another clue about the kinds of things that can activate programs. Different "initiations" offered by Metaphysical–New Age teachers and seminar leaders! Gads! It was beginning to sound very dangerous to become involved with such groups at all!

At this point, Lilly began to talk about an amazing "column of light" that she had photographed in her house. I was aware of the fact that this might relate to the "entry point" of the Reptoids who had raped her, but I didn't want to rock the boat of her personality alter that was present at the time, so I said nothing. I was hoping that this present part of her would seek the information that could be helpful to enable her to overcome her programming. She identified the column of light as a "portal" and was sure that it indicated her connection to her "guides".

Q: (Lilly) So, can the portal [in my house] assist me in any way with this [rip in my] aura? Will it do me any good? I mean, what's it for, anyway?

A: It can assist you in becoming possessed.

Q: (Lilly) Well, that's just wonderful!!! How did it get there? It's on the top of my head; it comes right down.

A: No, it is not a part of you.

Q: (T) How about asking where this portal came from? (L) Yes, what was the generative source?

A: More than one.

Q: (L) Okay, there's more than one generative source. So, it's a combination of factors. Is it part of the historical site? The space-time location? [Lilly's house was built on the old site of Florida Southern Methodist College, which had been struck by lightning and destroyed in a fire many years ago.]

A: Yes.

Q: (L) Is it part of the metaphysical activities taking place in the house itself? [Lilly held many classes in her home.]

A: Yes. Other occupants. More than her. [The "other occupants" could refer to Lilly's husband who had "mob connections," or so she said.]

Q: (Lilly) Do they mean live ones or dead ones?

A: Both.

Q: (Lilly) That's what I thought. (V) How can it be removed?

A: Changes in lifestyle.

Q: (L) The question I have is, she is in a situation where she is somewhat blocked in her directions. It seems that many sorts of sources seek to...

A: Obfuscation is illusion.

At this point, we began to discuss the various illusions that we are presented with that we have to learn about before we can penetrate and overcome them. At this point, the Cassiopaeans just tossed out a term that brought us back to the Greenbaum subject:

A: Mind programming.

Q: (L) What about mind programming?

A: We thought we would just throw that onto the table.

Q: (T) Mind programming! As in programming of one's mind?

A: Tim received some most recently.

Q: (L) And whom did he receive the mind programming from?

A: Cultists.

Q: (T) What form did it take?

A: Negative.

Q: (T) Not negative or positive, but what form was it presented to him as?

A: Hypnotic.

Q: (T) Was he awake or asleep at the time?

A: Both.

Q: (T) How was it conveyed to him?

A: Lights, fires, chants.

Q: (Tim) I haven't seen any of the [Wicca or Reiki bunch] since way back when. (L) Way back when, what is that, a couple of years? (Tim) Yes (L) Well, then that's still "recently" in cosmic terms I guess. Is that what is meant?

A: Yes.

Q: (T) I just wanted to make sure that this was not a long-distance thing... that they did not convey this programming from a distance and... (Tim) Yes, and that they still didn't have their hooks into me.

A: Close, though.

Q: (L) Close, though to what?

A: Response was to "Hooks".

Q: (L) Are you suggesting that this programming still has "hooks" in him and that some of the choices he's been making in his life in the last two years are the results of this programming?
A: Maybe.
Q: (Tim) I want to know; did I get married as a result of this programming?
A: Yes.

Naturally, with the response to Tim's question being so forthcoming, everybody wanted to know if *they* had become involved with their respective partners as a result of some type of programming.

Q: (L) Did I get married as a result of some similar programming?
A: No.
Q: (L) Did Lilly?
A: Yes.
Q: (V) Did I?
A: No.
Q: (T) Did I?
A: No.
Q: (T) Did Frank?
A: No.
Q: (L) Frank never got married! (T) Well, I was just making sure that everybody felt like they were in on all this! (Lilly) This Greenbaum program, was it due to my father?
A: Yes.
Q: (Lilly) Thought so! It was his military career and position. Was this programming done to my father?
A: You were "Greenbaumed".
Q: (L) Was Tim Greenbaumed?
A: No.
Q: (V) What about V?
A: No.
Q: (L) What about Frank?
A: No.
Q: (L) Laura?
A: No.
Q: (L) T?
A: No.
Q: (T) J?
A: No.
Q: (Lilly) So, I'm the only one here that's been Greenbaumed?
Q: (Tim to Laura) They told you before that you got mental programming of some sort, but now they are saying it wasn't Greenbaum?

A: Laura had more advanced work done on her.

Q: (V) That opens up a whole new can of worms. (L) And what do you mean by that?

A: Not now.

Q: (L) Is there any possibility, to some extent, that I have overcome this influence at the present time?

A: No. Was partial, then aborted, leaving fragments of trigger response programs that have been in remission.

Q: (L) Why was it aborted?

A: Because STO forces intervened.

Q: (L) And when was this?

A: Mid "fifties".

Q: (L) So it was when I was three or four years old. (T) I think we should go back to what we were talking about with Tim, because they brought it up. (Tim) Am I still receiving instructions from the programming? Am I still receiving programming from them?

A: Buried for future triggers.

Q: (L) Is there anything he can do to deactivate this programming?

A: Would take powerful hypnotic work. Beware of stresses of a most personal nature.

Q: (L) Do you mean sexual actions; activities might be triggers or connected to this?

A: Partly.

Q: (L) Any further clues for him? (T) What was it that they... what was given to Tim in this programming? What was he told to do, or what was the mind control about? (L) What were the instructions?

A: Discover.

Q: (T) Is it something Tim will be able to discover? Does he have enough information to work on?

A: Not by himself.

Q: (L) Is his wife and the new baby part of the hook to keep him in the program?

A: Yes.

Q: (Tim) Is the hook attached to the physical, emotional, spiritual, or what?

A: All. You were particularly vulnerable at the time. Remember, this particular group has an uncanny ability to get to those who have parental influences with a troubled past.

[Phone call interrupted, call was from Tim's wife demanding that he leave immediately and come home!]

Q: (L) Is Tim's wife Greenbaumed?

A: Yes.

Q: (Tim) Where did she receive Greenbaum programming?... Oh, I know, her father was in the Navy... (L) Why are we not surprised!!!

A: Yes. And V's father too, but fortunately in too low level a capacity.

Q: (L) Does the Greenbaum influence, or interaction last indefinitely throughout a person's life, if something isn't done to terminate or halt it?

A: Yes.

Q: (L) Mind programming... Lilly wants to know how extensive the Greenbauming was in her case. Was it extensive?

A: Yes and your husband, too!

Q: (Lilly) That's just wonderful! More pleasant things this evening! (V) I've been sitting in your position, where I've gotten a bunch of bad news one night, and I know how you feel! (F) It's not really bad news, though, because it's good to know... (V) It protects you to have the knowledge. But, it's tough to hear. It's tough to face the fact that you can be controlled. But, if you look at your life, and you see all the lousy choices you make and the problems you have caused yourself, then you have to think that something is getting in the way of being able to see what is really going on! (L) I guess you just have to ask yourself every time you make a choice, why am I *really* doing what I'm doing? Is it really me doing it, or am I being "directed". You have to be pretty coldly analytical to do this. You just can't let emotions influence you to do what you seem to "want". (Lilly) Is there anything to cure it? Can anything be done? Now we know for Tim, it's hypnosis. What about me?

A: Awareness is step number one.

Q: (T) Tim's wife is one of his triggers... (L) Well, Tim finds himself, we all, I mean, jeez! What do we do about these difficult situations that we plant ourselves in the middle of, due to programming? Then we have to extricate ourselves, at great cost and pain? Having done it already myself, I know how much pain...

A: No need to extricate, if necessary work is done, in some cases.

Q: (L) If two people who are married to each other are Greenbaumed, as you are suggesting is the case with Lilly and her husband, is it possible that they could be programmed to kill each other? I mean, he's been pretty violent toward her lately.

A: Maybe, but not always. The programming is mainly intended to produce erratic behavior, for the purpose of "spooking" the population so that they will welcome, and even demand, a totalitarian government. Think of the persons who have inexplicably entered various public and private domains, and shot large numbers of people... Now, you have "met" some of these Greenbaum subjects...

This little remark followed by the three dots sort of went right over my head. But it was clearly a warning!

Q: (L) So you are saying that their implanted triggers are set to activate at a certain point in future time, to create a mass chaos, in the public domain? What types of activity, specifically?

A: Better to discover that one on your own.

Q: (L) Okay, that's another one that's dangerous to know right now...

A: Now, some history... as you know, the CIA and NSA and other agencies are the children of Nazi Gestapo... the SS, which was an experiment influenced by Antareans who were practicing for the eventual reintroduction of the Nephalim on to 3rd and/or 4th density earth. And the Thule Society, which groomed its dupe

ALL THERE IS IS LESSONS

subject, Adolph Hitler to be the all-time mind-programmed figurehead, initiated the contact with the "Antareans". Now, in modern times, you have seen, but so far, on a lesser scale: Oswald, Ruby, Demorenschildt, Sirhan Sirhan, James Earl Ray, Arthur Bremer, Farakhan, Menendez, Bundy, Ramirez, Dahmer, etc.

Q: (L) Is there any particular individual who is currently being programmed to take a more prominent position in terms of this...

A: Later... you must know that Oswald was programmed to be the "patsy". So that he would say many contradictory things. Demorenschildt was both a programmer and programmed. Ruby was hypnotically programmed to shoot Oswald with an audio prompt, that being the sound of a car horn.

Q: (L) The question has been brought up, is there some way or means that one can distinguish or discern a victim of Greenbaum or other mind programming by some clues?

A: Not until it is too late.

Q: (L) Was Sandy Greenbaumed?

A: Yes. [...]

Q: (V) I'd like to know if any Presidents have been Greenbaumed?

A: Yes. Remember, the "Greenbaum method" is one of many in existence. It is a veritable potpourri.

Getting back to our more or less chronological story: we came back to the subject again the following week. Tim was again present, and very upset about many strange events of the intervening days. He was terrified that he had been "kidnapped" and "Greenbaumed", as we were starting to call it:

October 12, 1996

Q: (L) In an earlier session you mentioned that we ought to discuss the matter of mind control...

A: Programming is the word you need, not "control".

Q: (L) Tim has had some very strange events happening to him and he would like to know if he has been Greenbaumed?

A: Tim has not been "Greenbaumed," but mind programmed by those who have ties to a Wiccan organization as we previously described.

Q: (L) How does one determine the signs of someone who has been programmed, whether Greenbaum-type or otherwise? In specific, how could Tim tell?

A: Pay attention to the signs. Difficulty keeping up with the demands and pressures of life both before the programming and after. Feeling like you are losing control because everything is now even more "confusing".

Q: (T) Any specific signs?

A: We gave you one, now for 2: wife "acting up". Also, parental problems that have already begun.

Q: (L) How does one overcome or cancel this programming?

A: The same as always: Knowledge protects.

Q: (L) In what ways will knowledge help to cancel programming?

A: In ways directly affecting Tim.

Q: (L) I don't understand. How can knowledge help to cancel programming?

A: So that the awareness can be the foundation for being able to deal with situations, and possibly rectify some of them.

This obviously means that, unless one has an idea that they could be programmed, they will not learn about the ways and means of deactivation. I guess it is something like being an alcoholic: you have to admit that you have a problem in order to seek help.

Q: (L) Okay, in regards to this Greenbaum programming and the Nazi connection: On a couple of occasions you mentioned a group called the Antareans. Who were these human types or aliens?

A: Antareans were the name given by 4th density groups in contact with the Thule Society on third density Earth, before and during World War One.

Q: (L) What are they called now?

A: There is no one currently labeling themselves as "Antareans," in contact with anyone now.

Q: (L) So, they are no longer here?

A: No, not this particular group. There are others.

Q: (L) You said once that I was not Greenbaumed, but that something else was done. What was this?

A: The work that was attempted was more intense, but it was aborted because it turned out that your frequency resonance vibration was not proper for that particular type of "experimental" programming.

Q: (L) Does this mean that there was something about my vibrations that caused what they were trying to do to result in positive things?

A: Possibly, in an offhand way.

Q: (L) You also said that STO intervened and stopped this... Does this mean that there is some reason to protect me?

A: Okay... learning is an exploration followed by the affirmation of knowing [through] discovery. One day, you will know this. You are doing just fine. No more on that for this session.

And this last remark brings us back to the subject of the interactions with the Metaphysical Church group and their attempts to kill me and how this was associated with the green pool which was sort of a "symbol system" in my reality that there was something seriously wrong in my personal environment. The responses given to me should be taken to heart by those of you who have written to tell me how similar your lives have been to my own. Remember, according to Ra, there are approximately 65 million Wanderers on the planet. And, according to Ra and the Cassiopaeans, the Wanderers are prime targets for STS interference.

October 28, 1994

Q: (L) Okay, during the period of time I was getting the hassle from the metaphysical church group, my pool was green. Was this symbolic of the attack I was under?

A: Yes, but you left yourself open by association and buying too many concepts without careful examination. Investigate before buying and practicing in future, okay?

Q: (L) Investigate what? Ideas?

A: Yes. And concepts and especially practices.

Q: (L) The ideas of candle burning, salt, sage, shamanistic rituals and so forth? Is all this useless?

A: You are learning; remember when we say "good no ritual"?

Q: (L) In other words, your knowledge and your strength, which comes from your knowledge and knowing, is the point and the protection?

A: Precisely. This is extremely important.

Q: (L) Alexandra David-Neel quoted a lama who said we must beware of the children of our own minds as well as the children of the minds of others, such as thought forms perhaps created by higher negative beings. If we do not acknowledge that such things exist, are we then subject to being devoured by them?

A: Yes. Ritual drains directly to Lizard beings.

Q: (L) Even our saying of the Lord's Prayer?

A: It is okay to pray. Why do you think organized religion is obsessed with rituals?

Q: (L) Is the same thing true of modern day shamanistic practices and so forth?

A: Exactly.

Q: (L) What occurred to make my pool clear up?

A: You restored your own energy.

Q: (L) And it had nothing to do with rituals?

A: Correct. In spite of rituals but you were lucky could have gone the other way.

Q: (L) What prevented this from happening?

A: Divine intervention. [Energy surge]

Q: (L) Well, my life seems to have been full of incidents of Divine intervention.

A: Yes.

Q: (L) What is the purpose of this intervention?

A: To preserve and prepare you for work.

Q: (L) What is this work?

A: You are extremely valuable to all on your planet.

Q: (L) What particular value? Is this common to all people?

A: No.

Q: (L) Is this something meaningful? What is the mission?

A: Faith in your opening channel; you will learn as you go. We cannot tell you all at once.

Sorry. I tried. We still don't know what the "mission" is. We only know that there are, apparently, a *lot* of other people involved!

But we are also aware that the rules of the game seem to necessitate waking up against the obstacles of being prime targets of the STS control faction. And this can be *very* problematical when considered in the light of that most astounding revelation out of the mouth of one of the very victims of mind programming:

> "Master Programmer" was designed to turn Lilly into a dynamic New Age/Metaphysical teacher whose job was to travel the country, giving classes and seminars in many and various subjects, in order to *turn on the already installed programs of other greenbaum-type victims.*

We might just want to ask how many *other* prominent teachers and channels and "New Age Metaphysicians" are also "Master Programmers"?

AFTERWORD

As some readers may know, *The Wave* was originally published online, amounting to almost a thousand pages of printed text. Thus, we have decided to publish the series in multiple volumes, including the *Adventures Series* as well, which deals with events surrounding the writing of the original Wave material. All volumes contain extensive updates not published online. *Riding the Wave* introduces the concepts and theories related to the Wave.

In this volume we discussed many pitfalls that challenge the seeker in his or her journey. Despite our belief systems, we still fail and we still suffer. One of the reasons this is so is that most belief systems just provoke guilt instead of leading to understanding of symbols/forces *behind* the events of our everyday lives. Simply focusing on "creating love and light" or "changing the universe" or "creating a new reality by thinking and affirming and desiring" actually have a *backward effect*, because, they are *tacit admissions of lack*; lack of light, lack of perfection, lack of a perfect reality. Any change for the better in this life can only come from an objective look at the limits of our own beliefs, and learning to think in *unlimited* terms.

In our search for the objective nature of our beliefs and the ways they influence our lives, we've learned something of the nature of higher realms, that negative beings *do* inhabit them and influence our lives in insidious ways. To be free of the negative forces, we *must* be aware of them. The only thing that offers protection is *knowledge*. With the knowledge of higher worlds and their relation to our own, we can navigate *this* world with awareness of the various pitfalls and diversions that we all encounter, but that few recognize. What you don't know about *can* harm you, but vigilance in the art of discernment – of seeing the reality behind the symbol system of 3D reality – can offer protection.

When you ask a question – if the question is a burning one – your life becomes the answer. All of your experiences and interactions and so forth shape themselves around the core of the answer that you are seeking in your soul. How to be One with God, the universe? Love *is* the answer, but you have to have knowledge to know what Love *really* is.

Stripped to the Bone covers in more detail the message that knowing our limitations is what empowers us to overcome them. As such, it deals with such practicalities as mind-programming and the human/alien consortium, the ontology of evil, free will, humanity's dual nature, and the alchemical "integration of opposites". In *The Terror of History* I introduce the concept of "organic portals" and take a more historical approach, looking into the mysteries of Oak Island and the "Priory of Sion", as well as the history of the Jews.

Petty Tyrants and *Facing the Unknown* deal with the events surrounding the writing of the Wave. They detail the Matrix-like theological "drama of souls", the symbolic nature of reality, "petty tyrants", and the strange death of Morris Jessup. *Almost Human* is a look at the metaphysics of evil, encompassing cyclic catastrophe, conspiracy, psychopathy, and the true motivations of the power elite and their control of information. *Debugging the Universe* concludes the material that was first published online and deals more fully with the implications of what the C's have said about the nature of hyperdimensional influence, and the goal of true "seeker", in relation to the Self and the World. With the exception of *Petty Tyrants* and *Facing the Unknown*, the Wave books can be read in any order.

The fact is, in the past several years, we have made much progress in our understanding of The Wave and our relationship to it. I will be adding material to the end of this book version of the series – that will not appear on the website – that will include this information, and, finally, we will have a conclusion to *The Wave*. Whether or not that conclusion is correct remains to be seen.

I don't think we have very long to wait to find out.

RECOMMENDED READING

Harold Bayley's *The Lost Language of Symbolism*.
Joseph Campbell's *The Hero with a Thousand Faces*.
Carlos Castaneda's *The Active Side of Infinity*.
William C. Chittick's *The Sufi Path of Knowledge*.
Richard Dolan's *UFOs and the National Security State*. (2 volumes)
Umberto Eco's *The Search For the Perfect Language*.
Don Elkins, Carla Rueckert, and Jim McCarty's *The Ra Material*.
William James' *Varieties of Religious Experience*.
John Keel's *Operation Trojan Horse* and *The Eighth Tower*.
Andrew Lobaczewski's *Political Ponerology*.
Barbara Marciniak's *Bringers of the Dawn*.
P.D. Ouspensky's *In Search of the Miraculous*.
Nigel Pennick's *Magical Alphabets*.
Jessie Weston's *From Ritual to Romance*.

OTHER WORKS BY
Laura Knight-Jadczyk

High Strangeness
Hyperdimensions and the
Process of Alien Abduction

Weaving together the threads of
alien abduction, science, religion,
history and political conspiracies
to reveal the hidden slavery
of the human race.

PAPERBACK: 444 PAGES
ISBN: 978-1897244432

The Secret History
of The World
and How To Get Out Alive

Drawing on science and mysticism to
pierce the veil of reality. Over thirty
years of research unveiling for the
first time, The Great Work, and the
esoteric Science of the Ancients.

PAPERBACK: 872 PAGES
ISBN: 978-0976406364

AVAILABLE FROM
WWW.REDPILLPRESS.CO.UK
FOR MAIL ORDER CALL 01225 481635